THE FIERCE LIFE OF GRACE HOLMES CARLSON

The Fierce Life of Grace Holmes Carlson

Catholic, Socialist, Feminist

Donna T. Haverty-Stacke

NEW YORK UNIVERSITY PRESS
New York

NEW YORK UNIVERSITY PRESS
New York
www.nyupress.org

© 2021 by New York University
All rights reserved

References to Internet websites (URLs) were accurate at the time of writing. Neither the author nor New York University Press is responsible for URLs that may have expired or changed since the manuscript was prepared.

Library of Congress Cataloging-in-Publication Data
Names: Haverty-Stacke, Donna T., author.
Title: The fierce life of Grace Holmes Carlson : Catholic, socialist, feminist / Donna T. Haverty-Stacke.
Description: New York : New York University Press, [2020] | Includes bibliographical references and index.
Identifiers: LCCN 2020015049 (print) | LCCN 2020015050 (ebook) | ISBN 9781479802180 (cloth) | ISBN 9781479892006 (ebook) | ISBN 9781479804535 (ebook)
Subjects: LCSH: Carlson, Grace Holmes, 1906–1992. | Women socialists—United States—Biography. | Feminists—United States—Biography. | Catholics—United States—Biography.
Classification: LCC HX84.C37 H38 2020 (print) | LCC HX84.C37 (ebook) | DDC 324.273/7 [B]—dc23
LC record available at https://lccn.loc.gov/2020015049
LC ebook record available at https://lccn.loc.gov/2020015050

New York University Press books are printed on acid-free paper, and their binding materials are chosen for strength and durability. We strive to use environmentally responsible suppliers and materials to the greatest extent possible in publishing our books.

Manufactured in the United States of America

10 9 8 7 6 5 4 3 2 1

Also available as an ebook

For my Josephine, a brave girl with the heart of a fierce woman.

CONTENTS

Introduction   1

1. Beginnings   9
2. Conversion   41
3. Sisterhoods   80
4. Politics and Love on the Left   119
5. The Break   156
6. "Carlson's Continuing Commentary"   183

Conclusion   221

Acknowledgments   227

List of Abbreviations   229

Notes   231

Index   281

About the Author   291

Illustrations appear after page 118

Introduction

On November 25, 1992, Sister Anne Joachim Moore, of the Congregation of the Sisters of St. Joseph (CSJ), delivered a eulogy at Saint Mary's Junior College (SMJC) in Minneapolis for her dear friend and colleague, Grace Holmes Carlson. Sister AJ had worked with Grace since the early 1960s when the two wrote the founding plan for SMJC. Grace, who had been raised a Catholic in St. Paul, left the Church during the late 1930s and joined the Socialist Workers Party (SWP), to which she then devoted her life for the next fourteen years. She was the only female defendant among the eighteen Trotskyists convicted under the Smith Act on the eve of America's entry into World War II in 1941. In 1948 she ran for vice president of the United States under the Socialist Workers Party banner, but, in 1952, she left the SWP and returned both to her professional life as an educational psychologist and to the Catholic Church. During this second phase of her life, she dedicated herself to the educational mission of SMJC. She worked closely with Sister AJ to educate young women in the technical skills of nursing and in a liberal arts curriculum, both couched in a Catholic cosmology in which one's efforts were focused on service to God and to others.

In her eulogy Sister AJ remembered the many facets of Grace's long and productive life. She also captured much of Grace's personality. Recalling Grace's struggle to recover her voting rights after the 1941 Smith Act conviction, Sister AJ noted that it was not until the early 1960s that she had them restored. Grace "enjoyed describing [to her friends] the reaction on the young bureaucrat's face when, in completing the forms he asked her why/how she had lost these rights, to which her response was, 'Of course, by attempting to overthrow the government by force and violence.'" Sister AJ explained that "I think she loved that little episode connecting back to her exciting and thrilling days as a [n]ational figure, one to be reckoned with by the government. She was a fierce woman with a light, good-humored touch."[1] *The Fierce Life of Grace Holmes Carlson:*

Catholic, Socialist, Feminist is a historical biography of Grace Holmes Carlson (1906–1992) that examines the story of this complicated woman in the context of her times. In particular, it considers the significance of her experiences during the twentieth century as a member of the working class, as a Catholic, and as a woman.[2]

Even as she earned a PhD in psychology at the University of Minnesota in 1933 and built a professional career for herself by 1940, Grace continued to see herself as a member of and defender of the working class. Partly this identification came from her Irish and German working-class roots—her father was a boilermaker on the Great Northern Railway, and she grew up in St. Paul's Rice Street district—but it also was a result of her conversion to Marxism during the 1930s. These experiences shaped not only her life choices but also her perception of her life's trajectory. Over the course of her life, even as she rose into the middle class in terms of occupation and income, Grace continued to identify with workers and their concerns. Grace's story thus illuminates both how "working-class subjects come to be" and how class operates in the spaces between occupation, politics, life experience, social networks, and culture.[3]

Grace's life was also one marked by lived Catholicism in which that faith tradition—and the women and men of the formal, organized religious institution—shaped her commitment to social justice. Grace was raised in the Catholic faith, educated in parochial school by the Sisters of St. Joseph, and she later returned to the Church and to the Josephites, who found work for her at what became St. Mary's Junior College after she left the SWP in 1952. Her story contributes to recent historical scholarship on the importance of understanding the role of faith in workers' lives.[4] It speaks to how religion shapes working-class political consciousness and can sustain different types of political action.

Grace's years in the SWP also provide an atypical story of a woman in the role of a party organizer—a woman among many men within a movement that prioritized class-based concerns over gender equality—who nonetheless rose in the ranks of the party and translated its message to address women's struggles. Her career, and the lives of her female comrades at the party branch level that become visible in her extensive correspondence with them, illuminate both the possibilities and the limitations for women in the period between the "Lyrical Left" of the

1920s and the New Left of the 1960s. Grace's life was thus also part of the less familiar history of an alternative struggle for equality during the 1930s, 1940s, and 1950s among working-class women more generally and revolutionary Marxist women more specifically.[5]

Developments over the past few decades in the fields of both biography and working-class and radical history have opened the way for such inquiries. Since the late 1980s and early 1990s in particular, feminist theory has reinvigorated the historical study of individual lives, introducing, as Susan Ware has argued, "a different type of person as worthy of biographical treatment" and placing gender at the center of the "interpretive and narrative strategy," with equal attention paid to private and public lives.[6] James Barrett has recently urged historians of the political Left to explore what (auto)biography can "tell us about the personal identity and intimate relationships within the party and about the gendered quality of the communist experience." Asking questions of these subjects from the political Left, for whom there is often a "striking silence on personal issues," will enable scholars "to consider radicals and other working people, not simply as members of a particular social class or participants in social movements," as Barrett notes, "but also as individuals with personalities and private lives . . . that may have shaped their motivations and behavior beyond the political and social forces we find to be more familiar in our work."[7]

The appreciation of private lives, however, does not have to come at the expense of attention to structural forces but can come in recognition of the complex relationship between the two. As Nick Salvatore has described this kind of biographical approach, "The value, then, of understanding a particular life in its broad social context is precisely this: it examines the process of historical change through an individual who, like other humans, grapples simultaneously with complex forces both public and private." He argues that "the test, then, for biography is not whether the subject is representative, whatever that may mean, but rather what it is we might learn from a study of a specific life."[8] This biography examines the links between the many facets of Grace Holmes Carlson's private life and her extraordinary public career. These connections illuminate how working-class subjects have identified themselves in the past, how struggles for women's equality were defined and related to other social and political movements between the 1930s and the 1950s, and how some individuals who held the Catholic faith found theological and practical support for their commitments both to social justice and to women's autonomy even before the reforms of the Second Vatican Council (1962–1965).

In Grace's childhood, various factors shaped her identity as a working-class Catholic young woman who was committed to social justice. These included her natal family and childhood neighborhood, her local parish, her women religious teachers, and the impact of World War I and the 1922 shopmen's strike. Grace spoke about these formative influences during two interviews she gave to Carl Ross in 1987 and in several of the many speeches she delivered to nursing students and Catholic groups after her return to the Church in 1952.[9] Through her experience of World War I, as a working-class Irish and German girl, she had come to question government authority and the 100 percent Americanism that vigilante groups imposed on her city. As a result of her father's experiences during the shopmen's strike, she had deepened her understanding of the importance of worker solidarity. And Grace came to appreciate early on the importance of education for the development of her autonomy. It was not only her mother who instilled that lesson but also her women religious instructors in high school and college. Grace attended the College of St. Catherine (CSC) during the mid- to late 1920s, when a modern temper swept through American culture, shaking up assumptions about gender and sexuality. While yearbooks and campus magazines provide insight into the ways Grace and her young Catholic cohorts challenged stereotypes about women's proper roles, the sources are less forthcoming on the specifics of their take on sexual behavior. What is clear is how at CSC the Josephites reinforced the value Grace placed on higher education as a route to economic independence for women and how they set her feet on the road to a professional career.

What the Josephites did not expect from Grace as she went off to graduate school at the University of Minnesota to pursue a doctorate in psychology in 1929 was that she would gradually drift from the Church as she converted to socialism over the next decade. Grace maintained her commitment to social justice that she had developed in her youth as a working-class Catholic in St. Paul, but now channeled it in a revolutionary direction in a new city. Both her encounter with the 1934 Minneapolis strikes and her first job as a vocational rehabilitation counselor in the Minnesota Department of Education that she began in 1935 intensified Grace's evolving view that a socialist society was the only way to address the needs of workers and the exploited. In 1938 Grace entered the SWP as a delegate to its founding convention in Chicago. By September 1940 she left her job at the Department of Education—in part because of red baiting during the "little red scare"—to work full-time for the party, leaving the Church behind.

For the next twelve years Grace built a public career for herself in the SWP, working as Minnesota state organizer, running for elected office multiple times, writing a column for the party press, and working in both New York and Detroit to assist the party as needed. She built this career not only with her strong speaking, writing, and organizing skills but also with her strategic self-promotion among key leaders within the SWP, including National Secretary James P. Cannon and Labor Secretary Farrell Dobbs. Grace was elected to the party's National Committee in 1942 and served as its only woman member for many years. She had also gained notoriety in the party as one of the twenty-nine Trotskyists to be indicted and one of the eighteen who were then convicted of violating the Smith Act in 1941. Grace spent a year in federal prison in Alderson, West Virginia, because of her political beliefs.

Of vital importance to Grace's experiences within the SWP and to her survival as she served her sentence at Alderson in 1944 was her sisterhood of women comrades. That network, which included her biological sister, Dorothy Schultz, sustained her by providing a connection to the intellectual and social world of the SWP that she had left behind. Grace's rich correspondence during the year she spent in prison reveals not only the connections and concerns shared by her and her women friends but also Grace's relationship with the mostly poor and very young women incarcerated with her at Alderson. Both these experiences—Grace's interaction with her women Trotskyist comrades, who were working women and (in some cases) also working mothers, and her exposure to the poor women prisoners—served as the inspiration for the working-class Marxist feminism that Grace came to articulate in her writings for the *Militant* and in her 1945 "Women in Prison" speaking tour. Grace's experiences and writings (as well as those of other party women who wrote for the *Militant* in these years) were part of the Left's answer to the woman question during the 1940s. In her columns and her speaking tour, Grace offered a Marxist critique of capitalism as the solution to her and her party sisters' struggles and concerns as radical women. Their story adds to the history of feminisms on the Left during the 1940s and early 1950s, the period between the first and second waves. And Grace's evolving understanding of the woman question, specifically her critique of patriarchy that she articulated by the 1960s, speaks to the often overlooked connections between Old Left and New Left feminist concerns.[10]

It was not only Grace's ties to her female comrades that were so important to her political work but also those with men in the party. In addition to the platonic friendships and work relationships she forged over the years with men like James Cannon, Farrell Dobbs, Harry DeBoer, and her brother-in-law, Henry Schultz, Grace also engaged in a romance with Vincent Raymond Dunne for over ten years. Both Grace and Ray were married to other people at the time they pursued this relationship: Grace had separated from her husband, Gilbert, sometime in the late 1930s when she became more fully committed to the revolutionary Trotskyist movement, but Ray never left his wife, Jennie. As a result, only a few party insiders knew for certain about the affair. But Grace's and Ray's dedication to the SWP, among other factors, drew them together. Their relationship was just one of many within the SWP, including that between Grace's sister, Dorothy, and her husband, Henry, in which couples enjoyed sharing in the common work of the party. Private relationships became intertwined with public commitments and helped build and sustain the radical politics of those involved, who otherwise faced a world hostile to their beliefs.[11] Of particular importance to Grace's political career in these years was her run for vice president of the United States in 1948, the press coverage of which included deeply entrenched biases against women running for such high office—some of which still remain today.

Given Grace's high profile in the party by the late 1940s, her decision to leave its ranks in 1952 and to return to the Catholic Church came as a shock to everyone. Stemming from personal and spiritual reasons after the death of her father, Grace's break with the SWP was not due to political factionalism; she remained a Marxist and, unlike other high-profile defectors, never informed for the FBI. But because she had been blacklisted as a former high-level SWP member, she could not find a job. Her experiences during the early 1950s show the impact of the Second Red

Scare on individual lives, providing a case study of a woman's experience, which heretofore has been largely overlooked.[12] With the help of a local priest, Grace found work first as an administrative assistant at St. Mary's Hospital in Minneapolis and, then, as a faculty member who was deeply involved with the mission of Saint Mary's Junior College (SMJC). She also soon reunited with her husband, Gilbert, and began to rebuild her life with a new network of colleagues and friends.

That new life contained elements of the old as well as fresh influences and interests. Her return to the Church was driven, in part, by her need for the transcendent in her life, but she also could not bring herself to abandon the core of her radical political commitments. In a Church with many reactionary quarters, Grace found space to reconcile these two seemingly irreconcilable needs. During her years at SMJC from the mid-1960s until 1984, Grace embraced a unique form of Catholic activism that drew from the liturgical and Catholic Action movements, the ideas espoused by Catholic Marxists in the English *Slant* movement, and, ultimately, the reforms of Vatican II.

Through an examination of the many speeches she gave to student and religious groups in these years, the articles she wrote for the SMJC alumnae newspaper, and her correspondence with her new circle of friends (many of whom were priests), the specifics of her political concerns and her particular approach to them emerge. These included a continued devotion to fighting for civil rights and for peace, now also including attention to antinuclear campaigns, which were in the New Left but not of it in terms of Grace's analysis and methods. Through her insistence on striking at the heart of capitalist exploitation, which she believed was behind all inequities and challenges to peace, Grace maintained much of her Marxist thinking; in her continued belief in the importance of an organized political movement to effect revolutionary social change, she proudly touted her Old Left loyalties in the face of what she condemned as the individualistic and undisciplined approaches of New Left protests. And in her call for engagement with the pressing problems of the day as a gospel mandate for the lay apostolate acting within the Mystical Body of Christ to "restore all things to Christ," she functioned as a Catholic activist. In her roles as a teacher, administrator, mentor, and friend, Grace also continued her struggle for women's equality, now working to overthrow capitalist patriarchy by educating the masses through a variety of personal and professional interactions, particularly as she advised—and at times financially supported—women students at SMJC.

The long arc of Grace's life reveals fascinating continuities in her political consciousness that transcended the shifts in her particular partisan commitments. Her story also illuminates the workings of class identity within the context of various influences over the course of a lifespan. It reveals the vitality of working-class and left-wing feminisms that existed during what has been considered the doldrums of the women's movement. Her life in the SWP provides a window into the inner workings of the Trotskyist movement, particularly for women at the branch level, and into the social world of platonic and romantic relationships that were so central to sustaining that radical community. And her interactions with women religious, priests, and various institutions within the Church that informed her cosmology and activism are a rich source for understanding the contours of lived Catholicism in twentieth-century America. Grace, who was, as one of her friends called her, an amazing woman, may not have been representative of any one social group or historical category, but her life certainly has much to teach.

1

Beginnings

In the fall of 1922, Grace Holmes was just fifteen years old when her father, James, returned to his job as a boilermaker on the Great Northern Railway after having been on strike since July. Grace later remembered how her mother made her walk with him "out to the Jackson Street shops because they had pickets there and [her mother] was afraid something might happen to him." Grace, however, felt that what she did "was wrong." At the time she even went to confession, "saying that I have helped deprive the laborer of his wages." The priest, whom she describes as being "completely confused" by this admission, granted her God's forgiveness anyway. As she witnessed the collapse of the 1922 shopmen's strike, Grace turned to the sacrament of reconciliation to absolve her of what she believed was a sin: her complicity in undermining the strike and workers' solidarity. Even though she understood her family's difficult situation, she commented that her father's crossing the pickets still struck her as "something that was sinful."[1] Grace's understanding of the strike and of her father's predicament was informed by her faith; she saw it as a product of man's fallen nature, including that of her own father, who betrayed his comrades because of the desperate situation in which he found himself.

Throughout Grace Holmes Carlson's life, she remained committed to supporting workers in their fight against capitalist oppression and all who struggled for social justice. These commitments were formed during her childhood by various influences, including that of the 1922 shopmen's strike. Some of these influences were more structural or public, while others were more personal or private. How Grace grappled with these defining factors simultaneously, and developed into a young adult who prided herself on her questioning of authority and her devotion to worker solidarity illuminate the process through which working-class subjects like her defined themselves in the past.[2]

Chief among the things that influenced Grace were the members of her natal family and the experiences, values, and beliefs they shared with her. That inheritance included an Irish and German ancestry marked by a commitment to family, with deep working-class roots. Growing up in the city of St. Paul during the 1910s and 1920s, Grace experienced her ethnic and class identity in very place-specific ways. In the more solidly working-class neighborhoods, like that of north Frogtown, where Grace grew up, there was a greater degree of economic homogeneity, yet also some ethnic and racial mixing. As a result, inhabitants understood their daily challenges in class-based terms.[3]

Central to Grace's working-class childhood experiences were also her Catholic parish and parish school of St. Vincent's. There she was influenced by the priests trained in the diocese built by Archbishop John Ireland. They communicated the Church's evolving social teachings, which included a critique of the abuses and dangers of both capitalism and socialism and the defense of a living wage. And at St. Vincent's school, and then at St. Joseph's Academy high school, Grace was educated by the Sisters of St. Joseph. Their influence on her life was profound and did not end in her childhood. In these early years, the sisters helped Grace lay the solid foundation of academic training that would ultimately help her earn a professional degree. They also modeled for her the lives of educated women of faith who committed themselves to serving the least among them. The lessons Grace learned from the Josephites influenced her developing political consciousness as a young woman committed to social justice. They also contributed to her strong opposition to World War I and her criticism of what she saw as narrow definitions of patriotism. Grace Holmes's early formation thus included several inherent tensions that stemmed from the various, overlapping influences of her family, neighborhood, parish, and school. Each contributed to the working-class person she was becoming in her childhood and teenage years.

* * *

Although Grace often identified herself as an Irish girl, finding common ground in the humor of ethnic stereotypes with friends and comrades throughout her life,[4] she did not comment extensively on her family's immigrant history. Perhaps this inattention came from the fact that, when it came to her father's Irish side of the family at least, the immigrant past was quite distant. Her paternal great-grandfather,

Samuel Holmes, was born in Ireland in 1800 and came to the United States sometime before 1843, when her grandfather, Samuel J. Holmes, was born in New York. Grace's paternal great-grandmother, Catehene Holmes, was also born in Ireland and was twenty-three years younger than her husband, Samuel. Given the timing of Samuel J.'s birth in New York in 1843, Samuel and Catehene were not among the famine migrants who fled Ireland in massive numbers beginning in the late 1840s. Their ability to move west and purchase land corroborates their status as prefamine migrants. By 1850 Samuel Senior and Catehene, along with Samuel J. and two more sons, Thomas and William, were residing in Lebanon, Wisconsin, a farming community originally settled by Germans in 1843. Samuel owned four hundred dollars in real estate and worked as a farmer alongside neighbors from Ireland and Germany with similarly valued properties.[5] Although Samuel was unable to read or write, his being able to move from the port of New York to buy property out west indicates that he had resources. As Jay P. Dolan explains, "It cost about one thousand dollars in midcentury to start a farm—a sum beyond the reach of poor, unskilled immigrants." For the Holmes family, the farm was within reach, and they set down roots in Wisconsin.[6]

Eventually young Samuel J., Grace's paternal grandfather, struck out on his own and left the family farm. Sometime in the late 1860s he married Mary A. Henoran, who was born in Canada to parents originally from Ireland.[7] By 1872 Samuel J. and Mary Holmes had moved to Fond DuLac, Wisconsin, where Samuel appears in the city directory as a blacksmith.[8] The couple had two sons at that time, William L. and Thomas F., and had two more while still residing in Wisconsin: Samuel G. (born in 1876) and Grace's father, James A. (born in 1879).[9] By 1895, Samuel and Mary, along with young James, had moved to St. Paul. They settled into a rented home in the Ninth Ward on Lyton Place off Rice Street in a working-class district just north and east of the more predominantly German working-class Frogtown. The Rice Street neighborhood was distinctly working-class in character, with Rice Street itself being a commercial corridor for local residents that housed a streetcar line and various storefronts. On the blocks off this main thoroughfare were some modest cottages along with duplexes and small apartment houses.[10] In their living arrangements, the Holmeses found themselves in line with St. Paul's Irish working class: they lived in a somewhat ethnically mixed neighborhood because "the Irish population was dispersed more or less evenly throughout the city."[11] In their occupations, however, the Holmeses diverged from the norm for the working-class Irish in St. Paul, the majority of whom were unskilled laborers.[12] Samuel J. continued to ply his trade as a blacksmith while James, just fifteen years old, worked as a driver.[13] But they were still solidly working class, as their settling into a rented home in the Rice Street neighborhood indicates.

By 1900, James was working as a blacksmith's helper, perhaps attempting to learn his father's trade. At times he also worked as a packer for an express company, an unspecified laborer, and a clerk at an oyster house.[14] James eventually found his permanent occupation in the railroad shops, first as a boilermaker's helper and then as a boilermaker.[15] That choice of trade makes sense given James's earlier exposure to blacksmithing: working with iron and steel, making and repairing the steam engines for the locomotives, drew on some of the same skills as characterized his father's trade.[16] His transition to this work came during the same years when he left his father's house on Lyton Street and moved to 301 University Avenue West with his young bride, Mary Nuebel.

James and Mary met and courted in the working-class Rice Street district of St. Paul. Before they married, James had been living with his Irish family on Lyton Street. Mary was residing with her German family on University Avenue in south Frogtown. Unlike her father's side of the family, Grace's maternal side had a closer immigrant connection: her mother, Mary, was born in Germany in 1877. Grace's grandmother, also named Mary, and her grandfather, Frank P. Nuebel, had eight children, seven of whom survived into adulthood: Frank Jr., Carl, Tracy, Casper, Mary, Henry, and Joseph. The family arrived in the United States from Prussia in 1882.[17] By 1885 they were residing in Red Wing, Minnesota. Frank died there in 1891, an event that may have led his wife and some of their adult children to relocate.[18] By 1895, Casper, Mary (Grace's mother), Joseph, and Henry were living in an apartment in St. Paul at 301 University Avenue West.[19] Frank Jr. had established himself as a grocer with a business located at 312 University Avenue West.[20] Henry and Mary worked as clerks in the store. Casper worked as a driver, and Joseph became a soldier who served in the Philippines.[21] Frank Jr.'s status as a grocer placed him squarely within the norm for German immigrants in St. Paul, who, unlike most of the Irish immigrants to the city, "had arrived with some combination of necessary skills and capital, as well as a familiarity with the workings of a capitalist economy." As early as 1860, 26 percent of German-born males were engaged in trade and service in St. Paul (while only 14 percent worked as common laborers).[22]

It is unclear how Mary and James first met, but the two were soon rendezvousing often on Rice Street bridge. Grace later commented on this phase of her parents' lives, noting that given the busy character of the location, "How it could have been a romantic spot I don't know, but it seemed that way to them."[23] Mary and James were married on July 20, 1904.[24] They remained in the neighborhood, close to their family and jobs. At first they lived with the Nuebels at 301 University Avenue West, deploying a strategy common among the working class in pooling incomes to support the costs of rent and other living expenses.[25] This strategy became all the more necessary after Frank moved the grocery store to Western Avenue with his wife and children. His siblings had to find other ways to support themselves. Henry worked as a painter, Casper continued as a driver, and Mary married James.[26]

In these early years of their marriage, Mary and James had two daughters, Grace (born on November 13, 1906) and Helen Dorsey, who would be called Dorothy (born on December 5, 1909). Both girls were baptized in the Catholic Church at St. Peter Claver's parish by its pastor, Rev. Thomas Printon.[27] At the time, St. Peter Claver's was located on the southwest corner of Farrington and Aurora Streets, a few blocks south of the Holmeses' apartment on University Avenue West.[28] The location was also on the northern border of the Rondo district, "a narrow sixteen-block area bounded on the north by German working-class Frogtown and by the mixed neighborhood north of Summit Avenue on the south." The district was the heart of St. Paul's black community and housed "black professionals, businesses, cultural and political clubs, a newspaper," and six churches. In 1910, African Americans made up only 1.5 percent of the total population of the city of St. Paul, but from their homes in the Rondo they "created a leadership contingent who assiduously worked to guard community interests."[29]

That effort included getting St. Peter Claver's built. When the original congregation of mostly black Catholics raised money in 1892 for a permanent site to replace the church space they had been renting on Market Street since 1888, they were met with "some objection by the neighbors" to the lot they bought on the corner of Rice and Aurora Streets. The congregants did not give up. Among them was Samuel Hardy, who organized the First Negro Catholic Congress in 1889 and founded the first black newspaper west of Chicago. Hardy and the others secured the location on Farrington and Aurora as an alternative site. They established their parish there, further west from Rice Street and closer to the edge of south Frogtown, without resistance from white neighbors.[30] Founded as an African American parish, St. Peter Claver's gradually became a racially mixed one.[31]

Grace's exposure to this kind of interracial community may have contributed to her commitment to the civil rights struggle and her work in the St. Paul NAACP later on in her life by normalizing such interactions for her family.[32] When she was a baby and a very young child, her family attended St. Peter Claver's, which had a congregation of about four hundred black and white members in 1910.[33] Mary and James's decision to have their daughters baptized there most likely was due to the location of their residence at 301 University Avenue in south Frogtown during the early years of their marriage. St. Peter Claver's was just a few blocks from their home. And this was before the building of the Church of St. Agnes, which became the parish for German Catholics in that neighborhood after 1912.[34] Presumably the Nuebels worshipped at St. Peter Claver's, and when James married into the family, he and Mary continued the connection.

By 1914 both their living arrangements and their parish ties would change. Mary, James, Grace, and Dorothy, along with Mary's two brothers, Henry and Casper, moved to 158 LaFond Avenue in the north Frogtown area, west of Rice Street, where there were blocks of modest single-family homes.[35] Many of their neighbors were native-born Americans of German or Irish descent, but there were also second-generation Poles, Bohemians, and Russians, including one family whose parents' native tongue was Yiddish.[36] Grace and Dorothy were enrolled in St. Vincent's parish school. Located on the corner of Blair Avenue and Virginia Street, just off LaFond, it was a short walk from their new home. By 1920 James and Mary owned the house, a purchase made possible by his wages as a boilermaker for the Great Northern Railway and a mortgage, as well as whatever earnings Henry and Casper could contribute while they still lived there too.[37]

The adults in Grace's immediate family orbit had an impact on her developing personality and political consciousness. She had a particularly close relationship with her mother during her childhood, noting how she "was completely devoted" to her to the point of not fully appreciating her father. Mary "had relatively little education" but loved books. Grace later commented on how her mother "had the greatest influence on my life in terms of making me interested in reading and education, and being a kind of liberated woman if you can talk about it at this [time]."[38] The importance of education as a way to build a better life for herself and to establish her independence as a young woman was a message communicated to Grace at an early age by her mother. Mary not only emphasized the value of reading in their home but also supported her daughter's education from Grace's time at the local parish school to her years at the selective St. Joseph's Academy and through her enrollment at the College of St. Catherine.

But Mary's influence on Grace went beyond developing her appreciation of education as a means to intellectual and economic liberation. It also included cultivating Grace's compassion and empathy as Grace came to fill a caregiver role for her ailing mother. Mary suffered from Parkinson's disease—what Grace, as a child, thought of as "some kind of unnamed nervous disorder"—which made it hard for Mary to function at times. Although the disease usually affects people over the age of sixty, it can sometimes affect those under forty, as it did with Mary. Grace's devotion to her mother may have stemmed, in part, from this reality, which evoked her protective instincts and pushed her to mature beyond her years. Grace recalls how when she "was just young, ten, eleven years old," she would "go to the library and get books for her" mother. Mary was particularly interested in works dealing with "new thought," the popular philosophy that taught a mind-over-matter approach to health.[39] Perhaps Mary found hope in such readings. Grace does not comment on her mother's situation beyond these few recollections, but in them her devotion to her mother is clear.

Grace's relationship as a child with her father was equally complex. She admits in her recollections later in life that she was somewhat unfair to him as a child, not really appreciating how hard he worked to support the family because he was not around the house much to spend time with her and Dorothy.[40] But in those memories she also reveals her respect for him and the influence he had on her. In particular, she attributes to him and his identity as a worker her consciousness of her own working-class identity. It was not only their north Frogtown/Rice Street neighborhood that communicated to her the family's position among what she called the "low working class."[41] It was also James's role outside the house. He was, as she later described, "a worker all his life." Grace was aware of some of the other jobs her father had taken before he became a boilermaker, but it was his work for the railroad with which she and Dorothy most associated him. Grace remembered how "we thought that was a great kind of job, you know. We would go down to the shops to visit him and all this type of thing."[42] Sometimes she would bring "his lunch down to him" and he would take her "through the Round House."[43] She saw and knew the work her father did and was proud of it and of his identity as having been "a worker all his life." Grace remained loyal to this identity and took it on for herself even as she advanced through higher education into the ranks, occupationally at least, of the middle class: her heart and her identity would remain grounded in her awareness of her family's Frogtown/Rice Street working-class roots.

Grace gained this bone-deep sense of her class identity from observing her father and from living in north Frogtown. But she attributed the earliest formation of what she called her "pro-union and even pro-radical" ideas to her "German uncle who thought of himself as a real radical, thought of himself as a Marxist, although he didn't join the Party." Grace did not know how her Uncle Casper came to his radical politics—whether he brought them with him from Germany or was drawn to them once he arrived in the United States in the midst of the second industrial revolution—but he exposed her to the ideas during her childhood. Casper, who was also Grace's godfather, resided with the Holmeses both when they lived on University Avenue and when they moved to LaFond Avenue.[44] He spent a lot of time with Grace and Dorothy. They got to see him not only at home on his days off but also at his workplace, where they sometimes helped out. Grace explains how Casper "would rent some of the streams where watercress was growing, and he would pick watercress" to make a living. He subscribed to a radical newspaper and used old issues as wrapping paper for the greens.[45] Grace recalled how when she was "ages seven, eight and nine," she "would go with him sometimes and then I would sometimes help bunch the watercress before he would sell it to the restaurants and grocery stores and all of this type of thing." In the process she would read excerpts from the socialist newspaper used for the wrapping and, as they worked, Grace recalled how "he would talk a lot about radicalism." She later claimed that she was "kind of sympathetic toward this despite the fact that, of course, the church view was anti-Marxist."[46] At seven, eight, and nine years old, Grace may not have been fully aware of this tension, but she was beginning to find sympathy with socialist ideas even while she remained devoted to the Church. Her natal family thus shaped her young identity as a worker and exposed her to socialist ideas that would stay with her for the remainder of her life.

* * *

Grace also began to question authority at a young age. She acknowledged that this trait was nurtured, in part, from a somewhat unlikely source: the women religious who taught her at St. Vincent's parish school. The sisters, "who were from Ireland, born in Ireland," were, as Grace recalled, "very anti-English, very anti-English." When the Great War broke out, the sisters had the students "sing songs like 'I Didn't Raise My Boy to Be a Soldier' and a lot of other songs that later were determined to be kind of seditious, so we had to drop them." The experience cultivated in Grace what she called "a kind of anti-government position really very early in life." She also attributed her openness to the socialist ideas her uncle was sharing with her in these same years to this orientation, describing it not as a clear partisan position but "mostly a kind of attitude that I developed."[47] She may not have been able to fully understand or define that stance as a young grade school girl, but Grace was beginning to question authority and challenge the assertions of the capitalist state because of these influences.

As Grace noted in her recollections of her schoolday experiences, the women religious who taught her were Irish. Their ethnic identity explained their anti-English sentiment and their opposition to the war, which "may have been linked closely to the plight of their homeland." It also reflected the demographics of the parish. St. Vincent's, founded as a mission chapel in 1888, became the spiritual home to "125 families, predominantly Irish." The school, which opened in 1902, was originally "staffed by four Sisters of St. Joseph of Carondelet."[48] The Irish-born among them were more directly concerned with Ireland's struggle for freedom from English colonial rule; their antigovernment and antiwar positions stemmed from this ethnic politics. But they were not alone in opposing the war, especially before the United States entered the fight in 1917. Whether because of concerns similar to those held by the Irish-born sisters, or because of the more class-based anger at fighting what was perceived to be a Wall Street war that was common among many second- and third-generation Irish, such dissent "reflected the predominant Irish working-class sentiment in [Grace's] neighborhood and town."[49] In this way, Grace was not an outlier among her working-class neighbors, but rather stood in opposition to the elites of St. Paul (including Archbishop John Ireland), who by 1917 backed the war effort with overt patriotic rhetoric and displays.[50] The women religious who taught Grace at St. Vincent's and who dissented from that form of patriotism thus reinforced her working-class (and Irish working-class) identity.

The sisters also contributed to Grace's spiritual formation in ways that informed her developing political consciousness. Their Irish identity was but one part of who they were. Equally significant was their commitment to their religious order, the Sisters of St. Joseph. Founded by a Jesuit priest in France in 1650, the order was created to educate the poor girls of Le Puy. The sisters were not to be cloistered but, as was becoming the case with other orders of women religious emerging during the mid-seventeenth century, were to serve the growing social needs of their communities, either in education, hospitals, or orphanages.[51] The sisters were implored by the directives of their congregation to "show great charity towards all classes of neighbors, particularly toward the poor" and "to assist in Christ's redemptive work for the salvation of souls."[52] The Josephites' commitment to serving the poor and the dispossessed and their emphasis on the importance of education were values that Grace was exposed to as a young woman during her years at St. Vincent's and at St. Joseph's Academy. Those values later informed her commitment, understood as a gospel mandate, to social justice and to serving others.

The first Sisters of St. Joseph to arrive in the United States in 1836 from Lyon were requested by the bishop of St. Louis to help with such charitable, spiritual, and educational work.[53] As the ranks of the sisters expanded in subsequent decades, from both those coming from abroad and those joining the community from within the United States, the number and reach of the institutions they founded grew in kind.[54] By 1851, four sisters from St. Louis traveled to St. Paul upon the request of Bishop Joseph Cretin to open a school, and they created the basis of what became the thriving Josephite community in St. Paul.[55] As Carol K. Coburn and Martha Smith observe, "By 1920 they created and/or staffed fourteen parish schools (plus catechism classes in twelve other parishes), three academies, a music and art conservatory, two hospitals, two orphanages, and a women's college."[56] In this work they touched thousands of lives, including that of Grace Holmes.[57]

It was the underpaid labor of these women religious that made possible the expansion of these institutions, especially the Church's parochial school system.[58] So too did the contributions of the members of each parish, many of whom came from the ranks of the immigrant working class. St. Vincent's, whose boundaries included "University avenue on the south, to the several townships on the north, Chatsworth on the west, and Rice street on the east," was "a parish of working people" where "funds were never abundant."[59] Yet its members sacrificed enough not only to expand the church from the original small mission chapel built in 1888 to the Gothic stone structure that sat one thousand people in 1897 but also to fund the building of the school that was completed in 1902. Their sacrificial giving was supplemented by a few larger donations from more well-off benefactors.[60] "An imposing structure three stories high," St. Vincent's school was built on "spacious grounds, large enough, after providing ample playground for the children, to afford an enclosed park prettily laid out in the greensward and flower beds." The building itself was "of the colonial style of architecture from Twin City mottled pressed brick, with Georgia marble trimmings."[61] Over the entrance, "On the frieze, which is also marble, the appropriate inscription, 'Suffer the little children to come unto me,' is done in gold letters."[62] The school contained eight "large and airy and well lighted" classrooms that could hold a total of six hundred children. Each classroom had a crucifix on the wall.[63] The physical spaces served the dual purpose of the parochial school mission to educate its students and to see to their proper religious formation.

It was thus not just the Sisters of St. Joseph who taught Grace in grade school who had influenced her as a child but also the parish where she worshipped and attended school. For working-class Catholics during the late nineteenth and early twentieth centuries, their parishes were, as Evelyn Savidge Sterne has argued, "the most accessible and important institutions," where "the largest proportion of immigrants (first-generation) and ethnics (second- and third-generation) congregated on a regular basis." The Church was the institution "to which every Catholic could, theoretically belong," unlike "unions, political machines, mutual aid associations and saloons," which were limited by skill level, ethnicity, class, or gender. While not an exclusive female sphere, the parish provided opportunities for women to participate through groups like the Rosary and Altar Society and the League of the Sacred Heart. Parishes were where the Catholic Church met the local community and "functioned not only as sources of spiritual solace but also as dispensers of charity, promoters of upward mobility, and centers of neighborhood life."[64] These multiple functions were carried out in Grace's childhood parish, which had its own spiritual and social character that became one of the many influences on her young life.

St. Vincent's parish was named after and dedicated to St. Vincent de Paul, who lived in seventeenth-century France and devoted himself to serving the poor. Like the Sisters of St. Joseph whose order was founded in France in the same century, he too "brought charity out of the cloister and into the city streets." St. Vincent communicated in his works the idea that "each man is indeed his brother's keeper."[65] The parishioners of St. Vincent's in St. Paul embraced this legacy in various ways. In 1890, for example, the parish's literary and dramatic society "gave an entertainment at St. Paul Workhouse." In 1928 they "inaugurated the custom of putting a penny into the St. Vincent de Paul boxes as the Congregation leaves the Church." That year, between April and July, the working-class worshippers contributed $16,416.38 through the penny campaign.[66] No doubt many parishes had congregations that conducted similar works of mercy and charity. But St. Vincent's parishioners' special identification with their patron—whom they referred to in his prayer as the "heavenly patron of all associations of charity and Father of all unfortunate, who during life never rejected anyone who implored [God's] assistance"—may have added to the meaning of such efforts.[67] Being a part of such a parish during her youth, Grace was exposed to these works when she attended Mass and partook in the devotional life of the Church.[68]

Although St. Vincent's congregation was historically mostly Irish, it was not completely racially and ethnically homogenous. The parishioners also captured the spirit of St. Vincent by welcoming all those who implored God's assistance because they appreciated the spiritual brotherhood of mankind. That appreciation was expressed not just in terms of caring for the least among the community through works of charity for the poor but also in terms of receiving into the congregation all of God's children, including Chinese, African American, and Native American converts. Considered "living temples of the Holy Spirit," these converts were brought into the church after months of missionary work on the part of Father Laurence Cosgrove, pastor of St. Vincent's from 1889 to 1910.[69] In January 1904, one group of converts that received the sacrament of confirmation "represented ten different nationalities, including 6 Indians, 4 Negroes, 7 Chinese, 1 Gypsy, several Bohemians and a family of deaf mutes, besides many of the nationalities of Europe."[70] The extensive press coverage of the Chinese converts, from their baptisms in late 1903 to their confirmations in January 1904, indicated the uniqueness of such evangelizing in St. Paul and, indeed, in the United States at a time when nativist hostility towards the Chinese remained strong. Congress had just passed "yet another exclusion law" in 1902, "this time extending the period of [Chinese] exclusion indefinitely" from the ten-year ban applied in the original 1882 law and "continuing to deny naturalization to the Chinese already in the United States."[71] The baptism in December 1903 of laundryman Sam Lung marked the first time in the history of the parish that a Chinese community member was converted. In October 1904, five more "native Chinamen were baptized and received into the Catholic faith": Quam Sam, Kee Soon, Ho Lip Tang, and Ho Yon. Tang was a manager of a local restaurant and the other three men were waiters. In addition to reaching out to and welcoming these men into the parish community, the priests of St. Vincent's continued to baptize and receive African Americans from the neighborhood, marking this parish as a mixed one, although not to the same degree as St. Peter Claver's. In 1904, for example, "Thirty-five colored converts were baptized, made their profession of faith, and were received into the church during the month of St. Joseph."[72] Although the expanding ethnic and racial diversity of St. Vincent's parish may not have translated into widespread social harmony among all of the parishioners, it communicated a certain commitment to equality on the part of its priests, who considered all people as "living temples of the Holy Spirit." While there may have been a degree of missionary condescension in the interactions between Father Cosgrove and the converts, the remarkable presence of such a diverse population in the pews, and the theological basis of the equality of all God's children behind that presence, were parts of the world in which Grace grew up and may have contributed to her lifelong commitment to social justice for all peoples.

Grace's parish life also influenced her developing political consciousness by reinforcing her commitment to workers' struggles. That devotion stemmed not just from her identification through her father and her family's situation with the working class and not just from the radical ideas her Uncle Casper exposed her to as a child but also from the milieu of her Catholic parish and the archdiocese of St. Paul. Central to setting the tone for that archdiocese was Archbishop John Ireland. Ireland, who was appointed coadjutor bishop of St. Paul in 1875 and then ordained archbishop in 1888, grew up "on the streets of pioneer St. Paul, Irish, Catholic, and poor." That experience shaped him, as did the time he spent at the seminary in France where he was sent in 1853 by then bishop Joseph Cretin. As a poor Irish young man, Ireland was treated as an outsider, mocked as a misfit, and condescended to as a charity case. Once he returned to the United States and later became archbishop, he launched a campaign for "Irish uplift and Catholic institution-building" in St. Paul that favored Irish priests trained in the St. Paul Seminary that he built and controlled.[73] Those priests worked in the city's parishes (including that of St. Vincent's) and communicated not only the Church's dogma to the faithful but also its social teachings, which Ireland championed. Specifically, Ireland drew from the ideas expressed by Pope Leo XIII in his 1891 encyclical *Rerum Novarum*, in which the pope applied "Catholic tradition to the problems of modern industrial capitalism" to criticize both capitalism and socialism. In *Rerum Novarum*, Leo "reaffirmed the individual right to hold private property" while at the same time he defended the right of workers to organize in unions and "asserted that the state should guarantee a living wage."[74]

One of the foremost proponents of the living wage, articulated in specifically Catholic terms, was Father John Ryan, a priest who had been "educated in Bishop Ireland's schools and went on to teach at St. Paul

Seminary under Ireland's supervision."[75] Ryan thus was a product of Ireland's influence and became an extension of it, at times going beyond Ireland in his defense of workers' rights. A potent mix of Catholic teachings, along with the Irish republicanism, socialism, and populism to which he was exposed in Minnesota, led Ryan to develop his "interest in social questions," his "love of economic justice," his "sympathy with the weaker economic classes," and, ultimately, his living-wage theory, which he published in his doctoral dissertation in 1906.[76] In articulating his theory, Ryan "drew explicitly on *Rerum Novarum*" when he claimed "that an imperative higher than economic theories about free markets compels society to guarantee a living wage to its workers." He based his argument for the living wage not on social utility (as had been the approach of other economists) but on "sacred natural rights."[77] Ryan also emphasized the limits to individualism and the importance of the common good, insisting that the state needed to regulate economic behavior so that no one person could use another for his or her own economic gain or threaten the other's rights.[78] Guaranteeing a living wage through legislation was one of the progressive reforms Ryan advocated as a means to the greater end of preserving the God-given rights and dignity of workers.[79]

Archbishop Ireland supported Ryan in his work, appointing him as professor of moral theology at St. Paul Seminary in 1902. Ryan remained in this position until 1915, influencing a significant number of priests who were educated in his classroom.[80] By 1915, of the priests who served in the city of St. Paul, 78 percent were trained at the St. Paul Seminary, following Ireland's desire to control the formation and placement of clergy in his archdiocese.[81] Among the priests who served in St. Vincent's parish during the time of Grace's childhood, at least three could have been trained by Ryan, given the timing of their assignments: Rev. Timothy Crowley (who was assigned to the parish in 1908 and became pastor in 1912 after Rev. Cosgrove); Rev. John Sullivan (who served as an associate from 1912 to 1918); and Rev. Martin Griffin (who became pastor in 1922).[82] Even if these men had not been among Ryan's students, his message was made readily available to St. Paul's Catholics through popular publications. The *Catholic Bulletin* "published numerous articles extolling the social-justice teachings of Father John Ryan" after he left the city to teach at Catholic University in 1915, and it "also regularly invoked the social justice doctrines of *Rerum Novarum*" in its discussions of labor issues.[83] Ryan's many speeches and writings were also "quoted regularly in the *Union Advocate*." In some of these talks and publications, Ryan went much further than Ireland in defending workers' rights, calling for "protection of picketing and boycotts" in addition to the living wage.[84]

As a result, for many Catholic workers in St. Paul, there was not a disconnect between their commitments to their unions and their Church, between their fight for their dignity as laborers and their faith; indeed, many understood their struggle within the social teachings of their Church as stemming from the higher authority of their God-given rights. For some working-class Catholics, this reality meant that they did not find radical politics appealing: as Mary Lethert Wingerd argues, "Socialism seemed both unnecessary and irrelevant" and "remained on the political fringe." But for others, as was the case for Grace Holmes in the years before she left the Church and then again after she returned to it, it meant that they would not have to choose between their faith and their radicalism because they could see a continuity between the two in their struggle for social change.[85]

* * *

Grace's commitment to social fairness also may have been influenced by the broader environment of St. Paul. There a secular devotion to the common good and a sense of mutuality drove what Wingerd has defined as the city's unique sense of "common civic loyalty among a diverse population" that was "dependent on cross-class institutions that are grounded in urban neighborhoods."[86] Chief among such institutions was the Catholic Church. But both the common civic loyalty and the cross-class cohesion that undergirded it were tested during World War I. Grace, still quite young at the time, witnessed this fracturing of the older civic compact in her city during the war and the 1922 shopmen's strike. These experiences deeply affected her by sharpening her distrust of the government and reinforcing her belief in the need for working-class solidarity.

The common civic loyalty or civic compact that would come under strain during World War I originated in the geographic and socioeconomic reality of St. Paul where, without an industrial ring, elites "stayed put on Summit Avenue for generations" and "the intimate scale of the city fostered an interclass proximity that required daily interactions on many levels." As Wingerd has argued in her work, such proximity and interaction helped foster a climate in which cooperation and compromise in employer-and-employee relations prevailed. After the challenge posed by the industrial unionism of the American Railway Union (ARU) during the Pullman strike and boycott of 1894, James Hill, the Great Northern Railway magnate, but also other businessmen in St. Paul who relied on transportation as the life blood of the commercial city, came to favor what they deemed less disruptive, "responsible" craft unions instead. In Minneapolis industrialists moved out of the central city, organized themselves in the notorious Citizens Alliance, and fought viciously against any union presence in order to maintain control and profitability of their companies. But in St. Paul businessmen came to favor American Federation of Labor (AFL)–style unionism within the "insular civic identity of the city." A "long era of compromise" between employers and employees resulted that lasted from the 1890s through the 1910s.[87]

World War I tested this compromise and the common civic loyalty that sustained it, exposing the class tensions that were just below the surface in the city, including within the cross-class institution of the Catholic Church. When the fighting broke out in Europe, class-based differences quickly became clear. Businessmen in St. Paul hoped the war would bring new economic opportunities through government contracts, and so they put their support behind intervention. But most workers did not share this outlook. Germans, who in 1910 had made up 25 percent of St. Paul's population, supported neutrality, not wanting to see the United States enter into the fray against their fatherland. The city's unions dissented even more strongly, with the St. Paul Trades and Labor Assembly (TLA) asserting that its members were "'unalterably opposed to war.'" It maintained this position even after the AFL came out in support of intervention in March 1916.[88] For some in the city's ranks, this opposition was grounded in their ethnic identities as Germans, or as Irishmen and Irishwomen, like the sisters who taught Grace to sing "I Didn't Raise My Boy to Be a Soldier." But it was also rooted in their recognition of their very different economic interests from those of the businessmen who supported the war: any gains to the local economy would likely be short lived, and enjoyment of them depended on workers' physical survival if they were sent to the European trenches to fight. Even before the United States entered the war in April 1917, businessmen and professionals in St. Paul asserted their support for the conflict in ways that reinforced the emerging class divide. In January of that year they formed the Patriotic League of St. Paul, which, through public displays of patriotism, counteracted the demonstrations of the anti-interventionists. But the league also moved to suppress dissent by pressuring employees to join its ranks through the use of veiled threats and interrogations of their loyalty.[89] Workers felt the strain on the old civic compact in quite blatantly class-based ways.

And they felt that pressure not only in their workplaces at the hands of the Patriotic League members but also within the archdiocese of St. Paul and within their parishes. Archbishop Ireland supported the war despite—or indeed because of—the opposition to it among many of his working-class flock. Concerned to demonstrate the Church's loyalty to the cause in the context of the heated wartime atmosphere, he saw demonstrations of patriotism as essential to removing doubts about his fellow Catholics' standing.[90] This wartime posture came easily to Ireland because he had long been an ardent advocate for the Americanization of the Church in the United States as a part of his modernist stance. That Americanization did not merely include the embrace of patriotic rhetoric and the waving of the American flag by Church leaders at civic events but rather encompassed a broad agenda to have "Church and Age Unite!" to refute nativist claims that Catholics were ignorant and superstitious sheep beholden to the Vatican and incapable of being good citizens.[91] To combat those prejudices, Ireland worked tirelessly throughout his career not only to speak out on the right of workers to join unions and demand a living wage but also to work for temperance reform and in support of high-quality Catholic schools (from parochial grade schools to diocesan high schools and institutions of higher education).[92] He also joined with James Cardinal Gibbons and Bishop George Mundelein in calling for the Americanization of those schools in terms of their curriculum, where instruction would take place in English.[93] During his long tenure as head of the St. Paul diocese, Ireland did much "to reveal the church to America and America to the church."[94]

The priests in his diocese and many of the parishioners embraced this mission in the decades before the war. At St. Vincent's, they carried out overt displays of patriotism at the formal blessing and dedication of the new church building in 1898.[95] On the day of the celebration, "The exterior of the church was decorated with numerous American flags, two large silk banners being displayed from the steeple. The houses in the immediate neighborhood were also decorated with the American colors." Before the Mass, a grand procession of the many neighborhood social and parish spiritual groups formed at the corner of Rice Street and University Avenue and marched to the church, "following behind the standard bearer, who bore the American flag." Once this lay procession arrived at the church, it halted and opened its formation to allow Ireland to pass through with a procession of clergy and altar boys.[96] In a demonstration that blended secular and sacred, patriotic and spiritual, the clergy and members of St. Vincent's, with Archbishop Ireland presiding, dedicated their new church in a display that asserted their American Catholic identity within their working-class St. Paul neighborhood.

In 1902 parishioners constructed this hybrid identity again through their celebration of July Fourth. That year the members of St. Vincent's gathered on the parish grounds for a picnic. The special focus of the event was raising an oversized flag (fifteen by twenty feet) over the new parochial school building. The day's events began with a procession of thirteen girls from the parish who "were dressed in white frocks with red and blue sashes, to represent the thirteen original states." A member of the local Grand Army of the Republic (GAR) post then read the Declaration of Independence and Rev. M. Gallagher, one of the parish priests, delivered an address. The blending of civil and religious symbols continued when "the ceremony was concluded with the blessing of the flag by Rev. R. L. Cosgrove."[97]

There were thus working-class members of St. Vincent's who proudly displayed their patriotism during these parish events, both on church grounds and in the streets of the surrounding north Frogtown neighborhood where they lived. And that love for the United States did not disappear when war broke out in Europe in 1914. Instead, many in the community opposed the war either because of their ethnic loyalties, which were especially strong for the first generation (like the Irish sisters who taught Grace) or because of their class-based critique of a fight that they did not see as their own. Their positions differed sharply from that held by elite Catholics in the archdiocese, like Archbishop Ireland, who insisted on continued displays of loyalty and support for the war. These differences exposed the class-based tension in the Church that had lingered just below the surface.[98]

Especially once the United States entered the fight in 1917, the ethnic and working-class reasons for nonintervention were dismissed as illegitimate and were defined as anti-American by the war's supporters in St. Paul, including the middle-class and professional members of the city's Patriotic League. For dissenters of any stripe, it was a difficult time. Grace, who was ten years old, recalls how the father of one of her school friends, Helen Nash, was considered "anti-American" and was subjected to one of the "American first groups, which didn't have that name, but they used to march in front of his house." Most likely the group was the Patriotic League, which used such public displays to intimidate anyone who did not join its ranks or who spoke out against the war.[99]

It was also a difficult time for Germans in St. Paul and elsewhere in the United States.[100] Grace recalled how they "felt that they had to demonstrate their Americanism, you know," in the face of hostility and suspicion. Referring to her German heritage, she noted that "I had immediate experience with the impact of this hundred percent Americanism," but she does not offer any details.[101] Exactly what kind of prejudicial comments or harassment she or her mother or her uncles may have experienced during the war is not recorded. But in St. Paul the pressure placed on Germans to support the war was intense, resulting from the propaganda produced by the Minnesota Commission for Public Safety, which charged the state's immigrant population with disloyalty. The commission, given statutory authority at its creation in March 1917, was empowered "for the duration of the war to issue and enforce whatever orders" it felt necessary for public safety. It issued circulars condemning any expressions of dissent against the war and fired up a popular frenzy against Germans. In St. Paul that frenzy led to the closing of German restaurants and beer gardens, the dropping of German language classes from schools, the removal of works by German composers in the programs of performances at the city's Schubert Club, and even the removal of the statute of Germania from a building in the city's business district.[102]

Although many Germans "struggled against this outpouring of ethnic antagonism" by joining patriotic societies and supporting the United States in the war,[103] Grace later claimed that she "didn't subscribe to it," referring to that 100 percent Americanism attitude. She admitted that as a young girl in grade school at the time she "didn't do anything about it either" except that the experience of such discrimination based on such a rabid, narrow definition of Americanism led her eventually to find other approaches to understanding politics. Grace recognized the connection between her rejection of "the temper of World War I" and her later "attempt to study the Left in sociology and courses like that" when she could. The repression of the war did not cow her into subscription to a blind loyalty to America and its wartime agenda; instead, the memory of the experience nurtured her rebelliousness, contributing to the way she "just liked to think of myself as being an independent thinker."[104]

Grace admitted that at the time, when she was still in grade school and even in high school, this independent thinking "wasn't all that much." She had not yet struck out completely from the confines of her Catholic working-class world. Indeed, it was in that world where she found support for her questioning of government authority and what was really her nonconformity with the middle-class and elite support for the war in the wider city. "At that time," Grace recalled, "I kind of associated myself with the Irish sisters who were glad the war was over" when it ended in 1918.[105] They communicated their antiwar sentiments through teaching the students to sing antiwar songs in a way that also reinforced Grace's Irish and working-class identity. But her awareness that the sisters were pressured to "drop" the songs when they were "determined to be kind of seditious" seems also to have contributed to her critique of such repression and fueled her anti-authoritarianism.[106]

In addition to leading the students in these allegedly seditious songs until they were suppressed, the sisters communicated antigovernment sentiment less overtly through their politics outside the classroom; Grace recalled how "some of Sister Alberta McGee's relatives in Ireland were involved in the anti-English activities there, you know."[107] McGee served as principal of St. Vincent's school from 1916 to 1925, and her politics were known by the students.[108] Grace claimed that those politics, in combination with the antiwar stand of her other teachers, contributed to her "kind of independent sort of position" in which she "never saw herself as a great patriot" in the way that term was being defined in the official culture of her city, country, and Church at the time.[109]

Grace's emerging political identity was more in line with that of other ethnic workers in St. Paul who remained opposed to the war in large numbers and who defined a different, vernacular, working-class Americanism that included dissent against the war. The war as experienced on the home front in St. Paul not only contributed to the antigovernment attitude Grace was coming to embrace but also exposed the class tensions within her parish and in the wider city. Class tensions surfaced again during the 1922 shopmen's strike in a way that directly affected Grace and the evolution of her political consciousness.[110] Her father, as a boilermaker for the Great Northern Railway, joined in this nationwide strike. Her family's experience of this event reinforced Grace's understanding of the need for worker solidarity in the face of capitalist exploitation and contributed at a young age to what she called her pro-union sentiment.

As a boilermaker, James Holmes worked as a railroad shopman; he was one of "the over 400,000 men who built and maintained the nation's rolling stock." In addition to boilermakers, there were machinists, blacksmiths, electricians, sheet-metal workers, and railway carmen who labored in the railroad shops that were clustered in centers around the country. Together these workers made up the second largest manufacturing workforce in the nation, outnumbering "meatpacking and iron and steel workers combined."[111] In his study of the shopmen's strike, Colin J. Davis argues that "although separated from each other by craft skills," the members of these six trades "nonetheless enjoyed a close-knit camaraderie" and "felt a keen attachment to their railroad employment."[112] These factors aided them in their trade union organizing efforts, during which they otherwise faced an uphill battle against employers who, by the turn of the twentieth century, were imposing piecework and using spies to control their workforce. Each shopcraft (represented by unions like the International Association of Machinists, the International Brotherhood of Boilermakers, and the International Brotherhood of Blacksmiths) came to recognize "that the best guarantee for their survival lay in first organizing federations of crafts on individual railroads and then bringing these together in one nationwide bloc" to confront these employer challenges. They formed the Railway Employees' Department (RED), which was chartered by the AFL in 1909.[113] RED's efforts at organizing system federations were aided by the shortage of workers during World War I; unions became a vital partner in wartime labor and industrial relations to secure continued production and industrial-sector peace.[114]

When the war ended, however, shopmen faced the backlash of employers who wanted to roll back labor gains. The Pennsylvania Railroad began contracting out repairs to nonunion shops and cutting its workforce to regain control of the shop floor.[115] Other lines began to contract out, too, leading the members of RED at its April 1922 convention to support a strike "if contracting out and piecework were not discontinued." When the Railway Labor Board (a mediating body formed by the Transportation Act of 1920) announced a wage cut for shopmen in June to be effective from July 1, 1922, the die was cast. As Davis explains, "On July 1, shopcraft leaders reported that nearly 400,000 shopmen walked off their jobs: 60,000 machinists, 18,000 boilermakers, 10,000 blacksmiths, 11,000 sheet-metal workers, 160,000 carmen, 110,000 helpers, and 20,000 apprentices."[116] On the Great Northern Railway, where James Holmes worked, 7,685 of its 8,220 shopmen (or 93 percent) walked out, indicating a significant degree of solidarity behind the fight. In the communities along the Great Northern where it housed its shops, there was strong support for the strikers that helped prevent the infiltration of strikebreakers.[117] By July 25 the *Great Falls Tribune* reported that "the Great Northern Railroad cancelled trains and the 'grain harvest is in danger of congestion.'"[118]

Rather than negotiate a settlement that addressed the concerns of the shopmen on their lines, most employers wanted not just to defeat the strike but also to crush the unions in the process. They launched massive campaigns to recruit, train, house, and feed the strikebreakers. They hired private detectives to guard the worker replacements when local police, rooted in the communities, refused to do their bidding. And they intimidated and blackmailed merchants to prevent them from supporting the strikers with threats of moving their rail lines out of their town if they did not comply. Strikebreakers and their private detective defenders often used physical force against the strikers to enter the shops and keep them up and running. When strikers and their community-based supporters reacted against that violence with sabotage of railroad property or physical intimidation, employers appealed to the federal government for US marshals to protect the strikebreakers and for court injunctions to prevent strikers from picketing or communicating about the strike.[119] The injunctions made it extremely difficult for the shopmen and their union leaders in RED to continue the fight on a national scale. Those leaders responded by giving up on that struggle and focusing instead on securing the seniority rights of their members on the lines whose owners were willing to come to the table and negotiate a settlement.[120]

Many of the shopmen felt betrayed at this turn of events because the core issues of the wage cut and contracting out were not addressed; they still wanted to fight. But some began to return to work.[121] Their decision may have been reinforced by the difficulties of having been on strike for so many months without pay. Without a strong commitment from their national leadership to continue the fight to the end, these workers no longer saw the point of such sacrifice. By early October, "The number of returned workers increased to 'between 125,000 and 130,000,' over 65,000 miles of track (26 percent of the total)." By late October, Davis finds that "a liberal estimate of the strikers returning to work . . . was 150,000 men (37.5 percent of the total)."[122]

James Holmes may have been among those who, feeling betrayed by the RED leadership, returned to work that fall. James had originally joined in the strike when it began in July. Grace recalled that he "had stayed out a long time and they didn't have the kind of union benefits and so forth that they have now, so we had a pretty difficult time financially." On the one hand, she recognized how "it was understandable that he went back" to work when he did. He had a family to feed and a mortgage to pay. But on the other hand, Grace recalls how, at the time, her father's returning to work "seemed to me to be a very unfortunate kind of thing." To her it was a sin—an offense against God—and by going with him to the Jackson Street shop, she felt complicit.

The 1922 shopmen's strike, along with the impact of World War I in St. Paul, were formative events in Grace's life and in her later understanding of how her working-class consciousness developed in her childhood. As she experienced these events, she more closely identified herself with the antigovernment attitudes of the Irish sisters at St. Vincent's and her Irish and German family members and neighbors who opposed the war. And, by the time she was fifteen and forced to escort her father to cross the pickets, she had come to believe in the importance of the solidarity at the heart of the union movement. Because of her continued observation of her Catholic faith, she also understood these working-class commitments in specifically faith-based terms: scabbing was a sin, an offense against God, as was the capitalist exploitation that drove men to such desperate measures.

* * *

At the time of the 1922 shopmen's strike, Grace's faith formation and her developing social consciousness were being shaped once again by the Josephites, who were her high school teachers. Grace later acknowledged this dual spiritual and political legacy, commenting that she had a "good basis for a unified philosophy of life laid at St. Vincent's" that was then "built on" at St. Joseph's Academy (SJA).[123] She considered the Josephites "valiant women in the Biblical sense" and later acknowledged that it was her "privilege to have known many of them" as she was growing up. She recalled how "special heroines of my childhood—and adulthood—were Sisters Albertus (of St. Vincent's), [and] Elizabeth Marie and Mary John (both of SJA) to name only a few of those who had a significant influence on my life."[124] Grace attended SJA from 1920 to 1924, and there she learned from these women religious a core set of values that reinforced her already developing commitment to social justice and sensitivity to political and economic repression. Like her mother, Mary, who encouraged Grace to become a "liberated type of woman" through reading and education, her teachers at SJA pushed her and the other female students to settle for nothing less than excellence and to assume that they would become leaders through their educational achievements.

At the time she enrolled at St. Joseph's Academy, the school was already seventy years old and a well-established institution in the city. Founded by the Sisters of St. Joseph of Carondelet when they arrived in St. Paul in 1851, the school was originally housed in the small log cabin chapel that had been the first St. Paul's Cathedral. As enrollments grew, this accommodation was no longer adequate. In 1860, the sisters were able to purchase property on St. Anthony Hill. A three-and-a-half-story yellow limestone building opened there on Marshall Avenue for the students in 1863. New wings to the main building and additional structures were added to the campus in subsequent decades, and the site remained the permanent home of the academy until it closed in 1971.[125] Originally the school served boarding students, but, as St. Paul grew, day students began to enroll, particularly after the extension of the streetcars to the campus during the 1880s. By 1905 the academy's main site became a full-time day school, with the boarding students transferred to Derham Hall at the College of St. Catherine.[126]

One of the school's most ardent supporters and its special patron was Archbishop John Ireland, whose sister, Ellen Ireland, was among the members of one of the earliest graduating classes in 1858. She joined the Sisters of St. Joseph that same year, taking the name of Sister Seraphine Ireland; in 1861 she became the directress of the academy.[127] Under her guidance, SJA developed a rigorous academic and spiritual program that was accredited by the University of Minnesota in 1899.[128] With well-equipped science labs, vibrant drama and music departments, and a student-run literary magazine that was started in 1913, the academy enabled the Josephites to provide a broad liberal arts education for their students. As the academy's catalogue asserted, "In a word, the system of education is so arranged as best to cultivate the heart, develop the mind, train the hand, and refine the character."[129]

To cultivate the heart and refine the character of Grace and the other female students at the academy, the Josephites required them to be observant Catholics. The Josephites maintained the students' faith formation at the center of the curriculum in a number of ways. As the school catalogue emphasized, "Religion receives the prominence due it as the sure source of those virtues that give fragrance to life here below, and title to happiness hereafter."[130] Religion classes were, "of course, a regular part of the curriculum," with "diocesan priests assisting in that department."[131] The students' homeroom period was devoted to religious instruction three days a week, and on "the first Friday of every month, the regular home room meeting is replaced by a visit to the Blessed Sacrament" in the school chapel. That monthly exposition and adoration of the Eucharist was supplemented with an annual retreat. The school year also began with an opening Mass and the students attended masses for the Church's various holy days throughout the year.[132] At the center of their educational experience at the academy was the instruction in and expression of their Catholic faith, centered especially on the Eucharist; that focus reflected broader trends in the Church during this period, when the laity, encouraged by Pope Pius X in 1905, began to engage in more frequent reception of communion and when "Mass itself became an act of lay piety."[133] For Grace, who remained devout in these years, these experiences at St. Joseph's sustained the centrality of her faith and, as she later noted, laid down a "good basis for a unified philosophy of life."[134]

That unified philosophy included an appreciation of God's presence in the Eucharist and of his calling to make the most of one's gifts in service to him and to others. The Josephites' appreciation of the need for superior academic instruction for Catholic students to prepare them to be active and responsible participants in their communities was not a purely secular one; it stemmed from a spiritual understanding of the transcendent and temporal purposes of one's proper vocation. These women religious placed special emphasis on encouraging their students not only to meet high standards in the classroom but also to consider a range of vocations after graduation to serve God and his people. This emphasis stemmed both from the Josephites' commitment to serving others without distinction and from the currents of the Catholic Action movement that was developing within the wider Church at the time and that "invited Catholics to engage in their faith in socially oriented ways."[135]

From a position grounded in their Catholic faith, the Josephites also encouraged their all-female student body to achieve academically and to contribute to society in ways that bolstered those students' confidence and sense of self-worth in an otherwise male-dominated society. In the "study helps for high school students" that they reproduced in the student handbook from the University of Michigan's School of Education, they urged the pupils to "strive to excel" and not to "be contented to 'get by.'" The main curriculum included courses in math, science, history, English, and modern languages, and for those on the college preparatory track, Latin and philosophy too. In addition to this rigorous core, the Josephites offered "special activities for the various grades" that included an exploration of "city occupations open to women" for the sophomores, the "study of great American women" for the juniors, and discussions on the "choice of vocations and careers," "woman suffrage," and "higher education" for the seniors.[136] As one alumna remarked, "We were challenged to believe that no matter what we did or where we went, women were expected to be leaders, whether in their own homes or in the wider community."[137] Grace internalized this message, by striving to excel during her years at St. Joseph's and setting her sights on a college degree. She was not alone among her classmates. Prior to 1918 not many St. Joseph's Academy graduates went on to college; instead, "There was much greater interest in the two-year teacher training institutions." But by 1921, 28 percent of the graduating class enrolled in college. For Grace's class, graduating in 1924, that number increased to 30 percent.[138]

Grace's commitment to working hard and becoming a leader in her wider community included service to others, which was also supported by the school. In "My Promise to St. Joseph's Academy," which was reproduced in the student handbook, classmates pledged to "put service above self."[139] Opportunities for service abounded at St. Joseph's. Homeroom classes had "committees on visiting the sick and bereaved" and groups for organizing "Christmas boxes for the needy." When she became principal in 1919, Sister Hilary focused on "reawakening in the pupils a great interest in missionary activities." Propagation of the Faith units were revitalized in each homeroom; Grace became a promoter in her class, helping to raise funds to support the organization's missionary activities.[140] In addition to these charitable and evangelical efforts, one alumna recalled how the students also studied *Rerum Novarum* at the school. "Society cries out for citizens to search for the common good and find ways to protect the poor and vulnerable," she noted; "SJA and the Sisters of St. Joseph taught me to attempt to answer that cry."[141] Grace, who fought for the poor and vulnerable throughout her life—albeit in different ways and with different ends in mind at different times—internalized the Josephites' teachings at SJA on the importance of being her brothers' keeper.

It was through the support of others that Grace was able to attend St. Joseph's Academy. Her parents, James and Mary, had already sacrificed to send her and her sister, Dorothy, to St. Vincent's school, finding the money to pay their tuition because they (and Mary in particular) believed in the importance of a good education for their girls. When it came time to enroll in high school, Grace's parents may have tightened their belts again, but they were also aided by the various scholarship programs available at St. Joseph's. Such programs help explain how working-class young women like Grace and Dorothy were able to attend what was an otherwise selective and costly institution. St. Joseph's had "full tuition honor scholarships," which were "assigned to incoming pupils on the results of competitive entrance examinations," and financial assistance, "given on the basis of scholarship during attendance at the Academy in the freshman, sophomore and junior years," both of which were "financed by the school." There were also scholarships from "endowments or gifts" by various donors, including the Alumnae Association, Sister Seraphine Ireland, and Archbishop John Ireland.[142] The basic tuition for the classical academic course in which Grace was enrolled from 1920 to 1924 was sixty dollars per year. In addition, there were lab fees, lecture fees, a graduation fee, and extra costs for musical instruction that could add up to between one and two hundred dollars per year depending on how many options one chose.[143] In 1920, James was earning seventy-two cents per hour as a boilermaker for the railroad. Assuming he worked five days a week for fifty full weeks per year, he would make $1440 per year. Tuition for just one daughter would be almost 7 percent of that annual wage, and once James faced wage cuts in 1922—and then time on the picket line with no pay during the strike—making such payments became even harder.[144] During her years at St. Joseph's, Grace's earning a place on the scholarship honor roll no doubt helped make her education there possible.[145]

In addition to her coursework, Grace applied herself to a variety of other activities in high school. She became quite involved with the literary magazine, the *Academy*, penning short stories and reports for it during her junior and senior years. She served as its editor-in-chief during her senior year. Although her fiction writing was somewhat formulaic, it communicated values important to her. In "The Heart of a Shattered Oak," for example, Grace expressed some of her antiwar sentiment as she presented a rather melodramatic story of John, a soldier blinded at the front who returns home and loses all hope when his favorite oak tree is felled by lightning. Only the loving words of his mother save John from attempting suicide.[146] In "His Success," the melodrama continues as Grace delivers a critique of raw ambition in her story of a poor little rich boy overlooked by a professional father who was more concerned with advancing his medical career than spending quality time with his son. After the boy's father forgets his birthday because he is preoccupied with a new surgical procedure, the son suffers such a shock that he is sent into a fever that quickly kills him. The father is left "sitting besides the deathbed of his son, dead because of his neglect" pondering "over his 'success.'"[147] Despite their mawkish tone, these two stories serve as windows into some of Grace's values as a teenager. They communicate her recognition of the importance of familial love as well as her condemnation of both the destructive power of war and the obsession with social status.

In Grace's reports for the magazine, she takes a more clinical, and at times, humorous approach and also reveals her early interest in psychology and chemistry. In "Have You Ever Had a Blue Monday?" Grace reports her findings from an unscientific polling of seniors and freshmen to uncover why more of the former come to class on Monday unprepared to start the week's work. Locating the cause in the greater amount of time upperclassmen spend socializing on the weekend, she concludes, "From this it can be readily seen that after so much pleasure and so little studying, the average student would be loathe [sic] to return to the daily grind of school life on Monday."[148] In "Do You Regard Chemistry as a Useless Science?" Grace lays out in detail just how many things chemistry is integral to in everyday life, from medicine to food preparation to clothing production to popular entertainments like films.[149] And in "Seniors Have High and Lofty Ambitions," she analyzes the results of a questionnaire "given to fifty-two of the Seniors concerning their ambitions and plans for life," finding that 49 percent planned to go on to college, with most hoping to be teachers, some to become nurses, and others to enter into the arts or into the business world as secretaries.[150] In these early writings, Grace demonstrated her interests in investigating and assessing the world in which she lived and communicating her findings to others, interests she would build on in college and graduate school and during her early career as an educational psychologist.

In her articles for the *Academy*, Grace also demonstrated her passion for writing. In the "Seniors' Secrets of Success" section of the magazine, during her final year at St. Joseph's, the feature editor poked fun at Grace's devotion to the undertaking. "Grace Holmes' ability as a writer," the editor noted, "is, as far as I can observe, due to her habit of spending her afternoons at the Academy after partaking of a very wholesome meal of mashed potatoes."[151] But Grace also partook in other activities in high school, including her work as a promoter of the Propagation of the Faith. In addition to her writing and service work, Grace played volleyball (becoming team captain in her senior year), served on the student government committee and the entertainment committee, was a member of the junior debating team, and performed in two school plays.[152] These commitments speak to her seemingly endless energy and her interest in social activities, particularly those that honed organizing, leadership, and public speaking skills. These characteristics and abilities that she displayed as a teen were ones that she would maintain and develop throughout her life.

Grace later noted how at St. Joseph's she "liked all the regular high school things that the other girls did," and her participation in so many activities certainly seems to verify this assertion. Yet she continued to feel, as she had done in elementary school, that she was "different and independent." Indeed, she "prided" herself on her nonconformity even as she took on the leadership roles of editor and team captain in these years.[153] Some of this sense of difference may have stemmed from her working-class background. St. Joseph's was not as socioeconomically homogenous as St. Vincent's was. Select academies, like SJA, were originally opened to cater "to wealthy families, Catholic or Protestant, who had the means to pay tuition for their daughters' education." As Coburn and Smith explain, they were often "the 'cash cow' that enabled the sisters to work in parish education and receive little or no compensation." The separate fees for fine arts (which sometimes "exceeded the cost for standard tuition") were also aimed at middle- and upper-class families that could afford them.[154] Grace may have begun to sense the class differences that existed in St. Paul in a more direct way among her classmates with whom she interacted on a daily basis at St. Joseph's, even though the school was similar to St. Vincent's in being a Catholic haven. The comment in the *Academy* about Grace's diet of mashed potatoes may have been a class-based (and ethnic-based) one, meant more as a back-handed compliment than a straightforward statement of praise. Grace was not the only student at SJA on scholarship, but not all of her classmates were from her Frogtown/Rice Street neighborhood anymore. Her time at St. Joseph's Academy became yet another experience in her early life that contributed to her growing working-class consciousness.

* * *

By the time she graduated high school in 1924, Grace had been exposed to various influences in her home, neighborhood, parish, schools, and the wider St. Paul community. Together these factors contributed to the development of her Catholic working-class consciousness. She had become a young woman who questioned narrow definitions of patriotism and blind assertions of support for the government, a Frogtown/Rice Street girl who believed in the importance of unions and was intrigued by socialist writings, and, at the same time, a devout Catholic who was sensitive to the needs of the poor and exploited. From these beginnings Grace set off for college and then graduate school, where her life would take a different turn.

2

Conversion

Between 1924 and 1940, Grace came of age as an educated and professional woman. During her years at the all-female College of St. Catherine (CSC), under the guidance, once again, of the Josephites, Grace redoubled her commitment to her Catholic faith and to her belief in the liberating potential of education for women. When she went to graduate school at the University of Minnesota, Grace earned her PhD in 1933 before she married Gilbert Carlson, a law student whom she met on campus. She also continued working after she and Gilbert wed in 1934 when she was twenty-eight, establishing herself as a professional woman who balanced marriage with a career and political activities. At first, this arrangement succeeded. Grace and Gilbert shared a commitment to each other and to their respective careers. But eventually, when Grace became more deeply involved with the Trotskyist movement that first attracted her during the mid-1930s and left the Church in the late 1930s, Gilbert could not bring himself to follow her, and the two separated.

Between the time when Grace attended CSC as an undergraduate beginning in 1924 and when she began working full-time for the Socialist Workers Party (SWP) in 1940, she had also come of age politically. In these years she reaffirmed certain values (particularly her commitment to helping those who were exploited), more deeply developed other facets of her worldview (especially her identification with the working class), and embraced new concepts (specifically Marxism). Her conversion to Trotskyism stemmed, in part, from the elective affinity between her working-class Catholic identity and socialism as she understood it.[1] It took place in the context of the Great Depression and as a result of her exposure to new ideas and new social networks at the University of Minnesota. Also crucial to her identification as a Socialist was her experience of the momentous 1934 Teamsters' strikes in Minneapolis, during which she came to appreciate the violent reality of class conflict more deeply than ever before. Her introduction to some of the strike leaders pulled her further into the political orbit of the Trotskyists. Her work for the Minnesota Department of Education as a vocational rehabilitation counselor, which she began in 1935, intensified her maturing view that a socialist society was the only way to address the needs of workers and the exploited. As her political beliefs evolved, so too did her partisan affiliations: Grace first joined the Farmer-Labor Party, then entered the Socialist Party with the Trotskyists in 1936, and ultimately served as a delegate to the founding convention of the Socialist Workers Party in 1938. Grace, whose conversion to socialism was now complete, made the members of the SWP her new family and devoted herself to improving the lives of workers and the oppressed by fighting for the creation of a socialist society.

* * *

Before Grace became a Trotskyist, she maintained her concern for both the temporal and the transcendent and remained a devout Catholic. At the College of St. Catherine, which she attended between 1924 and 1929, the Josephites continued to play an important role in Grace's life. They modeled for Grace and the other women at CSC a professional life outside of marriage that inspired many students to enroll in graduate programs or begin careers outside the home to support themselves and their families. The College of St. Catherine, which celebrated women's capabilities in all fields, including in pre-professional education, shaped Grace's gender identity as a young adult. The Sisters of St. Joseph who founded the college in 1905 "were early proponents of increased opportunities for women."[2] Even when society continued to regard women as "intellectually and physically incapable of rigorous education" and defined them "almost exclusively as wives and mothers," the College of St. Catherine "created spaces that enabled their students and faculties to develop their own intellectual and social identities as women."[3]

The chief architect of the College of St. Catherine's strong academic program was Sister Antonia McHugh. McHugh, who took her permanent vows in 1898, earned a bachelor's degree in philosophy and education in 1908 and a master's degree in history in 1909 from the University of Chicago. With Archbishop John Ireland's backing, she became dean of CSC in 1914 and immediately began an intensive campaign of faculty development. Under her leadership the number of advanced degrees earned by the sisters rose from three to twenty-five, and with her support many of those sisters had the opportunity to study at Chicago, Harvard, Yale, and even institutions abroad.[4] McHugh also oversaw CSC's accreditation with the North Central Association in 1916 and much of its physical expansion through her organizing the College Board of Trustees. Her leadership moved CSC "from obscurity to recognition as a high-quality liberal arts college for women" by the early 1920s.[5]

In creating such an institution, McHugh stood out as a reformer in an otherwise conservative Catholic Church, especially when it came to defining proper roles for women. Although CSC included faith formation in its raison d'être, its mission as an institution dedicated to the higher education of women, with a liberal arts curriculum that McHugh modeled on the University of Chicago's, placed it at odds with traditional definitions of women's place in society then articulated both outside and within the Church. Preparing women academically to go on to graduate school or careers outside the home inherently challenged both the mainstream ideology of separate spheres and the Catholic ideology of true womanhood. The former, which celebrated women's domestic roles as wife and mother, had emerged in the context of the Industrial Revolution in the early nineteenth century. The latter, which shared with Protestantism a scripturally based interpretation of essential gender differences, had since medieval times also included an understanding of women's nature as tied to both the fall of man (through Eve) and its redemption (through Mary). Both ideologies sustained assumptions about women's inherent physical and intellectual inferiority that undergirded opposition to women's higher education and that defended the primacy of women's domestic roles.[6] McHugh and the other Josephites at CSC thus challenged accepted gender norms within both the national American context and that of their own Church.

One way they did this was through their own experiences as educated professional women who became models for their young female charges. At the College of St. Catherine, students like Grace saw women operating the institution at all levels, staffing it at all levels, and running it "with their own intellectual and physical labor."[7] As Jane Lamm Carroll argues, in this way the sisters became "exemplars of women living lives that were alternatives to the social roles of marriage and motherhood and that challenged the social assumption that women were or should be dependent on men."[8] McHugh and other Josephites not only ran the college but also did so as highly educated women, most with master's or doctoral degrees, working alongside equally well qualified lay people and priests.[9] They demonstrated that "the purpose of an educated woman was not 'being a good companion to an educated male.'"[10]

Grace and her fellow students at CSC followed the Josephites' lead in challenging the ideal of true womanhood. Traces of their renunciation are found in the pages of their college yearbooks. One page spoofed a "Household Hints" column, suggesting that the way to "dress a chicken" was with "furs in summer, low shoes in winter," the way to "take spots out of cloth" was to cut them out, and the way to "prevent cake from getting stale" was to "eat while fresh."[11] Another entry mocked the kinds of popular advice offered to women trying to lose weight, suggesting that "reducers" contort themselves into pretzel shapes, "taking care to roll the eyes," while loosening their joints with lubricating oil. It also advised readers not to forget to dance the Charleston and to remain on a diet of oranges.[12] In the many candid photos that filled certain sections of the yearbooks, the women are seen in relaxed, at times silly, poses with each other on the campus. In one picture, four women, dressed in their flapper best, lift their legs in a kick line.[13] While the yearbooks also contained more serious reflections on the importance of higher education, the variety of academic clubs and their activities, and the significance of certain annual traditions, they contained quite humorous entries, like those above, that showcased the women's wit and humor. But in that humor there was a serious message: these women were not at CSC to learn how to dress a chicken, clean clothes, or lose weight. They were there to stage Shakespeare plays in all-women productions, to run labs, and to master foreign languages. They were there to find themselves as young women, to make friends, to flirt, and to play. Some, like Grace—who was portrayed as a bookworm in one cartoon on a page humorously depicting the members of the senior class—were more academically focused. Others, like some of her classmates who were portrayed as fashion obsessed or sporty, were not.[14] But there was a clear sense that during their college years, the women of the College of St. Catherine were forging independent identities for themselves as what might be termed Catholic flappers.

The young women at CSC, including Grace, who might be considered Catholic flappers were of the same generation and lived in the same modernizing American world as other young women (and men) coming of age during the 1920s who were then redefining not just gender roles in broad terms but also the meaning of marriage and sex in ways that emphasized the importance of love, intimacy, and personal satisfaction.[15] The women of the College of St. Catherine would have been privy to these broader cultural shifts, even those students who came from working-class enclaves, because those changes were created and represented in the shared mass culture of movies, popular magazines, and urban amusements.[16] Indeed, part of what the young women of CSC were doing on campus through their appropriation of flapper dress styles and modern humor in challenging traditional gender norms was putting their unique stamp as Catholics on the 1920s New Woman.

Where CSC women's embrace of the new definition of sex and marriage may have diverged from that held by the middle-class Protestant college students who have been studied by Paula Fass was both in the area of birth control and in the assertion of "personal satisfaction." Fass's statistics on the acceptance of the use of contraception for married couples do not include data on Catholic college students.[17] Leslie Woodcock Tentler's research on Catholics and contraception reveals a growing popular acceptance of marital contraception among the faithful during the 1920s, but one that was rooted in either a "good faith ignorance" of the Church's official teachings against it or a selective application of those teachings to difficult working-class circumstances in which the guilt-ridden couple often agonized over the choice.[18] Neither reality reflected a positive embrace of the practice as a liberating component of a new attitude towards sexuality.

Similarly, any new attitudes towards sex and marriage in this period were inflected, for Catholics, with distinct confessional values. By the late 1920s, the positive understanding of marriage in the Catholic tradition had become more apparent in the pamphlet literature used in seminaries and, by the early 1930s, on college campuses in classes on marriage and parenthood. These tracts spoke of marriage and parenting as the "divine project for the development and increase of unselfishness in humankind." Only with the acceptance of the rhythm method in the early 1930s was sex in marriage decoupled from procreation and celebrated as necessary for "love, interpersonal communion, and the couple's spiritual development."[19] But here, still, the emphasis was not on individual self-fulfillment but on a deeper commitment to a shared marital vocation. And for the Catholic students at colleges like the College of St. Catherine, women religious, who were consecrated virgins, could not serve as role models in this regard.

Silences surrounding sexuality in the archives makes it difficult to trace exactly how Catholic college women may have diverged from the standards being defined by their Protestant sisters. There are no references to sexuality in the CSC yearbooks, even in jest. And Grace left no trace of her romantic relationships before her husband, Gilbert, and did not comment on the nature of her courtship or marriage with him anywhere in her papers. Many individuals like Grace who became active on the political Left purposefully crafted their own stories with an eye solely to the public aspects of their life; they did not consider personal facets of their life significant enough to warrant recording.[20] Such was the case with the interviews Grace gave to Carl Ross, which mainly constructed a narrative of her evolving political consciousness. But Grace does not fit this mold entirely: she saved in her papers the extensive personal correspondence she had with her many friends and with her sister, Dorothy, exposing that part of her life. Perhaps her silence with respect to Gilbert specifically stemmed from a more general or faith-based reticence to make public the intimacies of her marriage. Whatever the reason, there is no evidence of Grace's romantic or sexual experiences with Gilbert or with anyone else before her marriage, whatever they may or may not have been.

Part of the difficulty in understanding the precise ways in which Grace and her classmates understood their sexuality and gender roles is the tension that emerges in what little documentation does exist. On one hand, the yearbooks challenge traditional domestic roles for women with their light-hearted pieces spoofing housework and dieting. On the other, the school's magazine, *Ariston*, congratulated alumnae on their marriages.[21] At the same time, however, the magazine also touted the many academic and professional achievements of the students, faculty, and graduates, often more frequently and at greater length than the reports on recent weddings.[22] While there was joyful support for the vocation of marriage on the part of the students, the women at the College of

St. Catherine also focused on cultivating their personal, intellectual, and professional skills. This focus was nurtured by the mission of CSC itself, which, in turn, derived from the vision of the Josephites to advance opportunities for women.

But part of this focus also came from the nature of the student body at Catholic institutions like the College of St. Catherine, especially after 1920. Unlike the "elite women's colleges of the East, the so-called Seven Sisters," whose aim "was to produce intelligent and cultured women who could be cultured mates for successful men and educated mothers to future leaders," Catholic schools like CSC catered to students who "had more varied futures ahead of them," in part because of their increasingly working-class and immigrant backgrounds. Some of the graduates of the College of St. Catherine became middle-class stay-at-home wives and mothers, but after 1920 many were increasingly more likely to become career women or "single women responsible for their own financial affairs" who may also have been "continuing contributors to family incomes."[23] Grace and her sister, Dorothy (who began her studies at the College of St. Catherine in 1929), were among this growing working-class population at CSC. As early as 1914 the college actively recruited enrollment from working-class communities by advertising its financial assistance for qualified students. Although by the 1920s tuition cost thirty-five dollars per quarter (plus twenty-five dollars for room rent and eighty-five dollars for board and laundry), the college offered some scholarships and an early version of what by the 1940s would become a more coordinated work-study program.[24] As the Josephites at SJA did, those at CSC worked to open the doors of their institution to as many young women as possible. By the end of the 1920s, CSC would have a more diverse socioeconomic student body as a result.

At the College of St. Catherine, Grace and Dorothy rose to the expectation that they would become well-educated women who would be prepared for whatever path in life they chose. That expectation was set by the Josephites, who taught students across a rich curriculum of humanities, arts, and sciences under the assumption that the women graduates would pursue fruitful careers or further education so that they could contribute to society in a meaningful way.[25] The statistics bear out the impact of these expectations: "From 1913 to 1935 at least 21 percent of St. Catherine's graduates went to on to postgraduate studies," whereas, by comparison, "during the same period, less than 5 percent of the female graduates of the nearby coeducational Hamline University pursued graduate studies." And graduates of Catholic women's colleges, "like graduates of non-Catholic women's colleges, pursued professional degrees in law and medicine at proportionately higher rates than alumna at coeducational institutions."[26] Both the all-women environment and the presence of the Josephites, who espoused their message of service, made a difference in inspiring these women to advance their postgraduate education and careers.

Grace, who began her undergraduate studies at the College of St. Catherine in September 1924 and graduated in June 1929, was, by all accounts, dedicated to her studies. During her time on campus she majored in English and minored in chemistry. Her transcript reveals her exposure to the broad liberal arts curriculum created by Sister Antonia McHugh.[27] In addition to the courses in her major and minor fields, Grace took classes in modern and ancient history, math, German, general and educational psychology, ethics, art history, drama, and library science.[28] Her grades ranged from mostly As and Bs to the occasional C and only one D (in intermediate German).[29] Judging from the caricature of her in the yearbook as a bookworm, she was considered a serious student by her peers, just as she had been at SJA.

It is hard to discern from her transcript, however, the personal struggles Grace endured during her time at the College of St. Catherine. Her mother, Mary, who had been suffering from Parkinson's, began to decline in the early years of Grace's time at college. Mary's condition became so serious that Grace had to suspend her college career for a year, starting her sophomore year in 1926 instead of 1925, in order to care for her.[30] It must have been an extremely trying time for Grace and her family. Seeing a parent suffer physical pain is devastating. Being the primary caretaker for an ailing parent is emotionally and physically draining. Grace was just nineteen years old at the time, and so the pressure on her must have been intense. Even though she had been used to helping her mother in the past, bringing home books for her from the library, the kind of assistance she needed to provide now was much more labor intensive and intimate. But, because she was so devoted to her mother, and because her family presumably could not afford any other kind of care, she came home from college to help. For that year Grace remained by her mother's side in their home on 158 LaFond Avenue, preparing her meals, cleaning her clothes, helping her bathe and dress. Perhaps she also read to Mary, knowing how much she enjoyed books. In this work Grace embodied the spirit of service that the Josephites extolled. And in that labor of love she experienced her final moments with her mother. That time did not last long, however, as Mary succumbed to complications of her disease on May 11, 1926.[31] Years later Grace commented, "Some people felt sorry for me" because "my mother died when I was young." And she admitted, "I even felt sorry for myself." But she quickly reframed the memory, arguing that she was also very appreciative to have been "given the opportunity to develop independence of thought" at a very early age. After Mary's passing, Grace held on to the lessons she had learned from her mother in the short time the two had had together.[32]

Grace returned to the College of St. Catherine four months later and began her sophomore year. She resumed a full eighteen-credit course load and became involved in various extracurricular activities. As she had done at St. Joseph's Academy, Grace found time to write for the student magazine. She contributed poems and book reviews to *Ariston* but did not serve as its editor.[33] Instead, Grace also became a member of the science club and of the Ambrosian Round Table, a group that raised money to expand the college's library collections.[34] But she really committed herself to the College of St. Catherine's Campus Cast, becoming vice president of this drama club in her senior year. She not only served on its play-reading, costume, and stage-design committee but also performed in its production of *Troubadour's Dream*.[35]

Dorothy, who followed Grace to CSC, was equally engaged with campus life. She became one of the associate editors of *Ariston* in 1929, was elected president of the College Association in 1931, and served as one of CSC's delegates to the Inter-Collegiate World Assembly of the League of Nations at St. Paul High School in 1931.[36] Her address at this assembly (which was on "The Effects of the Economic Depression on Spain") won praise from a professor at Macalester College who wrote to Sister Antonia McHugh with his opinion that it was "in point of structure and delivery among the finest of those presented before the Assembly."[37] Dorothy's talents as a speaker were already evident. So too was her deepening interest in politics, which was nurtured through her participation in the League of Women Voters. Her affiliation with that organization also took her off campus and out of St. Paul when she attended the LWV's national convention in Detroit in 1932.[38] For both sisters, their time at the College of St. Catherine was one of intellectual and social growth inside and outside of the classroom.

But there was also continued spiritual growth. Although Grace and Dorothy were expanding their horizons at the College of St. Catherine through their academic pursuits and extracurricular activities, they still found themselves in a primarily Catholic community. CSC enrolled non-Catholic students, but it was a self-professed Catholic institution. That identity was made clear, for example, in Sister Antonia McHugh's message to the students in 1929 when she said, "What I should most like to see in your lives [is] a great abiding faith, that expresses itself in a spirit of service in the cause of Christ and the neighbor."[39] It was also evident (as had been the case at SJA) in the various ways in which observation of the Catholic faith was intertwined with the school experience at CSC. The academic year began with an opening Mass; special feast days, like that in November for St. Catherine, were celebrated in the chapel; crucifixes were displayed on the walls of the classrooms; annual retreats were held by priests from the nearby College of St. Thomas; sodality receptions were held on campus; reports were made in the yearbook of the students who joined the Sisters of St. Joseph upon graduation; and, in 1929, the golden jubilee of five women religious was celebrated with a special pontifical High Mass on campus.[40] Students were also required to take courses in the Old and New Testament, the sacraments, and Christian life.[41] At the College of St. Catherine, Grace and Dorothy thus found a secure place in which to maintain their Catholic faith. Neither Grace nor Dorothy showed signs of leaving the Church at this stage of their lives. Dorothy, in a welcoming address to Archbishop John Murray, who visited the campus in 1932, pledged "in the name of all the students loyalty to the new archbishop and co-operation in all his undertakings."[42] For a short time, Grace even considered entering the convent.[43]

At the College of St. Catherine, Grace and Dorothy also maintained their working-class identity, even as they became exposed to a broader world through their education and participation in various clubs. But for Grace, at least, that class identity became more complex. During the 1920s the college was becoming increasingly socioeconomically diverse with the Josephites' recruitment of working-class women like Grace and Dorothy. But there were still students there from middle-class and elite backgrounds. The student directory contained listings with addresses from Frogtown and Rice Street, but also from Summit Avenue.[44] As she had at SJA, Grace came to feel this class difference, but at CSC her reaction was not the same. She recalled how "one time we went out to see the waterworks and we were on a bus coming back and the bus ran right close to where I lived. Some of the girls were talking about, 'Oh, isn't this a terrible neighborhood' and all that, so I rode down to Rice and University and walked back because I didn't want to be known as being part of this; I was embarrassed by it."[45] Perhaps because Grace was beginning to see herself advancing through her education into a professional career, her reaction to the class differences she experience at the College of St. Catherine was, in this moment, one of shame instead of redoubled commitment to her working-class roots. This desire to distance herself from those roots spoke to her aspirations as a young woman on the cusp of adulthood. Ultimately Grace would embrace her working-class roots again as an adult, but only after she beat a new path for herself intellectually and politically in graduate school.

* * *

At the University of Minnesota, Grace left the familiar confines of St. Paul and entered into a new world of ideas and social networks in Minneapolis that dramatically reshaped her life. Through the culmination of various influences, which included her professors, her coursework in the sciences, her participation in certain student groups, her exposure to a more activist campus life in the context of the Depression, and, ultimately, her experience of the momentous 1934 Teamsters strikes, Grace began her journey down the path to socialism. Her political coming of age as a Trotskyist was a gradual one that, at first, did not include her leaving the Church. It also dovetailed with her sexual coming of age when she met and married Gilbert Carlson, a young lawyer with whom she shared a passion for social justice.

At the University of Minnesota, or "the U," as it is known colloquially, Grace encountered an environment that was quite different from that of the College of St. Catherine. As a secular, coeducational institution, the U did not provide the space to nurture her Catholic faith that CSC had. Instead, it was where Grace found kindred spirits of another sort. Through her academic work and extracurricular activities, she sharpened her understanding of socialism from the days when her Uncle Casper first exposed her to such ideas at the watercress patch. But this process did not happen overnight.

Grace's choice of major field contributed to this new education, in part because of its grounding in the sciences, which began to open up for her new ways of thinking about the world. Building on her limited coursework in psychology and educational psychology at the College of St. Catherine, Grace chose to major and minor in these two fields at the U, but her experience of these subjects in graduate school was fundamentally different from her time in the classroom at CSC. "Most of the faculty [at the U] were logical positivists, a philosophy based on atheism," Grace later noted. "I was very influenced by that," she admitted.[46] She explained how she "became extremely interested in science in those days, you know, and as a matter of fact there was kind of a background for a loss of faith in later years."[47] Being exposed to secular sources of authority and ways of understanding human behavior and emotions in a formal educational setting for the first time challenged many of Grace's existing notions of the field and of her approach to life. It sowed the seeds for a questioning of her faith that would bear fruit later.

At the same time that Grace's experiences at the U were laying the foundation for her conversion to socialism, they were also building the base for her future professional career. With the exception of a few classes, all of Grace's coursework in graduate school was in her major and minor fields of psychology and educational psychology. During her first quarter on campus, fall 1929, she struggled somewhat to adjust to the new environment, earning four Bs and one A. From the winter quarter of 1930 through her last quarter at the U (spring 1933), however, she excelled, earning straight As. She graduated with a 3.88 cumulative GPA.[48] In July 1930 she earned her master of arts degree with a thesis titled "A Statistical Study for a New Type of Objective Examination Question," in which she concluded, after analyzing data drawn from exams taken by students at the university, that a particular type of question (the "wrong word" question) was "satisfactory for incorporation into tests of educational achievement."[49] In June 1933 she submitted her doctoral dissertation, "A Study in Work Decrement." In this lengthier study

Grace presented her findings from experiments conducted over several years (between 1930 and 1933) in which she presented subjects with a mental test (such as learning a series of Chinese characters), then gave them "fatigue producing work" (usually in the form of mental multiplication) followed by a mental test again in the original subject to see if there was a decline as a result of the intervening fatigue. Her results showed that there was.[50] With this work Grace began to establish her area of expertise within educational psychology in mental assessment techniques.

Her doctoral research enabled Grace both to maintain connections with those from her past and to build new professional relationships. To secure subjects for her experiments, Grace tapped into the Catholic network in St. Paul by reaching out to her former teachers at CSC (Sister Jeanne Marie) and SJA (Sister Elizabeth Marie), who gave her access to their students. All of her work was supervised by her dissertation adviser, Dr. John G. Rockwell, then an assistant professor in the College of Education.[51] The two began a professional relationship at the U that would continue after Rockwell became the state commissioner of education in 1934.[52]

With her dissertation submitted and defended, Grace graduated in June 1933. The United States was in the midst of the Great Depression. The first wave of New Deal legislation that would eventually begin to alleviate some of the worst of the suffering had just been passed or was then being passed by Congress during President Franklin Roosevelt's first hundred days in office.[53] Grace recognized that she "was lucky" to get a job as a lecturer at the U, a position she maintained for two years. She recalled how in that role, "I was supposed to work miracles. For example, they would have the football players take 'How to Study' and then I was supposed to interview them and encourage them to study more." Noting, with some humor, the difficulty with assisting these college athletes, she remarked, "Good night! These boys were spending all their time practicing, you know, and they hardly had any time for studying. You certainly couldn't work miracles so it was kind of a tough job."[54]

While she struggled to find professional satisfaction from teaching the football players study skills, Grace found other outlets for intellectual stimulation that contributed to her deepening interest in politics and socialism. By 1932 Dorothy had begun her studies at the U in political science and economics and Grace became drawn into her circle of classmates. Dorothy knew Benjamin Lippincott, a professor of political science, whom Grace described as "a left-wing sort of professor." She recalled that when she was a lecturer, she "used to go to his class just to get a political education. So there's where I met a lot of these people who were left-wingers."[55] Grace not only was drawn into an orbit of left-leaning students but also was exposed to Lippincott's take on politics. An assistant professor at the time, having recently earned his PhD in 1930 at the London School of Economics under Harold Laski, Lippincott advocated distributive justice and greater government control of business to achieve that end. He had not yet published *On the Economic Theory of Socialism*, in which he and other scholars, whose essays he edited, made the case for the feasibility (and need) for socialism in the face of what they saw as capitalism's failure to foster economic progress.[56] But Lippincott may have communicated such ideas in his classes as he worked out the premise of the book. His emphasis on socialism's ability to better address society's needs was a message that the left-wingers in his class had already come to accept and was one that Grace found appealing too.

The idea that capitalism was incapable of meeting society's needs became all the more convincing as the Depression deepened. The urgent circumstances of the time contributed to the appeal that socialism had for some people in the United States during the 1930s. Even for those not attracted to socialism, the economic crisis spurred them to question what was happening. Grace recalled how "all the 'thinking' people on the campuses (the non-fraternity people) were forced to think about the social and economic problems. Unemployment among academic people was higher ... and employment and poverty were major facts of American life."[57] The Depression hit Minneapolis and St. Paul hard. As Charles Walker has charted, "In 1932, eighty-six per cent of the manufacturing plants in Minneapolis were operating at a loss. In the same year cost of living in the Twin Cities had dropped twenty per cent but pay rolls had gone down thirty-five." Walker notes that "by the spring of 1934 unemployed and dependents constituted almost a third of the population of Minneapolis and Hennepin County."[58] On the university campus, Grace and Dorothy grappled with these realities by becoming involved in the Social Problems Club. One of the things this student group did was invite speakers to campus to discuss possible solutions to the contemporary economic crisis. This extracurricular activity became another experience that contributed to Grace's political education at the U.

One year Governor Floyd Olson "came and gave a talk at the old Frederic Hotel." Grace recalled how impressed she was because "my gosh you don't get the governor of the state to come to an awful lot of these little two-bit sort of meetings, but he was really interested in young people," and he turned up.[59] Olson was the first Farmer-Labor Party candidate to be elected governor in America. He was initially elected in 1930 on a somewhat moderate platform and then reelected in 1932 and 1934 with a more progressive agenda in response to the deepening crisis of the Depression. He called for a graduated income tax, a state system of unemployment insurance, and significant increases in public relief. During his time in office he was able to implement the tax and relief policies.[60] Support for his agenda and candidacy reflected not only Minnesota voters' desire for action in the face of the Depression but also many of those voters' longstanding support for the Farmer-Labor Party (FLP), which was the electoral arm of the Farmer-Labor Association. Originating with an alliance between the Farmers' Non-Partisan League and the Working People's Non-Partisan League in 1917, which became a more formal merger in 1924, the organization maintained the antimonopoly concerns of its founders, which included "a moratorium on farm foreclosures, relief for the unemployed, banking reform, [and] a state income tax." As Tom O'Connell argues, the Farmer-Labor movement "reflected diverse social traditions" that included the socialist ideas brought by Finnish and Scandinavian immigrants to Minnesota, temperance and suffrage reformers' "crusading spirit," the farmer-solidarity and antimonopoly agenda of populists, and, by the 1920s, the organizing skills of some Communists. Its focus was ultimately "a more equal distribution of wealth through an economy based on small businesses, cooperatives, and public ownership."[61] As a working-class Catholic, Grace was attracted to the FLP message because of its emphasis on distributive justice, a goal that was shared, in some ways, with the social teachings of the Church since *Rerum Novarum* and John Ryan's articulation of the workers' right to a living wage. Her first partisan affiliation was with the Farmer-Labor Party, and she supported Olson's campaign in 1934.

Grace admitted that she did not become politically active to any real degree until after she completed her doctorate in 1933, arguing that she was just too caught up in her academic work to engage seriously with anything else.⁶² But once she graduated and was working as a lecturer, things changed. Her participation in the Social Problems Club with Dorothy was one outlet for her energies. The two sisters were not alone in their campus activism during the 1930s, a time when there were widespread student protests at colleges and universities around the country. It was during this "first student movement" when, as Robert Cohen describes it, "the old left was young." This generation of college students, unlike those of the 1920s, engaged with politics in response to the main domestic and foreign threats of the age: the Depression, the possibility of another world war, and the spread of fascism. As a generation who had a memory of the horrors of World War I from their childhoods and who were then exposed as young adults to various revisionist interpretations of that conflict as having originated only from the machinations of Wall Street and war profiteers, their antiwar sentiment was incredibly strong.⁶³

Their desire to avoid another war at all costs manifested itself in antiwar conferences and in protests against the ROTC on campuses beginning in the early 1930s and in antiwar strikes beginning in 1934. In that year about 10,000 students around the country participated. Gaining momentum, a second strike in 1935 saw close to 160,000 students join in, including 3,000 from Minnesota.⁶⁴ Grace was one of those who turned out for the strikes. Even though she was not an undergraduate, as a lecturer on campus and member of the Social Problems Club, she joined in the strike at the U in 1934 and listened to the speakers who had assembled on the steps of the Northrup Auditorium.⁶⁵

Grace expanded the reach of her political activism beyond the campus in these years too. In so doing she found herself smack in the middle of the sectarian disputes then running rampant among the various parties and organizations on the political Left. By the early 1930s, deep splits existed not only between the Socialist Party of America (SP) and the Communist Party (CPUSA) but also between those who remained affiliated with the Communist Party and those who had been ousted and formed the Communist Left Opposition in 1929. The SP had been established in 1901 by the more moderate and electorally minded members of the Socialist Labor Party, along with some former Populists. In 1919 many of the more militant native-born members of the SP, "left-wing trade union activists from the IWW [Industrial Workers of the World] and AFL [American Federation of Labor]," and recent immigrants in the foreign language sections of the party who "were inclined to hold firm to a more militant class-struggle perspective" broke away from the SP and formed the Communist Party. They were enthralled with the promise of the Russian revolution and wanted to connect their struggle to an international movement. Most of the SP's members (particularly its "Old Guard") denounced the Communists' links to Moscow, condemning what they saw as the CPUSA's devotion to its priorities over the needs of America's workers. After the death of Lenin in 1924, Stalin's rise to power included "tightened dictatorial controls" and an assertion of the Russia-first policy of "revolution in one country" that then also triggered factional splits within the international Communist movement. Some Communists were ousted from the Communist Party in 1928 because of their loyalty to Leon Trotsky's critique of Stalinism and their adherence to revolutionary internationalism, which put them at odds with those who remained within the Communist Party's ranks. In the United States, people like James Cannon, Rose Karsner, and Antoinette Konikow formed the Communist League of America, Left Opposition (CLA) in 1929.[66] The Trotskyists, as they became known, had a significant presence in New York, but also in Minneapolis, where many members of the Left Opposition came to communism from the leftist trade union ranks of the IWW. Many now worked in the coal yards or as truck drivers affiliated with Teamsters Local 574.[67]

Grace's early experiences of the sectarian disputes in Minneapolis revealed her initial political naiveté, but also her pragmatism. As she ventured off campus to join other protests in the city, she discovered just how deeply these partisan divides ran. Grace recalled, "Here I was just barely out of the Farmer-Labor Party, which I belonged to for quite a while, and here I met these Trotskyists" who "would start haranguing me about what was wrong with the CP." Grace remembered how "one time there was some kind of march on the state capital, you know, kind of like a hunger march or something like that, and I went to it and the Trotskyists, none of them came." She recalled how "they told me that I just didn't know what I was doing; that this was led by the CP." The Trotskyists were correct about the nature of the event. During the early 1930s such marches had been organized by the Communist Party around the country, and in 1932 a hunger march on Minneapolis's city hall was coordinated by the Communists. Grace most likely joined a different march (given that she was not politically active until after 1933), but she remembers what she called the Trotskyists' "terribly polemically minded" position on her attendance. From her perspective, as a young person new to the politics of the Left, refusing to cooperate with the Communists in what she felt was "a good thing to participate in" (an event that was "calling attention to the problem of hunger") seemed short-sighted.[68]

But, what Grace would come to understand as she entered more deeply into the world of radical politics was that the Trotskyists' polemical attitude came first from their principled opposition to what they described as the CPUSA's Stalinism. During the early 1930s their criticism also stemmed from a rejection of the Communist Party's "third period" policy, in which it believed that capitalism had reached its third and final period of development and, because capitalism was allegedly in its death throes, that no compromises could be made with other leftist groups that might stand in the way of the Communist International's self-appointed role as the only body to lead workers to complete the revolution to socialism. As a result of this policy emanating from Moscow from 1928 until 1935, Communist parties around the globe turned on other leftist parties and groups rather than creating a united front against the crisis of the Depression and the rise of fascism. Such was the case in the United States, where Communists fought verbally and physically with their political rivals during the early 1930s.[69] There were thus also these reasons for the Trotskyists' failure to support the hunger march, reasons that Grace did not yet fully understand.

Grace gradually came to appreciate these realities as she drew more closely to the Trotskyists in the city. It was through the Social Problems Club that she made the initial contacts. Dorothy led the way here for Grace, as she had with making the connection to Lippincott's classes. Grace remembered how it was Dorothy's "student political action kind of group" that "came to know some of the Trotskyist leaders and would go to some of their meetings." Once she earned her PhD, Grace began going to the meetings too; she recalled how "I used to go to some of these Sunday Forums" and her boyfriend at the time, who soon became her fiancée, Gilbert Carlson, "would come along with me too."[70]

Grace "became very interested in their program and in the people, like Vincent Dunne and the others," who would speak at what was then the headquarters of the Workers Party, which the Trotskyist Left Opposition had merged with by late 1934. She explained how "they seemed to be so much stronger characters than the politicians that I came to know in the Farmer-Labor Party."[71] And it was strength of character that was needed during 1934 when the Trotskyists, like Dunne, led the Teamsters in their strikes for union recognition and higher wages.

Grace was a witness to these historic strikes during the summer of 1934. As members of the Social Problems Club, she and Dorothy collected money for the strikers and took it down to the May strike headquarters in a renovated garage at 1900 Chicago Avenue.[72] There she and Dorothy met more of the men who were involved in the strike and had ties to the Trotskyists. At the Sunday Forums, which they continued to attend, they also heard the leaders discuss the workers' struggle. And through Gilbert, whom she married that summer, Grace became more familiar with the strike leaders for whom her new husband provided legal assistance.[73] Through these points of exposure to the Trotskyist leadership of the drivers' struggle, Grace deepened her interest in socialism. She later explained, "The leaders of Local 574 were socialists (Trotskyists actually) and my admiration for them, their courage, ability and intelligence led me to study their program and join the party in 1936."[74] Watching them in action impressed Grace. "I admired their dedication to justice," she noted. And that admiration began to convince her of the validity of their political convictions and to see those as a good fit for her. She believed that "in spite of the fact that these people were philosophical materialists, they were not materialistic people." From her experience of the strike and of witnessing the Trotskyist leadership of that strike, Grace began a new phase in her education in socialism, turning to the study of the Trotskyist program in earnest and, for the first time, engaging seriously with the works of "Debs, Trotsky, Lenin, Marx and Engels."[75]

One of the strike coordinators whom Grace and Dorothy met when they brought the funds that they had collected to the strike headquarters was Henry Schultz. Schultz was not a Teamster but an electrician who had volunteered to help the drivers in their struggle. Born in Minneapolis in 1902 to parents who had emigrated from Germany in 1892, Schultz was a member of the International Brotherhood of Electrical Workers (IBEW), Local 160, and had been working as a brakeman on the Northern Pacific Railway since 1928.[76] He "was assigned by the strike committee to the dispatcher's function," working closely with the strike leaders to send out pickets around the city.[77] Dorothy and Henry became romantically involved and began what became a lifelong relationship and a jointly shared participation in the struggle for workers' liberation. Both Dorothy and Henry, along with Grace, also deepened their ties to the Trotskyist movement in Minneapolis and St. Paul as a result of what they experienced during the summer of 1934.

With Henry working at the strike headquarters, Dorothy and Grace began attending the mass meetings that were held in support of the strike. Grace recalled "what a great impact the Drivers strike of 1934 had on all Minnesotans—on and off campus. You were either on the workers' side or the bosses'—the union or the Citizens Alliance," the notorious employer organization that had kept Minneapolis an open shop city until that summer.[78] The 1934 strikes exposed the depths of class conflict that existed in Minneapolis, both in the violent extremes to which the employers went to try to maintain control of their industries and in the remarkable solidarity of the workers who resisted them.

Employers in Minneapolis, including the owners of the various trucking firms, came together in 1903 and created the Citizens Alliance (CA) to oppose workers' attempts to unionize in the city. By 1934 there were eight hundred members in the CA and the organization had developed a notorious reputation for using labor spies and its influence with the mainstream press to crush organized labor.[79] When the truck drivers attempted to organize within Local 574 of the Teamsters and then demand union recognition and higher wages for their labor, they were met with the stiff resistance of their bosses and the CA in Minneapolis.

But the drivers had one important advantage in this struggle: the superior organizing skills of many workers who were also Trotskyists. Vincent Raymond Dunne, who was born in Kansas City, Kansas, in 1889 and grew up on his grandfather's farm in Minnesota after his father, a streetcar worker, was injured on the job, knew workers' struggles from having experienced them all his life. Before coming to Minneapolis and finding work as an express driver in the 1910s, Dunne had labored as a grain harvester in North Dakota and a lumberjack in Montana. He briefly became a member of the Western Federation of Miners (WFM) and became familiar with the militant socialism of those in the IWW during his time out west. Once back in Minnesota, Dunne brought that syndicalism and socialism with him and was drawn into the orbit of the Communist Left Opposition. Working as a weigh master in the coal yards during the 1920s, Dunne became friends with Carl Skoglund, a Swedish immigrant who was an organizer for Local 574 and who became, as Dunne recalled, his "first real teacher . . . as a revolutionary socialist."[80] The two became leading figures in Minneapolis's then small Trotskyist community.

It was not just their years of experience as workers that contributed to their success as union and strike organizers but also their political views. As Trotskyists, the two men believed that democratic, industrial unions were the vehicle through which workers could resist oppression and, under the leadership of a true workers party, bring about a socialist society that would secure the workers' political and economic independence. They were thus fully committed to organizing the drivers and ending the open shop in Minneapolis because they understood that struggle as part of a bigger revolutionary project. Their revolutionary Marxist perspective also enabled them to be "more resolute and far-seeing in [their] preparations for class-battle" while at the same time it positioned them to be "more adept at negotiating limited, transitional victories in the class-struggle" because they understood the "protracted nature" of that struggle and of labor organizing.[81] Dunne and Skoglund were joined in the 1934 strikes by Harry DeBoer, who began driving a truck after he left school at the end of the eighth grade, and Farrell Dobbs, a high school graduate who worked for Western Electric until he lost that job in the Depression and found work in the coal yards.[82] It would be through their experiences of the strikes that DeBoer and Dobbs would join the Trotskyists too.[83]

Along with Vincent's brothers, Miles and Grant Dunne, who also belonged to Local 574, these men led the effort to organize the drivers into the union, beginning in the coal yards in February 1934. Inspired, in part, by the recent New Deal legislative protection of section 7a of the National Industrial Recovery Act (NIRA), which provided a federal guarantee of workers' right to organize in a union of their own choosing, Dunne, Skoglund, and the others felt the timing was right to strengthen

Local 574.⁸⁴ Taking advantage of a cold snap early that month, they organized a strike in which seven hundred men walked off the job and through which they built momentum and solidarity for a union vote. Conducted in mid-February, the election resulted in 77 percent of the voting men choosing affiliation with Local 574.⁸⁵ The success in the coal yards inspired drivers across the city to join the Teamsters local; by April, Local 574's ranks grew to almost three thousand members. From this position of strength, 574's president, William Brown, and vice president, George Frosig, issued the union's demands on April 30 for "the closed shop, shorter hours, an average wage of $27.50 a week, and extra pay for overtime." The employers flat out refused the demands, and their continued opposition led the union to vote for the strike that began on May 16.⁸⁶

Because of the organizing skills of the Dunne brothers, Skoglund, and Dobbs, the strikers were ready for what became an intense fight in the streets of the city. From a special headquarters, fitted out with a radio system to dispatch flying squadrons of strikers to stop scabbing truck drivers, a commissary staffed by a women's auxiliary to keep the men fed and ready to picket, and a field hospital to attend to the injured in the fight, the Trotskyists in the Teamsters led the workers in their struggle. Clashes between the strikers and the police widened to include those workers who came out to support the strikers (including those in the building trades, who called a general strike in sympathy) and citizens whom the police made special deputies to increase their ranks. By mid-May some thirty thousand workers faced down two thousand police and deputies in a confrontation in which two of the deputies were killed. A truce was called and an agreement reached at the end of May in which the drivers' membership in the union was recognized, but that recognition did not extend to inside workers in warehouses and loading bays.⁸⁷

In order to secure union protection for all workers in the industry, which was central to the industrial unionism favored by Dunne and the other Trotskyist strike organizers, Local 574 voted to walk out again in July. Once again the Trotskyists deployed their organizing skills, setting up a fully equipped headquarters, deploying the flying squadrons, and holding mass meetings to keep up morale and maintain community support. It was at those mass meetings that Dorothy and Grace had deepened their connections to the strike (and for Dorothy, her personal connection to Henry, who was working the radio dispatch). This time around, the strikers also published their own newspaper, the *Organizer*, to counter the union bashing and red baiting expressed in much of the mainstream press at the behest of the CA.[88] Grace later recalled how through these various tactics, especially the use of the newspaper to remain connected with the strikers and to control the narrative of the strike, the Trotskyists proved that they were "better strike leaders than you find in most strikes." Dorothy, who also witnessed the events, agreed.[89]

As the strikers upped their game with even better organization, so too the employers redoubled their resistance. Determined to reopen the streets to trucks, which had come to a standstill once again in July and cut off the lifeblood of the city's economy, the major trucking firms demanded the police do more to protect their strikebreakers. On the afternoon of Friday, July 20, a scab truck in the market district was loaded with a few boxes of produce. Guarded by fifty police on foot and one hundred more in squad cars, the truck began to pull away from the loading bay and down the street when it was confronted by strikers in a pick-up truck. When the strikers' truck pulled up to and blocked the scab truck from moving, the police, without warning, opened fire on the strikers. Meridel Le Sueur described how under this barrage, "Lines of living, solid men, fell, broke, wavering, flinging up, breaking over with the curious and awful abandon of despairing gestures, a man stepping on his own intestines bright, bursting in the street, another holding his severed arm in his other hand." Others, "standing on the sidewalk," could not "believe that they were seeing this. Until they themselves were hit by bullets." Two men were killed and at least sixty-seven were seriously injured.[90]

Bloody Friday, as these events became known, "polarised class-alignments in the city," as Bryan Palmer has argued, "proving beyond any doubt that 'a class battle did exist. . . . [I]t made Minneapolis people take sides either actively or in their hearts.'"[91] Grace had already taken sides with the workers since her father's experience with the 1922 shopmen's strike. But now, as a young woman who was becoming increasingly drawn to Trotskyism, she saw from the 1934 strikes, and Bloody Friday in particular, just how violently and intensely capitalists were willing to hold on to power. The civic compact of St. Paul, buttressed by the Church's social teachings, found no place among the bloodshed in Minneapolis's Market District. Grace, who was not in the city that day but away on her honeymoon with Gilbert, read about the events and was "horrified."[92] Her heart was with the cause of the workers, and soon, she would take action beyond her volunteer work with the Social Problems Club, attending more of the Trotskyists' Sunday Forums to further her education in socialism as the only solution to the oppression of workers.

After Bloody Friday, Minneapolis was placed under martial law by Governor Olson. A federal mediator was sent in by the Roosevelt administration, which was anxious to have the strike settled. After several rounds of talks, an agreement was finally reached on August 21 that included recognition of Local 574 and a minimum wage. The Trotskyists and the strikers they organized had mobilized tens of thousands of supporters in a months-long struggle and had successfully broken the open shop in Minneapolis.[93] For those who took sides with them, like Grace and Dorothy, the victory communicated the importance of working-class solidarity in defeating injustice and exploitation.

Grace also shared these experiences of the 1934 strikes with Gilbert. The two had met as students at the U. While Grace was working on her PhD in psychology, Gilbert was in the law school earning his degree. They both graduated in 1933.[94] He and Grace continued to see each other while she worked as a lecturer at the university from 1933 to 1935. It was during those years when they also began attending the Trotskyist Sunday Forums together with Dorothy and other members of the Social Problems Club.[95] And during the 1934 strikes, they did what they could to assist the Teamsters; Grace and Dorothy brought donations from campus to the strike headquarters, and Gilbert offered his legal services to strike leaders who got arrested.[96]

Gilbert Edward Carlson was born in St. Paul on April 6, 1909. His father, Edward Carlson, was born in Sweden in 1879 and his mother, Ida Tessier, in Minnesota in 1886. When Gilbert was a baby his father worked as a fur dresser in a tannery and the family lived with Ida's parents in a rented home on Anita Street on St. Paul's West Side.[97] By the time Gilbert was ten, his father was working, along with Ida's younger brother, in a packinghouse and the family had moved to West Delos Avenue, still on the West Side.[98] At age eleven, Gilbert took a job as an elevator operator at the Minneapolis Club. He later graduated from high school and enrolled in the University of Minnesota's law school.[99] While a student, he continued to live at home with his parents, now sharing an apartment at 468 Bellows Street on the West Side with his maternal uncle, Amos, who worked as a telegraph operator in the packing plant, and Amos's two children, Maydean and Amos Junior.[100] Although they came from different neighborhoods in St. Paul, Gilbert and Grace thus shared in common their working-class roots and a strong work ethic that helped them be the first in their families to graduate from college.

The young couple also shared a concern for social justice that contributed to their finding common ground and falling in love. Spending time together at the campus Social Problems Club, they discovered their mutual liberal interests. Dorothy, who became friends with Gilbert at the time too, described him as a "nice person" with a "good sense of humor" who was "very smart."[101] No doubt his intelligence and humor were attractive to Grace, who valued, and indeed shared, the same attributes. As they got to know each other, Grace and Gilbert also discovered their shared concern for the plight of workers. By 1934 they acted on that interest and began working together for the Non-Partisan Labor Defense (NPLD).

The NPLD was created by Trotskyists as a "genuinely non-partisan labor defense organization dedicated to uniting workers and others for militant defense of all victims of labor struggle, whatever their affiliation, against reaction." Its methods included legal defense, publicity and educational activities, and aid to prisoners.[102] Grace later recalled how "Gilbert was picked to be a lawyer who helped out with some of the cases," including defending knitwear workers in Minneapolis who had been arrested for striking.[103] Charles Walker, a journalist and labor activist whose wife, Adelaide, was also working in the NPLD, got to know Grace and Gilbert during this time. He noted how Grace struck him as a "very effective, capable, thoroughly honest gal." By contrast, Gilbert came across to Walker as "a nice but inexperienced and not very aggressive or convincing guy."[104] Despite the differences in their temperaments, Grace and Gilbert had found common ground in their working-class backgrounds and their desire to fight for workers' rights. The two fell in love. The connection between political and romantic passions was neither unusual nor unique to Grace and Gilbert's relationship. As one Communist later recalled, "The excitement of a cause can be quite an aphrodisiac."[105]

In addition to sharing their work in the NPLD, Grace and Gilbert were both devout Catholics. The two were married in Grace's home parish of St. Vincent's on July 28, 1934, with Dorothy as their maid of honor. Father Martin Griffin, the pastor, presided over the sacrament.[106] Grace and Gilbert enjoyed a wedding breakfast with their guests at the Commodore Hotel after the ceremony and then drove off on "a motor trip to Canada" for their honeymoon.[107] Returning to St. Vincent's in Frogtown for the ceremony suggests Grace's continued ties to her working-class family's roots, whereas the choice of the reception venue and honeymoon signal a desire for middle-class respectability and the reality of the professional status that Grace and Gilbert had achieved with their graduate degrees and new careers. In some ways they were like many labor leaders of their generation who, as Elizabeth Faue argues, "were both of and outside their class. Upwardly mobile" Grace and Gilbert were similar to "the working-class children who became the leaders and cultural workers of the labor movement" and who "had trans-class identities."[108]

Grace's entering into marriage as a sacrament in the Church also is evidence that her drifting from her Catholic roots during the early years of her politicization among the Trotskyists was a gradual one. Dorothy's presence at the wedding also communicates that the sisters had not yet officially left the Church. Indeed, Dorothy married in the Church too. She and Henry celebrated their wedding on February 18, 1937, also at St. Vincent's.[109] At this point, neither Grace nor Dorothy (nor Gilbert, for that matter) saw their faith and their politics as incompatible. Dorothy later recalled that during these years she would often attend Mass and a Socialist meeting on the same day.[110] Given Grace's commitment to social justice, which had been formed, in part, by the Josephites, it makes sense that she would not see her work in the NPLD or her attendance at the socialist forums as necessarily contradictory to her understanding of her faith. For the time being, she and Dorothy and Gilbert remained in the Church while they learned more about the Trotskyists and their approach to workers' struggles.

* * *

During the early years of her marriage to Gilbert, Grace's life became increasingly devoted to building a better world for workers and the oppressed. With Gilbert she sustained her support for the NPLD and, after it was reconstituted as the Workers Defense League in 1936, for the WDL.[111] She also continued to attend the Socialist Sunday forums each week with Dorothy. It was in her new career in the Department of Education's Division of Vocational Rehabilitation, however, where Grace finalized her conversion to socialism. It was through that work that she came to believe that the only way truly to make the world a better place for workers and the oppressed was through the creation of a socialist society.

During the first few months of her married life, Grace remained a lecturer at the U. When a new career opportunity arose, Grace eagerly embraced it as a chance to do more than teach study skills to football players. When Dr. John Rockwell, "who had been [her] thesis advisor at the University, became the state commissioner of education" in 1934, he hired Grace a year later because, as she explained, "he wanted to bring in people who were actually prepared academically and were not just political appointees." Part of her duties was to "write scientific things about testing these people [their clients] for their vocational and intellectual skills," and so Grace was able to draw on her expertise as an educational psychologist who specialized in assessment methods. She was also tasked with "finding jobs" for the clients, an assignment that in the context of the Depression she found to be "very, very difficult."[112]

At the time she arrived at the Division of Vocational Rehabilitation in 1935 it was being revamped under its then director, Dr. Frank Finch, who focused the unit's work on "the administration of rehabilitation services on an individualized basis. To this end, trained psychologists were employed as case workers and intensive studies of the abilities, aptitudes and needs" of all disabled clients "were made before retraining programs were begun." Grace explained in a letter to Sarah Tarleton Colvin in September 1939 how this "program of ministering to the 'whole individual'" has "continued to expand under the new Director, D. H. Dabelstein." Colvin—a veteran of the women's suffrage movement, former Minnesota state chairperson of the National Women's Party, and FLP supporter—had been appointed by Governor Olson to the State Board of Education and was friendly with Grace. The two shared not only the belief in the need for women to be independent and politically engaged but also progressive economic views.

Although Grace's work at the DoE frustrated her at times, it advanced her conversion to socialism. Grace felt comfortable writing to Colvin with her take on things, which, by 1939, had become more radical. Using descriptive categories that reflected the normative assumptions of her time, Grace told Colvin, "It is my own conviction, however, that the problems of the physically handicapped workers depend for their complete solution on the establishment of a new society. Then emphasis will be placed on what individuals can do rather than upon the cruel and senseless competition of physically handicapped people with normal individuals." Echoing the shift in her politics by 1939 that resulted, in part, from these experiences in vocational rehabilitation, Grace concluded, "We may even hope some day to reach a state where services will be 'from each according to his abilities, to each according to his needs.'"[113] Grace later acknowledged, "This job pushed me toward socialism." She explained how "trying to find jobs for handicapped people during the Depression was terrible. It seemed immoral to me that people who were qualified weren't able to find jobs. There was something wrong with a system like that."[114]

During her time at the DoE Grace became active, both on the job and off, advocating ways to change that system. In November 1935, Grace had just been "appointed to direct the rehabilitation of those handicapped by tuberculosis in Hennepin, Ramsey and Stearns counties," by meeting with "patients soon to be discharged from Glen Lake sanatorium to aid them in choosing a new line of work which will not endanger their health."[115] It was this work that led her to see the faults of the system she complained about to Colvin in 1939. Grace also cowrote a paper with Dabelstein on "Vocational Rehabilitation of the Tuberculous," published in November 1940, in which they argued for the total-person approach and the development of better facilities for after-care and rehabilitation of such patients.[116] From her professional perch as a psychologist employed by the DoE Grace thus made clinical arguments for helping disabled people. She also used her expertise to call for more sweeping social change outside the DoE. As a guest speaker on "Health and Hygiene" at the St. Paul Trades and Labor Assembly's (TLA) unemployment conference in March 1940, Grace criticized the poor conditions of certain local hospitals and urged attendees to recognize the "relationship between poverty and ill health." Ultimately, she called for "a program of socialized medicine and hospitalization" to address the needs of disabled people, whose disabilities, she believed, were either caused by or worsened by economic disadvantage.[117]

In her role as a member of the education committee of the TLA, Grace went further and made the connection that unions were the organizations that would help spearhead such change, arguing that it was through them that workers needed to fight for better conditions across the board. Grace made this argument in St. Paul in February 1940 at the Fifth Annual Workers' Education Conference, an event cosponsored by the St. Paul TLA and the Workers' Education Department of the Works Progress Administration (WPA). There she praised the St. Paul Labor College, an institution sponsored by the TLA, for providing the "additional education" that workers who may have had to drop out of school needed "in order to function in their trade unions, in their daily life, in dealing with employers, in fighting for better conditions."[118] On its face, her comments fit easily into the tenor of the conference, at which sixty delegates from twenty-five AFL unions heard greetings from AFL president William Green about the importance of the organized labor movement and the Labor College's efforts to support it. She even shared the stage with labor reform priest Father Francis J. Gilligan, a student of John Ryan's "theology of social justice," who, like Ryan before him, taught moral theology at the St. Paul Seminary. Gilligan, who also had begun working for African American civil rights by the mid-1930s, was a strong supporter of labor schools.[119] At the conference he "emphasized the fact that 'knowledge is power,' and that the Labor College can play an important role in helping Labor achieve such power."[120] Although Grace would agree with this statement on its face, by early 1940 she had begun to understand the ultimate purpose and meaning of unions in a very different way from Gilligan and Green and many others in the AFL.

The reason for this disparity was Grace's embrace of Trotskyism, to which she had been increasingly exposed since the days of the 1934 strikes. That event, coupled with her activities at the U and followed by her experiences at the DoE, pushed her to question the validity of the capitalist system in ways that were different from the critiques of social injustices that had been part of her childhood working-class Catholic identity and different even from her progressive reformist stance as a young adult in the FLP. By attending the weekly Sunday Forums of the Left Opposition and getting to know the Trotskyist leadership in the local labor movement, Grace had honed her existing class consciousness in a way that led her to see things from a revolutionary Marxist viewpoint. Some of the elements of this viewpoint—such as her understanding that she was a member of the working class, her sense of solidarity with members of her class, and her supporting the realization of the dignity and free development of each person in society—were already parts of Grace's identity before she attended the U. But others—including her seeing working-class interests as counterposed to those of the capitalist class, her believing in the need for political and economic struggle to advance workers' interests, and her efforts towards bringing about workers' control of the economic and political systems—were new and evolved out of her experiences since 1933.[121]

Grace not only developed a revolutionary class consciousness in these years but also forged stronger ties to the revolutionary Marxist movement of Trotskyists in St. Paul and Minneapolis. When she formally joined them in 1936, it was as a member of the Socialist Party because in that year the Trotskyists had decided to enter the SP in the hopes of winning over more radical Socialists to their ranks. Between 1928, when followers of Trotsky were ousted from the Communist Party for rejecting Stalin's "socialism in one country" policy, and 1933, the Trotskyists in America were organized essentially as a Left Opposition to the CP. In 1933, as it became clear that there would be no reform of the Comintern away from what Trotskyists perceived as its Stalinist bureaucratic degeneration, they no longer considered themselves "a faction of the CP and set out to build a revolutionary Marxist party." Integrating with the class struggle was central to this goal, and that was most notably achieved during the strikes in Minneapolis in 1934. That same year, the Trotskyists merged with the American Workers Party (AWP) as part of this strategy, becoming the Workers Party of the United States (WPUS). By the spring of 1936, when Grace joined as an official member, the WPUS dissolved itself and joined the SP in the hopes of winning even more young radicals to the cause of building a new international revolutionary socialist movement.[122]

The Trotskyists' time in the SP was short lived, as disputes over domestic and foreign policy issues emerged between these revolutionaries and the more moderate electoral Socialists already in the SP's ranks. Ultimately, the Trotskyists were expelled by the moderates in the summer of 1937, but they managed to take some of the more radical Socialists with them.[123] Gathering in Chicago from December 31, 1937, through January 3, 1938, Trotskyist delegates from around the country, including Grace, established their own revolutionary Marxist party, the Socialist Workers Party (SWP). At that time membership stood at around one thousand. George Breitman, then a young Trotskyist from New Jersey who would later become an organizer for the SWP in Newark and Detroit and a member of the party's National Committee and Political Committee, recalled the exuberance of those gathered in Chicago. "The convention represented a milestone in the history of the American revolutionary movement," he said. "I am sure most of the delegates shared my conviction that we had participated in something truly significant: the launching—at last!—of the party that would lead the American workers in their coming socialist revolution."[124] Grace, too, recalled her presence at the convention with pride.[125]

At this founding convention, the delegates adopted the party's Declaration of Principles, in which they laid out the fundamental beliefs and goals of the Trotskyists and the reason for the SWP's creation. The first section makes the argument for why socialism was needed, articulating general tenets of Marxism. Beginning with the assumption that capitalism had failed (a belief that the crises of the 1930s reinforced for many leftists), it declares that socialism is "the only road" out from the oppression of war and fascism that capitalism breeds. The goal in confronting capitalism is "to wipe out its central and insurmountable conflict by taking the ownership and control of the natural resources, the productive plant and means of exchange, out of the hands of private individuals and corporations, and placing that ownership and control in the hands of society itself, to be used for the fulfillment of human needs and not for profit." Central to this struggle against capitalism, the declaration asserts, is the working class, who "can carry out socialization only through the conquest and maintenance of political power" by the "overthrow of the capitalist state" and "transfer of sovereignty from it to their own Workers' State—the Dictatorship of the Proletariat." But that workers' state is presented as a "temporary political instrument making possible the transition to the class-less socialist society." In that socialist society, "The entire population will be transformed into a community of free producers owning and controlling the total productive wealth and resources of society, and freely and consciously working out their own destiny."[126] The utopian dimensions of this vision of socialist society were attractive to its supporters.

In part 2 of the declaration, the Trotskyists explain the role of the revolutionary party in the process of ushering in the socialist society, and they make the case for their particular position among other parties on the Left. Trotskyists, like other Communists, believed that "without an adequate, firm, and strong revolutionary party, the magnificent heroism, militancy and self-sacrifice of the workers lead and can lead only to sporadic and unconnected battles for partial aims which achieve no lasting conquests." At their founding convention in Chicago, Trotskyists called "upon all revolutionary militants to join with us to build the SWP into the mass revolutionary party which will lead the working class of the United States to power." But unlike the Communists in the CPUSA, for example, who followed Moscow and supported Stalin's plan for establishing socialism in one country, the Trotskyists believed that the SWP, "together with the revolutionists of all countries united in the Fourth International, will achieve the victory of the International revolution and of world socialism."[127] Remaining true to what they understood as the original international revolutionary vision of Marx and Lenin, the Trotskyists in Chicago situated their new party within this global struggle. Several of the leaders of the new SWP, including James Cannon, Vincent Dunne, and Rose Karsner, even traveled to Mexico later in 1938 and met with Trotsky to plan the founding conference of the new Fourth International.[128]

Grace already knew Vincent Dunne, or Ray as he was called by his friends, since the days of the 1934 strikes and her attendance at the Trotskyist Sunday Forums with Dorothy, Henry, and Gilbert. James Cannon and his partner, Rose Karsner, would become important figures in Grace's life too. Cannon was born in Rosedale, Kansas, in February 1890 and shared with Grace an Irish heritage and a Catholic childhood. He also shared working-class roots. At age twelve, he went to work in a meatpacking plant. In 1908 he joined the Socialist Party, and from 1911 until 1913 he was a traveling organizer for the IWW. He left that role to settle down in Kansas City after he married Lista Makimson in 1913. In

1919, when the SP split, Cannon left with those who supported what would become the Communist Party. He was elected chairman of the national committee of that party as it came above ground and he headed its International Labor Defense from 1925 to 1928. Cannon also attended the Sixth World Congress of the Communist International in 1928 and there came into possession of Trotsky's "Criticism of the Draft Program of the Communist International." He was expelled with other followers of Trotsky that same year for sharing this critique of Stalinism and then became a leading figure of the Communist Left Opposition as it evolved from a faction in 1928 into the independent revolutionary party of the SWP a decade later.[129] Rose Greenberg Karsner, "a Romanian-born party worker" from New York who had married and divorced the socialist journalist David Karsner, became Cannon's life partner after he left Lista in 1923.[130] Rose, described later by a friend at the time as a "gentle, beautiful, and very capable young woman," first met Jim in 1921 in the then underground Communist movement and the two found themselves crossing each other's paths in the years that followed.[131] They remained partners in life and in politics for the rest of their lives and became close friends and comrades of Grace, Ray, and other Trotskyists in Minneapolis.

By attending the founding conference of the SWP in December 1937 and January 1938, Grace signaled her full participation in the Trotskyist movement. At first, her political affiliations were tolerated at the DoE, as were her union activities with the Minnesota State Employees Union, Local 10, and the TLA. She later recalled how, when Olson was still governor, Minnesota was a "liberal kind of state" and such political affiliations among public workers was not a big issue.[132] When she was a member of the more moderate electoral socialist SP, such connections were not particularly suspect in progressive circles. But this tolerance ended with the election of Republican Harold Stassen as governor in 1938 and his reelection in 1940. At that point, Grace was openly affiliated with the revolutionary Marxist SWP, not the SP. And, in terms of the broader political context, since August 1939 the country had entered a period that historians now identify as the "little red scare," which also contributed to the atmosphere of intolerance that Grace experienced first-hand at the DoE.

During this scare, fears of Nazi subversion that had developed after the exposure of a few German spy rings in 1938 were easily combined with (and at times surpassed by) longstanding anti-Communist sentiment in the United States. This merging of national security fears increased especially after August 1939, when Germany and the Soviet Union signed the Non-Aggression Pact and the CPUSA (which had up until then been a vocal opponent of fascism) did an about-face and condemned the fighting that broke out in September as a capitalist war. From August 1939 until June 1941 (when the Germans violated the pact and invaded the Soviet Union), the Nazi and Communist threat merged as one in the eyes of many Americans because of the CP's opposition to the war. President Franklin Roosevelt authorized the increased domestic political surveillance by the Federal Bureau of Investigation (FBI) of alleged subversive organizations, including the CP and the SWP, while Congressman Martin Dies (D-Texas) continued the work of his House Committee to Investigate Un-American Activities, which he began in 1938. Dies investigated over six hundred organizations, four hundred newspapers, and two hundred labor unions with alleged Communist ties. Many conservative and liberal anti-Communists supported these investigations. Indeed, in 1939, 79 percent of Americans approved of Dies's work. During this "little red scare," not just members of the CP but also anyone who had or was thought to have ties to the radical Left could come under scrutiny. That scrutiny could be conducted by the FBI and Dies or by state and local government agencies or by private groups, like the American Legion, that sought to expose and purge the presence of radicals in both the public and the private sector.[133] Grace—and soon thereafter her supervisor, John Rockwell—became casualties of such a purge in Minnesota.[134]

For Grace the problems began on April 1, 1940, when Rockwell wrote to her expressing his concern over her using her upcoming vacation time to attend the SWP's convention in New York without clearing those plans first with the Board of Education. Although he granted that she was "entitled to vacation" and "to spend your vacation as you see fit," he insisted that it was "subject only to the limitation that you recognize that you are a member of this Department, such that any action on your part which might possibly involve embarrassment to the Department should be fully cleared with the Department in advance."[135] Rockwell, who had been appointed by Governor Olson, was known to have "kept aloof from all political movements" in his role as commissioner of education and was conscious not to discriminate against any of his employees because of their politics, in accordance with the state's civil service laws. He knew of Grace's connections with the SWP before April 1940 but later explained that up until then he did not see those ties as having any bearing on her work for the DoE. Perhaps it was not until Grace's activities with the Trotskyists became more frequent and public after 1938, and took place in the deepening anti-Communist atmosphere of the little red scare, that Rockwell decided they were a problem.[136]

In her response, which she penned the same day, Grace explained that the Civil Service Board (CSB) rules contained nothing barring "a state employee from attending a political meeting," noting that she was not going as a delegate or alternate, which, she granted, was specifically banned.[137] Whatever may have transpired next between Grace and her former dissertation adviser is unclear, as there are no more letters between the two until after she tendered her letter of resignation on April 21. Sent to D. H. Dabelstein, the director of the Division of Vocational Rehabilitation, that letter merely stated that she wished "to submit my resignation from the position of vocational rehabilitation counselor . . . effective September 1, 1940."[138] Her official "report of separation" filed with the state indicated "personal consideration" under "reason for resignation."[139]

Grace was more forthcoming about her reasons for leaving the DoE in a letter to her colleague at Glen Lake, Dr. E. S. Mariette. After emphasizing how she "had a great personal satisfaction in taking part in the rehabilitation program at Glen Lake," she expressed her views on the need for "the establishment of a new society" in which to properly treat such disabled clients. "For the past four years I have taken an active part in the Socialist movement which I am confident will build this new order," she explained. "I am leaving the Rehabilitation Division now so as to be able to devote full time to this work, unhampered by the restrictions, written and unwritten, which are now placed upon State employees."[140] Those "unwritten" restrictions had emerged in the broader climate of repression just beginning to sweep over the DoE.

Even after she submitted her resignation and signed her report of separation with the state, Grace still faced criticism. On August 28, Rockwell wrote to her saying that he was "extremely disturbed" to read in the newspaper that she would be presiding over a memorial meeting for

Leon Trotsky, who had been assassinated by agents of Stalin in Mexico on August 21. He argued that "this Department can in no sense be interpreted as being interested in the Trotskyite or Communist program" and that her presiding at the meeting "cannot help but tend to create in the mind of the public the suspicion that this Department is engaged in the kind of political propaganda that should have no part in our educational system." Because her resignation would not go into effect until September 1, she was still a member of the department, and he insisted that her "actions must be governed in relation to the Department of which you are a member." Rockwell then threatened to suspend her if she went ahead with her plans.[141]

Grace refused to back down. In her response to Rockwell, she informed him that she had already called the newspaper and requested that it clarify its mistake of identifying her by her professional title so as not to confuse readers into thinking that she would be attending the Trotsky memorial meeting in her capacity as an employee of the state. But she refused not to attend and insisted that she had "never violated" the civil service regulations with respect to political activities.[142] Sticking to her guns, Grace presided over the Trotsky memorial held in Minneapolis at 919 Marquette Avenue, the SWP's branch headquarters, on August 29.[143]

Rockwell soon came under scrutiny too and his knowledge of Grace's political activities became one of the more heated issues that supercharged the case against him. On November 20, 1940, the Board of Education issued a resolution ordering his suspension from office for thirty days, during which time he would be given a chance for a hearing. The charges included his opposition to appointment of certain individuals supported by the board and his "inefficiency" as commissioner of education. On December 18, additional charges were adopted against Rockwell when the board passed another resolution asking that "all matters pertaining to actions of John G. Rockwell during his term" as commissioner be considered.[144] The timing of the board's suspension of Rockwell coincided with the broader context of the little red scare in the United States, which was manifesting itself in the local politics of reaction against progressives and leftists in Minnesota. The nature of many of the charges, which would only begin to come out in the hearings—especially those that dealt directly with Grace—reflected the anti-Communist agenda of the majority of the state's Board of Education.

The issue with Grace dealt with her radical politics and questions surrounding what Rockwell knew and how he handled that information vis-à-vis the board. The tenor of the questions posed to Rockwell during the hearings that were conducted between January and March 1941 and the amount of time spent on the topic (as well as the press coverage it received) communicated the intensity of the anticommunism of the board members as well as their assumptions about the nature of the radical politics targeted in their purge of the DoE. At one point in the hearings, for example, Rockwell was asked if he knew that Grace, as a member of the SWP, advocated the violent overthrow of the government. At another he was asked if there "were colored folks" at a party he held at his house as a fundraiser for one of Grace's trade union causes.[145] One newspaper slammed Rockwell for not firing Grace sooner and, confusing her role and duties at the DoE, argued that "these, might we call them rascals, who are in our schools and teaching our youth the advantages, so to speak, of Communism should either be sent out to hoe corn or sent where they belong."[146] Although Rockwell had defenders within local progressive circles (including Colvin, who was on the board), they were not able to prevent his ultimate dismissal from office.[147] The substantive charges regarding his handling of state aid and teachers' certificates, which were also addressed in the hearings, may have been enough in ordinary times to lead to his suspension, but it seems that the politics of the little red scare also helped drive the final nail in the coffin of his career at the DoE.[148]

Grace managed to escape this fracas at the DoE relatively unscathed. She resigned from the vocational rehabilitation division and had to leave the work she loved, but she landed on her feet by using the juncture as an opportunity to begin working for the SWP full-time. However, the furor surrounding her politics at the DoE would not be the last time her commitment to the SWP would come under scrutiny by representatives from the state. And the next tangle would be with the federal government, during which Grace would not fare so well.

Grace's resignation from the DoE and embrace of full-time SWP work was not, however, without any costs. Rockwell had been her dissertation adviser at the U and was the one who hired her as a vocational rehabilitation counselor. The two had become colleagues and friends during the years she worked at the DoE and Grace had even come to know Rockwell's wife quite well too. So as things began to fall apart for him in late 1940 and early 1941, Grace felt bad for "poor Rockwell" because so much of the animus directed at him during the hearings was related to her politics. She even attended the hearings to try to show her support, but given the climate, that may not have had the effect she had hoped for. Grace later recognized that "in one of these hearings I was pictured as the Trotskyist centerpiece of the case, you know" and that these were "difficult days."[149] After Rockwell was dismissed, the two fell out of touch.

* * *

By late 1940, Grace had become a committed Trotskyist. Between her time as an undergraduate at the College of St. Catherine and her career at the DoE, she had significant experiences that both reinforced her identity as an independent woman and deepened her class consciousness and concern for social justice in ways that led her to embrace the revolutionary Marxism of the SWP. She also met and married Gilbert Carlson in the midst of all of these changes. Unfortunately for their relationship, her becoming a member of the SWP and her increasingly public role in that party undermined the marriage. Like her friendship with Rockwell, it, too, would be a casualty of her political commitment but for different reasons.

Later in her life Grace spoke briefly about why she and Gilbert separated. She explained that it was in the aftermath of their becoming party members when Gilbert "was told by some priest friend that he couldn't be a Catholic and a Socialist at the same time, so we were going in different ways."[150] Gilbert remained devout and committed to the Church. Grace, however, admitted that she "wasn't a practicing Catholic" anymore by 1938 and so she did not face the dilemma that Gilbert did. But she found that she and Gilbert then "grew apart" as a result. Neither sought a divorce, but the two agreed to separate. The relationship that had once sustained a shared political commitment to social justice and workers' liberation now fell apart as husband and wife disagreed over how to pursue their political goals. Gilbert stayed with the Church and went back home to live with his mother. He continued to practice law and to defend his former comrades in the Teamsters. Grace stayed with the SWP and remained in the house the couple had rented, sharing it with "two girls from the Socialist Workers Party chapter in St. Paul" who "came in to live with [her]."[151] Grace began to apply her talents as a writer and a public speaker full-time to the cause of revolutionary socialism by 1940. For the next twelve years there would be no turning back as she, now separated from Gilbert, made the SWP the focus of her public and private life.

3

Sisterhoods

Female comrades were an essential component of Grace's life in the SWP. Albeit a coed world—indeed, one in which men dominated the top party leadership—it was one in which women, like Grace, forged connections to support each other within the movement. Their sisterhood was part of the broader "dense networks of family and friends" among those on the political Left during the twentieth century that Kathleen A. Brown and Elizabeth Faue argue proved so vital to the Left's existence in the face of government repression and surveillance. As Brown and Faue note, "The risks of opposition politics—in terms of political ostracism and social ostracism—were such that most activists could not survive without the encouragement of friends and family."[1] Grace's personal connections, especially to her biological sister, Dorothy, proved important during her run for Senate in 1940, during the strain of her prosecution under the Smith Act in 1941, and particularly during the year she spent in Alderson prison in 1944.

Grace's correspondence reveals the importance of this female network for her survival. It shows how Grace, her sister Dorothy, and their friends Rose Karsner, Elaine Roseland, Bea Janosco, and others sustained each other as any caring network of kin and companions would. Yet it also reveals how through that sisterhood these working-class women made significant contributions to the SWP at the branch level during the 1940s as party organizers, political candidates, and writers for the party press. As they committed themselves to working towards the creation of a socialist society, they grappled with their experiences as working women within a revolutionary movement in capitalist society. Theirs was thus a political sisterhood. Even as they expanded their work within the party, Grace's friends continued to face the demands of the double day. Grace's letters are a window through which becomes visible a group of working-class housewives sharing their daily concerns as they struggled to participate in the public work of the revolutionary SWP while the "children were climbing all over the kitchen."² In her letters, her writings for the *Militant*, and her 1945 "Women in Prison" speaking tour, Grace voiced a working-class Marxist feminism that belied the now debunked assumption that the 1940s and 1950s constituted the doldrums of the women's movement. The record she left behind shows that Grace was committed to advancing herself and other women in the party so they could bring about their liberation, as workers and as women, through the creation of a socialist society.³

* * *

When Grace resigned as a vocational rehabilitation counselor and became a full-time organizer for the SWP in September 1940, the party became the focus of her life, and her network of party friends became her new family for the next twelve years. Grace, along with her sister, Dorothy, and her brother-in-law, Henry, were members of the party's St. Paul branch.⁴ Because the Trotskyists in Teamsters Local 574 (which by 1940 was designated as Local 544) belonged to the SWP's Minneapolis branch, Grace, Dorothy, and Henry "used to think the real action was going on in Minneapolis so we would practically always attend two meetings a week, you know, both the St. Paul branch meeting and the Minneapolis branch." They also attended the Minneapolis branch's "educational meetings and trade union meetings."⁵

By 1940 Grace, Dorothy, and Henry not only became committed members of the SWP in the Twin Cities but also remained loyal to James Cannon when a faction fight tore through the party that same year. With the Nazi-Soviet Pact of August 1939 and the outbreak of World War II in September 1939 came the "most thoroughgoing internal struggle in the movement since its inception."⁶ SWP Political Committee members James Burnham and Max Shachtman led the faction that argued that the USSR was not, "as Trotskyists had traditionally argued, a degenerated workers' state (with a collectively owned economy worth defending in the face of imperialism, although requiring a political revolution to overturn the reactionary dictatorship of the [Stalinist] bureaucracy)." Instead they insisted that the Soviet Union was "a new form of oppressive class society" that "must in no way be defended by revolutionaries."⁷ As this fight played out in the SWP, Grace, Dorothy, and Henry, along with Vincent Dunne and others in the Minneapolis branch, gave their support to the majority led by Cannon in opposition to the Burnham-Shachtman faction.[8] The majority believed that the "doctrine and program of revolutionary Marxism" as proclaimed by the Fourth International meant that "the defense of the Soviet Union is the elementary duty of every workers' organization." After the minority raised its opposing view, a discussion of the issue was "formally opened in October [1939] and continued uninterruptedly for six months." That discussion, as Cannon later explained, included the publication of thirteen internal bulletins and "unrestricted distribution of factional documents." There were also "innumerable debates and speeches in party membership meetings." Finally, a special convention was called in April 1940 in New York, where the majority position won in a vote of fifty-five to thirty-one. When the minority leaders rejected this decision and began to attack the program of the party publicly, they were expelled and formed the Workers Party.[9]

Grace's loyalty to the SWP contributed to her becoming its candidate for the US Senate in Minnesota in 1940. But so too did the St. Paul and Minneapolis branches, which supported women's participation. Dorothy later recalled how "we had an exceptional situation" there because it was "very much a family movement" and "a lot of activity involved the women."[10] Although Dorothy noted correctly that this inclusivity was "not true in the unions" with exclusively male membership, Minneapolis in particular had a history during the Depression decade of the 1930s of having a "community-based labor movement" in which women played important roles in union auxiliaries, most notably for Teamsters Local 574 during the 1934 strikes. Working women also had a history of organizing themselves, as was the case among clerical workers in the Stenographers, Bookkeepers, and Tax Accountants (SBTA) Local 17661. Those efforts were led by Jewell Flaherty (Miles Dunne's wife) and Rose Seiler (who graduated from the U with a degree in sociology and political science and later married Teamster and Trotskyist Ed Palmquist).[11] Grace's background as a former member of Local 10, American Federation of State, County, and Municipal Employees, and as a delegate to the St. Paul TLA fit into this pattern of women's participation in the labor movement in the Twin Cities during the 1930s.[12] She was welcomed in the SWP as a valuable member who brought her trade union connections along with her stellar speaking and writing skills.[13]

Grace also was quickly pegged as an excellent political organizer, and that work contributed to her nomination as the party's candidate for the 1940 US Senate run. Her friend and comrade Harry DeBoer later recalled how "she spent most of her time, when she wasn't out giving speeches, in the SWP hall at 10th and Marquette in downtown Minneapolis." Commenting on what became one of her signature favorite beverages, he noted, "She usually had some coffee ready, and we came in and joined her in discussion of issues and problems." Referencing what would also become a hallmark of Grace's social interactions, DeBoer recollected how she was "a very good cook, and people got into the habit of dropping in for lunch. People paid her very small amounts of money for lunch, and those lunches turned into meetings." DeBoer remembered how Grace's "way of making things pleasant and homey was one of her very effective organizing techniques."[14]

Grace's domestic approach to political organizing played on older gender norms even as they flew in the face of them. The belief in women's innate difference from men undergirded the assumption that a woman's place was in the separate sphere of the home as a wife and mother. These ideas (although not always translated into reality for working women) had become enshrined in middle-class custom and in law and had kept women outside of or on the margins of electoral politics (and the workplace) throughout much of America's history.[15] After a "century of struggle," the vote was finally extended to women throughout the nation with the ratification of the Nineteenth Amendment in 1920.[16] As many scholars have documented, the absence of the vote before 1920 had not rendered women politically powerless or inactive; politics broadly understood included many avenues for women's activism during the nineteenth and early twentieth centuries.[17] But with the vote, women's participation in traditionally defined electoral politics did expand; Grace's run for the US Senate in 1940 took place in this context.

On both the national and the state level, however, this expansion was slow and limited. As Susan Ware notes, only twenty-eight women served in Congress between 1918 and 1940, and only one woman (Hattie Caraway) served in the Senate.[18] Susan M. Hartmann traces an uptick in the numbers of women elected to state legislatures from 144 in 1941 to 228 in 1945, and a "slight decline immediately after the war was followed by the election of 249 women in 1950."[19] In the two decades after securing the vote nationwide, women had thus broken into the world of electoral politics, but the numbers were still insignificant because of, as Hartmann notes, the yet "unshaken . . . cultural norms which defined politics as masculine." When it came to moving beyond such helper roles as "canvassers, election clerks, and inspectors" to becoming candidates, women continued to face the challenges of "habit and prejudice."[20]

Grace did not face the same degree of "habit and prejudice" in becoming a candidate in what was, in 1940, the then quite young SWP. On September 21, 1940, two weeks after the *Socialist Appeal* reported that Grace had begun her career as a full-time organizer for the SWP, it announced her Senate run. The Minneapolis branch, headquartered at 919 Marquette Avenue, and the St. Paul branch, headquartered at 138 East Sixth Street, were the nerve centers of the campaign. Its first order of business was to secure the two thousand signatures needed to get Grace on the ballot. Her campaign, managed by Chester Johnson, sent out ten thousand leaflets describing her platform along with the same number of a special issue of the *Socialist Appeal* targeting the working-class neighborhoods in St. Paul, Minneapolis, and Duluth. Grace spoke on the radio, before groups of African Americans and youth, and at two election rallies. By October her campaign had gathered twenty-six hundred signatures.[21]

In her campaign speeches, Grace articulated the critique of capitalism that she had honed since joining the party. "Capitalism is a great destroyer of human lives," she asserted. "Not only are millions of young men murdered in its bloody wars, but each year, hundreds of thousands of men, women and children die needlessly because of the failure of capitalism to provide them with the means of life—adequate food and clothing, warm houses and proper medical care."[22] Grace also engaged with the question of the war in Europe when she condemned her political opponents as having no real solution. "Their feeble anti-war declarations, lacking the necessary economic interpretations of the causes of the war, are as futile in this period as the action of a man who tries to hold back the tide with a broom," she declared. Grace promised that if she were elected to the Senate she would introduce a bill that, as the *Socialist Appeal* explained, would provide "the trade union movement with military equipment and instructors so that the workers might receive their military training not under the labor hating army machine, but under their own auspices."²³ Offering a Trotskyist interpretation of the war, she proclaimed, "In a world in flames, with every continent an armed camp, he who puts forth a pacifist program as a solution to the problems of war and fascism BETRAYS THE WORKERS, ... Only armed workers can lay the foundation for a society free and equal."²⁴

Grace thus voiced the SWP's position, which was neither pacifist nor isolationist in its opposition to the war as it was then being conducted. As Cannon later explained, the reason Trotskyists "do not support a declaration of war by American arms, is because we do not believe the American capitalists can defeat Hitler and fascism." Rather, "We think Hitlerism can be destroyed only by way of conducting a war under the leadership of the workers."²⁵ By September 1940 the war in Europe had been going on for a year. In the spring Hitler had launched his blitzkrieg attack on Holland, Belgium, and Luxembourg, and by late June the Nazis had taken control of France. President Franklin Roosevelt moved beyond the limited support for the Allies that he had secured through the cash-and-carry provisions of the 1939 revised Neutrality Act to more robust emergency wartime preparations in the wake of this blitzkrieg. In May he asked Congress "for a supplemental defense appropriation of nearly \$1.3 billion," and in September he signed the Selective Service Act, the first peacetime draft.²⁶ But there was still strong popular opposition to the United States entering the war.²⁷ Because of this antiwar sentiment, Trotskyists were hopeful that they could make a decent showing at the polls in November.²⁸ The SWP's antiwar and military policy, however, was very different from either the traditional midwestern antiinterventionism or the pacifism that fueled much of the antiwar sentiment in Minnesota. Positioning herself on the far left with the SWP's radical take on the war and the arming of workers, Grace did not have much chance of winning.

In her 1940 Senate run, Grace also called for "genuine economic and social equality for women," expressing her understanding, as a Trotskyist, that the latter could not exist without the former. She also demanded "full social, political and economic equality for the Negro people," which reflected her support for civil rights as a member of the St. Paul NAACP. Grace's inclusion of women's and African Americans' rights in her campaign stemmed not just from her personal commitments to equal rights but also from the strategy and principles of the SWP. The party touted her candidacy as having special appeal to working women, and its demand for civil rights traced back to its Declaration of Principles, which defined discrimination as a tool of the bourgeoisie to divide the working class.[29]

Despite the party's hopes, Grace did not do well at the polls. Her positions were just too radical for most voters, even those who opposed the war. And then there was the fact that she was a woman running for elected office in 1940 with the obstacles of habit and prejudice among the general electorate in her way. Overall, her vote total of 8,761 (or 0.72 percent of the state's popular vote) put her nowhere near the victor, incumbent Republican Henrik Shipstead, with 641,049 votes (53.01 percent), or the runners up, Farmer-Laborite Elmer Benson, with 310,875 (25.71 percent), and Democrat John Regan, with 248,658 (20.56 percent).[30] But, as the *Socialist Appeal* reported in the aftermath of the election, for the Trotskyists, "The total vote, though indicative of our support [in the urban centers], is of course not the chief value of the election campaign." Rather, it was the fact that "many people have been brought closer to us by hearing for the first time in this campaign the revolutionary Marxist program."[31]

Grace also advanced this interpretation. Writing to Rose Karsner that fall, she expressed satisfaction that "thousands of Minnesota workers and farmers heard our program over the radio and were thus introduced for the first time to the Trotskyist movement."[32] She was also proud that she had outpolled in Minnesota the combined vote of Earl Browder (who had run for the presidency on the CP ticket) and Norman Thomas (who had run for the presidency on the SP ticket).[33] Writing to Natalia Sedova, Leon Trotsky's widow, Grace noted that "it was a source of great satisfaction to me to have made so much better showing than the Stalinist candidate."[34] In her analysis of the campaign, Grace not only reflected the party line on the significance of her race as an educational tool but also voiced her ambition to lead the young SWP in such evangelization.

Writing to Farrell Dobbs and James Cannon after the election, Grace explained that despite having contracted bronchitis and developing an enlarged heart near the end of the campaign, she was fully recovered and eager to serve the party again.[35] Neither Farrell nor Jim needed reassurance. They wrote to Natalia expressing how "we are all very happy at this emergence of a woman leader" and told Grace that "there definitely is a place for you" at the party "center" in New York.[36] They also agreed to send Grace on a lecture tour in early 1941 to consolidate the support she had built for the party in her campaign.[37] Grace presented the SWP's antiwar message in a coast-to-coast tour that began in Milwaukee on January 2 and ended in the Twin Cities on April 9.[38] Farrell praised it as "an inspiration and a lift to all of the comrades" that was "responsible for some increase in party membership."[39]

Farrell also noted how the tour had made Grace "personally a much more valuable contributor to our ranks." The recognition of her worth to the party was made publicly in February, when a banquet was held in her honor in New York.[40] And moving beyond ceremonial acknowledgment of her importance, she was elected in November 1941 as an alternate to the SWP's National Committee (NC), "the highest governing body of the Party."[41] The next year, in October 1942, Grace was elected as a full member of the NC and served as its only female member.[42] Within two years, because of her strong speaking, writing, and organizing skills, her total commitment to the party, and her network of supportive comrades, Grace had risen from state organizer to NC member.

By the time Grace was elected to the NC, new events had thrust her even more in the spotlight of the national SWP. She, along with twenty-eight of her comrades from Minneapolis and New York, had been indicted under the Smith Act in June 1941 for allegedly advocating the violent overthrow of the federal government. Because of the way it interpreted the Trotskyists' past actions and speech, the federal government built a case in which it alleged that twenty-nine Trotskyists, including Grace and Dorothy, had violated the Smith Act. That law, passed in June 1940, made it illegal to "knowingly or willfully advocate, abet, advise, or teach the duty, necessity, desirability, or propriety of overthrowing or destroying" the government by force or violence or to advocate disloyalty in the armed forces.[43]

On June 27, 1941, federal marshals accompanied FBI agents as they searched through bookcases and file cabinets during their raid of the SWP headquarters in Minneapolis and in St. Paul. The federal officers gathered up mountains of SWP publications that had been on display for sale and distribution at both headquarters, along with two red flags and framed pictures of Lenin and Trotsky. Grace was present at the time of the raid in Minneapolis. The *St. Paul Dispatch* described how, as the agents and marshals awaited a truck to haul away all the literature they had confiscated, Grace engaged them in a political discussion about the "question of overthrowing the government by force."[44] The day after the raids, Grace denounced the events as "unwarranted" and declared that the SWP would carry on its business as usual.[45] She "announced that the third series of lectures on American history sponsored by the party" would continue that Saturday with a focus on the topic of the Bill of Rights, which she described as having "an especially timely significance" given the "recent violation of civil rights by the FBI in its raids."[46]

What the Trotskyists did not know for certain until it came out during the trial months later was that the FBI had been gathering information on the SWP and the Trotskyists who belonged to Teamsters Local 544 for over a year before the raids.[47] Through the use of both informants within Local 544 and agents who questioned members who, for personal and political reasons, opposed the Trotskyist leaders of their union, the Bureau gathered information alleging that various Trotskyists had spoken repeatedly about the need to overthrow the government by force. These allegations were presented by prosecution witnesses to the grand jury that was convened by US Attorney Victor Anderson in Minneapolis during the first two weeks of July.[48] On July 15, that jury returned indictments under the Smith Act against all twenty-nine defendants for allegedly advising insubordination in the armed forces and advocating the violent overthrow of the government.[49] The SWP was outraged at the indictments, denouncing them as a frame-up by Teamster president Daniel J. Tobin, who intended to purge the Trotskyists from Local 544 with the aid of both his political ally President Roosevelt and the Department of Justice. Many labor liberals, who saw a violation of trade union autonomy, and civil libertarians, who disliked the law's criminalization of advocacy, were also deeply concerned about this first use of the Smith Act.[50]

When the trial began in Minneapolis on October 27, 1941, Grace and Dorothy stood alongside twenty-six comrades. Grant Dunne, who had been one of the original twenty-nine indicted in July, had committed suicide on October 4. A World War I veteran, Grant had suffered from shell shock, which, along with the pressure of the impending trial, may have contributed to his taking his own life.[51] Deeply saddened by his death, the remaining defendants headed into the courtroom later that month.⁵² The prosecution laid out its case first, during which it questioned just over three dozen witnesses, including FBI agents who had infiltrated Local 544, and entered into evidence over 250 exhibits, including many of the publications that the US marshals had seized in the June raids.⁵³ When the prosecution rested on November 17, Judge Matthew Joyce issued a directed verdict dismissing the charges against five of the defendants, including Dorothy. Grace was now the lone woman among the twenty-three remaining defendants.⁵⁴

The defense opened its case on November 18 with the difficult task of both defending the SWP's revolutionary Marxist message and arguing that the party did not pose a clear and present danger to the government. Albert Goldman, a defendant who also served as one of the defense attorneys, used the testimony of James Cannon in particular, but also that of Farrell Dobbs, Vincent Dunne, and Grace Carlson, to show the jury that the SWP was a legitimate political party with a revolutionary agenda, but an agenda that it had a right to advocate under the US Constitution and one that did not equate to the advocacy of violent overthrow of the government.⁵⁵ When she took the stand on November 25, described in the local newspapers as the "slim, svelte Grace Carlson, only woman defendant in the trial," Grace did her best to clarify the specifics of the Trotskyist program and defend its legality.⁵⁶ She addressed what she actually said during her 1940 campaign and 1941 speaking tour because those words had been taken out of context and used against her by some of the witnesses for the prosecution.⁵⁷ Grace clarified that any violence she spoke of was not violence to be launched by workers against the government, but was the violence that the SWP predicted would come as the capitalist minority reacted to crush the workers' majority; it was workers' preparation to defend themselves against capitalist violence that she supported.⁵⁸ And when it came to the charges that she and the others had undermined the morale of the armed forces, she insisted that the SWP's position on members who were drafted was that they had "first responsibility . . . to be good soldiers" but that "we feel they are free to talk about the things they believe in, just as other soldiers are free to do that."⁵⁹

Grace's plea for free speech spoke to the heart of the defense's case. Goldman and the other defense attorneys (including Gilbert Carlson) made the argument that the Smith Act was unconstitutional for criminalizing advocacy (i.e., speech) in the absence of overt acts. They asserted that the SWP did not constitute a clear and present danger, thereby invoking a speech-protective implementation of that First Amendment test. The clear and present danger test had been articulated by Justice Oliver Wendell Holmes in the World War I–era *Schenck* case, but was originally used as a justification for speech restriction when the Court upheld the Espionage Act in 1919. In the years since that case, civil libertarians, and Holmes himself (along with Justice Louis Brandeis), had argued for the speech protective power of the clear and present danger assessment.[60] But this position was one that the courts had not yet accepted with respect to federal law, so the Trotskyists' advocacy of it was risky.

For the prosecution, the question was whether this group of Trotskyist antiwar dissenters had advocated the violent overthrow of the government in their speech and publications; the constitutionality of the Smith Act was never in question for the government, which stood by the right of the legislature to determine the need for such protective laws and which argued that it was not the courts' place to second guess that determination. Henry Schweinhaut, the special assistant to the attorney general, argued in his closing remarks that the SWP had been proven to be a real threat. Driving home his point about the clear and present danger posed by the defendants, Schweinhaut told the jury that even though Goldman also tried to portray the SWP as "a futile, a puny, a weak and a kindly little minority," so too were the Bolsheviks just before they took power.[61] Schweinhaut proclaimed that the Constitution was not a suicide pact: free speech protections did not extend to the use of such speech to destroy the very government that guaranteed them.[62]

Despite the best efforts of the defense team, the prosecution's argument won the day. The jury was charged on November 29, and on December 1, it found eighteen of the remaining defendants guilty of violating the Smith Act. Reentering the courtroom on December 8, 1941, the day after the Japanese attack on Pearl Harbor, the "18" (as they had become known in the SWP press) awaited their fate. For those convicted of advocating the violent overthrow of the government, and who remained committed to their antiwar stance, the timing was unfortunate. Dobbs later recalled how he felt for sure that the government would lock them up and throw away the key. As it turned out, he and Grace, along with Vincent Dunne, James Cannon, Felix Morrow, Albert Goldman, Carl Skoglund, and four others, were sentenced to sixteen months in federal prison. The remaining defendants received terms of one year and one day.[63]

The Trotskyists immediately began the appeals process. The judge issued a stay of execution of the sentences while that proceeded. Cannon also sent out a message through local leaders to members of the SWP around the country proclaiming that the work of the party must go on.[64] Grace abided by this call and dove back into her work as state organizer for the SWP in Minnesota. Dorothy, who was pregnant at the time, participated in a mass meeting coordinated by the Civil Rights Defense Committee (CRDC) in New York in mid-December to raise funds for the defendants. The CRDC was an organization created and staffed by the party that garnered support for the 18 from those outside the SWP, particularly from the ACLU and non-CPUSA Left-led unions.[65] Dorothy also served as campaign manager during the spring of 1942 when Grace ran for mayor of St. Paul.[66] Although that bid was unsuccessful, it demonstrated Grace and Dorothy's continued commitment to the SWP. Grace declared that she still believed that "only a socialist government can bring a lasting peace, and freedom and plenty for all."[67]

Ultimately, the courts were not convinced by the defense appeals. The Eighth Circuit Court upheld the convictions and the validity of the Smith Act in a decision it handed down on September 20, 1943.[68] The last hope for the 18 was now the US Supreme Court. But on November 22 it denied the writ, essentially refusing to weigh in on the constitutionality of the Smith Act at this juncture.[69] After the party's lawyers made one last-ditch effort in a petition for a rehearing submitted on December 1, the 18 ran out of options when the Court again refused the case, indicating that during war it would defer national security issues to the legislative authority of Congress.[70] Grace and the other convicted Trotskyists would now have to serve their time in prison.

* * *

Before the 18 began their prison sentences, they gathered in solidarity. The comrades in New York came together on December 26 at a farewell banquet.[71] Grace, who had spent five months in New York working as an organizer, was not present for this event because she had returned home to Minnesota on December 20 to see Dorothy, Henry, and their two children (Ann, now five, and James, twenty months old) before surrendering in Minneapolis.[72] During her time in New York, Grace had deepened her friendships with James Cannon and Rose Karsner. She also made new connections, especially with George Novack and Evelyn Anderson, who led the CRDC's fight for the 18's appeal, and with Miriam Braverman, an organizer in the New York branch who used the pseudonym Carter in her correspondence with Grace.[73] When Grace returned to Minneapolis in late December 1943, the leaders in New York sent her a bouquet of red roses and a telegram. "Although your stay was short in New York," it read, "the New York membership has grown to know you as a Trotskyist woman leader who is an inspiring example to our entire movement. Separation from the other comrades and they from you cannot sever the ties that bind you."[74]

Back in St. Paul with Dorothy and her family, Grace reconnected with her Minnesota comrades. On December 28, the Minneapolis Trotskyists assembled for their farewell event at the party's headquarters. Grace joined Vincent Dunne, Harry DeBoer, and the other Smith Act "class-war victims," as they were termed by the *Militant*, at an evening event of food, drink, songs, and speeches attended by over two hundred supporters.[75] Two days later, on December 30, the eve of their surrender, the comrades gathered again at SWP headquarters, meeting with those who came by "to give their last greetings and expressions of solidarity."[76] In her final moments of freedom, Grace surrounded herself with her comrades, who had become like family to her since she committed herself full-time to the SWP in 1940.

Grace came to appreciate her SWP friends even more when she was involuntarily separated from them. On December 31, 1943, she and the other convicted Trotskyists in Minneapolis gathered at 919 Marquette Avenue before walking together to the federal courthouse to surrender. At 2:30 p.m. they "formed ranks" and marched two by two down the street. Once they reached the courthouse, they were taken into custody.[77] As the only woman among the 18, Grace was held separately in the Hennepin County jail as she awaited her transfer to the federal correctional facility for women in Alderson, West Virginia. Her male comrades were sent to the federal prison in Sandstone, Minnesota.[78]

Of the county jail Grace recalled that it "was a rotten place to be anytime, but particularly on New Year's Day, you know." She remembered how "for a few days there I didn't have any literature, anything to read except for the kind of junky stuff that was around the place." Missing the rich collection of socialist tracts and copies of the *Militant* at SWP headquarters, Grace felt out of place among the popular magazines and tabloid papers left in the jail. Within a few days, however, Dorothy was able to remedy the situation for Grace. She and one of their mutual friends from the Minneapolis SWP, Elaine Roseland, "got together some books for me to read, so then it wasn't bad." They also were able to bring her "clean clothes and even some candy and cookies."[79] Grace's time in the county jail then became much more tolerable. It was also lightened by the occasional visit from Dorothy and Elaine. Maintaining her links to her family—both biological and political—became essential for Grace's survival during this first stage of her incarceration.

As the time drew closer for her departure to prison, Grace worried about her separation from family and friends. "If you look up Alderson on the map you will find that it is in Greenbrier County, in the southernmost part of West Virginia—a long, long ways from anywhere," she wrote to Dorothy and Henry. "According to the rule book, which George [Novack] brought back, only blood relatives are allowed in as visitors," she noted. "If this rule is strictly adhered to it would quite effectively cut my list of visitors." Pondering the reality of the distance and expense of such a trip for Dorothy, especially now that she had two small children, and for her father, in his advanced age, Grace commented, "One might almost say that it would wipe out any possibility of visitors." But she hoped that perhaps "concessions are made and that I might be permitted to see [SWP] people from New York."[80]

Still in the county jail on January 7, Grace wrote to Evelyn Anderson. The US deputy marshal who was to accompany her to prison had informed her that they would "probably start for Alderson by car on this coming Sunday morning." Grace lamented having to make "a three to four day trip in a car with this big, beefy, flatfoot," but assured Evelyn of her safety because the marshal's wife was accompanying them too. Asking her to "give my love to all the comrades [in New York], especially Rose," she admitted that she really missed them, "the meetings and the fun." But she also told Evelyn that she found "great satisfaction" knowing "how much the comrades will do for the prisoners. When the prison bars close round one," she commented in closing, "it becomes terribly clear that 'no force on earth is weaker than the feeble strength of one.'"[81]

Grace felt her isolation on the long drive down to Alderson with US Marshal Littel and his wife. Because they "drove much of the way along the same route which Bea, Elaine, Ray and I took last year" to the convention, she felt even more lonely: "The comparison was a pretty sad one." Although she appreciated that the Littels "tried very hard to be kind and friendly," Grace still felt the divide that her new status as a convicted criminal had created. While the Littels stayed in hotels whenever they stopped for the night, Grace was held in local county jails. The conditions in most of these rural facilities were appalling. Locked in a cell with seven other women and an open toilet in Huntington, West Virginia, Grace kept on her clothes and covered herself with her coat as she tried to sleep on the metal slab bed. Before she left this last stop on her way to Alderson, she did what she could for the "poor devils" who were being held there. "I left them some cosmetics, towel, etc.—not much to do but the best I could."[82]

When she arrived at Alderson, Grace found herself at the first, and, at the time, only federal prison for women in the United States. Established in 1927 and officially opened in 1928, the institution was modeled on a boarding school in both its architectural design and its correctional agenda. Grace described its appearance as that of "a well-kept college campus" with buildings "of red brick, trimmed in white, excessively neat and clean."[83] On the 159-acre campus was a main administration building that housed the medical offices, quarantine cells, and administrative offices. Beyond this main building there was a group of smaller brick cottages arranged in a horseshoe. Unlike the cellblock, the cottage unit was "a small institution in itself, with its own dining room, kitchen, living room, library, [and] inmate organizations.... For each woman, also, there is a small bedroom where she can create her own bit of home."[84] There were about thirty women per cottage, overseen by a female warder. Inmates, when not working on whatever job was assigned to them during the day—be it laboring on the prison farm, working in the kitchen or dining room, cleaning the bathrooms, staffing the library, or performing other tasks—spent their time in the cottage. Literacy classes were also offered at the prison, along with other academic, business, and home economics courses. This "intellectual training" existed alongside the "manual training" of the physical tasks and, together with mandatory Sunday religious observation, was intended to reform the prisoners.[85]

Mary Harris, the first superintendent of Alderson, who implemented this progressive model, thought the day-to-day experience of time there was more conducive to changing prisoners' attitudes and fostering their self-respect than that of traditional cellblock facilities. But as L. Mara Dodge has argued on the basis of her research of a similar cottage-style state prison between 1930 and 1962, "The surveillance of women within their small living units was much more intense and invasive than that experienced by male prisoners housed in larger and far more anonymous cell blocks." The cottage warders, "female correctional officers who lived in the cottages with their charges . . . were required to record all incidents that occurred on their watch, along with unsubstantiated suspicions, rumors and gossip."[86] As Harris explained the procedure at Alderson, "Every day there comes to the superintendent's desk a report of the conduct of every inmate, both in her cottage and on her work detail" so that "conduct difficulties can be detected before they become chronic." With "serious disciplinary cases," such as "high temper, [or] persistent rebellion," the inmate would first be "put in a room to think things over." If the inmate did not express remorse, then solitary confinement in the barred quarantine cells was deployed. The "most severe punishment of all," reserved for "cases of escape" and as a last resort for other problems, was "loss of good time"—i.e., eliminating the possibility of shortening the inmate's sentence because of good behavior.[87] Although there were no bars on the windows of the cottages, the repressive atmosphere of this type of prison bred the anxiety that came with such constant surveillance and reporting. Even after just a few days at Alderson, Grace recognized how "one of the big occupations here is cleaning up and straightening up," which was just one of the "strict rules" she had to follow that were enforced by daily inspections and punishment if violated. Grace admitted that "even so great an exponent of cleanliness and order as I am feels the strain a little bit."[88]

When Grace arrived at Alderson on January 12, 1944, her sentence notice stipulated that she had been allowed ninety-six days of good time, meaning that her "good conduct" term ended on January 24, 1945. If she did anything to violate that, she might have to serve out her full sentence until April 30, 1945.[89] Grace did not detail her experiences of being processed upon her arrival, but Helen Byran, secretary of the Joint Anti-Fascist Refugee Committee, who served time at Alderson in 1950 for contempt of Congress, wrote about the procedure. After being fingerprinted and then photographed with her prison number hanging around her neck, she was directed to shower with delousing shampoo. A physical followed that included an uncomfortable pelvic exam. Finally her personal items were catalogued and taken for storage and she was shown to her cell, where she was locked in for the first three days of her twelve-day quarantine.[90] Grace told Dorothy, "I wouldn't have minded this so much except that I had only popular magazines to read—nothing much to make one forget one's surroundings." But she explained that this strict isolation was about to end, and for the rest of the quarantine period her schedule would be "rise at 6:00, make bed and clean room, breakfast, 6:30, work at assignment (mine is to scrub bathroom floor, clean out sinks, shower, check all of the girls in and out of the shower) lunch at 11:00 a.m. wash and sew clothes in afternoon, supper, 4:00 p.m. social hour or so in evening lights out between 8:00 and 8:30 p.m." The routine kept Grace busy, but did not engage her intellectually at all. "So with that and other lacks," she explained, "I am not excessively happy but neither am I terribly uncomfortable." With an eye to others, as was often her way, she concluded, "People often must put up with more for less reason."[91]

Because "a job opened up in the Medical Office" when "one of the girls received an unexpected parole," Grace was moved out of quarantine and into a cottage two days early, on January 24. Her new routine allowed for a bit more flexibility: she slept and ate her meals and had time to read, bathe, and clean her clothes and room in the cottage each day, but she was able to walk across the grounds to the medical building where she had her work assignment from 7:30 until 11:55 a.m. and again from 12:45 until 4:55 p.m. She explained that "except for every Saturday night when we go to a movie and Sunday, when there is no regular work, this is my daily routine." Although life in the cottage was less confining than in the quarantine lockup, Grace told Dorothy that "you can easily see that my dreams of having a year of study and research have been pretty well shattered."[92]

What helped sustain her through this trying time was her connection to Dorothy and her women friends in the SWP. Her correspondence with them "became a lifeline to the outside world and connecting link to her political life."[93] In this respect Grace's experience of prison time diverged from that of other Alderson inmates whom the sociologist Rose Giallombardo studied during the 1960s; according to Giallombardo, they found it detrimental to "dwell persistently on events in the outside world" communicated through letters and found it easier to serve their sentence if they "suspend[ed] deep emotional involvement in outside events."[94] Grace took the opposite approach to doing her time. Even before she moved to Cottage 11, Grace expressed her gratitude for Dorothy's letter with the news from 919 Marquette Avenue "because by this time, the remembrance of all of the glowing speeches at the Farewell Banquet and the pleasant visits at the Hennepin County Jail is beginning to fade."[95] Through her correspondence, Grace remained connected to the sisterhood that had nourished her personal and political life before Alderson. She was allowed a limited number of correspondents during her time in prison that included Dorothy, Gilbert, Evelyn, Elaine, Rose, Miriam, and her friend from Minneapolis, Bea Janosco.[96] "I keep all of the letters I receive and re-read them at intervals," she explained to Dorothy. "They help to bridge the miles which separate us."[97]

Through her correspondence Grace also asked Dorothy and her friends to help her adjust to life at Alderson by providing her with some simple comforts. Chief among the items she asked for were books. Evelyn helped coordinate the mailing of those through funds raised by the CRDC.[98] Grace also asked for bobby pins, curlers, hair combs, and pins for her dresses. Because the removal of personal effects upon arrival at the prison constituted a "kind of symbolic death of the individual," such items took on added significance.[99] Early on in her sentence, as she was adjusting to the regimentation of prison life, she explained to Dorothy how such things "help me to feel a little more civilized."[100] Of all the gifts sent to her, photographs became her most prized possessions. She displayed pictures of Ann and Jim on the dresser in her room and treasured the images of her comrades that Elaine sent her. "There is no substitute for their personal presence," Grace noted at the time, "but it's much better than nothing at all."[101]

Beyond these tangible comforts, what Grace most needed from Dorothy and her SWP friends were intellectual stimulation and connection to the political and social goings-on that she had left behind. Early on Grace wrote to Miriam lamenting that "one of the worst effects of institution life is to restrict the cultural environment (I'm not trying to be funny). Most of the conversations are terribly subjective."[102] Although she would eventually find some satisfaction in her work at the prison hospital clinic, Grace deeply felt the absence of her comrades. "I am sick for home amid this 'alien corn,'" she complained to Dorothy, echoing Keats's reference to the Book of Ruth in "Ode to a Nightingale"; and she noted to Evelyn her hunger for "congenial companionship and stimulating discussions."[103] Grace did what she could within the confines of the prison to keep mentally active: she read the *New York Times* every day and wrote articles on public health issues for Alderson's newspaper, the *Eagle*.[104] But those things were not the same as the political and social engagement she had enjoyed with her comrades back home.

They did their best to keep her in the loop. From New York Miriam not only described the ways she and the others worked to keep the SWP going while their top leadership was imprisoned or called to war but also revealed how she began to take on increased responsibilities in the process. Through Miriam's letters, Grace heard about the New York branch's success with its *Militant* subscription campaigns, but also its struggles to maintain its robust programs. Miriam explained how with the draft, "Uncle Sam has been picking us off. Within the next few months we'll be practically shorn of men." The members who were still in New York were being stretched thin by competing demands. At one point they faced suspending the Sunday forum because the members were busy getting petition signatures for the 18's pardon campaign.[105] They were also engaged with producing the expanded six-page *Militant*. Feeling the pressures of these various demands in early March, Miriam wrote to Grace, "Please hurry back, because among other things, I need your energy to keep up with everything."[106] Yet Miriam managed to keep it all in hand and, although she admitted that she was at first "dreadfully nervous," she was placed in charge of half of the central branch after its reorganization that spring. By June she was helping to organize the SWP's mass meeting in New York with the ACLU and labor union supporters of the 18, and by July she reported to Grace that the branch was back to hosting its full slate of programs.[107] For her part, Evelyn kept Grace informed of the CRDC's efforts for the Smith Act prisoners, including its fundraisers and assistance to those who planned to visit the 18.[108]

From the Twin Cities, Dorothy, Elaine, and Bea sent Grace the details of the SWP's work there and, like Miriam's correspondence, theirs revealed just how much these women's roles expanded over the course of the year when many of the male party leaders were imprisoned or sent to war.[109] Dorothy had already been playing an important role in the St. Paul branch as an organizer. Like Miriam in New York, she had many balls in the air, working on the *Militant* subscription campaigns, the petition drives for the 18's pardon campaign, and the Sunday forums. It was in their participation in the latter activity, as a public speaker, where she and Elaine and Bea each blossomed while Grace was in prison. The women began preparing to take over more work at the branch even before Grace left for Alderson, in part because Grace pushed them to step up. Bea, who had been speaking at the forums since November 1943, agreed with Grace that Elaine and their friend Winnie Nelson needed to do more than just make the coffee.[110]

Encouraging that participation was hard work for Bea, especially after she had the competing demands of her new baby, born in December 1943, and was missing the mentorship of her more experienced comrade, Grace. Before her forum speech on Irish neutrality in March, she explained how she was "trying desperately to prepare" for it among all her other party and family demands. "I wish you were here to help me. At times like these, I miss you sorely indeed," she confessed. After the event went off without a hitch, Grace wrote back to Bea, providing praise while at the same time encouraging her friend to spread her wings more. "I think that you're doing pheonemenally [sic] well with the NAACP, WDL, Forum and regular organizational work," Grace said. "Dorothy tells me that your speech on Ireland was very, very good. I was glad to hear that you'd written an article on the FLP [Farmer Labor Party]. Tell me what appears and try to get in other articles now and then."[111] Bea, boosted by Grace's support, was preparing for her fifth forum in April. By May she chaired a panel discussion and helped coordinate a roundtable with Dorothy and their friend Winnie, experimenting with a new format for discussing current events at the branch. By June, when they organized their second roundtable, Bea wrote to Grace breathless at how "during the last two weeks, I have literally had more meetings than there were evenings."[112] By the end of the year, she, along with Elaine and two others from the Minneapolis branch, were elected to serve as delegates to the SWP convention in New York. Bea told Grace that at the preconvention discussions, "Elaine did very well. She is really developing a very good vocabulary and choice of words. . . . I know she felt more confident than she ever has."[113] And, describing her own presence at the New York convention, Bea explained how it was "a real milestone for me. I felt more than I ever have before that I was really a part of a movement."[114]

Dorothy, in addition to coordinating the roundtables with Bea and Winnie, became a more prominent figure at the Sunday forums during the year Grace was in prison. She played an important role in encouraging Elaine to speak at the forums too. Dorothy delivered the keynote speech at the SWP's May Day event and continued to work as a party organizer involved in the discussions over whether to run candidates in 1944 and in the planning of the homecoming banquets for the 18 at the end of the year. In addition to her work with the SWP, Dorothy was active in the WDL and in the NAACP. Yet Grace pushed her sister to do more, urging her to write reviews for the *Fourth International* and to turn some of her speeches into articles for the *Militant*.[115] Grace knew that a lot had fallen on Dorothy's shoulders since she and the other party leaders had been imprisoned, but she argued, "It's a good precedent that you are the responsible leader. Bea and Elaine and others have grown this year too."[116]

From Alderson, Grace was thus pleased to hear about the maturation of Dorothy, Bea, Elaine, and the other women and, continuing in her role as a mentor, sent along letters of encouragement. But Grace also sometimes felt frustration at being on the sidelines and unable to help directly.[117] Her isolation from the social world of the SWP proved painful for her too. In the Twin Cities, that world revolved around not only party headquarters but also Dorothy's house, where many informal Trotskyist gatherings took place. Dorothy, Elaine, and Bea wrote Grace detailing the supper parties and late-night socials they attended with the comrades, with music and dancing and drinking, sometimes until midnight.[118] In July, the women attended the popular raspberry festival fundraiser and wrote to Grace in great detail about what had always been one of her favorite events.[119] In November, when her friends in

New York coordinated a homecoming banquet for three male prisoners who had shorter sentences, Grace told Evelyn, "If I get any more of these mouth-watering descriptions of homecoming parties, I'll feel like breaking out of here and moving up my homecoming a couple of months. . . . Be sure that the accommodations provide for unlimited coffee."[120]

Grace truly felt like breaking out of Alderson when she first heard about Henry's illness in a letter Dorothy wrote on June 15. Henry was in the hospital with severe abdominal pain and fever. Because he had had his appendix taken out when he was sixteen, the doctors initially ruled out appendicitis but were uncertain what was causing his symptoms.[121] Grace wrote back immediately. "I know that you have enough fortitude to go through the situation (I've seen plenty of illustrations in the past) and I know that Henry is a good fighter and I know, too, that the comrades there will help all they can," she wrote to Dorothy, "but it does seem that Fate is turning the knife in the wound a little to have a thing like this happen now."[122] By the time the doctors discovered that Henry had not had his entire appendix removed as a teen, the remaining portion had become infected and caused a bowel collapse that required surgery.[123] Grace wrote to Dorothy with her frustration "at not being able to do anything positive toward helping along the situation."[124] But she was able to take some comfort in the phone call that the prison authorities allowed her to have with Dorothy in early July. Reflecting on her sister's incredible strength during this ordeal, Grace wrote to her after the conversation, "I'm doing all right and if you can pull Henry through, take care of the Party affairs, the children and yourself then you'll be doing about 3000% better than your share. I was all broken up last night over your telling me not to worry!"[125]

Much of what comforted Grace during this crisis was hearing that the comrades had stepped up, as she knew they would, to take care of Dorothy and Henry. Dorothy told Grace that "Elaine has been a tower of strength, coming over to help with things around the house, helping with the children, just being around to talk to." Reflecting on the power of their Trotskyist sisterhood, Dorothy proclaimed, "There's nothing like an organization! Bea, Winnie and Evelyn [DeBoer] got nurses when the hospital authorities said flatly, they weren't to be had" because of the wartime crisis.[126] The women not only helped Dorothy at home and in the hospital with Henry; they also brought Henry and Dorothy's struggles to the attention of the national party so that it, too, could help. When Dorothy took a job in an auto factory to help make ends meet because Henry's long recovery kept him out of work for months after the surgery, she was quickly reminded of her place in the SWP. In a letter to Grace, Rose wrote, "Dorothy, I understand, acted like this was her personal trouble, and had taken a job in industry, to make up for the loss of weekly income." She explained that "the center intervened however, sent a representative from Chicago and the necessary funds and ordered her to give up the job. She will have to learn, like the rest of us, that not only her services belong to the party, but also her troubles."[127]

Rose's comments reveal the two-edged sword that was the SWP's supportive network of comrades. On one hand, it was there to sustain its members in good and bad times. On the other, however, it also laid claim to them as members in a way that exerted its own pressures and expectations. Dorothy and Grace truly belonged to the party. Grace felt this side of her support network too when she was at Alderson. Twice she found herself questioned by Rose, who initially thought Grace was not fully committing herself to the party's goals: once, when Rose thought Grace was seeking early parole, which she did not approve of; and then, when Rose misunderstood the work Grace was doing in the prison clinic, which she thought was not as useful for the party as formal studying would be. It was only after Dorothy visited Grace and could explain to Rose in person what her sister was doing—that her work with the mental tests of the prisoners exposed her to a better understanding of the circumstances that landed them in prison—that Rose apologized.[128]

Even when Grace found pleasure in visits from comrades during her time in prison, she also quickly realized that she was, at times, under their scrutiny. Her comrades truly cared for Grace, but they also looked to her as a leader and expected her to be strong. The expectation was most pronounced in the report penned by Evelyn Anderson that was then shared with the CRDC's supporters, who had been raising funds for the defendants and their families. After Evelyn's visit in April, which was Grace's first since her time at Alderson had begun in January, she described their emotional reunion and the "eager talk" they engaged in during the three hours they were allowed to spend together. Evelyn emphasized how well Grace was doing on the whole, keeping up with current events as best she could with the newspapers and applying herself to her work in the prison clinic. But she also stressed how grateful Grace was for the visit, correctly noting her strong sense of isolation from the comrades back home. Evelyn also commented that "physically Grace was well, yes but, her eyes . . . only imprisonment, I thought, can produce such eyes."[129]

Because of these passages, however much they captured the real strain Grace was feeling being imprisoned at Alderson, reaction among her comrades was intense. Dorothy wrote to Grace inquiring about her health, worried that she was keeping something from her. Grace, who had tried to put on a brave face, was somewhat flummoxed and asked Evelyn to tell her what she had written in the report that had so upset everyone.[130] But a positive result came from the report too: the comrades soon realized how isolated Grace was and arranged another visit in June, this time with Henrietta Geller.[131] From then on Grace had a visitor about once a month: George Novack in July; Dorothy in August; Miriam in September; Bert Cochran in October; and Dorothy again, along with Henry, Bea, and Elaine, in November.[132] The party was both controlling and loving in its assistance and expectations. It arranged for visitors to provide moral support, but through them also watched for signs that Grace was serving her time like a good Bolshevik prisoner.

The report filed by Geller, along with several of Grace's own letters, also reveals the relationships that Grace was building with the other women prisoners during her time in Alderson. Here, too, things were complicated. Grace's attitude also evolved over time. As Grace was just getting adjusted to life in prison, her accounts of the other women reveal her shock and disgust with their ignorance and racism. Writing to Dorothy in February, Grace argued, "You have never seen unlovelier specimens of white womanhood, who still feel themselves innately superior, just by virtue of being white. The constant use of words like, 'n——r' and 'c——n' has me physically ill." Such repulsion at having to associate with people so different from oneself was not uncommon among new prison inmates.[133] But the experience was particularly jarring for Grace, who had come from a world in which she and Dorothy were active in the NAACP and not exposed to such racism in their inner circles. "I am not in a position to do much educational work, but I do the best I can," Grace said, indicating her belief early on that she should set an example for these women.[134] That plan proved difficult for Grace to implement at first because she continued to be repelled by what she perceived to be the coarse language and manners of her fellow inmates, despite the fact that the prison superintendent, Helen Hironimus, placed her in her cottage so that she could "be a good influence" on the others. Most of the women were quite young, "some only 16 yrs. of age," and were there because they had violated the May Act, a federal statute that "made it a crime to approach men in the armed services." For "these underprivileged girls, most of whom come from the mill towns and farms of North Carolina and Tennessee," prostitution was something they engaged in out of desperation.[135] "They are pathetic kids, I know," Grace said, "but they are so noisy and boisterous." Partly tongue-in-cheek, she told Evelyn, "I've been interested in sharecroppers' problems for a long time but I like my sharecroppers to be dignified and reserved and speak with low, well-modulated voices—especially when I want to read!"[136]

Over time, despite these socioeconomic and generational differences, Grace and the other women at Alderson began to warm to each other. Grace saw early on how poverty had contributed to the difficult circumstances these women faced. She told Evelyn that "these kids . . . have diseases that I've only read about—and made speeches about—like hookworm and some of the vitamin deficiency diseases."[137] She tried to understand where they were coming from, while at the same time communicating her beliefs about equality and brotherhood. Her education in psychology also served her well; she noted to Evelyn that "the Southern white girls, as a matter of fact most of the Northern whites soothe their own inferiority complexes with the feeling that they are better than the colored girls. It is not always comfortable to be an exponent of democracy under these conditions but I want my NAACP friends to know that they do not have to be ashamed of me."[138] To Miriam she argued that "few of these girls have had the chances to learn self-discipline that we did, and the lack of it is stamped on their faces and reflected in their words and actions."[139] By August Grace had deepened her sympathy for the inmates she had come to know through her daily interactions with them, including a young mother of ten from North Carolina. She was beginning to see her fellow prisoners, Betty, Rita, Agnes, Inez, and the others, as more than just clinical case studies. Grace wrote to Dorothy, "People really do try but the cards are stacked against them! I always knew that in a statistical sense but I'm learning about its meaning in individual lives now."[140]

In time, the women at Alderson came to respect Grace as she adjusted to life in prison and made personal connections with them. Although homosexual relationships became a part of doing time for many inmates, there is no evidence that Grace entered into such bonds with other prisoners; rather, she seems to have found her place within the fictive kinship networks that also functioned in the prison. Given her age, the nature of her crime, and her advanced education, she took on a mothering role.[141] After her visit in June, Geller noted that "all the girls look up to Grace" and that they sought her out to talk to her about their various problems. The women also got to know how much Grace loved coffee and how upset she was when she found out that each inmate only got one cup per day with breakfast. Geller explained how after the girls spoke with Grace, "She says she often finds four of five cups of coffee in front of her after they leave" at the end of the meal.[142] These acts of kindness continued in July, when the women heard about the crisis with Henry and "tried in countless ways to show their sympathy," cleaning her room while she was at work and giving her small handmade trinkets as gifts.[143] Grace did what she could to reciprocate. She gave her commissary allotment of "cookies, candy, fruit, etc." to one young girl whose family never wrote to her or sent her any money and she watched another young inmate's baby so that the woman could attend a dance being held in the prison.[144]

Besides her time with the women in her cottage, Grace got to know the inmates at Alderson through her work in the prison clinic but through a very different kind of interaction. Initially her duties were just routine clerical tasks, but when the chief physician, who "acts as an examining psychiatrist and interviews all the new inmates," discovered Grace's background as a vocational counselor with experience at Glen Lake sanitarium, she was eager to have her assist in developing the mental tests for the prisoners.[145] "I give the tests, correct them, keep the records and hand in the reports on them in addition to my regular job as record clerk in the Venereal Disease Clinic."[146] In this role Grace could have technically been thought of as an "inmate cop . . . prisoners who are in a position of authority over other inmates because of a work assignment." Yet, perhaps because of the kinship networks she forged with those in her cottage, she does not seem to have been thought of as disloyal and maintained the respect of the other prisoners.[147]

Grace's ability to remain connected to the inmates is remarkable given that she was also interacting with them in this clinical setting and was, at the same time, finding more common ground with the medical staff. In April Grace forged a professional friendship with one of the prison doctors, Dorothy Sproul, whom she converted to socialism and remained in touch with for several months after her release. Sproul seemed enamored with Grace, but there is no evidence that Grace ever returned such feelings.[148] In July a psychologist from Washington, DC, arrived at Alderson to observe the mental testing and addressed Grace by her title, as Dr. Carlson, which was a boost to her morale.[149] During her time at Alderson, Grace not only got professional satisfaction from being involved with the technical work of the clinic among the doctors but also saw the political importance of her efforts. She wrote to Natalia explaining, "My work assignment turned out to be even more advantageous to me than a year of luxurious study. The opportunity for this intensive clinical study of human behavior, especially of subjects who are products of the terrible economic and social conditions of the South, is one which would please any Marxist."[150] As she did her time at Alderson, Grace found ways both to live in the moment with her inmate kin and to remain connected to her party comrades and their larger revolutionary commitment through both her correspondence and her clinic work.

Grace's experience at Alderson was thus shaped by the relationships she forged behind bars and by those she maintained across the miles. It was also due to the nature of the prison at the time when she served her sentence. Elizabeth Gurley Flynn, who was imprisoned at Alderson because of her conviction under the Smith Act in 1949, had a different experience from Grace. At sixty-five, Flynn was much older during her incarceration, but Alderson had also become a very different institution from the time Grace had been there. Flynn, a CPUSA leader who was imprisoned at Alderson from January 1955 until May 1957, found it difficult to connect to the younger inmates, who "gossiped, played cards, and turned up the volume on the radio." Because there were "few people with whom she could identify," Flynn spent her evenings alone in her room reading. Like Grace, she came to see her "fellow inmates as victims of bad circumstances rather than bad people" and was able to connect with some of them when she worked in her mending job sewing for the prison.[151] Flynn played a mothering role to a few inmates, similarly to the ways that Grace did. But, unlike Grace, Flynn served almost a year of her time in what had become a maximum-security section at Alderson, confined to a small cell and largely isolated. It was only after she was moved into a cottage that she was able to have contact with her fellow Smith Act prisoner, Claudia Jones. But Jones was released over a year before Flynn, leaving her feeling alone once again. And by the time Flynn arrived at Alderson, most of the intellectual, physical, and spiritual training that had been a part of Mary Harris's reform program was gone and harsher punishments, including more regular resort to solitary confinement, had been introduced, making for a more tense and hostile environment in general. As Flynn noted of Harris's reforms by 1955, "Practically all of her methods and ideas have been discarded."[152] Grace's time at Alderson was by no means an easy one, and the cottage system had its own mechanisms of repression. But before the more draconian methods of incarceration that Flynn experienced were introduced at Alderson, Grace was able to find a role for herself with those who became her inmate kin while also staying linked to her SWP family in Minneapolis and New York through correspondence and visits.

After a year in prison, Grace was more than ready to return home to her family and friends. Dorothy had written to her in December, noting how her "Christmas joy is waiting until January 23," when she would meet Grace in West Virginia for the trip home.[153] Miriam wrote to Grace in early January, also counting down the days. "Well, baby, it won't be long now before we shall see each other. I hope you recognize me. I got a new coat, a mouton lamb, which is very classy, and a hat to match, which is even classier."[154] Grace was looking forward to her trip back home too. "I expect to look every inch a lady—assuming, of course, that the gloves and girdle get here on time," she joked, referring to the last few items she had asked Dorothy to send her. "If they don't, I'll be a lady, all but those inches."[155]

Grace returned home to Minnesota with Dorothy, after her release from Alderson on January 24. Once the two were back in St. Paul, Grace stayed with her sister, their father, James, and Henry and the children in the new house at 630 Fuller Avenue that Dorothy and the others had moved into when Grace was in prison. On January 28, Grace was among the special guests at the homecoming banquet "held in honor of the 18 prisoners in the Minneapolis Labor Case" at the Labor Lyceum. Organized by the Twin Cities WDL, the event brought together the recently released Trotskyist prisoners with their many friends and supporters in the SWP and WDL. Miles Dunne was the master of ceremonies. Grace, along with Vincent Dunne, Carl Skoglund, Max Geldman, and four other newly freed comrades, gave brief remarks of thanks for the continued support of their friends. Winnie Nelson, acting in her official capacity as treasurer of the WDL, presented checks from the CRDC of $150 to each of the ex-prisoners for "aiding them in readjusting themselves after prison life." And they all sat down to a feast of roast turkey with all the trimmings and, most special of all for Grace, plenty of coffee.[156] She was back home at last.

* * *

Ever the committed partisan, Grace did not remain still for long. After reuniting with her family and friends in the Twin Cities, she moved back to New York in February to pick up her work as an organizer. There she was able to reconnect with her East Coast comrades, including Miriam and Evelyn. Even before she was released from Alderson, Grace had begun thinking about what she was learning there and how she could use that unorthodox education to advance the cause of socialism and the SWP. Her time in prison also had contributed to a maturation of her understanding of socialism and a broader commitment to women's rights. She later noted in an interview how "this experience in prison just deepened my conviction that this was an unjust system, the whole capitalist system, and what it did to people." In particular, she began to take direct aim at the evils meted out by that system against women. Beginning in late June 1945, five months after her release from Alderson and when she had completed her parole, Grace launched her "Women in Prison" speaking tour.[157]

From June through September 1945, Grace spoke before twenty-two SWP branches around the country.[158] The *Militant*'s coverage revealed the essence of Grace's message: that women were "doubly oppressed victims of capitalist society" because they were robbed of their right to make a decent living in that society and then, when they were "forced to make a living by so-called illegal means," they were thrown in prison.

Most of the women she got to know at Alderson were young prostitutes (between the ages of fifteen and twenty). Grace argued that "these young girls ... were not criminals, but victims of a criminal social system."[159] Seeing poor young women trapped into lives of crime first-hand during her time at Alderson gave Grace the confidence to speak out against what she saw as the ultimate oppression of women under the capitalist system: their literal imprisonment. The answer, she insisted, was that "working people—common people must unite" to end poverty and crime and racial prejudice and "bring about the brotherhood of man" in socialism.[160] She proclaimed this message during her speaking tour, with the full financial backing and promotion of the SWP.[161] In so doing, she publicly crafted a gendered understanding of class-based oppression and articulated a socialist response to women's repression under capitalism. And she spread that message across the country before audiences that ranged between forty and two hundred members in size, thereby broadening the SWP's focus to include some of American society's most overlooked individuals: women prisoners.[162]

Through her "Women in Prison" tour, Grace was able to combine her commitment to advancing socialism with her specific concerns about women's exploitation in capitalist society, which had been focused in a unique way on women prisoners during her time at Alderson. But Grace had already been thinking about the "woman question" in socialist terms for many years before she began this tour in 1945. In her run for Senate in 1940, even though she did not provide specifics, she called for women's "genuine economic and social equality."[163] And in her daily interactions with her comrades in the SWP, Grace worked to make that equality a reality both for her female comrades by expanding their roles in the party and for women in general through the ultimate realization of socialism.

Grace's efforts can be glimpsed through her correspondence. She and Dorothy mentored their working-class female friends to become leaders in the party, particularly during the year Grace was in prison. Bea (who had been a business manager for a union newspaper), Elaine (who worked as a stenographer for an insurance company), and Winnie (who took a job as an office assistant once her son was old enough for nursery school) had competing demands on their time but believed in the importance of the SWP's mission.[164] The women in Grace's circle shared their joys and troubles, and their letters show how, for these Trotskyist women, their personal sisterhood was political. They supported each other not only as wives and mothers who struggled with the double day of paid public and uncompensated domestic work but also as Marxists who worked to create a socialist society in which the oppressions of capitalism would no longer exist. Their daily lives took place within this tension between the reality of their present and their dream of a socialist future.

To engage in the party work that they believed would bring about that future, Grace's friends had to balance the demands of pregnancies, children, paid jobs, and housework. For Grace's sister, Dorothy, this challenge spanned the course of many years while her children were still young. She was fortunate to have the support of her husband, Henry, who valued her work both at home and for the SWP, but caring for Ann and Jim (and then, after they were born in April 1946, their twins, Raymond and Vincent) was a full-time job that was ultimately left to her. In 1942, for example, both Henry and Dorothy traveled to New York for the SWP convention and brought Ann along. They were able to work late during the convention because they had a party friend in the city who was willing to babysit for them that night.[165] But most of the time, Dorothy bore the brunt of the childcare burden and either missed out on party engagements or struggled to juggle that work with her duties as a mother. When Jim was sick with the flu in December 1943, for example, she could not attend a fundraising party for the 18, and when they could not find anyone to watch the kids in January 1944, she missed out on the Sunday forum. Instead she remained at home trying to read one of Grace's recent articles as the kids were "climbing all over the kitchen."[166] Several times Dorothy had to end her letters to Grace because the children were crying for her or had begun to scribble on the page.[167] But as they had done for her when Henry was ill, Dorothy's SWP friends supported her in striking the balance. They were the ones who cared for Jim when he had a cold so that she and Henry could set up their new house when they moved in 1944. "It is times like this when I really appreciate what a Socialist society will do for the welfare of children," she told Grace.[168] The party network functioned like an extended family, but as Brown and Faue have argued, it was more significant than that: in the context of a world hostile to their radical beliefs, the party network also sustained the revolutionary politics of people like Dorothy and Henry.[169]

Grace and Dorothy's friend Bea Janosco would soon find herself grappling with similar conflicting demands when she had her first baby in December 1943, but, as with Dorothy, her SWP comrades helped her meet them. Even before Grace began serving her time at Alderson, Bea had become an active member of the local party branch.[170] Once she was expecting her first child, she had to make some adjustments to her usual routine. "Besides my regular duties" preparing for the Sunday forum, she explained to Grace, "I have been chasing around looking for the necessary appurtenances for taking care of a baby, of which there is a real shortage. It takes a lot of time and energy."[171] After the new baby came in December, Bea had to miss one of the forums while she convalesced in hospital. By the end of the month, she found a babysitter to assist her return to work.[172] Here again the SWP network came into play: Bea hired fellow party member Kelly Postal's twelve-year-old niece to watch the baby a few days a week.[173] At other times, Bea took baby, Judy, with her. In March 1944, when she and Winnie needed to take care of some WDL work at the U's campus, she planned to "to put the baby in the buggy and just make the rounds that way." In January 1945, in order not to miss the Sunday forums, she put Judy to sleep in a crib that had been set up at the party's headquarters.[174] Through a combination of her own ingenuity and backing from her Trotskyist comrades, Bea, like Dorothy, managed to stay active in the party while raising a family.

Grace, who mentored Bea, Dorothy, and the others as they took on greater roles in the party at the local level, was also inspired by them and their struggles. Beginning in 1945 (after her release from prison), she penned a regular column in the *Militant* in which she engaged directly with issues relevant to working-class women, interpreting them through a Trotskyist lens. In these articles—housed in the main body of the paper, alongside pieces on the war, strikes, and other "hard" news, not on a separate "woman's page"—Grace integrated working-class women's struggles into the narrative of the SWP's fight for the creation of a new socialist world.

In her articles Grace wrote acerbic critiques of capitalism and the culture it created to sustain itself by grabbing headlines from popular women's magazines, radio programs, mainstream newspapers, or official government reports and riffing on their inherent blindness to working-class realities and social inequalities. In an article from March 1945, for example, she mocks the advice given on the radio station WNYC by a public health lecturer who told women to "learn to relax by cultivating a hobby" and to take time to play with their children. With the pressures of working outside the home for some and the demands of caring for a household and raising children for many others, Grace imagined working-class women listening to this program asking "where, when, how?" Slamming the lecturer's advice for women to "sit down on the floor and play with your child," Grace imagines a working woman's response: "'A charming idea,' she thinks and perhaps after two-year old John Pierpont Van Renssalaer III has had his lunch and been cleaned up by his nurse she will go into the nursery and play with him."[175]

In other articles, Grace went beyond her criticism of American society's failure to engage with such class inequities as they affected women (as mothers and housewives)[176] to engage more directly with how that same society (and the capitalist system that undergirded it) constructed particular definitions of femininity and womanhood—definitions that Grace believed ultimately subjected women to the domination of that capitalist order and numbed their ability to revolt against it.[177] In an article from 1945, for example, Grace responded to a letter from a reader angered about a piece in *Life* magazine that celebrated an "American look" for women as consisting of "well-groomed, expensively dressed girls." The *Militant* reader, who was a self-described "hard-working mother and housewife," argued that "I don't look like those girls and the waitresses I worked with didn't either." Grace agreed with the reader and quoted Antoinette Konikow, the Russian-born Socialist, physician, and leading advocate of birth control since the 1920s, as insisting that "good health is the basis for good looks." Konikow was a founding member of the Communist Left Opposition in Boston whose opinions were respected by those in the party. Grace endorsed her position and reaffirmed that "the main reason why millions of American working women and working-class housewives do not have this so-called typical American look is that they cannot afford good health." She explained how the prescription of a good diet and adequate rest "is impossible for women who carry the double burden of industrial work and housework." Grace argued that the real American look for women should not be a full face of makeup but rather a look of "determination . . . determination to do something about the injustices of this system."[178] As in all of her criticisms of society's shortcomings, Grace linked the inequities (and oppression) she found inherent in America's consumer culture to their roots in capitalist exploitation.[179] But in this piece she linked that critique to a broader indictment of the ideal type of female beauty espoused by the culture, condemning it on both social and economic grounds as oppressive and as an unobtainable distraction to the mission of emancipation for workers *and* women.

Grace's focus on women's issues came from her understanding that women's equality would come through women's own education and empowerment so that they could join forces with other workers to advance the cause of socialism. Hers was not a middle-class, individualist understanding of women's equality that sought protection in the Equal Rights Amendment. Instead, it was closer to the labor feminism of union women in the postwar period who sought to address the economic needs of women in the workplace through unions in the fight for work access and fair wages, as well as through their continued support for protective legislation gained by the social feminists of the Progressive era.[180] Grace's working-class feminism was, however, also Marxist in its ultimate goal of overthrowing capitalism as the root cause of all oppression.

Grace wrote within the context of the SWP's understanding of the woman question as it was being articulated during and after the war. There was attention given to women in the party's press before 1940 but, hewing to a traditional Marxist understanding that women needed to be organized and mobilized as workers, those articles mostly focused on females in the paid workforce and on their union organizing struggles.[181] They echoed the influence on the authors' thinking of Marxist classics, like Friedrich Engels's *Origins of the Family, Private Property, and the State*. After 1940, and especially once the United States entered the war, the *Militant* featured articles by Antoinette Konikow, Mary Dante, Lydia Beidel, Marie Taylor, Larissa Reed, Rose Karsner, and Mille Fredreci that focused not only on women workers and their concerns on the factory floor but also on housewives and on women's other needs as members of working families.

Konikow, for example, continued to write about the importance of birth control in helping working-class women space their families and obtain some modicum of economic security "during the period of bondage under capitalism" until liberation came with socialism.[182] Reed railed against the ERA, quoting the labor movement's characterization of it as a "sweat shoppers dream" that would dismantle Progressive legal protections for working women.[183] Konikow, Taylor, and others wrote about the "double exploitation" of women working outside the home along with their continued domestic demands, which were made more difficult under wartime rationing. During the war years, other contributors to the *Militant* demanded more government-funded day nurseries to assist these exploited and exhausted women; at war's end they lamented the closings of those facilities that had been established but then were dismantled with postwar readjustment. Trotskyist women writers also offered a socialist vision of the future where there would be "community laundries [that] would free them from the never-ending round of washing and ironing," as well as "community nurseries, kindergartens, youth organizations" that "will not only keep children healthy and happy, but free the mother for a large part of the day" so she could work to help support the family.[184] And in a series titled "'My Day'— Experiences of a Working Mother," Fredreci presented an alternative to Eleanor Roosevelt's popular column with a specific focus on the daily woes and travails of women from the working class, describing things like her battles with her landlord to get the roof fixed and her "struggle to stretch a dollar" to feed her family.[185]

With the increase in the number of women working outside the home for pay during the war, the Trotskyist women writers in the *Militant* also celebrated what they saw as a moment ripe with political possibility: as one article proclaimed, "Transfer from Kitchen Sinks to Factories Will Develop Militant Armies of Class-Conscious Proletarian Women." Even in the pieces lamenting the struggles of working women and calling for support through day nurseries during and after the war, the ultimate goal for these Trotskyist women authors was the realization of socialism; they urged working women to begin that process by organizing in unions and called on all women, including housewives, to take an interest in politics so they could advance their class interests.[186] In so doing, these writers expanded the SWP's engagement with the woman question in ways that still aligned with issues of concern for labor feminists during the 1940s (including access to work, equal pay, and daycare) but that also included an understanding of the value of women's work in the home and the role of the housewife in the class struggle. In this latter vein, their arguments may have been informed by Mary Inman's insights in her 1940 work, *In Woman's Defense*.[187]

The echoes of Inman's work in the writings of the female Trotskyists in the *Militant* during the 1940s suggest that *In Woman's Defense* may have had a broader reach than that which Kate Weigand has traced solely within the CPUSA. Inman argued for organizing women in the home and for the recognition of the housewife as a worker. Weigand has demonstrated how, despite the Communist Party's criticism of Inman's work because of its focus on the domestic sphere and not the factory floor, many Communist women were influenced by her arguments, and even the CPUSA began to adjust its position on the woman question because of it. Weigand argues that other Communist writers drew from Inman's theories an appreciation for the connection between the personal and the political and of the cultural and social forms of oppression that women endured, including that of male chauvinism.

During the 1940s, Weigand explains, the approach to the woman question within the CPUSA began to move beyond "the classical Marxist analysis of women's oppression" that drew guidance from "Marx's *Capital* and *The Communist Manifesto*, Engel's *Origins of the Family, Private Property, and the State*, Bebel's *Women and Socialism*, and Lenin's *Women and Society*," in which that oppression was considered purely economic and male supremacy was dismissed "as a divisive concept imported to the working-class by bourgeois feminists and a serious symptom of false consciousness." By the mid- to late 1940s, after Communist women "who had been promised equality in progressive settings for many years, finally insisted on it," the party gradually "began to explore the notion that women's oppression included cultural and ideological components as well as economic ones." Weigand notes how, with the publication of Betty Millard's article, "Woman against Myth," in 1948, the CPUSA's approach to women's equality also began to shift. Millard drew from Engels to argue that "women's inferiority was not biological, but rather a historical phenomenon that originated with the evolution of private property," but she also insisted that it was not just class exploitation that "subordinated women" but also "religious doctrine, Freudian psychology, laws, customs, and language as well as 'day-to-day attacks'" in the media. The CPUSA's battle began at home, with the revamping of the party's woman's page in the *Daily Worker*: "cheesecake" content that had highlighted "scantily clad models" and "beauty contest winners" was dropped and Claudia Jones and Peggy Dennis "filled the pages with articles about women's history, their role in the peace movement, and their contributions to political struggles around the world."[188]

In comparison, the SWP had been ahead of the CPUSA on this curve, with serious content that had addressed women's issues being placed in the main body of the *Militant* for decades, even as that content remained committed to a traditional Marxist approach to the woman question in these years. As Grace's correspondence with her female comrades reveals, they had been living with the reality of and talking to each other about the connections between their personal struggles and their political work to bring about socialism for many years too. Grace, informed by these experiences and her time at Alderson, was one of several women on the Left (within as well as outside of the SWP) who wrote about the links between women's oppression and class struggle during the postwar years. Those women included not only the Trotskyist women writers for the *Militant*, like Konikow, Dante, Beidel, Taylor, Reed, Karsner, and Frederici, and those within the CPUSA, like Inman and Millard, but also those within the broader Popular Front Left, like Elizabeth Hawes, who in her writings during the 1940s outlined similar visions of access to birth control, community housing and laundries, and childcare for women.[189]

Although Grace and her friends did not use the term "feminist" to describe themselves, their letters voice the stirrings of women struggling for liberation. Their politics was very personal, but the personal was not quite yet fully political, in part because they shared their generation's understanding of a more traditional gender ideology but also, especially, because they were committed to revolutionary Marxism. They did not articulate a critique of patriarchy, which would become so central to second wave feminism. Instead, their struggles and Grace's articulation of a working-class Marxist feminism in her writings for the *Militant* and in her "Women in Prison" tour show a gradual evolution in thinking about the class-based experience of gender, which was coming to include a recognition of housework and mothering as productive work as well as some acknowledgment of certain cultural forms of oppression.

These ideas constituted the beginnings of what would become a more fully fleshed out feminism within certain quarters of the party by the 1960s, in particular that articulated by Myra Tanner Weiss and Clara Fraser in response to what they believed was the party's inadequate position on the woman question. Weiss and Fraser eventually came to the conclusion that the SWP needed to address questions of patriarchy in addition to the economic reasons for women's exploitation.[190] Their thinking was influenced, in part, by a controversy that erupted in the party press in 1954 known as the Bustelo incident, an internal debate that began with a focus on the role of cosmetics and fashion and became intertwined with larger questions about women and Marxism.

The Bustelo incident began with the publication of an article written by Joseph Hansen under the byline of Jack Bustelo, titled, "Sagging Cosmetic Lines Try a Face Lift," in the July 26, 1954, issue of the *Militant*. In that piece "Bustelo" slammed the nation's big cosmetics companies for "dumping more than $33,000,000 into ad programs for their products this next calendar year" to boost sagging sales in the context of rising unemployment in what he condemned as a campaign of mass fraud against women.[191] But Hansen's approach backfired with many women in the party. Louise Manning, a comrade from Los Angeles, began the debate when she wrote a letter of complaint to the editor explaining that she agreed with Bustelo's condemnation of the manipulations of the cosmetic corporations, but was upset because "one gets the feeling that it is the women who are being made fun of." Manning made the case that "in order to effectively attack these companies, we have to first understand why women are so vulnerable to their advertising schemes." She asserted that the desire for beauty was not a mere aping of bourgeois standards on the part of working women who "want to rise above the sweaty grind of the shop." According to Manning, "This striving has a progressive aspect because it is part of the rebellion of women against a position which denies them part of their rights as human beings."[192] Other *Militant* readers agreed and penned letters voicing their disappointment with Bustelo's analysis.[193] Marjorie McGowan joined in the condemnation of Bustelo, arguing, "If the women did not hunger for personal beauty in their bodies, in their clothes, in the environment, there wouldn't be any struggle, nor any revolution, nor any socialism."[194]

Such comments drew intense criticism from Evelyn Reed, who saw in them a misunderstanding of the class struggle and revolution. Reed believed that the comrades who were criticizing Hansen did so from a "contradictory position" in which they held the "notion that questions concerning women in the realm of sex, beauty, and so on transcend class lines." Taking a "traditionalist approach" to feminism rooted "in terms of classical Marxian premises and analyses," Reed insisted that "the *class distinctions* between women transcend their *sex identity* as women."[195] In direct refutation of the arguments advanced by Bustelo's critics, she insisted that "the class struggle is a movement of *opposition*, not *adaptation*, and this holds true not only of the workers in the plants, but of the women as well, both workers and housewives. It is because the issues are more obscured in the realm of the women as a sex," Reed insisted, "that some of our own comrades have fallen into the trap of adaptation" and justified the use of cosmetics as part of the revolutionary struggle.[196]

By the time the Bustelo incident erupted in 1954, Grace had left the party two years before. She was not there to weigh in on the debate, but as her writings from the 1940s reveal, she had one foot firmly in Reed's traditional Marxist camp, but also showed some signs of alignment with Bustelo's critics with her hints at what Reed termed "adaptation." Grace acknowledged the desire of women to look good "as members of the human race," a category that was distinct from and broader than that of class. Whatever the limitations of the traditional Marxist approach to women's liberation, those Trotskyists in the SWP who held that view engaged seriously with the woman question during the 1940s and 1950s, as Grace's experience in the party and the Bustelo incident shows. What is also clear from the 1954 controversy are the voices of the women comrades articulating how their desires for freedom as workers and as women would ultimately be met by socialism, even if they disagreed over how to engage in their sex-based struggles in the short term. Grace, who had left the SWP before this controversy erupted, would complicate her own understanding of feminism during the next phase of her life. But before she made that transition out of the SWP, Grace rose to national prominence as its candidate for vice president of the United States in 1948, supported by her network of both female and male party friends.

Figure 1: Father Laurence Cosgrove and workers ca. 1897 during the construction of St. Vincent de Paul's new church building in St. Paul's north Frogtown neighborhood, where Grace would later grow up. The parish, and its school, staffed by the Sisters of St. Joseph, influenced Grace's early commitment to social justice. Brick Laying Crew and Priest at Construction of the Church of St. Vincent De Paul, St. Paul, Photo HD6.73p257, Minnesota Historical Society. Courtesy of Minnesota Historical Society, St. Paul, Minnesota.

Figure 2: Grace Holmes, 1924, at Saint Joseph's Academy, St. Paul. Under the tutelage of the Josephites at the academy, Grace deepened her faith-based commitment to serving God by serving others. Photo of Grace Holmes, *The Academy: A Literary Magazine* (Saint Joseph's Academy, 1924), 29. Courtesy of Minnesota Historical Society, St. Paul, Minnesota.

Figure 3: Grace Holmes and her fellow graduates from the College of St. Catherine in 1929. Grace stands just to the right of center holding a bouquet of roses. At CSC, under the instruction of the Josephites, who designed a rigorous curriculum for their students and modeled professional lives outside of marriage, Grace came to appreciate more deeply the importance of education as the route to women's economic autonomy. Graduates of the Class of 1929, Photo 828, f. 7, box 166, University Archives Photograph Collections, Archives and Special Collections, St. Catherine University. Courtesy of Archives and Special Collections, St. Catherine University, St. Paul, Minnesota.

Figure 4: Police open fire on Teamster pickets who stopped a truck driven by strikebreakers on July 20 during the 1934 truck drivers' strike in Minneapolis. This event, known as Bloody Friday, further divided the city between those who supported the workers and those who backed the employers. Grace became a Marxist, in part, because of the polarizing events of the 1934 strikes. Police open fire on strikers who rammed truck guarded by police, Minneapolis. Photo HG3.18Tp39, Minnesota Historical Society. Courtesy of Minnesota Historical Society, St. Paul, Minnesota.

Figure 5: An SWP campaign office in St. Paul with posters in the window promoting Grace's and her sister Dorothy's respective Senate and congressional campaigns in 1940. Socialist Workers Party Campaign Headquarters, 540 Cedar, St. Paul. Photo J1.r15, Minnesota Historical Society. Courtesy of Minnesota Historical Society, St. Paul, Minnesota.

Figure 6: Rose Seiler, Dorothy Schultz, and Grace Carlson in Minneapolis at the time of the 1941 Smith Act trial. The three women were among the twenty-nine Trotskyists indicted under the Smith Act for advocating the violent overthrow of the government. The judge at trial issued a directed verdict dismissing the case against Seiler and Schultz. Carlson was convicted by the jury and sentenced to sixteen months in prison. Photo, Acme 10-29-41, courtesy of David Riehle.

Figure 7: Grace served her sentence in 1944 in a cottage like this one at Alderson prison. During her time there she got to know the other inmates and later denounced their imprisonment as the result of capitalist exploitation of working-class women. South Fronts and East Sides (North Side of Lower Quadrangle), Federal Reformatory for Women, Cottages, State Route 3, South of Greenbrier River, Alderson, Greenbrier County, WV. LC-HABS WVA, 45-ALD.V,1-C—1, Historic American Buildings Survey, Prints and Photographs Division, Library of Congress, Washington, DC.

Figure 8: Grace at a picnic with other SWP women. Although during the 1940s and early 1950s, Grace and her party sisters did much work that was traditionally associated with women (like preparing food for the SWP's many social events), they also played significant roles as party organizers, speakers, writers, and political candidates at the local level. Grace Carlson with women at a picnic, f. Photographs and Snapshots, 1930s–1970s, box 2, Grace Carlson Papers, Minnesota Historical Society. Courtesy of Minnesota Historical Society, St. Paul, Minnesota.

Figure 9: Vincent Dunne, Grace Carlson, Dorothy Schultz, and Henry Schultz at an SWP meeting ca. 1940s. Grace maintained a close personal and professional relationship with Vincent Dunne for over a decade during her time in the SWP. Their romance was not made public given that they were both still married to other people at the time, but it was a part of the all-in commitment of Grace to the SWP between 1940 and 1952. So too was her familial relationship with Dorothy and Henry: in these years the party was their whole world. Photo J1.6p2, A Socialist Workers Party Meeting, Minnesota Historical Society. Courtesy of Minnesota Historical Society, St. Paul, Minnesota.

Figure 10: Grace Carlson campaigning for vice president in 1948. During her campaign, Grace traveled around the country arguing that the "only road to peace" was through the establishment of a socialist society. Because of both her radical political message and her gender, the press coverage of her campaign was dismissive. Photo of Grace at podium, f. 1948 Presidential Campaign—Aug, 1948, box 1, Grace Carlson Papers, Minnesota Historical Society. Courtesy of Minnesota Historical Society, St. Paul, Minnesota.

Figure 11: After Grace left the SWP in 1952, she found herself blacklisted, but Sister Rita Clare Brennan, administrator of St. Mary's Hospital in Minneapolis, offered her a job as an administrative assistant. Grace with S. Rita Clare Brennan, f. Photographs and Snapshots, 1930s–1970s, box 2, Grace Carlson Papers, Minnesota Historical Society. Courtesy of Minnesota Historical Society, St. Paul, Minnesota.

Figure 12: Gilbert and Grace Carlson with their grandniece and grandnephews, July 1967. Having been separated for over twelve years while Grace was active in the SWP and romantically involved with Vincent Dunne, Grace and her husband Gilbert reunited after she left the party in 1952 and remained together until his death in 1984. Grace with Gilbert Carlson and children, f. Photographs and Snapshots, 1930s–1970s, box 2, Grace Carlson Papers, Minnesota Historical Society. Courtesy of Minnesota Historical Society, St. Paul, Minnesota.

Figure 13: Grace Carlson with Sister Anne Joachim Moore during a student reunion at St. Mary's Junior College in 1981. Grace worked with Sister Anne Joachim on the St. Mary's Plan, the founding document for what became St. Mary's Junior College in 1964, and the two remained close colleagues for almost two decades. Grace Carlson with Sister Anne Joachim Moore, 1981, St. Mary's School of Nursing, Series 8, Photographs, Box 11, Archives and Special Collections, St. Catherine University. Courtesy of Archives and Special Collections, St. Catherine University, St. Paul, Minnesota.

Figure 14: Grace Carlson in her office in the Old Main building of St. Mary's Junior College, 1983. After she retired from teaching in 1979, Grace remained a fixture on the SMJC campus through her work as an alumnae officer and her column, "Carlson's Continuing Commentary," that she wrote for the campus newspaper, *Good News*. Grace Carlson, 1983, St. Mary's School of Nursing, Series 8, Photographs, Box 11, Archives and Special Collections, St. Catherine University. Courtesy of Archives and Special Collections, St. Catherine University, St. Paul, Minnesota.

4

Politics and Love on the Left

During the late 1940s, Grace's life in the SWP continued to be enriched by the sisterhood that had sustained her during her year in Alderson prison. But her time in the party was also made meaningful by relationships with her male comrades. The wider social network of the SWP branches supported Grace and her fellow Trotskyists in their work as Socialists who sought to remake the world. Personal ties had long been important to their movement, seeing them through the dangerous 1934 strikes and the difficult 1941 trial. They remained essential to the nature of party life as members experienced the strains of the Cold War and Second Red Scare. Both the platonic comradeship that created an environment akin to an extended family and the romantic relationships that flourished among couples within the SWP (be they more traditional monogamous ones or "open, non-possessive, and occasionally, group marital relationships") contributed to the social and political world of Trotskyism.[1] Committed party members, like Grace, dedicated their lives to the movement. In an experience that was also true for many members in the CPUSA, their passion for the public cause of building a socialist world often became intertwined with the private relationships they engaged in with comrades pursuing common work.[2]

Grace's professional relationship and friendship with James P. Cannon and Farrell Dobbs remained important to her when she accepted the party's call to run for political office again during the mid- to late 1940s. In 1946 she was the party's candidate from Minnesota for the US Senate and in 1950 for the US Congress. In 1948 she accepted the party's nomination to stand for the vice presidency of the United States on a ticket with Farrell Dobbs, who was running for the presidency. In these campaigns Grace faced challenges as a revolutionary Socialist Workers Party candidate running during the Cold War and, as a woman, she experienced first-hand the sexism of the late 1940s political environment.

During the same years that Grace participated in these public political campaigns, she also engaged in a very private romantic relationship with Vincent Raymond Dunne. The origins of Grace's relationship with Ray Dunne are unclear, partly because she never spoke of it publicly nor left any overt evidence of it. But traces of the romance do remain and, considered in the context of other loving couples in the party, it speaks to the importance of shared political work among Trotskyists who built a community in which social and political commitments merged to sustain their movement in an otherwise hostile world.

* * *

In September 1945, Grace wrapped up her three-month "Women in Prison" speaking tour. Within two months of her return home, she was on the move again, this time to Detroit to assist the SWP local's leadership in quelling an internal factional threat and to institute an educational program. Vincent Dunne was also dispatched to Detroit to expand the SWP's labor fraction in the auto industry.[3] The timing was not coincidental: Trotskyists felt "exhilaration over the new possibilities that seemed to reflect a dissatisfaction with 'politics as usual'" after the war "and an openness, on the part of many, to new ideas."[4] The massive 1945–1946 strike wave was just beginning, led by 225,000 General Motors autoworkers who walked out in November 1945. "Frustrated by nearly four years of speedup, stretchout, cramped living conditions, and price inflation, millions of workers struck across the nation in 1945 and 1946." In the end, "4.6 million people engaged in nearly 5,000 work stoppages, costing employers a staggering 116 million work days." The United Auto Workers' strike against GM, in which workers demanded a 30 percent wage increase, lasted 113 days.[5] Once in Detroit, Grace worked with her comrades at the local SWP branch and published a dispatch from the strike in the *Militant*.[6]

Although she, too, was enthusiastic about the strike, heralding it as the kind of militancy that "will move capitalist mountains," Grace was aware of the risks attached to her new assignment.[7] One month before she arrived, fellow Trotskyist and UAW member Genora Dollinger and her husband, Sol, were brutally beaten by two men who had broken into their house. Dollinger, who had a public profile in the city as a union organizer, had also recently volunteered for the UAW's committee "to look into increased violence against labor union members." The local police "blamed the beating on union leaders," claiming that they wanted to put Genora in her place for "getting too 'high' in union circles," but Vincent Dunne, who visited her in the hospital, argued that "the culprits were thugs hired by the corporation."[8] Grace's assignment in Detroit was thus a potentially dangerous one.

Her comrades in Detroit valued her presence, and the SWP's Political Committee in New York agreed to keep Grace there until the end of June.[9] But the Minneapolis branch was eager to have her run for political office again. An electoral campaign was launched with a nominating convention on June 30. Grace went back to Minneapolis to run for Senate, and Dorothy, along with comrade Warren Creel, stood for US Congress.[10] C. K. Johnson, the campaign manager for all three candidates, issued press releases in which he interpreted the four thousand signatures they had gathered securing their place on the ballot as evidence of workers' desire for a true labor party, which, he argued, only the SWP provided since the merger of Minnesota's Farmer-Labor Party into the Democratic Party in 1944.[11]

Other press releases, picked up and run by the local newspapers, highlighted the candidates' biographies. Warren Creel was presented as the son of staunch Socialists and as a devoted union man. Dorothy, who had just given birth in April to twin boys, Raymond and Vincent, was put forth as a mother of four who "knows what it means to struggle to feed and clothe a family in this period of skyrocketing prices." Her leadership roles in the NAACP and Workers Defense League (WDL) were also touted as proof of her qualifications. Grace's professional credentials were highlighted alongside her background as a child of a railroad worker, as were her previous campaigns, her identity as one of the 18, and her work with the NAACP and WDL.[12]

Grace and Dorothy took to the hustings and to the radio to campaign, but ultimately to no avail. Dorothy pushed for antilynching legislation and condemned the Jim Crow practices of local institutions, like the Hotel St. Paul. Grace addressed the "menace of white supremacy" too, but also condemned Wall Street for entangling America's capitalist government overseas in ways that she believed were leading to conflict with the Soviet Union and possibly to World War III.[13] During their campaigns in 1946, Grace and Dorothy spoke to the hot button issues of the day: the rising cost of living that was resulting from postwar readjustment; the growing civil rights movement; and anxieties about the strength and duration of the postwar peace. But they proposed radical solutions—such as full employment for all workers, full equality for all minorities, and withdrawal of all American troops from foreign soil—that did not resonate with most voters.[14] Even though the SWP had secured "a 31 per cent higher vote" in 1946 than it had in 1940, with Grace's 11,421 votes topping the 8,761 votes from her previous Senate run, her percent of the total state vote was still minuscule (1.3 percent), and none of the SWP's other candidates came close to winning either.[15]

Despite this defeat in 1946, Grace was nominated in 1948 by the SWP's National Committee to stand as its candidate for vice president of the United States in its first national election campaign. That campaign took place in the context of the Cold War and what was becoming, by 1948, the Second Red Scare. In March 1947, President Truman defined containment of communism abroad as America's chief foreign policy goal. As the Soviet Union became defined as America's main geopolitical rival, anxiety rose over the possibility of Communist infiltration and subversion within the United States.[16] In March 1947 Truman also issued Executive Order 9835, which established the Federal Employee Loyalty Program, which gave the government the authority to screen its employees for any signs of political radicalism and to fire those it deemed disloyal. The attorney general then compiled a list of "totalitarian, fascist, communist, or subversive" organizations. Individuals with ties to groups on the list could be deemed disloyal, be subjected to firing or blacklisting by employers, or find themselves charged with contempt of Congress if they failed to cooperate if called before the House Un-American Activities Committee.[17] In June 1947 Congress passed (over Truman's veto) the Taft-Hartley Act, which restricted various union actions deemed "unfair labor practices" (like secondary boycotts) and, under the law's section 9h, threatened access to National Labor Relations Board elections for unions whose leaders refused to sign affidavits swearing they were not Communists.[18]

In the wake of these efforts to curtail political dissent (and trade union power), the SWP planned its first national election campaign to counter what it saw as a movement towards fascism in the United States. That campaign also emerged out of the party's understanding of its role in the changed circumstances of the immediate postwar period. But before the majority of members in the SWP, led by Cannon, could get behind this new vision, they had to deal with a challenge from a minority faction led by Albert Goldman and Felix Morrow. Goldman, who would defect from the SWP to Shachtman's Workers Party (WP) by 1946, argued that Cannon was turning the SWP "away from a Leninist-Trotskyist conception of a revolutionary party and toward a Zinovievist conception," meaning a monolithic party akin to that which Stalin had developed. As evidence of this assertion, Goldman pointed to the fact that his small minority faction had been censured for "organizing a discussion on the Russian question with some members of the WP" and for inviting members of the WP to attend socials and classes his group had planned. Goldman did not see the problem with such activities, but Cannon did. He asserted the Leninist nature of the party by noting that members did have "rights of free discussion" but that they also had duties, including "that all their political activity has to be carried out under the supervision and control of the party." According to Cannon and the party majority, the Goldman-Morrow faction had violated those duties. Goldman, frustrated by his inability to defend the minority position, left the party; Morrow was subsequently expelled.[19]

Before that break happened, the Goldman-Morrow minority had also believed that the obstacles facing Trotskyists in winning "the masses to the banner of the Fourth International" in Europe "required a more pessimistic analysis," a vision that did not mesh with the understanding of the party in the postwar era then being developed within the ranks of the majority. James Cannon and his supporters in the SWP, including Grace, kept faith with the revolutionary potential of the American working class. In the "Theses on the American Revolution," issued in the fall of 1946, they "argued that 'the workers' struggle for power in the U.S. is not a perspective of a distant and hazy future but the realistic program of our epoch.'" In a pamphlet published in April 1947, Cannon concluded that "our part is to build up this party which believes in the unlimited power and resources of the American workers; and believes no less in its capacity to organize and lead them to storm and victory."[20] It was this energy that informed the move towards the national campaign. In May 1947 Dobbs argued that it was time to grow the party from a "propaganda circle to a party of action," and by June there was discussion of its "preparing to run its own presidential candidate."[21] The national campaign began officially in February 1948 when the SWP's National Committee nominated Farrell Dobbs for president and Grace Carlson for vice president, their nominations to be ratified at the convention in July.[22]

In Minneapolis Grace packed her bags and left by train on June 23 for New York. Stopping off in Pittsburgh and New Jersey, she arrived in Manhattan on June 26. For the next four days she worked on her acceptance speech and caught up over meals with Elaine, Evelyn, and other party friends. The diary that she kept in 1948 logged these events in the briefest of terms, serving more like a calendar than a journal.[23] Grace does not record what she was feeling at the time, but no doubt the atmosphere among the Trotskyists was one of excitement at the launching of their first national campaign when their convention convened on July 1.

On the third day of the proceedings, Saturday, July 3, Grace delivered her acceptance speech before the assembled delegates and to radio listeners.[24] After expressing her gratitude and honor at being chosen as the party's first ever vice-presidential nominee, she launched into an hour-long speech on "The Struggle for Civil Rights." After asserting that the SWP stood for "full social, political and economic equality for the Negro people and all other minority groups," she criticized what she believed were the hypocrisies of the Truman administration's stand on civil rights, noting the continued segregation of the armed forces and existence of Jim Crow laws in Washington, DC.[25] Truman's call in his State of the Union Address in January 1948 for Congress to adopt some of the "legislative proposals included in the report of the [special] Committee on Civil Rights" that he had convened the year before had actually cost him the support of some in the Democratic Party. After his nomination in mid-July, southern segregationist Democrats bolted, formed the States' Rights Democrats (Dixiecrats), and nominated Strom Thurmond as their candidate for president.[26] Before this break from the Right took place, Grace voiced from the Left the SWP's criticism of Truman for not doing enough to advance civil rights. Touting her ten years' experience working with the NAACP in Minnesota, Grace presented her socialist take on the issue, arguing that racial divides were fomented by capitalists who wanted to keep workers distracted from their common class enemies.[27]

Grace also engaged in a line of argument in her acceptance speech that was new to her campaigning: claiming the legitimacy of America's revolutionary past for her party's positions. Casting the SWP as the heirs to "great American traditions of resistance to tyranny" as exemplified by the likes of Patrick Henry, William Lloyd Garrison, and John Brown, she insisted that the Trotskyists "speak for the persecuted minorities. If they can be deprived of their liberties who can feel his own rights safe?" And, broadening out her definition of civil liberties to include the rights of political dissenters and workers too, she argued that voters must resist the path to fascism that was being laid with the Taft-Hartley Act's restrictions. Referencing not only America's past but also more recent global events, she asserted that "the rich were able to place Hitler in power because of the failure of the labor leadership and the Stalinist party in Germany." Touting the SWP as the only solution to securing civil rights and halting workers' repression, she insisted that "only the most uncompromising resistance by all the oppressed and all the persecuted, can create the forces to smash the encroaching tyranny."[28]

After accepting the SWP's nomination, Grace remained in New York for another week, attending the convention's other events and meeting with her campaign manager, George Clarke, and her running mate, Farrell Dobbs. She also had time to socialize with her East Coast friends, joining Jim Cannon, George Novack, Evelyn Anderson, and Marvel Dobbs for meals during her stay.[29] She headed back to Minnesota on July 13 and five days later reported on the convention to the party members there. On Sunday, July 18, Grace attended one of her favorite gatherings of local comrades—the annual strawberry festival. Held at White Bear Lake, the event drew over one hundred people. Grace took the opportunity to deliver another campaign speech there.[30]

Grace did not have much time for reconnecting with her friends and family in the Twin Cities because just two weeks after getting back from New York she took to the road again, this time for a two-month, multicity national campaign tour. Grace began her tour in Salt Lake City.[31] For the next eight weeks she crisscrossed back and forth across the country, visiting Denver, Chicago, Detroit, Pontiac, Flint, and Cleveland in August, traveling to Toledo, Youngstown, Pittsburgh, Buffalo, Wilmar, Duluth, and back to Minneapolis in September, and making her way to Seattle, Milwaukee, New York, Camden, Philadelphia, Allentown, and

Des Moines in October.³² It was an intense schedule, aided at times by what Grace called the "miracle of modern aviation," but one met mostly by train travel.³³ The only region of the country she did not visit was the South. The party decided that it would be "too dangerous to arrange for mixed meetings of whites and Negroes in the South" and, because it did not have the funds for the security required to protect people's safety, it bypassed cities there.³⁴ Indeed, when the Progressive Party candidate, Henry Wallace, conducted his campaign tour through the region he was pelted with eggs and tomatoes because of his support for civil rights, and some of his supporters were violently attacked by protestors.³⁵

Publishing dispatches from the road in the *Militant* as she campaigned elsewhere, Grace reassured Trotskyist readers that "I have been taken care of very well and very generously in every city that I visited on this tour." She made special note of the comrades in Buffalo, who "crowded in more home-cooked dinners, parties and socials of all kinds into the schedule than any other place—for all of which I am very grateful."³⁶ No doubt such entertainments made the otherwise hectic schedule of campaign speeches and radio interviews not just bearable but enjoyable for Grace, who always appreciated mixing pleasure with political business. She also praised the efforts of campaign workers all along the trail, who helped arrange the various rallies and interviews for her to reach more voters. In addition to speaking before mass meetings at SWP branch headquarters around the country, Grace conducted many radio interviews, delivered a speech from a sound truck in Camden, and "spoke at three street corner rallies" in Harlem.³⁷ By October she acknowledged, "Campaigning is hard work, but I relish it."³⁸

During her campaign she delivered several key speeches. In one address, targeted for a radio audience, Grace built on the themes that she had explored in her acceptance speech in July, as well as on issues that had long been important to her. One of those issues was women's freedom.³⁹ "Millions of women bear the burden of a double oppression," she argued. "Exploited and abused like all workers, they are also discriminated against in industry, as well as having upon them the burden of the home." Perhaps as Grace spoke those lines she had in mind the struggles of Bea, Winnie, Dorothy, and her other women friends who wrote to her about the reality of that double burden. She also spoke about African Americans facing oppression with the continuation of Jim Crow throughout the country, especially in the South. "Tormented by these conditions, the oppressed are looking for a way out," but capitalists, she argued, continued to block them with measures like Taft-Hartley, House Un-American Activities Committee (HUAC) hearings, and FBI investigations that targeted unions, civil rights activists, and dissenters. Her assertion was no doubt informed by her commitment to the SWP's broader Marxist message, as well as by her years in the NAACP and her particular experience as someone targeted by the Smith Act and the FBI. As she did in her July speech, Grace connected the SWP's response to such repression to American traditions of resistance to tyranny: "Twice our people have faced a similar threat. Twice they have known how to meet it. In 1776 the farmers, mechanics and artisans, led by revolutionaries such as Sam Adams, Jefferson and Washington, destroyed the power of the British ruling class who sought to crush the birth of a new nation." And in 1860 Garrison, Brown, and Lincoln "personified the forces which waged merciless war against the slaveowners' attempt to perpetuate their outmoded system . . . and destroy the liberties of our people." Not shying away from invoking the use of violence in self-defense against such tyranny—including the tyranny of capitalism—she asserted that "the Socialist Workers Party, in these years of decision, comes forward as the continuator of these revolutionary traditions."[40]

In her "The Only Road to Peace" speech, which she delivered several times on the campaign trail beginning in August 1948, Grace invoked the dreaded specter of World War III. She warned of capitalists' maneuvers to bring such a conflict into being as they had done, she argued, with their manipulations for profit before World Wars I and II. Insisting that American capitalists, in seeking access to markets around the globe, were pushing the Soviet Union into the resulting Cold War, she voiced the SWP's position that "the only road to peace is that of revolutionary socialist internationalism." In the context of the Berlin crisis, which had erupted in June with Stalin's blockade of that city and had continued despite Truman's authorization of the airlift, Grace's words may have interested some voters who were looking for alternative solutions to the war scare fostered by that superpower standoff.[41] Grace explained that, as the Trotskyists had long argued, capitalists would resist "with strong-arm forces—Storm Troopers—fascist thugs and gunmen" any attempts of workers to build that revolutionary socialist internationalism. "But they won't win," she insisted, "because we are the many and they are the few." Again invoking the Founding Fathers, Grace quoted Thomas Paine by acknowledging that this "third American revolution" would "try men's souls" and not be easy, but she called on her listeners to join with her and the SWP to achieve its liberating goals.[42]

Grace was right that their struggle would not be easy and would be met with resistance. During the late summer of 1948, as Grace was campaigning around the country, the federal government continued to move against suspected subversive organizations and Communists through HUAC's investigations, the Federal Employee Loyalty Program, and even indictments under the Smith Act. The Second Red Scare was intensifying when in July the Justice Department charged twelve CPUSA leaders with violating the Smith Act, the same law that the 18 Trotskyists had been convicted under in 1941. In August, HUAC held blockbuster hearings during which Communist defector Whittaker Chambers identified Alger Hiss, a former State Department official, as being a Communist member of a spy ring in the 1930s. And that same month, but with less national attention than the Hiss case, a Trotskyist World War II veteran, James Kutcher, was fired from his job at the Veterans Administration in Newark because he had been caught up in a federal loyalty probe that identified him as being a member of a group—the SWP—that had been added to the attorney general's list of subversive organizations.[43]

On the campaign trail, Grace responded to these events. In a letter to President Truman, she protested Kutcher's treatment and argued, "His case marks the climax of a series of the most abominable malpractices by the Federal Government which make a mockery of the U.S. Constitution and reduce the Bill of Rights to a fiction." Condemning also the SWP's placement on the attorney general's list without prior notice, a hearing, or a chance to confront its accusers, she demanded that the president remove the party from the list. Truman's response, she said, would indicate whether he really was committed to civil rights or whether he had "turned the helm of government in the direction of a police state and thought control."[44] Although her letter, and similar protests penned by Farrell Dobbs, did not bring about any change in the Truman administration's policies, Grace did not stop condemning what she saw as the government's civil liberties abuses.[45] Along with her comrades in the SWP, she denounced the Smith Act prosecution of the CPUSA leaders. Although the Communists had supported the prosecution of the Trotskyists in 1941, the SWP decried these new indictments in 1948. Grace voiced the Trotskyists' recognition of the broader civil liberties implications of the government's actions: "Today they are prosecuting Communist Party leaders, tomorrow they will attempt to silence all militants in the trade union movement." Citing this prosecution, as well as the case of one of their own comrades, James Kutcher, Grace pointed out the prescience of the SWP: "All of these events symbolize the sweeping character of the march of reaction which we foretold from the courtroom in Minneapolis seven years ago."[46]

That march of reaction was sometimes voiced in the press coverage of the Dobbs-Carlson campaign. While most newspapers reported the announcement of the campaign in a neutral, matter-of-fact tone, a few voiced overt anti-Communist sentiments. In particular, some Minnesota papers jumped on the reference to Grace's connections with the State Department of Education in her campaign press release and echoed the cries for expanded loyalty investigations in state and local governments that were then being made by countersubversive anti-Communists around the country.[47] In one article from the *St. Cloud Sentinel*, the editors wondered, on the basis of the SWP press release, whether "Dr. Carlson is NOW or merely WAS a counselor in the State Department of Education." Asking "how many more socialists and communists and their like are holding positions in our University and/or State Department of Education," they called for "a little investigation in our own backyard." The *Le Sueur News-Herald* commented on the Dobbs-Carlson campaign announcement by stating, "From all we can learn the University is fast getting rid of the Mrs. Carlson type of instructors, a job which should have been tackled long ago. If the election of these two will take them far away from this state we hope they make it." Referring to Grace's positions as an instructor at the U and as a counselor at the DoE, the *Good Thunder Herald* echoed the desire of the *St. Cloud Sentinel* for a purge even as it mischaracterized the nature of Grace's former work at both institutions: "In those two spots she had a dandy chance to get at the kids we spend millions to educate, and we cannot help but wonder who put her there." The anti-Communist hostility that had permeated the Rockwell hearings during the little red scare of 1940 resurfaced with a vengeance in the context of the blossoming Second Red Scare in 1948.[48]

Although some of the press coverage of Grace's 1948 campaign included such hostility, most did not. Instead, other trends in the coverage emerged, some of which had to do with her being a Trotskyist candidate but more having to do with her being a woman candidate. The trends in the coverage of Grace's campaign for the vice presidency in 1948 fit quite closely with those uncovered by Erika Falk in her study of media bias in nine presidential campaigns launched by women between that of Victoria Woodhull in 1872 and that of Hillary Clinton in 2008.[49] Although Falk investigated women presidential candidates, there are similarities between the press coverage for those women's campaigns and that for Grace's vice-presidential bid.

One such pattern noticeable in the press coverage of Grace's campaign was its identifying her as a wife. Although almost all the stories on Grace also laid out her professional credentials as a woman who held a PhD, had worked at the DoE, and had run in several other political campaigns before, some still described her as "wife of a lawyer" and referred to her as "Mrs. Carlson" instead of Dr. Carlson.[50] Falk found this trend for the women presidential candidates she studied, too: "Women had their families mentioned on average once in every five articles," whereas the men's families "were mentioned about half as often." She found that "on average, women's honorary titles were dropped in 32 percent of the references" in four of the races she examined, where the "rate for men was just 11 percent."[51] Falk also found a greater quantity of "physically descriptive information gathered for women candidates" that she categorized as including references to their appearance, attire, attractiveness, age, and stature.[52] Once again the press coverage of Grace's campaign fit these trends too. She was described alternately as a "frail" forty-two-year-old, a "pert 41-year old . . . brunette," a "youthful, energetic holder of a doctor of philosophy" who appeared in a "jaunty summer dress," and "an attractive woman in her thirties" who had "flung her chic hat into the vice presidential race."[53]

Some of the press coverage of Grace's campaign trafficked quite heavily in gender stereotypes in ways that revealed the persistence of sexism in the broader culture. Not all voters were ready to accept the legitimacy of a woman candidate for national office. One article, in the tabloid *Picture News*, featured a photograph of Grace in which her facial expression was one of awkward surprise with the caption "Mrs. Carlson is prepared for violence." After visually demeaning the seriousness of her candidacy and platform, the article reported that even though Grace tried "to keep sex from beclouding the issues in her campaign," she was heckled by a man in Pittsburgh who accused her of lying about FDR and said, "That's just like a woman! Never knows when to shut up!"[54] In the German-language paper, *Milwaukee Deutsche Zeitung*, an editorial titled "Pretty Woman" managed to address some substantive issues. It engaged with Grace's political critiques of her opponents and challenged her claim that the SWP "engages in no compromise with the present day social order" by pointing out that it was running a campaign in which it was "striving . . . for political recognition." But the editorial also opened and closed with sexist assertions. "Republican and Democratic candidates like Harry Truman, Thomas Dewey, Earl Warren, take their wives with them on their campaign trips," it began, "in order to show them off and in order to make an impression upon the male electorate." But, the *Zeitung* argued, "The group which is in the field under the name of the Socialist Workers Party has gone a step further and has put forth a woman as candidate for the vice-presidency." In the final paragraph of the report, the editors comment, "Mrs. Carlson, it must be acknowledged, is unusually presentable—despite her Doctor's degree. In view of her charm, her party should put her forward as the presidential candidate, and instead of putting party platforms into the hands of the voters, they should put her picture in their hands. Millions of votes would thus be cast for her."[55] This chauvinist framing of the piece undermined the legitimacy of Grace's candidacy.[56]

But such sexist attitudes were ones Grace confronted on the campaign trail. As she worked to "get in as much Trotskyism as possible" during the short radio interviews she did around the country, she encountered similar bias. She provides a glimpse of her reaction to such prejudice in one of the dispatches she penned from the road for the *Militant*. In "A Week in Ohio" Grace reported on her interview with WTOD's "Women's Page on the Air" program. Grace reprinted the list of questions she was asked, which included some basic biographical inquiries and queries about her role in the SWP. The final question, however, cast her in the light of the domestic sphere and distracted from what could have been a more substantive discussion of policy issues. "In your tours around the country, I imagine you've picked up a great many cooking recipes that are particular favorites in sections," the interviewer asked. "Can you tell us about some?" Grace explained to her readers how "inasmuch as I'm the best cook among all the vice-presidential candidates (maybe even the presidential candidates) I was able to give Toledo's citizens the recipe for a very good Italian dish, Liver Rocco."[57] Instead of balking at the request or condemning it in the pages of the *Militant* for her readers, Grace rolled with the punches. As long as she could "get . . . as much Trotskyism as possible" into the conversation, she did not directly challenge such sexist cultural assumptions.

Much of the media bias that Grace faced took the form of two different but related patterns. Even though she technically was not the first woman to run for the vice presidency of the United States (that distinction belongs to Marie C. Brehm of the Prohibition Party, who ran in 1924), the press coverage of Grace's candidacy claimed that she was.[58] In so doing, it undermined the legitimacy of her place in the electoral battle. "Although the 'first woman' frame may help candidates in the short term by increasing the perception of their novelty and resulting in more press coverage," Falk explains, "the effects of reinforcing the notion of women as out of place and unnatural in the political sphere may be longer lasting."[59] Stories on Grace's run repeatedly included the terms "first woman" or "only woman" either in the headline or in the text or both.[60] Even SWP publicity material used such terminology, but, given the party's platform, which supported civil rights, that use signaled the Trotskyists' commitment to inclusion rather than an assumption that Grace was somehow an unnatural candidate.[61] The mainstream press, however, did traffic in the belief that women were incapable of political success. Closely related to the emphasis on Grace's being the first and only woman candidate in the 1948 national race was the reportage of her not really being a viable candidate. The *Minneapolis Morning Tribune*, for example, headlined that "Grace Carlson Hopes—But Her Race Is Futile," while the *Milwaukee Sentinel*'s read, "Unusual VP Aspirant Concedes Chances Nil."[62] Although coverage in the *Sentinel* and several other papers was based on discussions with Grace, who admitted the challenges she faced in the race, the mainstream press's decision to highlight her lack of viability may have been due, in part, to her gender.

Communicating the message that Grace's campaign was futile also stemmed from the fact that she was a Trotskyist with a criminal record. She recognized the practical challenges of gaining enough votes to come anywhere near close to winning. But, as in her previous campaigns, she insisted that electoral victory was not the main goal. Grace acknowledged that insofar as the SWP's revolutionary goals were concerned, "I don't think we are going to win by election campaigns . . . but we are making a step forward in educating the working class toward revolution."[63] There was also the reality that, as a convicted felon who had not had her civil rights restored, Grace could not vote for herself and, if elected, she would not be eligible to take office.[64] She and the other Trotskyists who had been convicted under the Smith Act in 1941 had applied for a presidential pardon in 1944 to no effect, despite the herculean efforts of the CRDC's petition campaign.[65] Despite Grace's interest in applying for a pardon again in 1948, disagreements within the party over its effectiveness derailed the effort.[66]

The SWP was ultimately unsuccessful in its 1948 presidential campaign. It could not get on enough state ballots to have any real chance in the Electoral College and did not appeal to enough voters in the states where it had.[67] In 1948, American voters turned out in support of the two major party candidates, giving Truman a little over 24 million votes, or 49.5 percent, and Dewey a little under 22 million votes, or 45.1 percent. Truman secured 28 states and 304 electoral votes (one of which would be switched to Strom Thurmond, giving Truman a final count of 303); Dewey won in 16 states with 189 electoral votes.[68] As Andrew E. Busch has argued, the election ultimately communicated "an affirmation of the New Deal, of containment, and of a halting progress on civil rights."[69] The SWP's revolutionary socialist agenda was far to the left of these positions—indeed, one of Grace's favorite targets on the campaign trail after Truman and Dewey was Henry Wallace, whom she slammed as an "unashamed champion of decaying capitalism."[70] The Dobbs-Carlson campaign trailed the other party tickets, including that of the Socialist Party, the Prohibition Party, and the Socialist Labor Party, tallying only 13,613 votes.[71]

Despite this poor showing, Grace believed she and Farrell "got a fairly good number of votes" and insisted that they "were pleased with it, anyway."[72] They remained committed to the SWP and continued to pursue its revolutionary socialist agenda even as the Cold War intensified. In 1949, the Soviets developed an atomic bomb and China became a Communist state. With these events abroad, the Second Red Scare widened at home. By 1950 Senator Joseph McCarthy launched his investigations of alleged Communist infiltration of the US government.[73] After her failed vice-presidential bid in 1948, before these events took place, Grace returned to Minneapolis and worked as an SWP state organizer alongside Vincent Dunne, who was now National Labor Secretary of the party. Farrell Dobbs remained in New York, where he continued to serve as a member of the National Committee and Political Committee. All three of them—along with the SWP as an organization and countless other Trotskyists around the country—remained targets of FBI surveillance.

Both the party's headquarters in New York and branch offices around the country were under surveillance by agents who gathered information from informants and wiretaps. Individual party members were also watched. Details of their lives were gathered by informants, who had infiltrated the party. Informants fed those details to FBI agents who filed reports, which the FBI director then forwarded to the Justice Department as he continued to try to make a case for the Trotskyists' illegal activities. J. Edgar Hoover secured authorization from the Justice Department for the electronic surveillance of the SWP on the grounds of the alleged threat of sabotage from Trotskyist intervention in unions and the possible violation of the Foreign Agents Registration Act of 1938 resulting from the SWP's failure to disclose its revived association with the Fourth International.[74] As the Red Scare expanded in scope, Hoover took advantage of new tools of repression. The 1950 McCarran Act, in addition to requiring the registration of Communist and Communist-front organizations with the attorney general, "finally authorized the custodial detention plan the FBI had been unofficially implementing for years."[75] Now the president was authorized "in the event of war or insurrection, to detain all persons he reasonably believed might participate in 'acts of espionage or sabotage,'" with "no provision for judicial review and no right to confront adverse witnesses."[76] By July 1950 "there were nearly 12,000 people on the Security Index; by the end of 1954 there were over 26,000, most of them Communist Party functionaries and other activists." Some of the Trotskyist 18 were listed among this group, including Dobbs and Dunne.[77]

FBI surveillance, which included agents' interviewing the employers, neighbors, and friends of the investigation's subject, often led to blacklisting. The Trotskyists' responses to this harassment varied. After years of struggling to make a living, Ed Palmquist renounced his association with the SWP and attempted to start his life over again in Alaska. Carl Skoglund was hounded by the FBI and, as an immigrant, by the INS, which used the threat of deportation to harass him for years after his release from Sandstone prison in 1945. But his commitment to the SWP never waned.[78] The same was true for Grace in these years. She continued to believe that the only road to peace was revolutionary socialism.

With this belief, Grace energetically confronted obstacles to her attempt to run for political office in 1950. Because of her 1941 felony conviction, she remained ineligible to run for state office in Minnesota, but she was able to put herself forward for US Congress in the state's fifth district, which included parts of Hennepin and Ramsey counties.[79] After the party gathered the required number of signatures to place Grace on the ballot, however, it received word that the Hennepin County auditor declared the petition invalid on the grounds that only 194 out of the required 500 signatures were those of registered voters as required by law. Although Grace and Ray vehemently disagreed—and Grace even began her own recount by cross-referencing signatories in the city directory—the auditor held firm. Ray made note in the local press how it was "a radical party in name alone [that] is suspect. This is the insidious way a fascist system creeps in." The targeting of the SWP only, he argued, was "in the spirit of the times."[80] Determined to get on the ballot, Grace secured a new petition with 1,379 names (even though she never conceded that there was a problem with the original one) and filed again in early October. This time the petition was accepted but almost immediately faced a court challenge. When the judge in that case found against Grace in mid-October, she was off the ballot again, but, with the aid of party lawyers, she immediately appealed to the Minnesota State Supreme Court.[81] Making the case that "the state courts have no jurisdiction over the question of the qualifications of Congressional candidates," Grace's legal team was victorious and on November 1, she finally won a place on the ballot for the November 7 election.[82]

The results were rather dismal: on November 9, the unofficial tally showed Grace polling a distant 1,305 votes, far behind the victor, Republican Walter Judd, with 71,242 votes, and the runner-up, Democratic-Farmer Laborite Marcella Killen, at 47,758. But once again, Grace remained optimistic. "We are quite happy about the vote we received," she wrote to her lawyer, Mike Myer. And finding a silver lining, she argued that "the SWP vote is higher on a percentage basis than the SLP vote and is almost as high as the Progressive Party vote. In the year of a Big Republican sweep and considering the fact that we had less than a week to campaign, we think that we did very well."[83] Despite yet another failed campaign, taking place in an era of heightened political repression, Grace kept faith with the SWP and her comrades. For the time being, she remained devoted to the movement that had become her second home and to its followers, who had become her extended family.

* * *

Grace was not alone among individuals on the political Left during the first half of the twentieth century who, in their daily life, found personal connections essential to maintaining their political activism. As Brown and Faue have argued in their study of the US Left between 1919 and 1950, it "was sustained and enhanced by the very elements of everyday life it refused to consider important theoretically," including marriage, sexual unions, friendships, family ties, correspondence, visiting, shared celebrations, and cultural activities. All of these things helped to "forge the Left politically and to sustain its activism." Grace understood this connection, noting how the Trotskyists in the Twin Cities were "'social socialists' who liked to have parties and picnics and that type of thing." The "dense networks of family and friends" that Brown and Faue explore were particularly important for people on the Left because they provided a shelter against the cold winds of rejection and isolation. This meaning was felt not just for those in the SWP but also for those in the CPUSA, where Brown and Faue found many similarities in these relational dynamics. Grace certainly experienced the nurturing quality of her network of women comrades during her years in the SWP. She also had platonic friendships with men in the party, including with Cannon, Dobbs, and others, that were equally valuable in this regard. But Brown and Faue note how marriages and sexual relationships were also often at the center of these supportive networks. For Grace, this was true too. Part of the reason why her marriage with Gilbert ended in separation by

1940 was her expanded role in the SWP and his unwillingness to share in that part of her life. The importance of having "common work" with one's romantic partner—a characteristic that Brown and Faue identified among the many couples they studied—was strong enough for Grace that it led to her separation from Gilbert. It also contributed to her romantic connection to Vincent Raymond Dunne. Their relationship was grounded in their joint commitment to the SWP.[84]

Grace and Gilbert had engaged in common work in their efforts for the NPLD and WDL during the late 1930s. But by 1940, when Grace became a full-time organizer for the SWP and made her first run for Senate, her commitment to the party had become a problem for their marriage. Gilbert, who remained a progressive concerned about social justice and labor issues, could not bring himself to leave the Catholic Church and devote himself to the SWP as Grace had done.[85] Although the two separated and lived apart for more than a decade, they remained in touch and were amicable. And, as the press coverage of her campaigns shows, their separation was not publicly touted: on the campaign trail she was still known as the wife of the lawyer Gilbert Carlson. Grace also received allotment checks from Gilbert when he served in the military during World War II.[86] But they were living separate lives. Gilbert acknowledged this when he wrote to Grace in December 1943 as she faced the reality of starting her prison sentence after the failed Smith Act conviction appeal: "It is at times like these I feel keenly the distance that separates us. . . . I can only wish you better happiness since I know you have had no easy time."[87]

Despite the fact that the two were living apart, they corresponded periodically over the years. It is hard to determine how frequently Grace and Gilbert wrote to each other because notations in her papers indicate that she did not preserve some of the communications she received from him. In a notebook she kept in 1943, Grace made a list of thirteen letters from Gilbert that she had received between April 1943 and January 1944, but those letters are not in her papers.[88] The collection includes a few missives written by Gilbert during the time she spent at Alderson, from January 1944 until January 1945, and messages from him communicated by Dorothy in her letters to Grace are also archived. There may have been other notes from Gilbert, but it is difficult to know with any certainty.

In the prison correspondence that has been preserved, it is clear that Gilbert was not Grace's first priority. Although he was one of her authorized correspondents at Alderson, she sent him only one direct letter.[89] Her other messages for him were included in her letters to Dorothy, who would forward them on to Gilbert. It was also through Dorothy that Grace learned that Gilbert had been called up to fight in the war. He was then serving in the army's 2675th Regiment in Italy. In March 1944, his unit was attached to the Allied Military Government responsible for assisting in the removal of refugees from the front lines. In April his regiment was fighting at Cassino and, in May, Gilbert was promoted to lieutenant. In most of their exchanges, made through these letters to and from Dorothy, Grace mentioned facets of her life and work in prison and Gilbert communicated what he could within the strictures of military censorship of his experience in the war.[90]

Occasionally emotions were revealed, however. In one letter, Gilbert notes to Grace how he was "sorry that we are as far apart in miles and problems. Had things been different we might have been happy since as on many points we agree very closely."[91] In another Grace tells Gilbert that she was "very, very lonesome. There are no congenial companions here. But so are you lonesome and so are millions of others lonesome in this weary world. It won't be that way forever though and that is something to hold on to."[92] And in response to Gilbert's telling her about his running into his cousin Amos at the front, she wrote, "I appreciate how much you left unsaid when you wrote [of Amos], 'He has a very nice wife and much to go back to.' These aren't the best conditions under which to express sentiments like these but I want you to know that I wish things were better for you."[93] Things did eventually get better for Gilbert in that he returned home safely from the war, but not to his wife because he and Grace remained separated. There is no record of any correspondence between the two for the seven years after Grace's release from Alderson in January 1945.

What there is, instead, is evidence of Grace's relationship with her comrade and lover, Ray Dunne. When Grace first got to know Ray during the 1934 strikes, he had been married to Jennie Octavia Holm for twenty years. Jennie was born on October 23, 1885, in Sweden, the eighth and final child of her parents; her mother died giving birth to her. Jennie grew up on Oland Island, Sweden, with her surviving siblings, Alma,

Nanny, Agda, Selma, Ida, and Arthur. All of them except Nanny and Agda eventually immigrated to Minnesota. Jennie arrived when she was just thirteen years old and began work, first in a laundry and then as a cook for a wealthy family. Jennie and Ray met in 1912, "when she was working as a waitress at the Great Northern station" and he was "a patron at the lunch counter." Evidently Ray liked her pancakes, for which she became well known in family circles. He soon fell in love with the strong, independent Jennie. The two were married on May 29, 1914, at the Holy Rosary Catholic Church on 2424 Eighteenth Avenue South in Minneapolis. Ray's brother Paul was his best man and Jennie's sister Ida, with whom she remained close all her life, was her maid of honor. Ray and Jennie had two children, Vincent Jr. (born in 1918) and Jeannette (born in 1920). During the Great Depression they also took in three children whose parents could not support them.[94] During the 1934 Teamster strikes, Jennie "cooked and helped at the women's auxiliary at least a few times." There is no evidence that Jennie ever joined the SWP, but she and her daughter, Jeanette, did attend certain party "dinners, fundraisers and events." Jennie did not travel with Ray when he went to Mexico in 1938 to meet Trotsky or on any of his many speaking and organizing tours during the 1940s and 1950s. When he was out of town on party work, which in certain years was quite often, Jennie held down the fort at home, which after 1941 was in their basement apartment on 2883 Holmes Avenue.[95]

The precise origins of Ray's romantic relationship with Grace are hard to pin down given the sources available and the fact that Grace and Ray kept the relationship a secret throughout both their lives. Only Dorothy and Henry and a few close friends knew about it at the time. But if the exact timing of when the relationship began cannot be defined, some of its contours can be. Grace and Ray had many opportunities to spend time with each other as they worked together at the SWP headquarters in Minneapolis during the late 1930s. By 1941, the two also shared the experience, along with the other indicted and convicted Trotskyists, of the Smith Act trial. When Grace separated from Gilbert and then left the Department of Education to work for the SWP full-time in 1940, there is also the possibility that she already may have been involved romantically with Ray; that affair may have been a contributing factor to her split from Gilbert. But this possibility is difficult to substantiate.

Grace insisted in the interviews she conducted with Carl Ross in the 1980s and on the videotaped interview she did at Tamiment Library in 1987 that the reason she split up with her husband was that she had left the Church and he had not. Somewhat defensively, she pushed back at the line of questioning in the Tamiment interview about her separation from Gilbert by emphasizing that "we weren't doing things together" and snapping, "There, that is the reason why, okay!"[96] Without corroboration, however, such defensiveness cannot be evidence for the relationship with Ray being the cause of her split from Gilbert.

There is also the possibility that the break with Gilbert may have been due to other factors, perhaps related to Grace's childlessness. If she had decided to use artificial birth control in their marriage, that decision may have not only deepened the rift between her and Gilbert (if he disagreed) but also contributed to her leaving the Church. The Church's condemnation of the use of artificial birth control, even in marriage, was a teaching reinforced in the 1931 papal encyclical *Casti Connubi* in reaction to the growing secular birth control movement of the 1920s. Adhering to this social teaching was difficult and painful for many faithful and led to many "anguished Catholic consciences." This was especially true for those among the working class for whom the financial consequences of large families intensified the stakes of such a wrenching choice.[97] Grace's decision to leave the Church (and Gilbert) may have been due to her refusal to adhere to the birth control ban that was being more widely enforced after 1931.[98] Grace, who was married in 1934, may have refused to follow the Church's teachings as part of both her sexual and her political coming of age; as she was drawn into the Trotskyist orbit, it would not have been surprising if she came in contact with Antoinette Konikow's tract on birth control, *Voluntary Motherhood*, which went through five editions between 1923 and 1938.[99] And she would have had access to birth control as a married woman in Minneapolis through the clinic run by the Minnesota Birth Control League.[100] But again, it is difficult to corroborate these suppositions. According to one FBI report, which contained information from the internal security division of the Minneapolis police from 1941, Grace allegedly "expressed the desire not to have any children as they might interfere with her career." The report also noted that "her husband Gilbert . . . disagreed with her on that point, as on many others."[101] Even though this source might substantiate the conclusion that Grace decided to use birth control and that such a decision seemed to contribute to her split with Gilbert (and perhaps her departure from the Church), without additional evidence it is hard to know for sure.

What can be traced out in Grace's correspondence and in FBI reports on Ray Dunne are the moments of opportunity that she and Ray had to strike up a romance before they served their time in prison from December 1943 until January 1945. In October 1942, Grace and Ray drove with Bea and Elaine from Minneapolis to New York for the SWP convention.[102] Perhaps the relationship bloomed during that long trip or in the convention hotel? Another opportunity was the period from July until late December 1943 when Grace and Ray were both stationed in New York City, she as a local organizer and he to assist the party center. Officially they had separate addresses: Grace was residing at 239 West Thirteenth Street, Apartment 6, while Ray stayed at Jim Cannon and Rose Karsner's place on 128 West Eleventh Street. According to the FBI—which used a combination of surveillance by agents on the ground, information gathered from informants who had infiltrated the party headquarters, wiretaps on phones, postal intercepts, and even "trash covers" (in which they searched the subject's garbage)—Dunne received almost no mail at his address for the duration of his stay.[103] But again, all of this is merely suggestive.

It was while Grace and Ray were imprisoned and kept physically apart—she at the women's federal correctional facility in Alderson, West Virginia, and he at the federal penitentiary in Sandstone, Minnesota—that the two generated evidence of their romantic relationship. Grace's and Ray's carefully written expressions of love and longing for each other's company peek out from the pages of letters between Grace and Dorothy that otherwise exchange news of quotidian goings-on and discussions of SWP happenings. Grace would include messages for and questions about Ray in her letters to Dorothy, and Dorothy would write with news from and about Ray that she learned via Henry, who was one of Dunne's authorized correspondents. It was a cumbersome system, but one that allowed Grace and Ray to stay in touch around the prison censors and within the limitations of their authorized list of correspondents.

Early in their prison terms, Ray wrote to Henry asking him to "tell Dorothy to send my very warmest personal greeting to her sister. I embrace her, notwithstanding the barriers and the distance."[104] Grace, who received this message through Dorothy, wrote back a week later telling her that she was "most pleased, of course, over the last letter, with the 'quote' from Ray. I know that section by heart now; I have read it so many times."[105] In another letter, Ray told Grace how he had "been reading Browning a bit," opining that because "we read him together so many times," the poet would not mind his taking the liberty of paraphrasing him.[106] Dorothy transcribed Ray's memory of the last stanza of Browning's poem, "Evelyn Hope," for Grace:

> I loved you,—all the while
> My heart seemed full as it would hold
> There is a place and to spare for your sweet smile
> And the red of your mouth and the hairs soft fold.
> So hush,—I will give you this rose to keep—
> See, I shut it within your lovely hands
> There, that is our secret! It will keep;
> You will wait and remember and understand.[107]

In her response, sent via Dorothy, Grace commented, "I am very devoted to Browning, but even more devoted to the author of the paraphrase."[108]

It was clear in Grace's letters that her heart was with Ray. More than once Grace would discuss Gilbert and Ray in the same letter to Dorothy; the shift in tone from caring friend to pining lover was palpable.[109] In Ray's communications to Grace, his special affection for her is also clear. In April he asked Henry to communicate to Grace via Dorothy that he was anxiously awaiting a copy of the article Grace had written for the Alderson newspaper, the *Eagle*. "I'll read it at sun up in the morning and remember that she had given it to me," he wrote, "and also that she had seen the same sun an hour before." In November he wrote how happy he was when he got messages from Grace. "The Smokies always seem a little nearer when I read some of your quotations." And he frequently sent "special and warm greetings to Grace" in his notes to Henry.[110]

At the same time, however, Ray never separated from Jennie and kept her as one of his authorized correspondents. In late spring 1944, Dorothy and Henry had not heard from Ray for a few weeks because he had used up all his allowances communicating with his wife. She had recently had an operation on her leg and Ray's attention temporarily turned fully to her. And on at least one occasion, Jennie visited Ray at Sandstone. His daughter, Jeannette, recalled driving up with her mother and some others to make the trip to the prison to see her dad.[111] By mid-May, however, Henry received a letter from Ray in which he was eager for information on Grace. Ray wrote to Henry that he was "hungry for the first hand news of Evelyn's visit to Grace. How she looked—how she felt—what she said about herself and others, in short a word from West Virginia."[112]

The depth of the connection that Ray and Grace shared can also be measured in the time they spent together as a couple before they served their prison terms. Dorothy and Henry knew about their relationship, as most likely did some of Grace's closest female friends, like Bea Janosco, who in a letter to Grace reflected on the "good old days" when they would all socialize together.[113] In a separate letter to Grace, Dorothy related how her daughter, Ann (then only five years old), had commented that it "doesn't seem like Christmas" because "Gracie isn't here—or Ray Dunne."[114] Grace and Ray came as a pair to many social engagements—including Christmas celebrations at Dorothy's house. Their relationship, although kept secret from Jennie and the public, flourished within a small network of party insiders.

And it flourished in the shared celebrations and social events that were part of the movement culture of the SWP in Minneapolis and St. Paul. Spending birthdays and holidays together was important to the community that the Trotskyists built and that the couples within the party enjoyed. Such community, based on intertwined personal and political ties, was also an important part of party life in the CPUSA; although the two movements diverged sharply on ideological grounds, they had much in common when it came to their movement cultures and the all-in quality of their members' commitments.[115] Connections with party friends, especially with Ray, remained vital for Grace when she was at Alderson. Even behind bars she saw to it that Dorothy sent a present from her to Ray for his birthday and reminded her to ensure that "my warmest personal greetings go with the gift."[116] And, as Dorothy related to Grace, Ray recalled "feeling that on St. Patrick's Day our memories are bound together—the office café, the F[armer] L[abor] lecture series, the planning the trip to Minneapolis this time last year. 'Best of all,'" she quoted him writing, "'on next St. Patrick's Day and—yes before that! I look forward impatiently to the time we can claim our right.... Yes indeed, better, oh! Much better times ahead!'"[117] Grace responded that she "heartily concur[red]" with Ray's sentiments and was also looking forward to the next St. Patrick's Day, when they could all be together again.[118] And similar feelings washed over Grace when she wrote to Dorothy on April 29. "Tomorrow is May Day," she penned. "Last year, I was chairman of the meeting at which Ray made a campaign speech. It will be heart-warming to think back on it and even more heart-warming to think of next May 1."[119]

As Grace's recollection of May Day points out, she and Ray also bonded over their shared political work. That work began at the SWP headquarters in Minneapolis (and during their time together in New York City in 1943), well before their prison sentences, and would continue for many years after. Her prison correspondence reveals how she initially had been taken under Ray's wing in this work when she first joined the party. In one letter to Dorothy, she recounted how she had reluctantly agreed to speak at the weekly prayer meeting in her cottage at Alderson despite her insistence that she had "no religion" and asked Dorothy to "be sure to let Vincent know about this because he launched me on my public speaking career." She followed up by asking her sister to "tell him, too, that after six weeks of concentrated, solitary thinking, I am more than ever grateful to him for what he taught me. I can only wish that I could have learned more of his patience, but I am practicing the patience that I did learn from him."[120]

Although she may have started out her career in the SWP as Ray's student, by the time of their imprisonment in January 1944 she had become a partner with him in both the professional and the personal sense. When Grace and Ray returned home to Minneapolis in January 1945 after serving their time, they were reunited with each other and with their comrades in the SWP. Over the next five years, the two remained devoted to their work for the party and to each other. That commitment to the SWP often meant they would spend periods of time apart on assignments in different cities or on speaking tours and campaigns. But Grace and Ray became something of a dynamic duo in the Minneapolis branch, which remained their home base in these years.

At first, the two were able to reunite in Minneapolis after their release from prison in January, but, despite the protestations of Dorothy and Bea, who hoped Grace would stay longer and enjoy time with Ray and their friends, Grace resumed her position as a local organizer in New York.[121] Because of parole conditions, it was not until May when Ray was able to join her and take up his new role as the party's National Labor Secretary. An informant (whose name remains redacted in the FBI file) intercepted correspondence between Grace and Ray at the time and told agents that the two were "having a clandestine affair" and that Dunne "contemplated living at the apartment of [Carlson]" in New York. In Ray's FBI file, an agent notes that "according to this correspondence, they plan to meet at the station in New York City on Friday, May 4, 1945, not advising other National figures in the SWP of Dunne's arrival, and thereafter would live together at the [Carlson] apartment until May 6, 1945, when she was to go to Boston to make a May Day address, at which time he would make his presence in New York known." The agent then reported how "from the tenure [sic] of her correspondence it appears that they have been carrying on an illicit affair for some time and plan to continue to live together after Dunne arrives in New York City."[122] If this information is accurate, Grace and Ray spent this time in New York working for the SWP and deepening their romantic connection.

As devoted comrades, however, Grace and Ray did not have much time together in Manhattan: Grace began her "Women in Prison" coast-to-coast speaking tour in June 1945. The couple found ways to connect while she was on the road. On the basis of a letter from Grace to Evelyn dated July 1, 1945, that was intercepted by the FBI before it was delivered, the Bureau reported that Ray planned to "be with her, Grace Carlson, at the Park Avenue Hotel in Detroit, Michigan where Grace was going to stay until July 13, 1945."[123] In August, as Grace continued her tour, Ray returned to the Twin Cities, where he spent most of his time at the party's headquarters in Minneapolis.[124] Grace joined him there and the two resumed their joint work in the branch in September. But by November they were back out on assignment again: Ray was sent to Cleveland and then Detroit to deal with challenges presented by those identifying with the Goldman-Morrow group in those branches and to assist in labor organization; Grace joined him in Detroit later that same month to organize educational programs for the local. From November 1945 until March 1946, the two were based in Detroit, enjoying their shared work for the SWP and, presumably, the time they could spend together as a couple behind closed doors.[125]

By June 1946 Grace and Ray were both back in Minneapolis. FBI reports asserted that, according to the information supplied by a highly confidential informant in that city's SWP branch, the two were still romantically involved. Also according to these reports (and as referenced in correspondence between two other party leaders), Grace underwent surgery for cancer that month.[126] It is unclear what kind of cancer this may have been or how long Grace suffered with it because she does not mention this at all in the interviews she gave later in her life. Grace did have a history of food allergies and heart problems, going back at least to 1940. Her correspondence shows the cardiac condition becoming an issue for her again in March 1943, when she was hospitalized for a week for an enlarged heart. Her physician, Dr. Fred Wittich, recommended she get EKGs every six months beginning in September 1943. But there was never any mention of cancer before 1946.[127] By the summer of 1946, however, Grace needed an operation to remove a tumor. Farrell Dobbs sent an update on Grace's condition to James Cannon in New York on June 13, noting that the surgery went well and that "she is doing as good as can be expected." Dobbs also revealed that the "doctor seems to think that once she recovers from the operation she will be in better physical condition than she has been for quite some time," indicating that the disease must have been causing her some level of pain or discomfort prior to its discovery.[128]

According to Ray, who wrote to Jim the following month, "Grace has recovered remarkably well and although she is far from being her strong self, is participating quite actively in what is turning out to be a whirl-wind signature and election campaign."[129] By early July she had accepted the party's nomination to run for the US Senate from Minnesota and in August filed her petition to get on the ballot. By September she was actively campaigning.[130] During this latter part of 1946, she and Ray were based in Minneapolis together, with Ray traveling occasionally as labor secretary and to attend national party meetings in Chicago or New York.[131] The same pattern characterized much of 1947, with Ray going back and forth to St. Louis to help organize brewery workers but also running his campaign for mayor of Minneapolis in the spring with Grace as his campaign manager.[132]

Grace's calendar book for 1948 provides insights into her daily comings and goings during that year. It reveals that she spent almost every day at the SWP headquarters in Minneapolis involved in some sort of party work when she was not out on the road campaigning. It also shows that when she was in Minneapolis, she was at the party headquarters between two and four nights a week for supper with Ray and other party friends. Every Monday they attended the Minneapolis executive committee meeting, every Wednesday the Minneapolis branch meeting, and on Sundays either the St. Paul branch executive committee meeting or the Sunday forum at the St. Paul branch. They also worked on fundraiser bazaars, organized various socials held at the headquarters, coordinated different picnics throughout the year, pitched in on mailings for the *Militant*, and staffed election campaigns. Except for the few weeks here and there throughout the year when Ray was out of town on labor secretary business or the two months from August until October when Grace was on tour during her vice-presidential campaign, the two spent most of their time together at the party headquarters in Minneapolis.[133]

That closeness sometimes bred contempt, and, if the FBI reports are accurate, Grace and Ray found themselves crossing verbal swords more than once over the years. On August 20, 1946, during the beginning of Grace's campaign for the Senate, a source identified only as T-1 claimed that Grace argued with Ray over her role in the party. T-1 was either one of the highly confidential informants in the Minneapolis party branch given "temporary symbols" to identify them, or possibly some form of technical surveillance, like the phone tap placed in the Schultzes' home where Grace had been residing since July. "I'm an intellectual who wants to make a mark as an intellectual," T-1 reported Grace as saying. "I place my lot to the workers in the Party. I could have gone to New York and could have been an intellectual there . . . I thought we understood each other but it does not look like we do." Claiming that Ray was "making a fight" against her, Grace allegedly said she "felt like a failure" but also that she felt that she could not discuss these things with Ray "because you never let me talk about myself," and that she could "never say anything to you and expect you to say 'Why, ya, sure.' I don't have to have your approval on every word."[134] Exactly what had precipitated this outburst—which according to T-1 was fueled by alcoholic drink—is unclear. But, if true, it reveals a tension in the relationship between the comrades and lovers that centered on Grace's perception that Ray did not fully appreciate or support her intellectual talents. Why that would be, given that all indications up until this point were that the two had a harmonious working and personal relationship built on mutual admiration, is not clear.

But the relationship between Grace and Ray was experiencing some stress. Other FBI sources provided additional accounts of further quarrels between the two powerful personalities in later years. Having shared political work could fuel romantic relationships, but it could also fray them when disagreements crept in. In the early summer of 1947, two confidential informants in St. Paul fed information to agents who reported that "Carlson was becoming more and more quarrelsome and irritable. She was often quarreling with Vincent Dunne concerning some technical aspect of Leninism and resented Dunne's speaking to her in 'accusing tones.'" Allegedly she also "often rationalized her behavior by saying, 'Who could have done any better?'" The same two informants told their Bureau contacts that Grace had "another violent quarrel with Dunne" on June 26 "when she severely reprimanded him for creating an embarrassing situation at a dinner which was attended by a group of Trotskyists."[135] Whether that situation was political or personal is not stipulated, but again, if the report is accurate, it sheds light on the complexity of Grace and Ray's relationship: as with many romantic partnerships, there were fights that stemmed from both personal and professional disagreements.

In January 1948 the friction was reported to be personal, but it also clearly had political implications. This time it was Ray who lit into Grace, criticizing her for "her flippant attitude and child-like behavior," which he feared was "causing internal strife within the ranks of the SWP." Allegedly Ray warned Grace, "'You're wisecracking yourself into a bad situation. You've got to cut it out.'" Concerned about her having made "unkind remarks" and having an "antagonistic attitude" toward certain members in the branch, he told her, "'I think you must control yourself. . . . I don't permit myself to say anything unless I think it's the right thing to say.'" And reminding her of the example she was setting through her behavior, Ray remarked, "'You're a great figure in this movement. You can't allow yourself to do these things. You're a psychologist. Do you think these people are so stupid they don't understand..."' The FBI file does not indicate what, if any, response was made by Grace.[136] She certainly could have an acerbic tongue and did not suffer fools easily, but Ray tried to remind her in this moment of what he had long ago taught her—the importance of patience in organizing work—and to warn her of the consequences of her comments on the people they were trying to keep in the SWP's ranks.

The disagreements between Grace and Ray were rooted not just in these matters of political substance and organizational style but also in personal strife that flared because their political lives and work were so intertwined with their love life. As Brown and Faue observed in their research, "Due to the intense pressures of oppositional politics . . . the Left could both foster and sometimes threaten sexual and marital unions."[137] Political disputes cut deeper because of the romantic link between Grace and Ray. An FBI report from November 1948 captured one such example. A source "related that Carlson criticized the subject [Ray] because of his 'demanding tone of voice.' He, in turn, rebuked her for her arrogance and 'too much talk attitude.' He pointed out to her that he did not like the way she was running the meeting. The quarrel became so violent," the source reported, "that Carlson in a rage cried that she would ask to be transferred from the Twin Cities leadership before taking any more insults from Dunne."[138]

The quarrels between Grace and Ray reveal them struggling with these intertwined personal and political frustrations. They also show Grace's deepening disappointment with Ray. By 1948 the two were not always seeing eye to eye. Indeed, in one episode in early November 1948 that must have reinforced Grace's sense of the emotional (and perhaps political) distance that was beginning to creep into her relationship with Ray, he "criticized her for speaking rudely of George Clarke," her campaign manager during her vice-presidential run. The reason for her making the "derogatory remark with respect to Clarke," according to an FBI report, was that "Clarke had made improper advances to her."[139]

If Grace was disappointed in Ray for not defending her in the incident with Clarke, he occasionally registered disappointment in her for not doing enough for the party. His anxiety may have been heightened due to the increased pressure the SWP was under during the Second

Red Scare. In April 1949 Grace attended a hearing at the state capital in Minnesota on an antisubversive bill that was before committee and then made a report to the SWP branch. When "she admitted to Vincent Raymond Dunne that she had not actively participated by speaking against the bill," according to an FBI report, "Dunne severely criticized her for not talking at the right time," and a "heated argument ensued." Grace "told Dunn[e] that the next time there was a hearing, he could attend."[140] In September the two engaged "in another of their periodic arguments"; this time (according to T-1) "both blamed the other for their negligence in losing the address of a potential party member."[141] As the repression of the Second Red Scare intensified during the late 1940s, the stakes of such incidents for the party were high and may have contributed to the tension between the comrades and lovers.

Even though their relationship included these "periodic arguments," Grace and Ray continued to work together in Minneapolis over the next few years. Aside from the national tour he took as the party's labor secretary from November 1949 through January 1950, Ray was reported by the FBI to be at the SWP headquarters in Minneapolis almost every day. He, "together with Grace Carlson," was described in FBI reports as dominating the local. For the next year and a half the two remained on the executive board and continued to devote themselves to the party's attempts to organize labor fractions as well as to its work coordinating various social and political gatherings, like the annual strawberry and raspberry festivals, the annual Trotsky memorial meeting, and the *Militant* picnic.[142]

Grace and Ray were not the only couples whose lives centered on the SWP. The same was true for Dorothy and Henry Schultz, Jim Cannon and Rose Karsner, Myra and Murry Weiss, and Genora and Sol Dollinger. These relationships exhibited some of the same patterns found in Grace and Ray's and charted by Brown and Faue. For these couples, having common work in the party was central to their romantic bond, and their total commitment to the party also impacted their relationships and families in a variety of ways.

On one hand, the shared work and full devotion to the SWP nurtured these couples and provided them with a complete social and political world. Dorothy and Henry almost exclusively socialized with party people and, like Grace, spent most days at the party headquarters, but in St. Paul rather than in Minneapolis. During Henry's health crisis in 1944, it was the party and its members who stepped up to support Dorothy. In their routine daily life, it was Bea and John Janosco, Elaine Roseland, Winnie Nelson, and, later on, Jeanne and Bill Brust who were their constant companions. Dorothy and Henry's coordination of and participation in the SWP's various political events and social gatherings filled their calendar.[143] Their son Raymond recalled how it became something of an inside joke among his siblings that all of the Schultz children were born in April, which was nine months after the annual strawberry festival. Their parents' ties to the party impacted their family in other ways too: the Schultz home was the site of many SWP socials and informal late-night meetings. Raymond recalls how one time he and his twin brother, Vincent, heard voices coming from what they thought was the closet in their bedroom, but it turned out to be the conversation from adults gathered in the kitchen below that had traveled up the chimney that went through the closet on the way to the roof. For him, his parents' commitment to the party was one part of his childhood, which included attending SWP picnics and festivals too. For his sister Ann and older brother Jim it was not recalled with equal fondness. Jim resented his parents' commitment to the SWP, which he saw as a type of religion that contributed to his and Ann's neglect. Ann also later confessed to another family member that she had been abused by someone in the SWP who frequented the Schultz home. Possibly as a result, she left home when she was only sixteen.[144] Dorothy and Henry's commitment to the party thus dominated their marriage and shaped their family in ways that were not always positive.[145]

Commitment to the working-class movement (for some, first within the Communist Party and then within the SWP) forged bonds between many couples. As Bryan Palmer describes the common law marriage of Jim Cannon and Rose Karsner, it was "a lifelong comradeship, a love relationship sealed in political collaboration."[146] Although it was not without challenges, especially given Jim's problems with drink, the relationship was rooted in a shared political commitment. In his prison correspondence to Rose, Jim wrote more about his plans for the party, proposals he and the other Trotskyists at Sandstone had discussed, and ideas for publications in the *Militant* than he wrote lengthy romantic musings. Although he certainly did communicate his love and concern for Rose, he also maintained their "political collaboration" through his prison correspondence.[147] The glue of common work was thus important not just for Grace and Ray but for many couples on the political Left—both within and outside of the SWP too—during the early to mid-twentieth century. Harvey O'Connor and Jessie Lloyd, independent socialists who never forged official party associations, spoke of the value of such shared politics. Jessie described Harvey as her "soul-mate both for fun and for purpose," and their life together as one full of "joy as well as activism."[148]

But such collaboration and commitment to a bigger movement sometimes also affected couples by placing a strain on their relationships if they were tasked with assignments that took them away from each other (and their children) for extended periods of time. Such was the case with Jim and Rose early on in their relationship, before they were expelled with fellow Trotskyists from the Communist Party. Palmer acknowledged the stress caused by their "geographic removal from their children" during the late 1920s.[149] For Genora and Sol Dollinger, another couple that thrived on their political collaboration within the SWP, it was separation from each other that they accepted as part of their complete commitment to the party. Their willingness to be selfless for what they understood to be the bigger and more important cause of their lives (individual and shared) resulted in periods of time in which they lived apart. Genora and Sol did not really want to reside in separate cities but, when the party made it clear that it did not want Sol to leave Flint and Genora recognized that she still had work to do in Detroit, they accepted the temporary separation. As Carlton Jackson explains, "Each put the interests of the party before the welfare of the other."[150]

To some extent the same was true for Myra Tanner Weiss and Murry Weiss. Although Myra expressed her sadness at their separation in June 1953 when Murry went to New York to edit the *Militant* and she remained behind waiting for a decision from Jim Cannon as to where she was most needed, she also understood that there was a larger commitment at stake. "Already it seems like years since we have been together. 3,000 miles and two weeks since we parted," she wrote Murry. She also noted how "everyone feels very unhappy to lose you from LA but the comrades here of course are not provincial and appreciate the importance to you and to the Party of your work in the center."[151] Unlike the

Dollingers, however, the Weisses were sexual nonconformists, who, as Alan Wald has uncovered, "sometimes strategized their love affairs for political reasons—including Myra's with Trotsky's grandson—and inspired a commune of young people in Los Angeles." Myra and Murry engaged in a relationship that "was an inviolable political collaboration that was maintained even while the two conducted other heterosexual liaisons." Other Trotskyists engaged in similar open relationships; some, like that between George Novack and Evelyn Reed, "lasted until death," while others, including that between Myra and Murry, did not.[152]

Although the all-in nature of life in the SWP was nurturing for many couples, be they sexually conformist or not, it could also be demanding, as the temporary separations of Jim and Rose, Genora and Sol, and Myra and Murry show. If one member of the couple did not have a full commitment to the party, the relationship often did not last long. Such was the case with Grace and Dorothy's good friend Winnie Nelson and her husband, Norman. Their marriage began to deteriorate even before he was sent to North Africa with the medical corps during the war. By July 1944 Winnie began to confide in Bea and Elaine that she had "decided to cut herself loose and live her life alone again" after holding on to her marriage to Norm for several years in fear of losing custody of their son, John. Once John was old enough to be in school full-time, Winnie felt more confident in her ability to support them both and had the courage to tell Norm she wanted to end the marriage. Elaine wrote to Grace at Alderson in July explaining that Winnie "did not go into detail about their differences but I gathered it began from his attitude and approach to the movement and then branched out in other little, but nevertheless important things."[153] In this case Winnie remained loyal to the party and sacrificed her marriage because, along with other minor problems in the relationship, Norm's view on the movement diverged from hers.[154] A similar break occurred in the marriage of Rose Seiler and Ed Palmquist when he began to pull away from the SWP after years of harassment by the FBI and blacklisting by employers because of his association with the party and his 1941 Smith Act conviction. Rose remained dedicated to the SWP and an active member in its Seattle branch, but Ed, who had divorced Rose and moved to Alaska, was no longer involved with the party by the early 1950s.[155] And when Marie Creel "dropped away altogether," pulling out of SWP activities in Minneapolis and even resigning from the WDL executive board in 1947, Grace registered concern with leaders in New York about the loss of her as a member and about the possible effect of Marie's departure on her husband, Warren Creel. Warren had also "asked for a leave of absence from active party work, saying that he feels overworked" but also citing a "need for bettering personal relations between him and Marie." Granting him the leave, Grace explained that she and Henry and Ray hoped to help Warren so that he would not leave the party too.[156]

Being supportive of couples in the party stemmed not just from a concern over the welfare of those individuals but also from a desire to ensure that their first commitment remained that of the welfare of the party and their ability to serve it best. Sometimes these concerns led to rather intrusive interventions into comrades' romantic and sexual lives. In her revealing memoir, *Not without Love*, Constance Webb recalls many such encroachments. As a young woman, her comrades pressured her to have sex with her boyfriend, Norman (who would later become her first husband), because, as one of them explained to her at the time, she and Norm were too young to marry and had college ahead of them, "but to wait all those years because of some misplaced bourgeois conception about virginity in marriage would be fraudulent." If she and Norm repressed their sexual desires, her friend explained to Webb, "neither you nor he will be able to concentrate on the most important aspect of your lives—the creation of a Leninist-Trotskyist party."[157] Later in Webb's life, after she married C. L. R. James, the Trinidad-born Trotskyist intellectual who cofounded the Johnson-Forest tendency, she faced continued interventions into her private life. James Cannon counseled her to leave James because of the challenges they faced as an interracial couple. Other comrades recommended she stay with him but advised her not to visit him when he was held on Ellis Island facing deportation for a visa violation because of the possible impact her presence might have on his legal case.[158] Of the latter pressure Webb recalled thinking, "I always believed that a wife or husband should be with her or his mate in times of crises. But, as usual, I acceded to these dictates despite feeling angry."[159] Theirs was a very crowded marriage with certain members of James's inner circle barging into their apartment at all hours of the day and night and even, at times, flirting shamelessly with him in front of Webb as they vied for attention from and influence over him.[160]

Less intimately intrusive were the interventions Bea and Dorothy made, along with Grace and Ray, who wrote from prison, into Elaine's relationship with Mark Braden, a comrade from Chicago she met while attending a "two-week vacation school sponsored by the Detroit branch of the party to improve her knowledge of Marxism and Trotskyist principles." None of Elaine's friends thought Mark was a suitable mate for her, seeing him as a rebound relationship after Elaine's brief wartime marriage with another man collapsed. After much discussion about the matter among themselves in the fall of 1944, they gently but firmly told her what they thought. Under such concerted pressure from her closest comrades, Elaine eventually came to agree and dropped her plans to move away from Minneapolis to be with Mark.[161]

* * *

The total commitment to the party and the shared work that sustained so many platonic and romantic relationships thus cut two ways: it fostered a supportive but also a demanding environment in which comrades were loving but also intrusive. Grace experienced both characteristics of the SWP community during her years in the ranks, but, as one of the true believers who was deeply devoted to the party, she did not question the nature of the political world that had also become her personal home. Grace shared in the belief that the freedom of workers (and of women) would ultimately, and could only, be met by socialism. Her dedication to the SWP led her to serve as its candidate for the vice presidency of the United States in 1948. Her devotion to Trotskyism sustained her continued work as a party leader after that election and supported the committed romantic relationship she engaged in with Ray Dunne. As long as she kept the faith with the SWP, she and Dunne were a dynamic duo in the party, especially in the Minneapolis branch, sharing in the work of revolution. It would not be until certain events shook that faith that her life would take a dramatically different path.

5

The Break

By early 1952, Grace had been an active member of the SWP for over a decade. As a local executive board member, state organizer, and National Committee member who was "always running for office someplace," Grace centered her professional life on the SWP.[1] Her personal life, too, was deeply intertwined with this Trotskyist world. Not only did she have her extended network of women comrades as friends, but she also had her biological sister, Dorothy, with whom she worked and socialized on almost a daily basis. And then there was her romantic involvement with Ray Dunne that was a significant part of her life during these years. Her decision to walk away from the SWP in June 1952 struck Dorothy and all her comrades like a bombshell.[2] Grace's break with the party also constituted a break with her life as she had known it for more than a dozen years.

Grace's reasons for leaving the SWP were, she insisted, purely personal and stemmed from her reaction to her father's death in September 1951. That event triggered a spiritual shift in her that led her back to the Catholic Church. Soon thereafter Grace also reunited with Gilbert. How much her failed relationship with Ray or the pressures of the Second Red Scare influenced her actions is difficult to substantiate, but those factors may have also played a role. Even after Grace left the SWP, she continued to experience the brunt of McCarthyism, finding herself blacklisted by employers and harassed by the FBI. For Grace, Catholic priests and women religious came to her aid during this difficult time, helping her to readjust professionally and supporting her reunification with Gilbert. Acutely aware of other Catholics who left Communist organizations and returned to the Church in these same years, Grace was adamant that she would not be among those who chose to inform on their former comrades. Instead, Grace reconciled her conscience as a Catholic who was a philosophical Marxist committed to pursuing social justice, now outside of the SWP.

* * *

In almost all of the accounts she gave about her reasons for leaving the SWP in 1952, Grace discussed the death of her father.³ James Holmes continued to reside with Dorothy, Henry, and their children after they moved into their new home on 630 Fuller Avenue in 1944. From there James went to and from work at the roundhouse until he retired sometime between 1945 and 1950.⁴ He also helped Dorothy out at home, especially with the young twins, Vincent and Raymond, who were born in 1946. Raymond recalls their going with their grandfather to Lenways bar on University Avenue, "about three blocks from our house." There he and Vincent would get orange sodas while James partook of stronger libations. Raymond's "memory is of [James] as the perfect picture of the grandfather image . . . kindly, comforting always present." But he acknowledges that James did go to Lenways often and that while Dorothy "never said so directly," he "was sure she thought her father could not hold his drink."⁵

With no surviving correspondence between James and his daughters, it is difficult to assess their relationships precisely. But the fact that James resided with Dorothy and her family indicates a sense of obligation and closeness that remained even after she and Grace had grown. James was integral to the family unit, not just for whatever financial help his wages may have brought during the years he was still working but also for the support he provided at home, however unorthodox his methods. When Grace was working as an organizer in New York in 1942, Dorothy explained how Ann's understanding of the "whole family" included grandpa. And when Grace was at Alderson worrying that the children would forget her, Dorothy noted how young Jim would say "hello" to the picture of Grace that James kept in his bedroom.⁶

Whatever the exact nature of their domestic world, it suffered a painful blow on the evening of September 3, 1951, when James suffered a hemorrhage of his esophageal hiatal hernia and died at the age of seventy-two. Henry signed the death certificate.⁷ Grace was not present when James died because she was attending the SWP's plenum in New York City, but she spoke several times after the fact about the impact of her father's death. In July 1952, after she announced her resignation from the SWP, she told the *Minneapolis Morning Tribune* that "death is such a tremendous thing" and that she realized after James's passing that she "didn't have all the answers."[8] Grace later explained how James's death "was a very traumatic situation for me," but clarified that "it wasn't that I thought his death was so tragic—he was old and he'd been sick . . . but then the whole philosophical question came up: Who would make up to him for everything that he had missed in his life?" Sounding a note of guilt, she continued, "All the problems that he'd had (and I certainly had been one of them.) That's when I went back to the church." In an interview with *SCAN* (*Saint Catherine's Alumnae News*) in 1986, Grace articulated her feelings a bit more fully, noting how when James died, "It made me think about the meaning of life. My father had worked hard and he had a lot of problems and I was one of them. And now he was dead, and there would be no one to make up to him for all he had missed in life. I thought about how people have disappointments in love and disappointments in their children, and how Marxism can't really help those things."[9] Although she never clarified what it was she thought James had missed in his life, Grace was coming to realize that something was missing from hers: a connection with God.[10]

For years since she had joined the SWP, Grace had thought of herself as someone who did not profess any religion and, as result, she took no part in the religious devotions of the Catholic Church. With James's death she began reading Catholic literature again, coming to the works, including those of St. Thomas Aquinas, with what she described as a "new understanding."[11] As she grappled with these spiritual stirrings, Grace realized that she "wanted to return to religion" but that she "had quite a sense of guilt about it." She later explained that "I thought I was seeking personal satisfaction and betraying the movement." She spent months struggling with her feelings. In May she began meeting with Father Leonard Cowley, then the young pastor of St. Olaf Catholic Church in downtown Minneapolis.[12] Founded in 1940 to "be a living sign of the presence of Christ in the heart of the city," St. Olaf's was considered by its first pastor, Father James Coleman, "an ideal field for making converts" with its downtown location. Standing on the corner of Second Avenue and South Eighth Street, St. Olaf's "became an oasis for many who had nowhere else to go."[13] It was here where Grace found her way back to the Catholic Church.

But Grace did not make her intentions known until June 18, when she officially resigned from the SWP in a letter to James Cannon. Prior to that communication, she carried on her business as usual in the party.[14] She even had been nominated by the SWP's National Committee at its September 1951 Labor Day Plenum to run once again for the vice presidency of the United States alongside Farrell Dobbs, who was picked to run for president. Although the nominations had to be ratified by delegates at the national convention in July 1952, party locals and branches around the country had already begun petition drives to get the candidates on the ballot.[15] It was full steam ahead with the Dobbs-Carlson ticket until Grace made her shocking announcement.

In the letter to her old friend and comrade Cannon, Grace wrote, "This is to announce my decision to resign from the Party and to ask that my name be withdrawn as the Vice-Presidential candidate. I am planning to return to the Catholic Church and it will be immediately clear to you and to the other National Committee members that I would be unable to serve as a candidate." She then hinted at the months-long struggle she had just endured, telling Jim, "I hope that you will believe that this was not an easy decision to reach. One does not break with comrades of sixteen years standing for light reasons but I believe this is the only path for me to take."[16] Grace later told the *Minneapolis Star* that she also called Jim and that "he asked her to reconsider." He then flew out to Minneapolis to try to change Grace's mind.[17]

Jim initially met Grace at St. Olaf's in Father Cowley's office, but then the two went to a nearby saloon where they spoke privately. Despite all his efforts to convince her otherwise, including pointing out his understanding of the Catholic Church as the "most reactionary and obscurantist force in the entire world," Grace would not budge. Cannon was concerned on multiple levels. First, he was deeply saddened and worried about the loss of his good comrade Grace. But he was also thinking about the repercussions for the party of her leaving. After meeting with her in Minneapolis, Jim called New York to report that "she has told the priest she is not going to give any information against us" and that "she still believes in socialism and is against capitalism and is not going to make any scandals against us at all." The Minneapolis branch members had gotten wind of Grace's decision, and Jim planned to meet with them to make sure morale remained, as Henry reported it to be, "unimpaired."

Cannon was in damage-control mode: "Our objective in the whole thing is to prevent any publicity before the convention or during the election campaign." Thinking ahead, he argued that "after the convention when another candidate is nominated, then any publicity will be a localized affair—she is no longer vice-presidential candidate."[18]

Cannon was hoping to wait until the party's convention in July to discuss the issue fully with delegates from around the country, but Grace's decision made the front page of the *Minneapolis Star* on Sunday, June 30. Jim quickly wrote to all SWP locals and branches reporting that the members in the Twin Cities were "an inspiration" to him in their commitment to the party: "There is not a single defection or sign of weakening anywhere in the party ranks." He also reported that the comrades there planned to send twenty delegates to the convention—including Dorothy—to show their continued loyalty. Jim included a copy of the article that he had prepared for the *Militant* to explain to the SWP membership Grace's decision to leave.[19]

The article, "How We Won Grace Carlson and How We Lost Her," appeared in the July 7 issue of the *Militant* and laid out Cannon's interpretation of her defection. He dismissed Grace's explanation that her decision was based on a "question of 'philosophy.'" Instead, Jim portrayed Grace as a woman who had been ground down by years of political repression and finally broke under the pressure. "Grace Carlson is a victim of the reactionary atmosphere in general and the witch hunt in particular," he argued. "Her sudden action in resigning from the numerically small and persecuted Socialist Workers Party for the rich and powerful Catholic Church, is only the final effect of the many successive blows of persecution, poverty and discrimination which had been inflicted upon her during the long time she fought on the side of the poor for the great ideals of socialism." Jim was correct in noting the political repression that Grace had experienced over the years, from the 1941 Smith Act trial to her year in Alderson prison in 1944 to the various manifestations of the Second Red Scare she experienced first-hand, including being a member of an organization on the attorney general's list and facing challenges to getting her name on the ballot in her later campaigns. But Cannon's characterization of Grace as a victim—as someone who "didn't answer my reminders [of the evils of the Catholic Church] with any argument or justification, but with the bitter tears of a defeated and broken woman"—dismissed her return to the Church as merely an excuse made by a "tired" woman who was looking for an "escape."[20]

In writing his narrative this way, Jim was able to treat Grace sympathetically, if condescendingly, as a victim of the same capitalist and reactionary forces that the SWP struggled against. It also allowed him to indicate to the party members that the fault here was with Grace's inner weaknesses in the face of such reaction, not with the program of the party. Because Grace made it clear in her interview with the *Star* that she wanted "it understood that I'm not becoming an informer on my friends of many years" and because, as Cannon noted, she "did not express any differences with the party program nor grievances against its people," he did not attack her on political grounds.[21]

The arguments laid out by Cannon in this article were also articulated by him in a statement that had been quoted by the *Minneapolis Morning Tribune* on July 1. In the aptly titled article "Priest, Party Clash on Mrs. Carlson," he and Father Cowley presented very different interpretations of Grace's decision to leave the SWP and return to the Church. If Cannon used Grace and her story to make a larger point about the embattled place of the SWP in Cold War America, Cowley held up Grace's reconversion to communicate a bigger message about the Church and faith in the modern world. Cowley noted how he had "been seeing Mrs. Carlson for the past six weeks," and he insisted that he could "affirm that her return to the church has been determined completely on ideological and theological grounds." He acknowledged that "she is undoubtedly a liberal and so will remain," explaining that she had "deviated from the church's time-honored teachings only because she was rightly concerned with the most liberal ideas of humanitarianism and wrongly concerned with the notion that the Catholic church censured these concepts." Cowley's interpretation was only partly correct, however. Grace was more than just liberal, and the Church had certainly censured socialism. That condemnation, no doubt, had influenced her earlier choice to leave the Church. For Cowley, who was concerned with helping Grace redeem her soul by her returning to what he understood to be the one true Church, Grace had merely erred temporarily and would be welcomed back by a loving and forgiving God who had been waiting patiently for her to knock on his door again. "Her faith has glowed like an ember throughout the past 16 years and has recently broken into a flame," he said. "I am happy that she has returned to her God."[22]

Like Cannon's interpretation, Cowley's contained a kernel of truth. Grace not only had experienced the reactionary forces of American politics for many years during her career in the SWP but also had moments when her faith flickered as she confronted those challenges. The pull of Grace's faith, despite her leaving the Church, was particularly noticeable during her years in prison. Acknowledging these ties is not to diminish her insistence that she had no religion during the time she remained outside the Church, but rather to reveal the complexity of her political and spiritual consciousness in that same period. In June 1944, Grace wrote Dorothy that "it really took a special effort of the will not to pray when I was alone here, feeling frustrated at not being able to do anything positive toward helping" with Henry's recovery from a ruptured appendix.[23] Two months earlier Grace had sent a note to Gilbert in which she recognized the pull of the Catholic faith on her, explaining,

> You will be surprised to learn that I attended High Mass this morning. Don't attribute this to any sudden conversion, though. I was invited to go to hear the Easter singing by the choir director who also teaches the music appreciation class which I attend. Except for a few funeral masses, this was the first mass which I've heard for seven years. There is a terrible lag between a human being's intellectual convictions and her emotions and feelings! Although I no longer have any belief, I was deeply moved by the service this morning—the more so, of course, because I was lonesome and the music brought back memories of far, far happier days.[24]

Chalking up her spiritual stirrings to "emotions and feelings" that were distinct from her "intellectual convictions," Carlson resisted any solace they might bring her as she reasserted her lack of religious belief. Years later, when she began to reflect on her father's death and how Marxism was no longer providing her with all the answers, Grace embraced her faith again.

Perhaps drawing on her readings of Aquinas, she found ways to reconcile that faith with her intellectual convictions.[25] The day after she formally resigned from the SWP, "The ban of excommunication, automatically placed on Trotskyites by the Church then, was lifted . . . and on Friday she went to communion for the first time in 16 years."[26] But Grace emphasized again how she wanted people to know "that I hadn't changed my political ideas, and it is still very important to me that people understand that I changed my religious attitude, not my politics."[27] The *Minneapolis Morning Tribune* reported at the time, "She has not left behind her deepest economic and social convictions which motivated her through her political career. She still is opposed to capitalism and United States participation in the Korean War."[28] And as Grace later explained, "I did remain a Marxist in my own mind."[29]

Grace's insistence in 1952 and for decades after that her choice "wasn't political at all and I resented [it] terribly when anybody tried to make it that" was rooted not only in her understanding of it as a truly personal and spiritual decision but also in her awareness that other former Communists-turned-Catholics had politicized their experiences during the Cold War years in ways that she did not want to follow. In her interview at the time with the *Minneapolis Star*, Grace explicitly said she refused to become an informer or to write books "like Budenz." And in her interview with Ross over thirty years later, she recalled how when she left the SWP, "That was the time when Elizabeth Bentley . . . Is that the name, Bentley? A couple of people had left the Communist Party and had returned to religion . . . and they were going around giving speeches and all this type of thing. Somebody got in touch with me, wanting me to do the same thing, but I refused absolutely."[30] Given the repressive climate of the Second Red Scare in which she made this decision, Grace's actions were principled and brave. Because she had not rejected Marxism and still valued her comrades in the SWP, even though she knew she could no longer socialize with them, Grace could not approve of nor place herself in the same category as Budenz and Bentley, who had become infamous in left-wing circles for betraying their comrades in the CPUSA.[31]

Louis Budenz was "a baptized Catholic who graduated from law school in 1912" and served as the "publicity director of the American Civil Liberties Union" before joining the CPUSA in 1935 and becoming managing editor of the *Daily Worker*. He broke with the party in 1945, returning to the Catholic Church with the spiritual guidance of the then famous radio priest, soon to be television sensation, Monsignor Fulton Sheen. Budenz initially took a teaching position at Notre

Dame. But he then cooperated with the FBI (which had been tipped off to his reconversion by Sheen) and began a "long and controversial career as an anti-Communist speaker, writer and government witness." His testimony during the 1949 Smith Act trial of eleven CPUSA leaders was essential to the success of the government's case, and by 1950 he had developed the reputation in Washington "as the nation's leading expert on Communism," who would testify before House and Senate committees investigating Communist infiltration of the government. Budenz also published an autobiography and other sensational accounts of his time in the Communist Party.[32]

Unlike Budenz, Elizabeth Bentley was not raised a Catholic. From a family with deep New England roots, Bentley attended Vassar College as an undergraduate but remained a lonely outsider for much of her life. According to her biographer, Kathryn S. Olmsted, Bentley's need for acceptance among her peers more than any deep ideological commitment contributed to her entry into the Communist Party in 1934 after her graduate study at Columbia University. By 1938 she had moved into the party's underground to become a courier in a Soviet spy ring, largely because of her romantic relationship with one of its key leaders in the United States, Jacob Golos. Bentley soon was charged with overseeing certain key contacts in the ring. After Golos's death in 1942, and because she feared for her life as she became a liability to the NKGB, she walked into the FBI's field office in New York in November 1945 and began talking. The information she provided during that interview and before HUAC in 1948 fueled government investigations into numerous alleged Communist spies in the federal government, including Alger Hiss, Harry Dexter White, and Nathan Silvermaster. Bentley also testified in the Rosenberg case. As she struggled to rebuild her life after the CPUSA, she was encouraged by Budenz, whom she had known in the party, to convert to Catholicism, which she did in November 1948, also with the aid of Sheen. She, too, wrote a sensational autobiography about her time as a spy.[33]

Bentley's and Budenz's defections and subsequent informing (and public testimony) helped fuel the Second Red Scare and aided the federal government in its investigations of Soviet spies and in its prosecution of Communist Party leaders.[34] Grace did not want to follow in their footsteps. Although she, too, like Budenz and Bentley, was guided back to the Church by a priest who, like many bishops at the time, communicated with the FBI in support of a common anti-Communist mission, Grace resisted the pressure to inform.[35] Unlike Budenz and Bentley, Grace had never engaged in espionage and, although she left the SWP, she did not fully refute her political beliefs; she remained a self-described Marxist who opposed capitalism. In addition, she did not believe there was anything criminal about those beliefs or her comrades' behavior that warranted her informing in the first place.

On the day she met with James Cannon at St. Olaf's, Father Cowley "advised S[pecial] A[gent] William P. Effertz that he had a meeting in his office" with them both. Grace did not know about Cowley's contact with the FBI, but she later noted that she "was not surprised to receive calls from the FBI and the Immigration Service, who expected me to cooperate with them."[36] The pressure began almost immediately after she announced her decision to leave the SWP. In an INS report from 1954, the investigator noted that "Special Agent Nugent advised that that agency [the FBI] has been attempting to cultivate Mrs. Carlson for the same purpose [to inform] since her defection from the SWP in June, 1952," but that she "has steadfastly refused" and "was not cooperative." After an agent interviewed her directly in April 1954, his report concluded that "Mrs. Carlson refused to cooperate with this Service as an expert witness or as an identifying witness" and that "she has steadfastly refused to cooperate with the Government to the extent of testifying against her friends." The report also noted, "Mrs. Carlson stated that she left the SWP solely for one reason, and that was the absence of God in their program." Although she "showed some willingness to cooperate to the extent that she would give general well-known history of the organization and its founding," Grace was deemed by the investigator as unlikely to "change her attitude toward testifying in the near future."[37] Grace corroborated the impression of the INS agent when she later explained the position she took in the face of this pressure to inform: "I never worked with the Justice Department or the Immigration [and Naturalization] Service. They also wanted me to report on whether people like John Jenasko [sic] were party members because they were ready to deport him because there were problems with his citizenship but I never testified." She clarified that "I would tell them if somebody were <u>not</u> a member, you know, if I could help in relieving this person. There were people who were what we used to call 'sympathizers,' but people from the FBI . . . thought maybe they were members. If I had a chance to clear their names legally I would do that. But I never testified ever in this whole thing."[38]

As the INS and FBI records reveal, "this whole thing" went on for quite some time and both agencies continued to pressure Grace for several years after she left the SWP. In addition to dealing with this harassment, Grace had to grapple with being blacklisted. She could not return to the Department of Education after the controversy that led to her resignation in September 1940 and to the purging of Rockwell several months later. Now that the United States was in the full throes of the Second Red Scare, with the war in Korea raging abroad, anti-Communist sentiment was running high at home. Because she had been a well-known figure in the Twin Cities, especially since the extensive coverage of her 1948 vice-presidential run and the reports on her defection from the SWP in 1952, "No employer would touch the controversial Grace Carlson of the headlines."[39] She needed to rebuild her life without the network of comrades who had been so central to it for the past twelve years.

* * *

By the time she made the decision to leave the SWP, Grace knew that she would have to break with her dear comrades. "I have appreciated the friendship of the Minneapolis members and will not forget you singly or collectively," she wrote them at the time of her departure, "but I know of the logic of politics, so I do not expect to be able to continue these friendships in the old way."[40] Even though she knew that she would never inform on her party friends, she also recognized that it would be difficult for them to trust her. And because so much of her social life had been connected to the party, she knew that she was closing herself off to that world too. There would be no more informal gatherings around the coffee pot or Grace's famous lunches at headquarters, no more strawberry festivals at White Bear Lake, no more holiday parties or late-night get-togethers at Dorothy's house. One informant for the FBI reported in 1963 that after Grace left the SWP, "She never returned to party headquarters for even a visit nor did she associate with party members after this with the exception of her relatives the Schultzes." Two other sources informed the FBI that Grace "had no dealings with the local S.W.P. since that time."⁴¹ The *Minneapolis Morning Tribune* reported that "Mrs. Carlson's parting with her Twin Cities Trotskyite friends occasioned more sorrow than bitterness on both sides."⁴²

Particularly painful for Grace was the initial estrangement from Dorothy. Grace later recalled how "another problem I had is that my sister stayed in the party. She didn't leave when I did and had nothing to do with me for two or three years."⁴³ An FBI agent who interviewed her in 1963 explained how Grace said that "immediately after her defection from the SWP in 1952, her relationship with her sister and family was quite strained." These must have been very difficult days for Grace, and for Dorothy, who had been practically inseparable all their lives. Grace admitted, "I had a tough time when I first left the party because I had no friends anyplace." Several years would pass until, as an FBI source noted, she began to "visit the Schultz home with more frequency" because "there was more or less a mutual agreement not to discuss politics or religion." And even then, according to the informant, "the main purpose of the visit was to enable Mrs. Carlson to visit the Schultz children."⁴⁴ It would not be until 1963, after Dorothy and Henry left the SWP, that the family would truly be reunited.

Grace had also cut herself off from Ray Dunne, but, unlike her relationship with Dorothy, hers with Ray would not be healed. An FBI informant reported in 1963 that "there has never been the slightest indication that there was ever any association on a personal basis or otherwise between V. R. Dunne and Mrs. Carlson after her defection in June 1952."⁴⁵ Grace and Ray, who had for so long been comrades and lovers, had now definitively split. Ray's private response to all of this has not been recorded, but FBI files reveal some of his actions in the wake of Grace's leaving in which he was focused on minimizing the fallout on the party. After Grace announced her departure, Ray and Dorothy signed a "confidential directive [that] was circulated to the SWP members in the Twin Cities area" calling for a membership meeting on June 24, 1952, and describing Grace's exit as "a serious crisis" that had "arisen in the work of the Party." When Ray was contacted by a reporter from the *Minneapolis Star* the next day and asked about Grace's defection, he "refused to comment."⁴⁶ At the convention in New York in July, Ray finally spoke openly about Grace's withdrawal and was reported by an

FBI informant as having said that "the best thing for the party was to forget it" and move on.⁴⁷

It is difficult to know precisely whether Ray and Grace broke things off as a couple before or right after she left the party and, if before, whether that breakup influenced her decision to leave. Given the nature and greater frequency of the arguments the two were having during the late 1940s as reported in the FBI files, and the impressions of party insiders at the time, it seems likely that the breakup came first. In fact, some Trotskyists claimed that Ray broke up with Grace and that that "was the real reason that Grace left politics, not her becoming religious." Those party members, who were very upset over Grace's leaving the SWP, blamed Ray.⁴⁸ Such an interpretation dismisses her explanation for leaving the party. It also assumes that her connection to the SWP was primarily maintained through her romance with Ray and thereby downplays her own contributions as an organizer, political candidate, and National Committee member, as well as her other (platonic) connections with male and female comrades. Perhaps her breakup with Ray contributed to her decision to leave the SWP, but there were clearly other significant factors too.

One of those factors was Grace's desire to reconnect with God. Although she never explained it this way, her search for the preternatural may have been connected to her realization, after the breakup with Ray, that she could not find true happiness in the mundane alone. As she explained to a priest friend many years later, it was the need for the transcendent that led her back to God and the Church. She noted that "I have been deeply concerned with the problems of human beings for over thirty years while I was in and out of the Church. I would still be out of the Church, if I had been able to find a true spiritual satisfaction in human relationships alone." Over the course of her life, she had come to learn that "human beings—even the best and bravest—fail one. If there is no Perfect Being, Who can offer perfect love, then one's search for love and understanding becomes a mockery."⁴⁹ With that realization she began extensive conversations with Father Cowley. He explained to her that she did not have to choose between her God and her "opinion on social problems so long as it doesn't conflict with moral principle."⁵⁰ And with that clarification she concluded that she could not but return to the Church.

It was not an easy reconciliation at first. Grace not only was cut off from her many close friends in the SWP (including Dorothy and Dorothy's family) but also was back in a Church that contained many right-wingers. She had not abandoned her Marxist principles and now confronted a future without the robust political exchanges she had relished for so many years. Grace recalled how when she returned to the Church, "It was the McCarthy period and a lot of the Catholics that I met made me sick to my stomach." She remembered one evening at her cousin's house where she "couldn't take much of any part in the conversation" and "just sat there thinking to myself, 'What am I doing with these people?'"[51] But Grace stuck it out and quickly found more comfortable corners within the Church where she could simultaneously pursue her spiritual devotions and her leftist politics.

First, there was her parish at the time of her conversion, St. Olaf's in Minneapolis, where she began attending Mass daily. Over the years Grace also became good friends with priests there other than Father Cowley, in particular Father Michael McDonough, with whom she shared progressive political opinions and found more pleasant company than with her cousin's conservative cohorts.[52] In addition to St. Olaf's, there was the Newman Center on the University of Minnesota campus where Grace found initial support. In 1952 Father Cowley was the Newman Center chaplain. After Grace left the SWP, her only friends were, as she noted, "the few I had around the Newman Club."[53] Saint John Henry Newman was an Anglican vicar at St. Mary's in Oxford during the 1820s and an intellectual leader in the "Oxford Movement" that sought to reform the Church of England. He ended up asserting the "true catholicity" of the Roman Catholic Church and converting in 1845. The Newman Centers that were organized on US college campuses beginning in 1883 were named after him and were intended to provide a spiritual home for Catholic students at non-Catholic universities.[54] Grace found both spiritual shelter in the center at the U as well as her first group of friends after her leaving the SWP. In addition, it was the Newman Center that gave her a job when she was no longer drawing a paycheck from the party. She was hired "to catalog its library" and worked there from June until November 1952, earning $175 a month.[55]

In providing Grace with her first job after she left the SWP, the Newman Center was functioning in a way that was not unusual for organizations associated with the Catholic Church. As Ellen Schrecker has argued, the Church "operated an economic and institutional safety net for repentant former Communists" during the Cold War years. Not only were the more well-known defectors, like Budenz and Bentley, aided with teaching positions in Catholic colleges but Grace, too, would be assisted in her readjustment to life after the SWP by Catholics and Catholic organizations.[56] As a blacklisted former Communist during the height of the Second Red Scare, Grace "had a hard time getting a job and tried several little things." She soon managed to secure something more permanent with the help of Father Cowley. "I was finally given a job [as a clerk] in the pediatrics department over at St. Mary's Hospital," she later explained.[57] Grace began this secretarial job in November 1952. Cowley had put her in touch with Sister Rita Clare Brennan, "the newly named personnel director of St. Mary's Hospital in Minneapolis." Sister Rita Clare knew about Grace's story from the local press, but was willing to give her a chance because she also spoke with fellow Josephites who had known Grace from her years at the College of St. Catherine and vouched for her.[58] Those women religious, who had been such a formative influence on Grace during her childhood and young adult life, again became important figures in what was becoming her life's second act. They extended to her not only kindness and acceptance when she sorely needed both but also employment and spiritual kinship.

The Sisters of St. Joseph had operated St. Mary's Hospital, then located at 2414 South Seventh Street in Minneapolis, since 1887. In the early 1900s they established a school of nursing at the hospital to meet the growing demands for more, and more technically skilled, nurses.[59] Grace worked in the secretarial position in the pediatrics department from November 1952 until August 1955, when "she was transferred to the Training Division of the School of Nursing" at the hospital. There she served as the school's social director. Mary Liber, who became the assistant director of the Training Division in 1957, told FBI agents in 1963 that when Grace first began working at the nursing school, she did not teach. "There appeared to be some reservation on the part of the management at the hospital to have her on the teaching staff," the agent noted in his report, "in view of [Grace's] known and publicized communist background." So although the Josephites in the Twin Cities welcomed Grace back among them, they initially proceeded with caution due to the political climate of the Second Red Scare, which had not fully eased by the late 1950s. The FBI report noted that "Mrs. Liber stated that it was not felt by any of the staff members at the time that [Grace] was not capable or that she might inject the Party line, but she was denied the opportunity to teach in view of the hospital's vulnerability to criticism."[60] Although they may have been willing to give Grace a second chance, the women religious were not certain how parents, alumnae, and donors might react to her presence in the classroom.

Although it may not have been the most intellectually stimulating position, Grace threw herself into her new job. As social director of the nursing school, Grace tapped into both her years of experience as a public speaker and her background in high school and college drama clubs. In December 1955, students at St. Mary's staged "The Enchanted Christmas Tree," which Grace directed. The following year they put on a version of Dickens's *Christmas Carol*, and Grace took the director's chair once again. In April 1957 she wrote her own skit, "The Mad Bomber," which was staged as part of the program to welcome incoming freshman.[61] Never one to sit still or do the minimum amount of work required, Grace also created her own space for intellectual engagement when she began to give public speeches again. This time, however, she was not presenting herself as an SWP candidate. In April 1956 she delivered a lecture entitled "Return to God" at the hospital. In December she spoke on "The School as a Learning Community" at St. John's University and on "The Paradox of Communism" at the University of Minnesota.[62]

That latter speech, along with the "Return to God" lecture, were ones Grace would deliver many times before different audiences over the years after she left the SWP. Although her notes for the "Return to God" speech are not among her papers, there are letters expressing the thanks of the groups before which she delivered it. Once again Catholic organizations provided Grace with support. In the fall of 1953, she spoke before the 4th Degree members of the Knights of Columbus as well as the members of the St. Paul and Minneapolis Serra Clubs, a lay group dedicated to promoting vocations to the priesthood and religious life. She gave the same speech in February 1956 to the Women's Confraternity Club of St. Cecilia's Church in St. Paul and in May 1957 to the Catholic Daughters of America's communion breakfast.[63] Grace also gave "The Paradox of Communism" lecture multiple times. In addition to her delivery at the U, she gave the speech before the Catholic Nurses of St. Joseph's Hospital in February 1957, the Sociology Club at St. Thomas's College in March 1957, and Maryhouse (a Catholic Worker house) in June 1957.[64]

Although she tweaked her notes for each venue, the core message of this lecture remained the same. Grace argued that there was a paradox of communism in that the follower adhered to a belief in materialism and not God, yet also remained dedicated to "a cause outside himself and a willingness to suffer privations and lose his life for the cause." At the same time, many Christians "cling to life and material possessions." Having "lived in both worlds," Grace presented herself as someone who "could help to interpret the paradox of communism." She urged her Catholic audiences to think of the group and not get too caught up in personal piety. She encouraged them to discuss big ideas, including the most pressing social and political issues of the day like the "H-bomb, race questions . . . internationalism." And, at the same time, she called on them to "be witnesses. To be doers and not hearers only," as they drew on Catholic thought and the Holy Spirit to solve those problems. Grace was no longer preaching socialism as the only road to peace, but a modern, engaged Catholic activism.[65]

By 1957 Grace had demonstrated by her actions that she had definitively severed her ties with the SWP. She was building a new life for herself that centered on the Catholic Church. She attended Mass daily, dedicated herself to her job as the social director of the nursing program at St. Mary's Hospital, and shared her unique insights as someone who had returned to the fold with fellow Catholics on a lecture circuit of faith-based organizations. Grace had made a good impression on her colleagues at St. Mary's and was invited to teach classes in social studies and psychology. As one FBI agent noted, "It is reported that the general feeling at the hospital is willingly to accept her for what she is now and not to be concerned overly much with her past."[66] On April 20 Grace signed her first annual contract to teach in the Department of Nursing at the College of St. Catherine (CSC), which had taken over the full degree program from the hospital's school in the 1940s. She was to begin on June 1 and started out in her new role as an instructor at $330 per month.[67] By February 1958, her supervisor, Sister Mary Jane, recommended her for a raise to $340, citing her excellent teaching ability and "her spirit of cooperation and loyalty," which were "a real stimulus to students and faculty alike."[68]

Even before she began her new teaching career, Grace was thinking and speaking about education. Two of her public lectures, "Marks of an Educated Woman" and "The School as Learning Community," expressed ideas that became essential to Grace's approach to teaching and mentoring. In "Marks of an Educated Woman," which she delivered to nursing students in 1956, she urged her listeners to "discard the idea that you don't need book learning to be a good nurse and a good mother. Ignorance never helped anybody!" She insisted, instead, that students must cultivate love of wisdom and the courage to seek it, humility, generosity, and an awareness that "no man is an island." Her practical advice for intellectual development included many of the things she had done herself all her life, like "extra-curricular reading, lecture-concert series, activity programs—intellectualized." She also listed "special groups; poetry reading; music appreciation; journalism; letter-writing [and] literacy contest[s]."[69] In "The School as Learning Community," a speech that she gave at St. John's University for the Regional Conference of Young Christian Students in 1956, Grace emphasized the importance of the "life of the mind" and the need to educate students who could become leaders. Her prescription was to engage in "great dialogue" about ideas, not idle chatter about "hi-fis—dances—boys," and to confront the forces that threatened the rights of others, including "anti-Semitism, Jim Crow, Nationalism, greed, anti-unionism." Grace also argued that as "propagandists for Christ," Christian students should direct their intellect to the glory of God—specifically by respecting and working to protect the rights of others—as they sought to "restore all things to Christ."[70] In these speeches Grace voiced several themes that she returned to during her years at St. Mary's, including the need for all women (and men) to have a broad liberal arts education, even if they were training for a technical career; the importance of lifelong learning and the development of the intellect; and the application of that learning to engage in and to change society as a gospel mandate.

Shortly after Grace was hired to teach, the nursing school's full degree program was moved again from CSC into a reorganized St. Mary's Hospital School of Nursing. In 1957, the dynamic forty-one-year-old Sister Anne Joachim Moore was called back from her assignment in

North Dakota to become the first director of the new school. Before she joined the Josephites in 1949, Moore had earned a three-year diploma in nursing from the original St. Mary's Hospital nursing program in 1937 and served as a nurse in England during World War II. On the GI Bill she earned her BA in nursing in 1946 and, after joining the Josephites in 1949, finished a law degree in 1950. As she took up the directorship of the new St. Mary's Hospital School of Nursing, Moore also completed a master's degree in education from the University of Minnesota. She implemented her new credentials immediately on the job as she and the faculty reorganized the school's curriculum "away from the apprentice-type training of the hospitals and toward a broader education for nurses."[71] Grace transferred with other faculty members from the Nursing Department at CSC to the new St. Mary's Hospital School of Nursing and became a close colleague of Moore's. The two energetic and committed women became the brains behind the founding plan for what became St. Mary's Junior College.

Before Grace and Sister AJ wrote what became known as the St. Mary's Plan, Moore "began exploring the idea of a 'single purpose' junior college for nursing education." She had read about the impending demand for college education as the baby boom generation matured, and she seriously considered establishing a program for an associate's degree in different healthcare fields. Moore also wanted to build the two-year junior college on the "open door" model of the Carnegie Commission of Higher Education, i.e., a college that would serve students who could not attend traditional four-year schools "whether because of inadequate preparation, cost or geographic distance." In this way, the student body would be distinct from that at CSC. In her thinking Moore was in line with contemporary ideas circulating among those who would support President Lyndon Johnson's War on Poverty and Great Society reforms to expand economic opportunity. But Moore's desire to serve students who were "disadvantaged by poverty, racial prejudice, physical, psychological, and educational" disabilities also came from "her congregation's historical commitment to caring for society's outcasts and those without power." Grace, who was educated by Josephites from elementary school through college, shared in this vision of caring for the "dear neighbor."[72]

In 1963, the St. Paul Province of the Sisters of St. Joseph approved Sister AJ's request to plan the new junior college. Moore recalled how "as I formulated the idea of St. Mary's Junior College, I often talked over ideas and plans with Grace, a responsive, indeed, eager participant."[73] The two women worked on the founding document, known as the St. Mary's Plan, which they released in 1964. In the document Sister AJ and Grace praised recent advances in technical education but argued that such education needed to consist of more than just vocational training. Their vision was one of the "student as a learner, not as a worker." Their idea for the new junior college was to be one in which the "students in technical programs are urged to develop a sense of social responsibility" not just pursue their own self-advancement. Central to that vision was a program of liberal studies that "helps to free our technicians from what might become a too-great concentration on limited concerns of a specialty" and to allow for a "greater sense of social responsibility."[74]

Sister AJ and Grace thus also maintained a focus on the new school's larger faith-based mission. In the plan they argued, "For all our technical students, Man is made the focal point of their studies in technical and general areas. In the philosophy of this Catholic college both the Man who serves and the Man who is served are esteemed because every Man is believed to have a divine dimension. A basically important objective of the college is based upon this Judeo-Christian principle: 'To develop a person assured of the significance of spiritual values strongly imbued with a desire to serve God and his neighbor.'" Chief among the goals for St. Mary's Junior College were "to develop a member of the health team who is convinced of the importance of treating the 'whole man'" and "to develop an individual genuinely sensitive to the rights of others." Ultimately their vision was one in which, through the technical and general educational requirements of the new college, they would prepare nurses for their "immediate goal" of a career in a health field, but that goal was also to be "presented as an opportunity to develop his God-given talents and to utilize them in the service of man."[75]

For some observers, the ambitious educational vision in the St. Mary's Plan may seem at odds with the intended student body of disadvantaged students if the assumption was that those students would want to focus more on vocational training for real-world results. Grace, however, disagreed and was often heard to say, "There is nothing too good for the workers!" That imperative came both from her Marxist and her trade union background (which included her early commitment to workers' education as a member of the St. Paul Trades and Labor Association) and from her own life experience as a working-class girl who made good via the educational opportunities she was afforded by the Josephites. She and Sister AJ wanted to educate the whole person and open students up to the possibility of a richer life in mind and spirit that would be turned toward bettering society and, ultimately, serving God in serving others.[76]

Peter D'Heilly, who began teaching at the new St. Mary's Junior College (SMJC) during the summer of 1965 and became good friends with Grace, noted that "one could not be a faculty member of SMJC without accepting and championing the SMP [St. Mary's Plan]." D'Heilly recalled Grace's influence in helping make the plan come to life on campus. As a "promoter of SMP," he noted, she "was a force to be reckoned with as a colleague." Grace became a "mentor and friend of the [general education] faculty," which D'Heilly helped lead once he became associate dean of general education in his second year at the college. "We had many faculty who worked hard to promote non-traditional liberal arts coursework which had SMP as its focus." Grace and Sister AJ "were a team" in this work of seeking "ways to further the goals of the SMP."[77]

Bill Morgan, who had completed his coursework for a PhD in American Studies at the University of Minnesota in the spring of 1966, was hired to teach at SMJC that same year. He experienced first-hand both the success of the St. Mary's Plan in action and Grace's strong personality in supporting it. Bill and Grace attended faculty meetings together during which she expressed her "very strong views about curriculum and mission." He remembers her as someone who was "strong-willed in her opinions about educational values and objectives," sometimes to the point of being abrasive. But Bill "tended to look aside from that because [he] always sensed there was a lot to learn from her." Bill also valued Grace as a friend and mentor. It was Grace who pushed him to complete his dissertation when, under the pressure of teaching full-time, he felt himself floundering.[78] Her support and the general spirit of academic life at the college made Bill feel at home. "Of all my teaching experience, St. Mary's offered teachers and students alike a wide latitude of freedom of thought—spiritually, politically, and socially," he later noted. "I think I was the only Protestant on the faculty," Bill remarked, "but I was treated like one of the family."[79] Grace's presence and influence were an important part of that experience.

* * *

For Grace, working at SMJC became one of the focal points of the new life she had built for herself since she had left the SWP in 1952. Not only had she thrown herself into writing the St. Mary's Plan with Sister AJ and into supporting the creation of the new junior college, but she also developed professional and personal ties with many of the women religious who were her new colleagues. The Josephites were one part of the new network that sustained her in these years. Grace found venues other than SMJC in which she broadened her personal and intellectual engagement, too, including St. Olaf's parish and the Newman Center. At those Catholic institutions, Grace volunteered her time and talents in various ways and built new friendships with priests and lay people as well.

Grace's connections with women religious included not just Sister AJ Moore, with whom she worked at SMJC, but also several other sisters at the college and in her parish during the late 1950s. Her correspondence with them is not extensive, but it reveals the nature of the relationships she had with them. Grace engaged with some sisters, like Sister Fides, on a mostly professional basis, communicating about upcoming classes and course plans. She also traveled with some of the sisters to Philadelphia in April 1959 for the National League of Nursing convention. With others, however, she had a more personal connection, receiving notes in which the women religious sent their prayers for her health when she was ill and thanking her for flowers she had sent them when they were not well or had a special anniversary to celebrate. Sister M. Germaine of the Religious of Our Lady of Charity of the Good Shepherd (RGS) appreciated how Grace and Father McDonough remembered her on her silver jubilee and noted how much she treasured them both as an "inspiration of selflessness and generosity." She also praised Grace for her commitment to tending to the needs of others in her volunteer work running weekly discussion meetings at the Home of the Good Shepherd, a halfway house for wayward girls run by RGS. "Only God can reward you for all that you are doing for us and for His Little Ones and we love you!" Sister Germaine later wrote Grace a get-well card in which she noted, "I think that you are too self-sacrificing and do not think of yourself at all and so have overdone." In the many short notes Grace received from these women religious, there was a common theme: an appreciation of Grace's thoughtfulness, selflessness, and hard work in her interactions with them and with the institutions where she worked or volunteered.[80]

One of the places where Grace continued to spend time even after she began her new teaching career at SMJC was the Newman Center at the University of Minnesota. Her first connection to the center was Father Cowley, who was serving as its chaplain in 1952 before he was ordained bishop in 1958. Father George Garrelts also got to know Grace through her work at the Catholic student center. He recalled meeting her when she first came to the Newman Center in the summer of 1952 and was working in the library. The two maintained an intermittent correspondence over the years. Peter D'Heilly recalls how Grace also "cooked many an outstanding meal for [the center's] cafeteria." She sometimes half-jokingly complained about Garrelts's exploiting her culinary talents, referring to him as "his Lordship." Garrelts, for his part, thought of Grace as a "brilliant woman who prefers to do her own thinking" and as a "very fine person with a keen sense of responsibility."[81] She not only donated her time to the center with her excellent cooking but also made a monetary donation.[82]

Grace made something of a habit of giving her time, talents, and treasure to Catholic organizations. In addition to her volunteer work at the Newman Center, she also ran weekly catechism classes for disabled children at St. Olaf's. Drawing on her expertise in educational psychology and her seemingly endless reserves of energy, Grace organized and ran what her friend Father Michael McDonough jokingly referred to as the "Carlson School of Special Education."[83] He and Grace first connected at St. Olaf's during her reconversion in 1952 when McDonough was a young associate priest in the parish. They became good friends and remained in touch over the years when McDonough served as the chaplain to St. Mary's Hospital and later took a position as a religion instructor at SMJC.[84] He also corresponded with Grace from time to time, sometimes sending humorous notes with inside jokes about people in the parish or his and Grace's shared liberal Catholic positions.[85]

In addition to her activities at Good Shepherd and St Olaf's, Grace continued her public speaking engagements. In February 1958, she and Father McDonough participated in a rally at Cretin High School organized by the Archdiocese of St. Paul's Confraternity Center (ACC) on the theme of "Laymen and the Crisis of the Modern World." McDonough presented on "The Sacred Liturgy: The Indispensable Source of the True Christian Spirit" during the afternoon's general session. Grace delivered the keynote at the opening of the two-day rally the evening before. She had been invited by Rev. Raymond Lucker of the confraternity, who noted that her task would be to "point up the world crisis in which we are living, the urgency of the world situation and the place of the Christian Layman in the world." He believed that her "own reading and background and [her] personal experience" would "contribute a great deal to the talk."[86]

Grace's notes for this speech show how she drew from her recent experience of returning to the Church, specifically her recognition of the need for the transcendent to give meaning to one's life, which might otherwise be mired in the mundane. Beginning with commentary on the parable of the Pharisee and the publican, she argued that "hatred of pharisaical self-righteousness is deeply imbedded in our personal lives. But what of our social lives—our public lives—our national lives?" She noted that Americans tended to see virtue in our superiority as a first world nation and in our technological achievements, but that the "crisis in the modern world is that technological development is sought as an end in itself. That this secularist-materialist view of progress has become a religion competing with Christianity." While she acknowledged that even Pope Pius XII appreciated the potential of technology to free people from back-breaking toil and, thereby, enable them to have a deeper life of the spirit, she also warned that "'technological spirit' is a spiritual danger" when it restricted people's gaze to material things only.[87] In his thank-you note to Grace, Lucker noted that "the whole rally was a big success and its success was due in no small part to your presence."[88]

Grace's ability to inspire listeners "to serious thinking" on the subjects about which she spoke contributed to the many invitations she continued to receive during the late 1950s. In addition to her participation in the ACC rally in February, Grace delivered speeches for members of the Knights of Columbus and St. Helena's Cana Club, as well as for students at Cathedral High School in the fall. As during the period immediately after her break with the SWP, Grace found intellectual engagement on the circuit of supportive Catholic institutions. In the thank-you letters from the organizers of the events at which Grace spoke was a common theme: appreciation for Grace's "wealth of experience" that she brought to her presentations. All believed that the listeners benefited from hearing her, and one organizer noted how he and the audience "gained a greater appreciation of our blessings and responsibilities as Catholics" from her speech.[89] The time that Grace spent speaking to these groups was thus as meaningful for them as it was stimulating for her.

But it was through the connections she made at SMJC, St. Olaf's, the Newman Center, and the Home of the Good Shepherd where Grace rebuilt her world of friends. While she got intellectual stimulation from lecturing before different audiences and from teaching at St. Mary's, her personal satisfaction came from the time she spent with her new colleagues and friends. As she had done at the Minneapolis SWP headquarters, Grace used her cooking skills to build connections. Peter D'Heilly fondly recalls how her "friends benefited greatly" from her talents. "She provided excellent soups to people who would return the containers. She brought treats to share at lunch. She joked a lot about her creations," including the famous "chocolate pudding to the fourth power." Grace not only brought her delicacies to work and to places where she volunteered but also invited her friends into her home for memorable dinners. Father Garrelts took the liberty of sending a paella recipe to her in advance of his next visit in his thank-you note after one such dinner. And Peter recalls how "liquor and wine were part of the feast. Grace's weakness was gin martinis." The only meal he remembers not going off well was a "tomato aspic pie" that had to be "washed down" with strong drink.[90]

Central to these gatherings was Grace's husband, Gilbert. As Peter notes, "To be invited to her home was to partake of the wonderful camaraderie of Grace and Gilbert" along with the amazing food.[91] The couple's reunification was a gradual one that began after Grace left the SWP in 1952. In her interview at the time with the *Minneapolis Morning Tribune*, she noted that she and Gilbert were "seeing each other again." After being apart for so long—and only having been together as a married couple for a few years before the lengthy separation—she and Gilbert needed time to reconnect. "I guess we've got to get to know each other all over again," she commented.[92]

Gilbert was still residing at 1370 Goodrich Avenue in St. Paul when he and Grace began to reconnect. He had moved back into that home with his natal family after he and Grace separated. In 1940 Gilbert shared the house with his parents, Edward and Ida Carlson, along with his Uncle Amos and cousin Amos and his maternal grandmother, Augusta Tessier.[93] By 1952, when he and Grace began seeing each other again, Ida had other ideas for her son's future. Even before Grace and Gilbert separated, she had had concerns about her son's wife. Grace recalled how Ida considered her "unladylike . . . for being more active and talking so much and running for office." Now, after Grace and Gilbert had been separated for over a decade—and Grace had been convicted of a federal crime and served time in prison—Ida was hesitant to support the reunion. "I had difficulty there," Grace recalled, "because his mother wanted him to stay home." Ida even called Father Cowley "and told him she thought this [reunification] was wrong." But, as Grace noted, Cowley "scolded her about not respecting Catholic marriage and all this type of thing" and so she backed down from her opposition.[94]

Soon Grace and Gilbert were fully reunited as husband and wife, sharing an apartment together in Minneapolis. Gilbert continued to work full-time as a lawyer in his practice downtown while Grace began teaching at St. Mary's. He also became involved in the nursing school. In April 1963, "It was he who went to the Minnesota Secretary of State to register the articles of incorporation of St. Mary's Junior College," bringing his legal expertise to the aid of Sister AJ. He then became one of the first lay members of the Governing Board of SMJC, where he served as secretary and became a "wise counselor for the president and administrative staff for many years." Gilbert even taught a course on the "Legal Aspects of Nursing." He was appreciated by the many friends he made at the school for his "gentlemanly joviality, his wit, and his engaging conversations."[95]

Gilbert soon became a "familiar fixture on campus." On the days he wasn't there for meetings, he would often pick up Grace to drive her home. Bill Morgan remembers how "the softest feelings I ever saw Grace showing was when she talked about Gilbert."[96] Because neither Grace nor Gilbert spoke about the process through which they found their way back to each other, it is unknown exactly how that took place or if there were other bumps in the road besides Ida's initial opposition. By the early 1960s, however, the two were a beloved couple in the SMJC community and among their many friends whom they hosted at dinners in their home. Raymond Schultz, Grace's nephew, remembers visiting his aunt and uncle when he was a tween: "They were together and from my knowledge had always been so."[97] However they managed it, Grace and Gilbert had healed the many years of separation that they had experienced and began a new life together as a married couple.

* * *

When Grace decided after many months of soul searching to leave the SWP in June 1952, she walked away from what had been her whole world for over a decade. She left her work as a state organizer and National Committee member. She would no longer run for public office as a Trotskyist. All of her friends and comrades in the movement and the wonderful social engagements they shared were now no longer a part of her life. And, particularly painful to her was her estrangement from Dorothy and Henry and their children. Yet Grace found a way to rebuild her life as she returned to the Church that had been, as she explained, "the center of my life as a girl."[98] With the spiritual guidance of Father Cowley and the trust and support of Sister Rita Clare and, later, Sister AJ and other women religious and priests, she not only secured a job but also carved out a career for herself at St. Mary's Junior College. Tapping into the Catholic network of organizations, Grace found outlets for her creativity and intellectual energy as she volunteered at St. Olaf's and the Home of the Good Shepherd and delivered lectures to various lay groups around the Twin Cities. And with her characteristic energy and 110 percent commitment to her efforts—along with some well-placed offerings of soup and chocolate pudding—she made new friends among her colleagues. In addition, she successfully reunited with Gilbert and built a new life with him as his wife. But Grace's story was more complex than just coming full circle. She may have returned to the Church and to her marriage, but she did not abandon her Marxist principles or her commitment to supporting women's self-advancement. She would continue to pursue her vision of social change and feminism through her speaking engagements, her volunteer work, and her mentoring of female students at SMJC through and beyond her retirement from teaching in 1979.

6

"Carlson's Continuing Commentary"

By 1963 Grace had created a new life for herself at St. Mary's Junior College as a respected professor and a beloved colleague. She had also successfully reunited with Gilbert, and she would soon fully reconcile with Dorothy. During the years when she taught at SMJC, and as she remained active in its alumnae association after she retired in 1979, Grace found a new political voice for herself. She became a Catholic activist who continued to embrace elements of her Marxist beliefs as she took advantage of opportunities at St. Mary's to "teach and practice social justice."[1] She called for a Catholic lay apostolate that engaged as a Christian duty with the pressing issues of the day, including the efforts to end the war in Vietnam, to promote women's self-advancement, and to halt nuclear proliferation. Echoing facets of the pre–Vatican II liturgical and Catholic Action movements, along with the Church's social encyclicals, Grace made the case for that active Catholic lay apostolate before the reforms of Vatican II. But, echoing her Marxist past, which she never fully shed, she also remained critical of what she saw as misdirected individualistic acts that did not strike at the center of economic and political power or that alienated the masses. She not only talked the talk in her speeches and correspondence but also walked the walk in her work with women students, whom she mentored to be independent, well-educated citizen leaders, and in her lay activism in her parish and other volunteer outlets.

As Grace's political consciousness evolved in these years, drawing on both her Catholic and her Marxist roots, her personal life became focused not only on her colleagues at St. Mary's but also, once again, on her sister, Dorothy. The two rebuilt their sisterly bond after Dorothy and Henry broke with the SWP in the early 1960s. Grace resumed her role as the doting aunt to Dorothy's children and provided a sympathetic ear when her sister needed to express her worries about the struggles that tore at the fabric of the Schultz family. Grace and Dorothy also continued to share their interest in promoting political change, with Grace now acting more behind the scenes in her educational work at St. Mary's and Dorothy taking to the front lines in various progressive causes after she and her family moved to Madison, Wisconsin, in the early 1960s. After Gilbert's death in 1985, it would be in Madison, with her sister, where Grace would spend her final days.

* * *

When Grace left the SWP in 1952, she reintegrated herself into a Catholic Church that was undergoing changes in its understanding of the liturgy and of lay participation in that liturgy and in the wider world. As she underwent her reconversion, Grace concluded, in part because of the changes happening in the Church, that she could maintain her political commitments to social justice and accept her faith again. During the years that followed her return to the Church, her religious and political consciousness took the shape of a Catholic activism tinged with Marxist insights.

In the many speeches she delivered from the late 1950s through the late 1960s, Grace repeatedly called for a Catholic lay apostolate that engaged with the concerns of the secular world. Beginning as early as 1957, she spoke about the "general agreement" in the Church "that every one should be a lay apostle" but recognized that this goal remained a challenge for many. The "feeling of responsibility—of community—of oneness with members of the Mystical Body [was] not deeply felt," she noted. Referring to the "theology of the laity" that she had been reading, she told her audience of Catholic nurses, "The Incarnation sanctified human affairs. To do God's work in the world." She called on the nurses to "participate fully in parish life" at the same time as they focused on their careers.[2] Grace recognized the challenge of living one's faith in the world, both because of the competing demand that work placed on people's time and because of the difficulty some had with really feeling "one with the Mystical Body." Speaking to a group of Catholic students in 1958, Grace asked them if they were truly living out their faith's call to use their particular talents in the service of God and others, "even with squares [and] jerks." Urging them to "lead a life of grace" in which they "dare to be different" by avoiding gossip and entering into substantive conversations about pressing political concerns instead, she called on the students to be "propagandists for Christ." Grace argued that "everyone in every group in which you work and play should know that you are a Catholic. And not just a Catholic, but a Catholic apostle."³

In these speeches, Grace was grappling with an understanding of the Catholic faith that was at once focused on the transcendent and the temporal—on loving and serving and uniting with God *and* with humankind. She acknowledged the "tension between vertical movement toward God and horizontal movement of human interest and natural knowledge," but she saw a resolution of that tension in lay Catholic activism.⁴ In her "Christianity and Communism in the World Today" speech, which she delivered several times between 1958 and 1963, Grace called for a "spiritual revival" among Catholics, who needed "to show forth Christ in our lives" when ministering to the poor in the world as a just alternative to acquisitive capitalism. Christian capitalists had lost ground to communism in certain poor countries, she argued, because they had been "more capitalist than Christian" and were not responding to the needs of the people. She drove home her case in another speech in 1965, quoting Rev. Peter Riga, that "to be a Christian is not purely to serve God, but it is also a dynamic social ethic, a service to mankind; it is not merely a theology, but also an anthropology."⁵

Grace (and Riga) were expressing ideas about the Catholic faith that had been in development during the decades leading up to the Second Vatican Council. In the context of the United States, those ideas were rooted, in part, in changes in the makeup and posture of the Church during the early to mid-twentieth century. Beginning in the 1920s, the Church in the United States moved from the enclave status of its immigrant phase, with a separatist mentality that had developed in the face of Protestant hostility, to a more assimilated, middle-class, educated Catholic community. By the 1930s the faithful of this Church were participating more fully, not just in the liturgy but also in broader society, as evidenced in their New Deal–era involvement in or creation of organizations like the Association of Catholic Trade Unionists (ACTU) and the National Catholic Welfare Conference (NCWC).⁶

The drive for greater participation both in the Mass and in the secular world was fueled by the impact of the liturgical movement, the Catholic Action movement, and the concept of the Mystical Body of Christ. The liturgical movement emerged in the late 1920s out of the writings of Virgil Michel of the Order of Saint Benedict (OSB) and other Benedictine monks at St. John's Abbey in Collegeville, Minnesota. It was also communicated around the country by priests who embraced the movement's message of promoting "forms of parish worship that emphasized congregational participation over contemplation."[7] Educational conferences and publications also spread these ideas among an increasingly educated laity. The movement translated into greater lay participation in the Mass, even before the switch to the vernacular during Vatican II, with the aid of missals and the dialogue Mass, in which the congregation joined in the liturgy by singing and reciting certain prayers rather than sitting in passive silence.[8] This increased participation in the Mass drew from and dovetailed with Pope Pius X's 1905 call for Catholics to receive communion more frequently (weekly, even daily), and embraced the notion that through the consumption of the body of Christ in the Eucharist, Catholics became part of the Mystical Body of Christ. With that understanding of connectedness to the Church and to one's brothers and sisters in the Church came a related sense of duty to act in the world. It was in this context in 1931 that Pope Pius XI defined Catholic Action as "'the participation of the laity in the apostolate of the hierarchy.'" That movement, under the direct supervision of the hierarchy, "invited Catholics to engage in their faith in socially oriented ways" and resulted in the plethora of Catholic organizations that mushroomed in subsequent decades, including the Catholic Worker movement. That organization, established in 1933 by Dorothy Day, promoted the living out of Jesus' teachings on caring for the poor and advancing peace through both its urban houses of hospitality and its farm communities. In advancing a social apostolate for the laity, the pope and the religious and lay intellectuals who promoted it always emphasized its theological basis. As Katherine E. Harmon explains their position, "One could draw 'all things to Christ,' the central message of Catholic Action, only by committing the self to Christ in the heart of Catholic life, the sacrifice of the Mass."[9]

Before Grace left the Church in the late 1930s, she was exposed to these ideas through the faith formation she had received under the Josephites in St. Paul as a girl and young woman during the 1910s and 1920s. When she returned to the Church in 1952, she became familiar with these concepts in a new way. By then the idea that each person was part of Christ's Mystical Body had already begun to "pervade popular spirituality." The focus on the Mystical Body that became especially prevalent by the 1940s and 1950s supported lay people's attempts to witness their faith in the world.[10] The logic of a "spirituality in harmony with contemporary life" was popularized by the activities of Day in the Catholic Worker movement, which became even more well known among the laity with the publication in 1952 of her autobiography, *The Long Loneliness*. For more intellectually inclined Catholics, like Grace, there were also the writings of the Jesuit priest and scientist Pierre Teilhard de Chardin, which inspired many during the late 1950s. He too emphasized the connection between faith and action in the world, and Grace, who had several of his books on her shelves at home, referred to his works in her speeches during the early 1960s.[11]

After her return to the Church in 1952, Grace also made direct connections with Benedictine monks at St. John's Abbey and St. John's University in Collegeville, who were promoters of the liturgical movement. Her initial contact with the monks may have been made through Benedictines who came from St. John's to assist with the weekend masses at St. Olaf's in Minneapolis, which was Grace's parish at the time she returned to the Church. Or it may have stemmed from her speaking engagements at St. John's University in the mid-1950s. However it was initiated, Grace soon established a correspondence with Godfrey Diekmann, OSB, and Emeric Lawrence, OSB. With Father Emeric she forged closer ties, as her more frequent and detailed letters with him between the late 1950s and early 1980s attest.[12]

Grace had thus tapped into broader currents flowing in the Catholic Church in the decades before Vatican II that stressed the importance of the laity as brothers and sisters in Christ who had a mandate to do God's work in the world. Those currents "sowed the seeds for the frenzied activity that followed the Second Vatican Council."[13] The council, which was held at the Vatican from October 11, 1962, to December 8, 1965, was convened by Pope John XXIII to bring the Church into the modern era. Out of these meetings, the twenty-six hundred bishops, who had gathered along with a few hundred expert advisers, produced sixteen decrees dealing with a wide range of issues. Two of the decrees that had a direct impact on expanding the activism of the laity within and outside of the Church were *Lumen Gentium* (The Dogmatic Constitution of the Church) and *Gaudium et Spes* (Pastoral Constitution on the Church in the World Today). *Lumen Gentium* "stressed that the church is a pilgrim people, not an unchanging institution." It developed the notion of the Church as the People of God based on the belief that "by virtue of baptism, every Christian is called upon to minister in the name of Christ."[14] *Gaudium et Spes* stressed that the faithful had to "'decipher authentic signs of God's presence and purpose'" in the world and become "'witness to Christ in the midst of human society.'"[15]

By 1965, when the council concluded its business, there were many areas in human society where Christians felt the need to bear witness to their faith. For some, like Day, the challenges of poverty remained a focus of their efforts. For others, like Father Francis Gilligan and the priests he trained in St. Paul and like many women religious from around the country, the black civil rights movement demanded their participation as they fought for the social and legal equality of their brothers and sisters in Christ.[16] Grace, who had long fought for social justice for workers, the poor, and African Americans, continued to champion these causes. As her work with Sister AJ Moore on the St. Mary's Plan showed, she believed in shaping the mission and curriculum of SMJC so that it served as broad a socioeconomic constituency as possible. On campus she remained active in the NAACP. And her continued volunteer activities at the Home of the Good Shepherd also demonstrated her ongoing commitment to young wayward women.[17]

In addition, Grace used her voice as a layperson in her new parish, St. Leo's in St. Paul, to educate her fellow parishioners about questions of inequality. She and Gilbert had moved from Minneapolis to St. Paul during the mid-1960s and made St. Leo's their new spiritual home. In February 1969 Grace wrote a letter to a parish priest responding to his criticism of the "alleged 'negative' character of the Prayers of the Faithful" that she had been writing as a member of St. Leo's liturgy committee. Arguing that the intercessions that the priest had written over the preceding few years tended towards "too much of a 'my country right or wrong' approach to be comfortable for me," Grace refuted his critique of her contributions. "To refer to the 'negatives' about our society—racial prejudice, poverty, undemocratic practices—and to pray that we may overcome them seems more honest. It also seems like a better teaching method for upper middle class parishioners, who might be happy enough to forget the 'negatives' in this country."[18] In this remarkable letter Grace expressed her continued commitment to social justice that she understood as intricately connected to her Catholic faith. And she referenced her equally strong commitment to education as an important means to advance such causes.

For Grace and many other Catholics, calling for an end to America's involvement in the war in Vietnam became another important way to witness their faith in the world. The United States first became involved in Vietnam by providing financial support for France's reimposition of its colonial control over the Southeast Asian country after World War II because of America's emerging foreign policy of containment. After France's defeat at the hands of the nationalist and Communist Vietminh in 1954, the Geneva agreement established what was intended to be a temporary partition of Vietnam until a national referendum in 1956. But the United States soon propped up the regime of Ngo Dinh Diem, the leader of the non-Communist Republic of South Vietnam, who refused to take part in a nationwide election. The United States continued to supply Diem with financial support and military advisers even after the eruption in 1960 of full-scale attacks against his regime by an indigenous rebellion. Viewing the insurgency through the Cold War lens of containment, the United States remained committed to halting what it insisted was an attempt by North Vietnam to spread communism to the South. President Lyndon Johnson deepened US involvement when he deployed US military forces in 1965. Troop numbers escalated from fifty thousand in 1965 to more than five hundred thousand by the end of 1968, with no end in sight. As news reports emerged of the continued viability of the enemy despite these increases and of the brutal tactics used by American forces—including the burning of Vietnamese villages and the use of napalm—many Americans began to question the purpose of such a counterrevolutionary war and to denounce their country's complicity in such heinous acts.[19]

The movement that developed to oppose the war was diverse in its makeup and tactics. Pacifists from organizations like the Fellowship of Reconciliation and the Committee for Non-Violent Action found common ground with Old Leftists in the SWP and younger activists in the party's Young Socialist Alliance, along with members of civil rights groups, like the Congress for Racial Equality and the Student Non-Violent Coordinating Committee, and groups emerging from the

New Left, like Students for a Democratic Society and the Student Peace Union. College campuses, including that of the U, became hotbeds of the teach-in movement that began in March 1965. But protestors also coordinated marches in Washington, DC, beginning in April 1965, that included thirty thousand people, and demonstrations that expanded to cities around the country, including San Francisco and New York in 1967, with upwards of four hundred thousand people turning out in Manhattan.[20]

In a commencement address she delivered in August 1965, Grace addressed the growing antiwar movement as a place where Catholics could demonstrate their faith. Arguing that "student participation in anti war demonstrations [is] legitimate," she called on the graduates to think about such civic engagement as flowing from their own moral code. Grace urged the students to "bear witness to the everlasting truth of these values not because someone else says that they are right but because you believe that they are right. This internalization [is] the authentic morality." Grace then reminded them, as they went into the world to begin their careers as nurses, that they "may dare to be different" by evincing their Christian faith in whatever they did.[21]

Exactly how to bear witness to one's faith while opposing the war became a bone of contention among those on the Catholic Left, and Grace found herself taking sides in this debate in her personal correspondence with her friend Father Emeric. "The Catholic Left" was the name given by the media at the time to a group of antiwar protestors, many of whom were Catholic and many of whom were also priests and women religious, but not all. These antiwar activists were inspired to oppose America's involvement in the war in Vietnam not only because of the call for social engagement found in the liturgical and Catholic Action movements and in the decrees of Vatican II but also because of Pope John XXIII's 1963 encyclical, *Pacem in Terris*, which they interpreted as an invitation to nonviolent civil disobedience in the aid of pacifism. Many also drew from the writings on peace and nonviolence by the Trappist monk Thomas Merton.[22]

After the US bishops came out in support of the war in 1966, many disappointed liberal Catholics looked elsewhere for moral leadership on the issue. By 1967 some in the Catholic Left came to believe that marches and demonstrations were not sufficient to stop America's war machine.

They began to take direct action by targeting draft boards and destroying draft cards to impede the functioning of the Selective Service. By pouring animal blood over the cards or by burning them with homemade napalm, the activists engaged in what they believed was a symbolic protest of the violence of the war itself. Catholic Left members engaged in such "actions" around the country, with major ones taking place in Baltimore in 1967, in Catonsville in 1968, in Milwaukee in 1968, and in Chicago in 1969. Among those involved in some of these bigger actions were the Berrigan brothers, Philip and Daniel, who were both priests. While some championed them as heroic, others had qualms about their tactics. Thomas Merton believed that even the destruction of property crossed the line and abandoned the commitment to nonviolence, while many in the student Marxist Left mocked those who engaged in the draft board raids as "mindless, moralistic masochists."[23] Grace, too, had her concerns about the direct-action tactics of the Catholic Left and expressed them in an exchange with Father Emeric.

In August 1970, shortly after Father Daniel Berrigan was captured by the FBI, Father Emeric wrote to Grace expressing his feelings of admiration for his brother priests who had put themselves on the line in their fight against the war and his sense of guilt for not doing enough himself. Berrigan had gone underground for months after he and the other Catholic Left defendants in the Catonsville Nine case lost their legal appeal. Grace wrote a lengthy response to Father Emeric in which she revealed her take on the direct-action protestors. "Now as to the Berrigans and their tactics," she wrote, "it's all right for you to be 'a little envious of their courage,' but you should be knowledgeable enough to be critical of their mistaken, individualistic, petit bourgeois approach to social problems. The enclosed clipping, recording a 91% opposition to draft office break-ins as a method of demonstrating against the war, offers solid evidence of the futility of their tactics." Grace argued that if one believed in advancing change with support of the majority of the population, then one's tactics needed to match one's goal. "Terrorist tactics, even if utilized by a poet-priest, alienate the majority. They win support only among the small minority who want to believe that gifted individuals can effect social change by individual acts of daring, rather than through the more laborious process of educating and propagandizing."[24] As the newspaper clipping Grace included in her response to

Father Emeric showed, she was not alone in condemning the "terrorist tactics" of the Berrigans. But her critique did not stem from a conservative reaction against such actions as disrespectful and unpatriotic, but rather from a Marxist one in which she sustained her opposition to the war and denounced the limitations of such an approach.

Allowing her Trotskyist past to come through in her analysis, Grace argued that "today's student and intellectual terrorists are very like the Russian Narodniki [sic] and the French anarchists of the 1880s," who became impatient with the masses and engaged in individual acts. She also referenced Lenin's critique of such "impatient leftist" actions in *Left Wing Communism—An Infantile Disorder*. Continuing to make her case for the need for more disciplined tactics that won the masses to the ranks, she ended her letter by arguing that "daily propaganda about the need for social change, winning hearts and minds to the Movement, and at the appropriate time, helping to organize the socialist forces—these are the important tasks, even if they seem unglamorous. To feel guilty about not doing enough is commendable, but to make invidious comparisons between the role of a teacher-monk and that of an individualistic political activist is wrong. One can be an avant-gardist without going to jail!"[25]

In response to Grace, Father Emeric brought up her past, specifically her Smith Act conviction and the time she served at Alderson. "Re: the Berrigans. O.K. You win, at least the first round," he wrote. "But I'd still like to argue a little. If you don't get mad at me, I recall to you that someone else went to jail for an ideal. Was there a difference?"[26] Grace's response was sharp and repeated her core critique of the draft board actions. "As to the Berrigans and going to jail for an ideal—there was a difference between our case and theirs," she insisted. "In our case we stressed the free speech aspect and won wide support among trade unionists, civil libertarians etc. We could not be charged with a bizarre example of deliberate lawbreaking—pouring blood over draft records—so bizarre and esoteric in its symbolism that workers would be turned away."[27]

In the notes for her speech, "Review of Catholics and the Left," which she delivered in November 1968, Grace articulated many of the ideas that she later expressed in her exchange with Father Emeric in 1970. She took aim at the broader New Left, including the activists in the Catholic

Left, and carved out her position as a Catholic radical with an Old Left approach. She defined herself as a "Christian against capitalism" who was "a propagandist for Christian socialism." And she explained that, as such, she was "prejudiced against those who muddy the waters by individualistic acts: demand dialogue in churches undemocratically; offend sensibilities by vulgar language; burn draft records or pour blood on them." She argued that the "basic error of New Left—Catholic or not is anti-intellectualism . . . 'I feel therefore I am,'" and contrasted that new movement to the Old Left of which she had been a part, in which "not to 'do your thing' but to do the thing that will advance the movement" was the focus in order to bring "an end to racial and social and economic oppression of man by man."[28]

Grace also openly expressed this criticism of the New Left to her students at SMJC in their discussions and debates on campus. Peter D'Heilly recalls her "barking and shouting at students who believed in the 'dawning of the age of Aquarius' and others who believed that progress and long awaited change would just 'happen.' She told them that revolutionary change was only won by enormous effort and never because people fought over 'two bit' issues."[29] Grace's view of the differences between the Old Left and the New Left was rather rigid and was biased in favor of the Old Left. It therefore ignored the connections that existed between the two movements that scholars are now coming to appreciate, both in terms of individual participants, like A. J. Muste and I. F. Stone, and in terms of organizations, like the SWP.[30] But for all these limitations, it captured a certain truth about the inherent tensions between the goals and tactics of the two movements.

Grace's Old Left perspective blended with her Catholic activism to produce the hybrid Catholic Marxist approach that she took to contemporary issues during the 1960s and beyond. Those included her reaction to Catholic lay activists within the Church itself. In May 1968 she declined an invitation by Dr. Robert Breitenbucher to join the Association of Christians for Church Renewal (ACCR), explaining that although she supported renewal in the Church, she believed that it was something that lay people, priests, and sisters needed to do together.[31] The ACCR was founded in St. Paul and Minneapolis in 1967 and in March of that year had "produced for Archbishop Leo Binz . . . an unsolicited report that recommended the convening of a lay congress and the division of parishes into 'neighborhood church communities' with greater lay oversight." Most of its members came from the middle class.[32] Grace wrote to Breitenbucher with her concerns over the "petty bourgeois" profile of the ACCR's membership. Admitting that she found herself to be a "petty bourgeois element these days," she argued, "I am enough of a Marxist to believe that you can't make a revolution without the support of the workers." She also complained about the ACCR's targeting of the bishop. "I am not primarily interested in taking power away from Bishops, but away from the big economic interests in the country—and their government."[33]

She made this same argument in two other letters. In one, to Father Emeric in 1968, she denounced "lay people and religious, who have just discovered social action and demand that all resources and energy of the Church be immediately translated into bringing a program of 'love' into social relations. Then with clenched fists and tightened jaws, they picket the Chancery office and demand of the bishops what they never had the guts to ask for from their own bosses in the Bar Association or the Medical Association or the Chamber of Commerce."[34] In the other, to Mary Berres, the executive secretary of the Catholic Interracial Council (CIC), Grace responded to a letter from the CIC to her parish social action committee asking for help with the archbishop's annual charity appeal. Grace explained that she shared the CIC's concern for the poor, "but I think that it is very naïve to think that the Catholic Church can solve the problem of poverty in this archdiocese or in any diocese. The Bishops of the Church do not have any real economic power in this country. Such power is in the hand of the 'economic royalists,' as the old phrase goes." She argued, "If the CIC members who are in the Chambers of Commerce, Manufacturers Associations, etc., would make an all-out demand on these organizations, I should see more sense to their protests. Although the Bishops are irritating to some of us, they are really just two-bit opponents in the basic struggle for social, political and economic justice—and some, like Bishop Shannon, are allies."[35]

Instead of joining the ACCR, Grace told Breitenbucher that she was thinking of setting up a *Slant* group, like the one in England. "I hope we can study the application of Marxism to Christianity and perhaps engage in some united-front efforts with other radical groups," she told him. This was not the only time Grace spoke admiringly about *Slant*.

She also referenced the organization and its manifesto in her "Review of Catholics and the Left" speech that she gave in November 1968 and in her "Contemporary Atheism" speech from April 1967. In the former speech, she spoke of *Slant* as an example of Christians against capitalism and in the latter as a movement within the Church that gave her "new hope" as a radical Catholic.[36]

Slant was a movement that was formed in 1964 among "a group of undergraduates at Cambridge University and their clerical advisors," who launched a journal of the same name in which contributors examined traditional Catholic theology "to promote the social goals of the Gospel." As Jay P. Corrin explains, "For them, these goals implied a socialist revolution." These young members of the Catholic Left in England, including Terry Eagleton, were among the first cohort from the working class to gain access to their country's elite educational institutions as a result of post–World War II reforms, and they brought their class-based experiences with them to "fill in what [they] felt was the missing political dimension of Christian renewal." As Corrin explains, their definition of Christianity "required an understanding of its historical roots. And if it can be recognized that Christianity is a revolutionary movement of liberation rather than a belief in abstract doctrinal statements—that is, a religion primarily concerned about a change in humanity's actual condition, which is, of course, possible only through political means—then it can be seen that Christianity is not incompatible with Marxism in the broadest sense" in its concern for the liberation of humanity and the creation of a community based on equality. Those in *Slant* rejected liberal models of reform and embraced Marxism because, for them, "It is only the political left that works against the status quo, which is promoted by undemocratic elitist social and economic forces that militate against the radical promises of a Christian transformation."[37]

For Grace, this approach to her Catholic faith and her activism in the world made complete sense. It also explains why she found Dorothy Day's movement "a little sappy" and of no interest to her in its personalized and decentralized approach to social ills, particularly its experiments with rural communities. Grace found ideological and spiritual brethren in *Slant* instead, with its focus on Marxist political opposition. Grace even began "a discussion with a number of selected students" and initiated a branch of *Slant* at SMJC among them and some faculty members.[38] In so doing she practiced what she had preached to Father Emeric: working to effect social change "through the more laborious process of educating and propagandizing."[39]

Taking a democratic approach to socialism was a part of that laborious process for Grace. In October 1963, eleven years after she left the SWP, she decided to seek a presidential pardon for her 1941 Smith Act conviction. According to the FBI agent who interviewed her as part of the process, Grace explained to him that "it has always been her desire to participate in the normal democratic procedures and particularly in the electoral contests." He also noted that "her inability to be able to vote as the usual citizen has been mildly embarrassing to her in her relationship with her students" because she "constantly encourages" them "to be good and active citizens and urges them to participate in their democratic duties in respect to the elections." She even organized voter registration drives on campus.[40]

After interviewing Grace's friends, colleagues, and neighbors, the FBI concluded that "CARLSON has had no dealings or apparent interest in SWP since defection and is a very devout Christian, who goes to church daily. She is reported to have led an exemplary life since 1952 and is considered unusually capable, charitable and of high moral standards and principles."[41] Most likely because of Grace's clear disaffiliation from the SWP, her reconnection with the Catholic Church, and the testimony of the priests and women religious on her behalf, President Lyndon Johnson granted her a pardon on October 20, 1965.[42] Grace finally had her civil rights restored and was able to fully participate in the liberal political order even as she continued to believe in the need to overthrow capitalism, now as a Catholic Marxist instead of a Trotskyist.

* * *

When FBI Agent Effertz interviewed Grace and her friends and colleagues in 1963, he noted that Grace had begun seeing Dorothy and Henry and their children again. By that time the Schultzes were living in Madison, and Dorothy and Henry were no longer active members of the SWP. That reality eased the reconciliation between the two sisters. As Peter D'Heilly recalled, "Their relationship somehow transcended Roman Catholicism and atheistic socialism. Grace at heart remained a socialist and the two sisters proved that blood is thicker" than water.[43]

Being there for her sister, Dorothy, and for Dorothy's children remained an important part of Grace's life that she was able to reconstitute after her sister left the SWP.

According to Dorothy it was internal friction within the SWP that led her and Henry to leave its ranks. Tensions had begun to emerge in the Minneapolis and St. Paul branches during the 1950s, when members, experiencing the pressures of the Second Red Scare, disagreed over organizational tactics. The party was also under severe financial strain resulting from declining membership. The "painful question of money" was just one feature of what Ray Dunne described in 1955 as the SWP's "modern dog days." With the aging of many of the party's most experienced cadres and with an "assist" from the FBI that continued to harass members, the SWP struggled to survive. By May 1955 the St. Paul and Minneapolis branches merged in an attempt to remain viable.[44] But the merger led to "spats and strains" that evolved into a "fratricidal internal conflict" by 1958.[45] Dorothy and Henry and their supporters from the old St. Paul branch chafed under what they felt was the too centralized approach of Ray Dunne and the Minneapolis cohorts.

Dorothy later explained that she and her supporters were used to having discussions at meetings involve everyone, but that after the merger the Minneapolis group insisted on having the executive committee direct things. Dorothy felt that decisions seemed to be made ahead of time, often coordinated by Ray, before subjects even got to the floor for discussion.[46] Although Dorothy later remembered the dispute that erupted in the branch as being one over the techniques of leadership, evidence from the period seems to indicate that it really was a question of who was in the leadership role. Dorothy and Henry had been used to running the show in the St. Paul branch. After the merger, they complained about what they now felt was the undemocratic approach of Ray's leadership. Internal party correspondence at the time between Carl Feingold, who was sent by the National Committee as an organizer to help settle the rift, and Farrell Dobbs, the party's national secretary in New York, hints at this more complicated picture and adds another dimension of criticism that was then leveled against Dorothy and Henry by the party center. Dorothy and Henry's objection to Ray's approach of organizing the branch business was recorded, but so too was Feingold's take on the Schultzes having formed a "clique" with Jean and Bill Brust and others in the branch that expressed "a softness and conciliatory attitude in the regroupment arena." That softness included a willingness to welcome other political groups to the party's labor forums, including representatives from the CP, so as to engage in a vigorous debate of current issues. Such a position, however, reminded Feingold of the Cochranites, a faction that had been expelled in 1953, in part for their "conciliation with Stalinism."[47]

Led by Bert Cochran, Harry Braverman, and "other tested cadres," the Cochranites, as they became known, believed that the SWP was too weak on its own to effectively counter the nation's repressive Cold War foreign and domestic policies, which were perceived as bringing the country closer and closer to fascism. Members of this faction offered a variety of alternative possibilities for finding other forums to overthrow capitalism, including entering the Communist Party (and eventually democratizing it) or orienting towards independent radical groups, including what remained of Henry Wallace's Progressive Party. Such strategies were deemed heretical by the SWP majority, including Cannon, who refused to "liquidate" the SWP or engage in conciliation with Stalinism. The disagreement ran too deep for reconciliation.[48] Feingold's hearing echoes of the Cochranites' positions in the Twin City situation may have been off the mark—there was never an equal political disagreement in the latter case—but it spoke to the wounds that the 1953 split left behind. The party center was concerned about the spats in the Twin City branch not only because they were undermining the leadership of the local and impairing its smooth operations but also because it worried about a rebel clique becoming the nucleus of a possible damaging faction.

The disagreements among the Twin Cities comrades, however, did not develop into a political split but were expressed in nasty personal attacks. Dorothy described the branch meetings during this time as "hellish."[49] The SWP's Political Committee (PC) was also not pleased with what was happening. After the party's national plenum, held in New York City in February 1960, the PC held a meeting with Henry (which was also attended by Carl Feingold) during which it instructed Henry to stop caucusing against the Twin City branch's leadership. It warned him that if he did not stop, the PC would bring charges against him and his group.[50] In the year that followed, Dorothy and Henry, who maintained their opposition to the branch leadership, essentially boycotted the branch meetings.⁵¹ Their son, Raymond, remembers that once his parents withdrew from active participation in the Twin City branch, it "resulted in me never again seeing many of the people who hung out at our house."⁵²

Dorothy and Henry still thought of themselves as Socialists and remained connected with the SWP as "members at large" when they left the Twin Cities in the fall of 1961.⁵³ One of the main reasons they moved to Madison was the job Dorothy had secured as the undergraduate librarian at the University of Wisconsin. After several years of what she described as restlessness, Dorothy had gone back to school, earning an MA in Library Science from the University of Minnesota. No doubt the tensions in the SWP Twin Cities' branch also contributed to the Schultzes' desire to relocate and start fresh. FBI files note how both Dorothy and Henry were dropped as National Committee members in June 1961 and, although Henry was subsequently elected as an advisory member of the National Committee, by 1964 they essentially had nothing to do with the party anymore.⁵⁴

Initially Dorothy set up the Schultzes' new home in Madison on 3128 Lakeland Avenue with Vincent and Raymond. Henry commuted to his job in St. Paul until 1962, when he was able to find work as an electrician in Madison and join the family full-time. The Schultzes then moved into their home on 2414 Willard Avenue. Jim, who was attending college in Minnesota, did not join the family at this time. Ann, who had left the family home in St. Paul during the early 1950s as a rebellious teen, ultimately ended up back in the family fold, first in St. Paul by the mid-1950s and then at the house on Willard Avenue in Madison in 1962.

Despite her criticisms of the party's effects on her family life as a child, Ann ended up joining the SWP during the mid-1950s. At first she attended party socials and participated in the Marxist education classes Dorothy had held at the Schultz home in St. Paul, but by 1954 she was attending party meetings in the Twin Cities. In 1956 Ann spent the summer at the SWP's training school in New Jersey, located at its Mountain Spring Camp, seventy-five miles outside of Manhattan. There she met Tom Leonard, a party member from New York. He left his wife to be with Ann. The two wed in the fall of 1956 and lived for a year in New York City until they were transferred by the party to Minneapolis, where Tom worked as the educational director. In 1960 Ann and Tom were relocated again, this time to Denver, where he was to help lead its branch and Ann became branch treasurer. By August of 1962, however, their marriage began to fall apart and Ann filed for divorce. She traveled back to Madison with their two children, Laura (born in 1958) and David (born in 1962), and moved in with her parents, Raymond, and Vincent on Willard Avenue. Ann then matriculated at the University of Wisconsin in September 1962.[55] According to Grace, by 1963 Ann, too, had "become inactive in party affairs."[56]

A partial rapprochement between Grace and Dorothy had begun even before the Schultzes left the party, within a few years after Grace left the SWP in 1952. Raymond recalls how, when he and Vincent were about ten years old, they and their mother would go to Grace and Gilbert's home for visits. During these encounters, Dorothy sat in the kitchen talking with Grace and Gilbert while the twins sat in front of the TV in the living room. At Christmas time, Raymond fondly remembers receiving presents from his aunt and uncle, "almost always pajamas . . . for which I always wrote nice thank you notes." In exchange, he and Vincent would give Grace and Gilbert homemade pomander balls (oranges studded with cloves and sprinkled with cinnamon). "They loved these presents," he recalls, "and they were ones we could afford to make" because the Schultz family was on and off welfare at the time. Once Dorothy began working as a librarian and "had more money," Raymond remembers them getting "smelly soap (lavender)" for Grace and Old Spice aftershave lotion for Gilbert. When he was in his twenties, Raymond took Dorothy to St. Paul to spend Thanksgiving with Grace and Gilbert. By that time, Dorothy was no longer in the SWP. Raymond remembers that "some current topics might come up" in conversation but that "we never talked socialism" or about the past.[57]

Avoiding discussion about socialism or the past was one way the two sisters initially found their way back to each other. Especially when Dorothy was still in the SWP, such topics were too problematic to broach. Once she and Henry left the party, Dorothy and Grace found ways to share their enthusiasm for current events in a manner that did not undermine each other's viewpoint. They were beginning to leave behind much of the old dogmatism. Grace had come to recognize how she had become "terribly polemically-minded" during her years with the Trotskyists, noting that among her comrades, "Polemics counted more than the ideas in a sense. It wasn't just winning you over to socialism; it was winning you over to their branch of socialism." When she first entered the movement, she could not understand this position, or how "the polemics were just fierce and families were separated," as had happened between Ray Dunne and his brother, Bill. But later in her life, after she left the SWP and looked back on her own experiences in the party and on the estrangement from Dorothy, Grace came to understand the cost of such dogmatism.[58] She and Dorothy healed their relationship by coming to respect their differently motivated takes on contemporary issues. For Grace, this entailed her Catholic Marxism, which informed her activism in the form of her teaching and mentoring the students at SMJC, her involvement in the *Slant* group on campus, her volunteer work at the Newman Center and Home of the Good Shepherd, and, once she regained her citizenship rights, her participation in electoral campaigns as a voter. For Dorothy, that meant taking to the front lines of antiwar protests on the University of Wisconsin campus during the late 1960s and, later, providing financial aid and working for progressive political campaigns and strikes in Madison.[59]

The two sisters also rebuilt their relationship by focusing on family matters. A chief concern for Dorothy during the mid- to late 1960s was Henry. After the Schultz family moved to Madison, Henry found work as an electrician. But in December 1964, at the age of sixty-two, he sustained a very serious head injury on the job after falling off a scaffold onto a cement floor. The over-fifteen-foot drop nearly killed Henry. To relieve the pressure on his brain from bleeding, doctors had to drill three holes in his skull. According to Raymond Schultz, his father "recovered physically, but suffered from mental issues and depression" as a result of the fall, "mainly due to not being able to work again." The mental issues may also have been due to "long term effects of the head trauma he suffered in the accident," which were not fully understood at the time. Raymond recalls how his dad "slowly alienated most people he knew by constantly arguing with them about politics at first but then on to virtually everything."[60] Dorothy echoed this observation in her correspondence with Grace during this period. Even four years later, she noted how Henry "does get so patterned in sitting around the house, watching television, not having anyone to talk to." Dorothy became increasingly worried, and even urged Grace to intervene by asking her to write to

Henry with whatever insights she might have as a psychologist to help him overcome his antisocial behavior. "This is no responsibility of yours, I know," she wrote Grace, "and maybe it is too much time and effort for so little possible return. I suppose I am pushed by the fact that there seems to be so little left for him."[61]

Whatever responses Grace may have penned to her sister have not been saved in her papers, so it difficult to know how she felt about all of this. According to Dorothy, Grace had declined to speak to Henry about his troubles when he asked her in person during a trip to the Twin Cities why he may have been having difficulty getting along with people. Perhaps not wanting to upset Henry further or maybe because she was afraid to make things harder for Dorothy, Grace uncharacteristically held her tongue. It was after this encounter that Dorothy asked Grace to write to Henry with her thoughts, but there is also no record of any such letter. Despite these silences in the archives on Grace's part, Dorothy continued to pour out her heart to her sister. Grace provided an outlet for Dorothy to express her worries as Henry's condition began to tear her family apart.

Soon things with Henry worsened; "his rigidities and occasional flareups" added tension to the house, which was already under strain due to the problems Ann was struggling with during these same years. Dorothy worried that Laura, Ann's young daughter, was "afraid of him at times."[62] Henry's drinking did not help things. His constant arguing, Raymond recalled, "eventually led to my mother forcing him out of our family home." Henry then "lived in different rooms around the eastside" of Madison for a while until he was hospitalized for minor surgery. Henry never recovered and passed away on September 24, 1969. Raymond believes that his father "died because he was so unhappy that he lost the will to live."[63]

During the same period when Dorothy wrote to Grace about these struggles with Henry, she also expressed her deepening concern about her daughter, Ann. After divorcing her first husband, Tom Leonard, and returning from Denver to Madison in 1962, Ann remained in Wisconsin for a few years with their children, Laura and David. She remained enrolled at the university, where she studied journalism and met Gene Galazan, a fellow student who was active in the Young Socialist Alliance. Ann seems to have been drawn back into the SWP orbit, despite her mother's objections. Ann and Gene also joined in protests that were held on the University of Wisconsin campus against the Vietnam War in 1964 and were married in 1966. When Gene got a job as an instructor at the University of Southern California in 1967, he moved to Los Angeles. According to FBI reports, Ann went with him at first and connected with the local SWP branch there. But by July 1967, she returned to Wisconsin and told her brother Jim that she was planning to file for divorce.

Dorothy took in Laura and David when, in early 1968, Ann decided to move back out to California in the hopes of securing a teaching job.[64] Originally she planned to send for Laura and David in June, once the school year ended, but she soon wrote to Dorothy that she was not ready to take them. Although Dorothy does not spell out Ann's struggle with alcohol in the letter to Grace in which she says it was a good thing that Ann recognized her own limitations with respect to the children, it becomes clear in other correspondence that her daughter was fighting this demon along with her failing marriage to Gene. Dorothy told Grace, "I am very distressed by the extent of her maladjustment and pain—a maladjustment which seems to have started at such an early age that I cannot see how I can avoid sharing responsibility—whether I know why or not." Keeping all of this from Henry while he was still alive and grappling with his own problems since his head injury added to Dorothy's pain.[65]

Grace provided emotional support to Dorothy during this trying time. After Ann returned to Madison and was hospitalized for her drinking, Dorothy wrote to Grace describing how she was beginning to resign herself to the limits of what she could do for her daughter. Dorothy and her sons met with Ann and the medical team in what Dorothy called a "very bruising session." During that intervention, the doctors apparently emphasized what they felt was Ann's tendency to run home whenever things became hard for her. Dorothy rejected this analysis, arguing to Grace, "There was some real misunderstanding of the economics of the group living at the house and more emphasis on some psychological reaction. No small part of this misunderstanding could come out of a failure to understand a radical past in which a more group approach to problems existed." Perhaps recalling the days when she struggled with Henry's appendix surgery and relied heavily on her SWP comrades, especially her sisterhood of female Trotskyists, Dorothy chafed at the doctors' critique of the group approach. Yet she also wrote to Grace, "For whatever it might be intended, it is clear that Ann cannot adjust within the framework of the family help as we have tried." Refusing to give up entirely either, she noted, "If there is anything which can arise in which we can help the children or Ann, I think we shall be eager to do it." She told Grace, "This is a bitter period, and I try to immerse myself in work or reading to keep from a sickness in my heart."[66]

But things seemed only to go from bad to worse. Three days after Ann was released from the hospital in Madison, she decided to travel to California again. On the way, she "had been terribly depressed, went out on a drinking bout on Saturday," after having been sober when she left the hospital, "had the money she had stolen from her, [and] was almost in pieces." Once in California Ann ended up in Gene's apartment, but he finally admitted that he "was not prepared to re-establish a home relationship." At the end of her rope, Ann decided to admit herself into Synanon during the summer of 1968. Founded by Charles Dederich in 1958, Synanon was one of the first drug rehabilitation centers in the country. Located in Santa Monica, it had "pioneered the idea of the ex-addict as drug counselor and of 'tough love' therapy" to foster "a culture of recovery." Before such institutions existed, the options for alcoholics and drug addicts were either the hospital (which Ann had already experienced) or prison. By the 1960s, Synanon received extensive positive press coverage in *Life* and *Time* for allegedly succeeding in keeping 80 percent of the addicts it treated clean.[67] Dorothy explained to Grace that Ann would be there for at least three or four months and that she and Jim and Vincent were all chipping in to cover her costs. Dorothy remained hopeful, telling Grace, "The only other step left was commitment." For the time being, Laura and David remained with Dorothy in Madison.[68]

In addition to being there for Dorothy as she grappled with these painful moments, Grace did what she could for Ann. Once her niece was settled in at Synanon, Grace sent Ann letters expressing her love and support and her sadness at hearing about her pain. She also sent small gifts when she could. In February 1969, Ann wrote Grace thanking her for the "beautiful red, blooming tulips" she had sent her for Valentine's Day. Ann also told Grace that now that she was at Synanon, her "pain was in the past," something she was coming to recognize in her truth-telling sessions of self-discovery at the center. But it was also clear from Ann's letter that, for whatever personal growth she may have been experiencing, she was becoming dependent on the sheltered "life style" at Synanon. She explained to Grace that they had "a whole way of life here that the society out there does not have," with "no wars, no physical violence," and "no prejudice, no discrimination of any kind" and that their "personal lives are not ruled by economic and material circumstances." She told Grace, "This is where I want to live. I find it more and more difficult to conceive of going back out there in that rat race." In part, what Ann was describing were the changes happening at Synanon, where, over time, the rehab center that had functioned like a commune was evolving into something more akin to a cult.[69] It was in this setting that Ann continued to struggle for many years to put her life back together. Although Grace and Dorothy were able to forge anew their bond as sisters through their shared concern for Ann (and for Henry), they ultimately were not able to solve the problems of either loved one.

* * *

Unable to save Ann from the pain that had contributed to her addiction and failed marriages, Grace remained concerned for her niece but was limited in what she could do to help her. Grace also remained concerned for the future of her young women students at SMJC, but for different reasons. Just as she had witnessed her female comrades in the SWP struggle to balance their work in the party and any paid jobs they had with their commitments as wives and mothers during the 1940s, so too did Grace see some of her former students grapple with similar challenges during the late 1950s through the early 1970s. But unlike Bea, Miriam, Dorothy, and Grace's other friends, who not only had their Trotskyist sisterhood to support them but also a Marxist feminism to inform their struggle, the SMJC graduates that Grace worried about did not. By mentoring them with insights that she also articulated in her speeches and by establishing a special emergency fund for those in need, Grace supported the professional success of SMJC's women students. In the context of her renewed Catholic faith, she articulated a justification for their careers as nurses who combined work with family and, in the process, modified her understanding of the feminist struggle.

Between the late 1950s and early 1970s in particular, Grace expressed concern for a pattern she was seeing among the women graduates from SMJC. Soon after obtaining their degree, enough of these women were dropping out of their new jobs as nurses when they married and had children to cause Grace to sound an alarm. These women's actions tracked those of nurses around the country after World War II and reflected changes in the profession. As demand for skilled nurses increased, employers dropped the marriage bar to hiring and so, even as younger, newly married nurses may have dropped out, many married women in their thirties whose children were school age or older returned to work to meet the demand for their skills. This trend of marrying young and entering or returning to the workforce over the age of thirty-five was true for women in the United States across the board during the 1940s, 1950s, and 1960s. Married women represented 20 percent of the nursing workforce during the 1920s, 42 percent by 1949, and 66 percent by 1966, but "older married women accounted most for the increase."[70] For Grace, the decision of younger women not to remain in nursing (or their inability to do so) once they married and had children was a problem: she argued in one speech in 1960 that if nursing school was just a way to spend time before marriage, that was "not the attitude of a professional woman," and it did "not deserve applause."[71]

For Grace, the imperative for women to engage in meaningful work that was independent from their role as wives and mothers came both from her own experience as a professional woman and from her renewed Catholic faith. Acknowledging that there were, of course, many historical and biblical sources that asserted the idea of female complementarity to men that had undergirded the notion that a woman's place was in the home, she rejected them and, instead, cited the ability of women religious and single women to succeed in their private and public lives on their own as evidence of women's innate equality. Drawing on the logic of Catholic Action, she also argued that the "creator must have endowed women with qualities of mind and soul to do his work," which included work outside the home that made a difference in society. Grace thus claimed both social and theological grounds for her assertion of female equality. She had become like other Catholic feminists, who "regularly explained their feminism in terms of their commitment to a gospel mandate for social justice, liberation, and radical equality."[72]

Grace's specific prescription for these young women to strike that balance between the demands of family life and work evolved over time.

Early on in her career at SMJC, in a speech she delivered in 1959, she argued that the "pressure of child-bearing and child-rearing may not permit women to do great creative work" or to take "jobs outside the home," and so she called for them to find other ways to "realize the potentialities of mind and soul," such as through volunteer work.[73] Not squandering one's education and finding an outlet for it in a way that would make a broader social contribution was her initial advice to her female students. In some ways this accommodationist position, in which the burden of adjustment was on the individual woman, echoed the advice she gave to Bea, Elaine, and her other SWP friends when she encouraged them to stay active in the party in whatever way they could, even as they struggled to balance the demands of marriage and children. But Grace's advice then also assumed that such accommodation was a transitional position, taken while the women worked to overthrow capitalism and thus ensure their eventual ultimate freedom. In 1959 she was not advocating that kind of revolutionary change to her audience of nursing students.

But just one year later, she articulated a different kind of revolutionary change. Most likely due to her years of working closely with the young women students at SMJC, Grace's approach to the challenges that women faced as they struggled to combine a career with family life shifted to include a demand for an accommodation from men and society as a whole too. In "The Professional Woman Today," delivered in 1960, Grace lamented the continued "long uphill climb for women" in the professions, where they were still mainly "concentrated in clerical jobs." Part of the problem, she argued, was women's failure to commit to careers and their leaving jobs for marriage because of society's expectations that such a choice was best for them and for their families. Grace rejected this thinking by questioning the idea that "dedication to family [had to] exclude dedication to profession" and by asserting that "major commitment to home and children should be true for men too" so that women were not forced to leave work and bear the burden of family life alone. And she condemned the "growth of 'momism' overprotectiveness" in childrearing, which impeded women's commitment to their careers, as unhealthy for both the mother and the child.[74] The feminism that Grace articulated here was different from the Marxist feminism she espoused during the 1940s because now she began to challenge patriarchal structures directly rather than only capitalist oppression.

She was not alone among women from the Old Left who came to such conclusions and began to connect and contribute to what was emerging as second wave feminism. Myra Tanner Weiss had done so in her critique of Evelyn Reed's and Joseph Hansen's positions during the Bustelo incident of the mid-1950s, and Clara Fraser broke with the SWP during the 1960s in part because of what she believed was its failure to address all sources of women's oppression.[75] Even though Grace had long severed ties with the SWP, she may have read Weiss's and Fraser's works and been influenced by them, but it is more likely that her critique of patriarchy came from her witnessing her married students' struggles after they graduated from SMJC. Her evolving feminist analysis led her to join with younger activists in the women's groups then developing at SMJC with which she became affiliated during the 1960s. Grace's broadened understanding of women's struggles through these experiences represented one connection between the Marxist feminism of the Old Left and the second wave feminism emerging during the 1960s and 1970s.[76]

In her call for men to make a commitment to home and children so that the burden of the work-life balance did not fall solely on the individual woman, Grace also echoed critiques of the gendered assumptions sustaining capitalist patriarchy that were being articulated among labor feminists in these same years. Those women saw the problem of the double day as something that could not be solved by individual women being forced to make personal accommodations to its demands. As Dorothy Sue Cobble explains, "Rather than adjust to men the issue was 'adapting the man's world to women'" in a way that "would involve the fundamental restructuring of the work world." As women in various industrial and service-sector jobs increased their ranks, they increased their numbers in their unions and pushed those unions to demand concessions to advance a fundamental restructuring that included things like the six-hour day, childcare facilities, equal pay, and maternity leaves.[77] Many nurses around the country had already made gains in these areas starting in the 1950s, when they were able to leverage the demand for their skills with employers to accommodate their needs as working wives and mothers. But even in this profession, as the numbers and Grace's observations show, married women with young children continued to face obstacles to fulfilling their careers and so it was mostly older married women who struck the balance. Even then they did so by using the justification of providing a vital service to society rather than that of meeting their own professional needs.[78] As late as 1972 Grace called for specific changes to assist women in their professional advancement as nurses that were akin to those demanded by the labor feminists during the 1940s, 1950s, and 1960s. In her speech "Women's Role," she argued that the way to secure women's equality was through their organized efforts in unions and "other groups for equal pay" and through more "women in politics!" where they could implement policies like "adequate day care centers etc." For Grace the imperative was now not only feminist but also Catholic: only through such organized efforts could women achieve "true self-actualization in the service of God and man."[79]

Beyond doling out advice in her speeches, Grace also worked with women students as their teacher and adviser at SMJC. In her words and in her deeds, she inspired many of them to think independently and to commit to their careers as nurses. Julie Ann Bloemendaal thanked Grace for helping her find the "starting place" in her life for which she had been searching. Joanie Machart wrote to Grace noting that "by your example you have guided me on the path of becoming, I hope, a good Catholic nurse and woman." Laure Campbell, who was a student at SMJC from 1970 to 1972, remembers how when she decided not to participate in the formal graduation ceremony, "Grace sat me down and asked many probing questions about my reasons, whether I meant to make a statement by not participating, and whether I had given sufficient thought to the matter." Laure recalls that "her goal was not to change my mind, but to help me identify the experiences, concerns and beliefs that led me to the decision." And in July 1970 Nina Leewright wrote Grace expressing her "sincere thanks for all your help & understanding during my 2 years at St. Mary's." She noted how "so often I never thought I would see graduation day" and expressed that she was "so very thankful for people like you who were interested in me as an individual with my worries & difficulties."[80] As she had done with her network of women friends in the SWP, Grace provided emotional support and advice to these women students. By taking them seriously as young women and encouraging them to stay on the path to their careers, she lived out her commitment to nurturing female self-advancement through education.

Grace also supported many students financially. As she neared her retirement in 1979, she wanted to do more to help with retention rates at St. Mary's. After talking with counselors on campus "who explained the many impediments to education: jobs, children, finances and family responsibilities," she decided to set up the Grace Carlson Student Emergency Loan Fund. The fund, which was established by 1982, provided "small, no-interest loans to pay a babysitter, fix a car, tide over the grocery budget, or remedy some other financial crisis." Grace argued at the time that she was motivated by recognizing that students at St. Mary's had "so much to think about, so many responsibilities." She acknowledged that "many are single mothers with children. I wanted them to have what I had—independence." Peter D'Heilly described Grace's motivation as "both Christian and personal. She had the means and was wont to share it." At its inception the fund was helping twenty-five to thirty students per month, and the director of financial aid at the time predicted that "over the course of their years at St. Mary's, nearly a third of the student body will take advantage" of it. She explained that "the typical loan is about $100" and that "most students pay their loans back within 60 to 90 days," but that they made a big difference in keeping the students on track. Grace was happy to do this for them. She reflected on her life and acknowledged how privileged she was to get a good education. "At a very early age, I was given the opportunity to develop independence of thought. Everyone should be able to do that."[81] Through her loan program she helped countless women do just that.

* * *

Although Grace and Gilbert both retired from their "'official' involvement with the college" in March 1979, Grace remained engaged in student life. One way she did that was through her creation of the emergency fund. In the fall of 1979, Grace also began her stint as an author of a column in the SMJC's newspaper, *Good News*, called "Carlson's Continuing Commentary." In her first installment, she explained that she was "still comfortably ensconced in Room D235 (next to the statue of the Sacred Heart) with the records and memories of a 24-year span of students at St. Mary's Nursing School and Junior College." From that office Grace planned "to visit with—and perhaps counsel—new students." She also announced that she would be working with the campus alumnae association. For the next five years she would thus remain connected to SMJC and pursue her interest in promoting women's economic and intellectual freedom.

In her "Commentary" column in *Good News*, Grace highlighted different female alumnae success stories. Among those she profiled was Joan K. Saari, a graduate of SMJC's Special Education Associate Program (a program that Grace had created). Saari worked at the Vineland center, "a healthsports center for disabled people." She also wrote about Rita Royayne, a graduate from St. Mary's School of Nursing in 1950 who had become, by 1980, the director of nursing services at St. Mary's Hospital.[82] Through these and other examples, Grace celebrated the success of SMJC's graduates and advocated the importance of education in getting those graduates to where they were. The articles were practical and inspiring.

In her work with the alumnae association, Grace not only engaged with the workaday duties of seeking continued financial support from graduates for SMJC but also attempted to inspire those graduates to take action in the world on pressing issues. A big part of her job in helping coordinate the annual alumnae day during the early 1980s was fundraising.[83] For Grace, however, an equally important task was crafting the content of the alumnae days. Grace helped organize events that reflected the interests of the former students and that also challenged them. Combined with the efforts of all the other faculty and staff committee members in alumnae relations, her work resulted in successful reunion events during the early 1980s. They included one in 1984 that showcased Dr. William Hedrick speaking on "Nuclear Warfare, the Prime Public Health Issue of the 1980s, and a Professional Health Care Response."[84] Incorporating substantial intellectual and political elements with social activities had by this time become a hallmark of Grace's approach to life; she shared that outlook with the SMJC community through her work with the alumnae association.

Grace invited Dr. Hedrick to speak at the 1984 reunion in part because she had taken up the antinuclear cause at that point in her life and because she believed it was an important issue that the alumnae should address as educated healthcare professionals and responsible citizens. As early as 1981, Grace promoted engagement with the issue when she shared with her "Continuing Commentary" readers information on the organization with which Hedrick was affiliated, Physicians for Social Responsibility (PSR), and its insights into "the medical aspects of nuclear war and the hazards of nuclear proliferation." Founded in 1961, PSR "made its mark by educating the public and policymakers about the egregious impacts of developing and testing nuclear weapons on human health." That included sharing the work of pediatricians and dentists who documented the presence in baby teeth of Strontium-90, "a highly-radioactive waste product of atmospheric nuclear testing." Their research contributed to the creation of the Limited Nuclear Test Ban treaty in 1963.[85] The organization faded out by the early 1970s, but was revived in 1978 by a younger generation of doctors led by the dynamic Helen Caldicott, an Australian physician who was then working at Harvard Medical School. Caldicott rebuilt PSR into a national organization that had ten thousand members by the end of 1980. Heightened tensions between the United States and the Soviet Union were then emerging, and the US government's response, which included President Jimmy Carter's commitment to install more missiles in Western Europe and President Ronald Reagan's push for the neutron bomb and MX missile, disturbed Caldicott and other antinuclear activists. PSR shifted its focus from warning about the health implications of nuclear testing to teaching—through symposiums, guest lectures, media appearances, and direct mailings—about the dangers of nuclear war. By 1982 PSR membership stood at thirty thousand, with 153 chapters in 48 states.[86] Grace became one of the organization's supporters. Its focus on the scientific and medical proof of the folly of nuclear war appealed to her as an intellectual and as a professional.

But, for Grace, opposing nuclear weapons stemmed from her embrace of Catholic activism too. In her "Continuing Commentary" column, Grace also publicized the efforts of the Benedictines, who, "moving beyond a mere sense of social responsibility [had] introduced a moral imperative into the opposition to the use of nuclear weapons." Grace connected her readers not only to the point of contact for the PSR at St. Mary's (the hospital chaplain, Father Jim Studer, OSB) but also to the petition campaign for a nuclear weapons moratorium that had been launched by the Benedictines. Their goal was the immediate halting of "the testing, production, and deployment of all nuclear warheads, missiles and delivery systems."[87] Grace shared this information with the readers of *Good News*, hoping to inspire the students, faculty, and alumnae to take up the cause with her.

Grace maintained her office at St. Mary's for five years after she retired. From that perch she remained engaged in campus life and in the work of social justice she found so rewarding. Through her emergency fund for students, her promotion of women's education in her "Continuing Commentary" column and alumnae association efforts, and her antinuclear advocacy, Grace pursued that work as an extension of her Catholic activism. In a speech she delivered in May 1981 during one of four special community days held by the Sisters of St. Joseph to reflect on their ministry, Grace explained that her passion for social justice that the sisters instilled in her was fulfilling only when it proceeded with "divine guidance and divine inspiration." She expressed her gratitude to the Josephites for allowing her to "teach and practice social justice" in a Catholic context at SMJC.[88] Grateful for these opportunities, she donated to the college the profits from two cookbooks that she published after she retired.[89]

Grace's lifelong commitment to social justice thus had taken on this new shape in the decades after she left the SWP. Although she would sometimes still reminisce about the "excitement, conflict, struggle and successes of SWP leadership" in the old days and even "sing old socialist anthems" when gathered with friends "on certain social occasions when [they] all had ample drinks," she would not remain in that place for long. When "Gilbert would announce that it was 'time,'" she would stop singing and change the subject so as not to "embarrass him with stories/songs of 'olden days.'"[90]

Gilbert, who tolerated Grace's reminiscing about the old days up to a point, remained a left-leaning Democrat. He and Grace had found many ways to share their life together despite any political differences. In their two-story townhouse at 837 South Cleveland Avenue in St. Paul, across the street from St. Leo's Church, they continued to host many of their mutual friends at the famous dinners that Grace cooked even after they retired from their official duties at SMJC. The two also "were avid readers," and their home was filled with books. And both Grace and Gilbert were remembered as being "practicing Catholics, active volunteers and generous supporters of parish . . . and larger church charity."[91]

Through his work on the governing board, Gilbert, like Grace, had also become a beloved figure at SMJC. In 1979, at the reception held in honor of him and Grace when they retired, he "was presented with a Distinguished Service Medallion by the Board in recognition for his many contributions to SMJC and the Board." *Good News* reported that "in responding to all the adulation, Gilbert's wry comment 'I want to thank you. I'm particularly thankful that Grace was here to hear it all' brought the house down."[92] In the article Gilbert was portrayed as understated with his dry, quiet humor. Grace was presented as her active and larger-than-life self; after accepting a gift from the faculty and staff, she reminded them how "when confronted with a rapt and captive audience she would take full advantage."[93]

Throughout the years since their reunion in 1952, Grace and Gilbert forged a loving connection despite their very different personalities. The two, of course, did share much in common, including their Catholic faith, their commitment to SMJC, and their left-leaning politics, that contributed to their marital bond. On the occasion of their twenty-fifth wedding anniversary, in 1959, one of Grace's students wrote them both expressing her admiration: "I pray if marriage is my vocation, mine will be as rich as yours is, and that I and my husband will possess some of the qualities I admire in the two of you."[94]

Over the years Gilbert and Grace also each dealt with various health issues as they aged and were there to support each other. Grace continued to suffer from various allergies and had to monitor her heart. As she got older, and continued to enjoy her favorite gin martinis, she developed ulcers and diverticulitis too. In 1973 Gilbert underwent hip replacement surgery and, with Grace at his side, made a good recovery from that initial procedure.[95] But by March 1978 he underwent another surgery to treat his hip joint, which had been severely damaged due to the advanced stage of his rheumatoid arthritis. After "a 3 ½ month stay at St. Mary's [Hospital] confined to a bed and wheelchair, unable to walk," Gilbert finally returned to his St. Paul home with Grace largely due to the efforts of the hospital's Home Health Care staff. With that support, Grace was able to continue working at the college.[96]

A few years later, however, when she and Gilbert were already retired, his health took a turn from which he ultimately did not recover. In 1984, because of Gilbert's declining health, Grace had to stop working at the alumnae office at SMJC and on her column for *Good News*. Instead, she remained at home with Gilbert and cared for him, much as she had done for her mother during the final year of her life. The complications of Gilbert's rheumatoid arthritis contributed to a "general debility" that he suffered for eight months. His history of chain smoking may have also added to his health problems. Grace honored his wishes to take "all reasonable and available measures" to prevent his death, but, ultimately, even the medical teams could do no more. In his final few days he suffered from bilateral pneumonia. He died on May 13, 1985, in St. Mary's Hospital.[97]

* * *

After Gilbert's death, space seemed to open up for Grace to reflect on her radical past more freely. Even when her husband was still alive, she had begun to reconnect with some of her old friends from the party who had either left or been expelled from the SWP by the mid–late 1960s, including Miriam Braverman and Jean and Bill Brust.[98] Grace also managed to reconnect with her dear friend Bea Janosco, sending her a card with one of her "favorite Shakespeare sonnets" in 1981. Bea wrote back recalling how they had "many good years, didn't we" and admitting that she "would be a very ignorant person today if I had not spent those years in the labor movement and the party."[99]

Beginning with these small steps in her correspondence with old friends, Grace slowly began to open up more about her years in the SWP. It was not that she had not spoken about that time before. Indeed, she addressed her commitment to Marxism and her years in the party quite openly in many of her speeches, especially in the years just after she left the SWP in 1952. But in most of those speeches, she situated her radical past within a narrative arc that moved her out from the SWP and into her new life as a Catholic activist. Not until Gilbert passed away did she begin to explore her radical past more independently from the life she had rebuilt for herself after she left the party. Perhaps she had not done so before because she had been separated from Gilbert during her years in the SWP (and had been involved with Ray Dunne) and did not want to dwell on that time while Gilbert was still alive; or, perhaps, especially during the 1950s and early 1960s, when the FBI continued to hound her for information about her former colleagues, she felt the pressure of the

Red Scare and decided it was best to avoid extensive recollections about that past. By the late 1980s, when that pressure from the FBI had long been lifted, when her relationship with Dorothy had long been healed, and after Gilbert had passed away, Grace became more open to such reflections.

It was around that same time, beginning in the early 1980s, when younger members and former members of the SWP, scholars, and activists from other radical parties began approaching Grace and asking her to share her memories with them. George Breitman wrote to Grace in the spring of 1981 requesting her help as he worked on a book about Carl Skoglund. He also sent her copies of some of the material released during the SWP's lawsuit against the FBI.[100] In the suit, which had been filed in 1973, the SWP charged that for decades the FBI had "engaged in massive violations of the constitutional rights of the SWP, [its youth organization, the] YSA, and their members," through its surveillance and harassment.[101] What that lawsuit eventually revealed was that the SWP had long been a target of the Bureau's counterintelligence program, or COINTELPRO, in which the "express goal was to 'disrupt,' 'discredit,' and 'neutralize' domestic protest groups." It took thirteen years, five decisions in district court, three major decisions in the court of appeals, and three applications to the Supreme Court, but the SWP eventually forced the FBI to release "tens of thousands of pages of files" that "contained evidence of thousands of unlawful acts committed by the FBI and its informers."[102] In 1986, Judge Thomas Griesa of the United States District Court of the Southern District of New York "found the FBI guilty of violations of the constitutional rights of the SWP . . . and of [its] members," and he ruled that the government could not use any of the FBI's files on the party or its members that had been compiled through illegal methods.[103] Griesa also ruled "that the FBI's COINTELPRO operations against the SWP . . . were 'patently unconstitutional and violated the SWP's First Amendment rights of free speech and assembly.'"[104] Grace did not record her reaction to this important verdict, but perhaps the thawing climate for political speech it represented (in comparison to the Red Scare and COINTELPRO years) also contributed to her willingness to share her memories. She agreed to correspond with Richard Valelly and Alan Wald too; each was writing his own study of the political Left in those years.[105]

In 1987 Grace sat down for an interview with Carl Ross, a former Communist Party district secretary. Ross was gathering interviews with former leftists and labor leaders for the Twentieth-Century Radicalism in Minnesota Project, which is now housed at the Minnesota Historical Society Library. Grace met with Carl twice: once on July 9 and once on July 14. In these interviews she discussed the wide sweep of her life, from her childhood in St. Paul through her years at St. Mary's. Although some of what she discussed tracked the narrative she had created for herself in her speeches that she had been delivering since she left the SWP, many of her insights were new or more fully fleshed out. These included the recollections of her childhood, her experiences during the 1941 Smith Act trial, some details of her time at Alderson, and her thoughts on the dogmatism of the political Left.[106]

By the time Grace met with Ross in July 1987, she had already traveled to New York City for an interview at New York University's Tamiment Library on May 1. She had been invited, along with Dorothy, George Novack, and Felix Morrow, for an event that focused on the history of these former Trotskyists and their experiences with the 1934 Teamsters' strikes and the 1941 Smith Act trial. Grace and Dorothy were interviewed together. They talked about the things that influenced their political radicalism, the 1934 strikes and the Trotskyist leadership of the strikes, the conflict with Tobin and the 1941 trial, Grace's reasons for leaving Gilbert, the place of women in the SWP, and her time at Alderson. At times the sisters disagreed about their take on something, but even those mild tiffs were experienced in good humor, with Dorothy noting, "We're arguing" to the interviewer. Unlike the early years of their rapprochement, when they could not discuss politics or the past, the two now revisited the time they had spent in the SWP at some length.[107]

After the trip to New York, Grace returned to the book-lined apartment in St. Paul where she had moved after Gilbert's death. A year later she gave another interview, this time to the editors of SMJC's *Good News*. In that exchange she revealed that she was moving to Madison in the fall. Raymond later recalled how by this time, with Grace in her early eighties, it was getting hard for her to live alone. "It seems reasonable to move," she told the editors, "although I really like Minnesota." Putting a positive spin on things, she then commented, "But that's kind of a prejudicial attitude, isn't it? After all Wisconsin has quite a progressive history!"[108]

Dorothy, who had been living in Wisconsin for decades at this point, had certainly appreciated that progressive history and did her part to play a role in it. Raymond recalled how during one antiwar protest at the University of Madison in 1967, when the National Guard and Madison police used tear gas on students and chased them off the Library Mall, Dorothy stood in the hallway in front of the library where she worked "with her hands on her hips facing off against [them]. She seemed to be saying, 'No you don't. NOT in my library.'"[109] Dorothy, who became an associate professor of library science at the university, also spoke out at the University Senate on behalf of women faculty. As a member of the Association of Faculty Women, she increased the library's holdings in women's studies and pushed for a women's studies librarian, a position that was created in 1977. That same year she copublished, with Miriam Allman, *Women's Studies Resources: A Core Collection List for Undergraduate Libraries*.[110]

After she retired in June 1980, Dorothy opened a restaurant and bar on Williamson Street. She named it "Mother's Willy Street Pub," and when asked about the name she would tell people it was "because I own it." Raymond recalls how the pub "quickly became a place for young leftists and 'politicals' to hang out." Dorothy and Ann, who had moved back to Madison by this time, shared one part of a side-by-side duplex; Jim and his wife, Diane, lived in the other. David, Ann's son, eventually ended up in Madison too, working in the pub. Dorothy, Ann, Jim, and Vincent were also members of the Wisconsin Alliance, "a small but active group in local politics." They knew many people in union circles, too, who also used the pub as a gathering place in these years.[111]

Unfortunately for Dorothy, mixing family with business did not work very well. According to Raymond, "The business followed the pattern of many small businesses and failed" after a few years. Raymond was able to help his mother sell the building, but at the cost of his relationship with Jim and David. Dorothy eventually relocated to a house on Thompson Drive. When Grace decided to move to Madison in 1988, she at first found her own apartment. She and Dorothy were now physically closer, and the sisters were able to help each other. As Grace aged, however, she needed even more help. Her vision declined rapidly and she worried about falling. Eventually, "Grace paid for the addition of a room with a bathroom on the backside of [Dorothy's Thompson Drive] house" so she would not be living on her own. Once again the two sisters were together, as they had been for so many years on LaFond Avenue in St. Paul.

*　*　*

For this final stage of Grace's life there are very few surviving records. Living with her sister, Dorothy, she had no reason to correspond with her anymore. Any letters she may have written to her nieces and nephews or to her remaining friends have not been preserved in her papers. She lived in Madison for the last four years of her life and became "a faithful member of St. Bernard Catholic Church." Peter D'Heilly recalls that during this time when Grace lived with Dorothy and close to her nieces and nephews, "She experienced much love there." Even as she had to slow down because of her failing eyesight, Grace found ways to remain engaged through her parish and family life. One can only imagine the lively conversations she must have had with Dorothy around the kitchen table.

"At the approach of her own death," Sister AJ Moore later recalled, Grace "directed that no extraordinary means be used." As a devout Catholic, Grace believed that death was not the end; she looked forward to her soul reuniting with God in eternity. She had been by the side of her mother and Gilbert when they had made that journey. Now, she had her sister Dorothy with her when her time came. After "a brief illness" Grace died, at the age of eighty-five, on July 7, 1992.[112]

Conclusion

In death, as in life, Grace had Dorothy by her side. And, as was true for so much of her life, she also had the Church. Her wake and funeral mass were held at her parish of St. Bernard's in Madison on Thursday, July 9, 1992. Father John Hebl officiated. On Saturday, July 11, Father Mitchel, who had traveled from Grace's former parish of St. Leo's in St. Paul, presided over a special memorial service at the chapel of the Resurrection Cemetery in Mendota Heights. A dedicated activist to the end, Grace had requested that in lieu of flowers her friends contribute to Physicians for Social Responsibility.[1]

Grace's passing was also commemorated by the SMJC community. In the fall 1992 issue of *Good News*, an obituary announced, "Dedication and spirit endears staff and students to Carlson, who dies at 81." Although the editors got her age wrong in the headline, they captured the essence of Grace in the text. "'Nothing is too good for the workers,' Grace Carlson would say. When she joined the St. Mary's Junior College staff in 1955 to teach psychology, she applied her socialist philosophy to her work as a teacher—nothing was too good for the students." The editors cited Grace's efforts to "make education accessible to students, especially single-parent students" through her emergency fund. And they quoted Peter D'Heilly, who recalled how Grace "saw St. Mary's as an institution that gave people a second chance and as a way for students to prepare for a career in helping others, which was a primary focus of her life too."[2]

As Grace's life shows, her faith was a primary focus for her as well. Her story serves as a reminder of the importance of taking religion seriously as it is experienced by people in the past, as a fundamental factor in their lives and in how they chose to live their lives. The Catholicism Grace experienced in St. Vincent's parish and through the Josephites who were her teachers at St. Vincent's school, Saint Joseph's Academy, and the College of St. Catherine shaped her political consciousness as a girl and young woman. Her dedication to social justice and serving others as a gospel mandate can be traced to these formative experiences. Grace's story also reveals the complexity of Catholicism as it was lived by those in the past. The social activism of the Josephites, along with the commitment to the living wage and workers' dignity communicated by Archbishop John Ireland and Reverend John Ryan, reveal the diversity that existed within the institution of the Catholic Church. So too did the liturgical and Catholic Action movements that fed into the changes of Vatican II and that so inspired Grace to find a comfortable home in the Church after her return in 1952. Although many scholars of labor and working-class life may overlook the power of faith in motivating individuals like Grace in their social and political activism, her story reveals how for those who chose to embrace it, faith could function as a formative and driving force for progressive change.[3]

Grace's life also demonstrates the complexity of class identity as a social category that is forged from multiple, intertwined experiences and perceptions and that evolves over time. Grace's understanding of herself as a member of the working class came first from her childhood experiences of her natal family's limited economic means and the socioeconomic composition of her childhood neighborhood and parish, from her awareness of fellow working-class families' opposition to World War I, and from her exposure to the 1922 shopmen's strike. As she mixed with girls from Summit Avenue at SJA and CSC, Grace became more conscious of her class difference, even admitting to being embarrassed by it. Yet, even as she began to rise out of the working class through her access to higher education and her professional position at the Minnesota Department of Education, Grace continued to identify with the working class as a union member and, after her political conversion to socialism in the context of the Depression and the 1934 Teamsters strikes, as an SWP organizer. In terms of her income as a party organizer, Grace was no longer in the professional ranks. Politically and ideologically, too, she identified with the working class and fought for workers' liberation during her many years in the SWP. But after she broke with the party, and then became a professor at SMJC, Grace reentered the ranks of the middle class in terms of occupation and income. Her reunification with her husband, Gilbert, who was a successful attorney, bolstered this middle-class status.

Even though by the 1960s she admitted to finding herself something of a "petty bourgeois element these days," she continued to identify as "enough of a Marxist" in her understanding of the need to have the support of the workers to effect revolution and maintained her interest in and concern for the fate of the working class.[4] That identification contributed to her condemnation of the Berrigans and other facets of the New Left that she believed were missing the mark. Her continued commitment to Marxism also drove her interest in *Slant* and her belief in the need, as she explained to Father Emeric, for "daily propaganda about the need for social change, winning hearts and minds to the Movement, and at the appropriate time, helping to organize the socialist forces."[5] For Grace, these were the important, if unglamorous, tasks that she undertook when she penned socially conscious prayers of the faithful at St. Leo's parish, when she advised women students at SMJC to think independently, and when she supported the antiwar and antinuclear movements.

Perhaps some will see an inconsistency in the relationship between Grace's professed political ideas and her actions in her years after returning to the Church. As someone who advocated aiming at the source of economic and political power to effect real social change, she certainly spent a lot of her time working within the liberal order and remained committed to what was, despite its progressive wings, a conservative and patriarchal Roman Catholic Church. Although Grace denounced immediate reform efforts that did not strike at the heart of capitalist oppression, she engaged in her own charitable endeavors that aided many individuals in the short term; her work at the Home of the Good Shepherd and her fund for SMJC students stand out in this regard. Yet, Grace saw these undertakings as ultimately contributing to more far-reaching change. When asked about her fund, for example, she argued that she hoped it would help those students have the opportunity to access the education they needed to think independently and to have economic autonomy, positions that were revolutionary in many ways for the empowerment of women and from which those women could push for even greater social and economic equality.[6]

Grace's commitment to women's self-advancement and equality falls under a similar category of complexity, not necessarily fitting neatly into academic classifications. When she was a child and young woman, her mother's communication to her of the importance of education for economic and intellectual autonomy made Grace, as she described it, "a kind of liberated woman." The Josephites, who modeled the fruits of learning for women, reinforced this identity for her and set her feet on the path to her own academic advancement and intellectual freedom in graduate school at the U. Although Grace's experiences at the U contributed to her leaving the Church, they also led her to Marxism and a different understanding of women's advancement. Echoing Marxist classics, like Engels's *Origins of the Family*, Grace came to understand women's oppression as historically constructed with the rise of capitalism and believed, along with most Socialists in her day, that the answer to the woman question would come with the overthrow of capitalism and the establishment of socialism.[7] But Grace also experienced the struggles of women as a woman, and as a sister and friend to women during the 1930s, 1940s, and 1950s, in ways that began to expand her Marxist approach to this issue to include an understanding of the value of women's work in the home. This perspective was expressed in the arguments made by her and other women in the SWP (and on the broader political Left) during the 1940s for the need for women to have childcare support along with continued workplace legislative protections so that they could contribute to the revolution. Grace and her female comrades were coming to realize the challenges of trying to participate in the revolutionary party while the "children were climbing all over the kitchen."[8]

But it was not until after Grace left the SWP in 1952, returned to the Catholic Church, and began her work with female students at SMJC that she began to articulate a critique of patriarchy. The feminism that she voiced in her speeches during the late 1950s and 1960s included a defense of women's innate equality on theological grounds and a questioning of patriarchal structures so that women could advance professionally to serve God and effect social change. Perhaps somewhat unexpectedly, given the patriarchal nature of the Catholic Church, Grace's renewed faith allowed her to question the gendered assumptions undergirding capitalist patriarchy in ways that she had not done as a Marxist. She advocated for women's full self-actualization as their right as children of God. From this unconventional path she connected her Old Left Marxist feminism with currents pulsing in the second wave feminist movement of the 1960s and 1970s.

* * *

After Grace died, her former colleagues and her friends at St. Mary's were not content just to publish an obituary in the campus newspaper. On November 25, 1992, they also organized a memorial service for Grace on campus as part of their "Thanksgiving Remembrances." After the opening prayer, the academic dean of the college, Mary Broderick, gave a brief introduction. She was followed by Sister Anne Joachim Moore, who delivered the eulogy. A period of "memory sharing" came next for those gathered. And, as Grace would have enjoyed, the service ended with a lunch.[9]

Sister AJ, who had worked so closely with Grace for almost twenty-five years, spoke about the many facets of her friend's life. "Hers was a distinctive personality," she asserted. "There was nothing run-of-the-mill about her." Sister AJ first recalled their teaming up to transform St. Mary's School of Nursing into SMJC. "Grace was wonderful to have in the middle of it all," she recalled, "a lively woman of wide, deep interests who took to the idea of SMJC like a magnet." Sister AJ remembered the intensity with which Grace worked on the St. Mary's Plan and the "very good and heated fights" she engaged in with the faculty over what shape the nursing program should take. "Grace was a fierce woman," she observed of her friend's dedication to the college and her involvement with its creation and development in its early years. Perhaps because of that fierceness, students from each class at all of the alumnae events "ask first of all for Grace—then they break up in laughter and fond emotion as they relate what she meant to them—for many, Grace was SMJC."[10]

But Sister AJ also remembered the other parts of Grace's life. "My memories of her range from Cherries Jubilee to corn relish by the quart, gallons of homemade soup laced with vodka or bourbon or wine (all the alcohol having evaporated during the cooking—but the idea was so like Grace)," she recalled. There was also Grace's "impromptu recitation of long poems of dozens of stanzas learned in her childhood, along with her sister Dorothy," as well as her attempts at singing the "Internationale." "She was no singer," Moore admitted, "but her gusto and enthusiasm were a treat and great tension releaser—as well as a great tension creator." And there were even Grace's "tales of Trotsky and her experiences with Trotsky's wife; descriptions of her life in Alderson prison," and "her shelves of books which she shared generously like a small lending library." In addition to her students and friends, the children of many of her students also loved Grace. Sister AJ recalled her "coterie of little children admirers" to whom she gave dollar bills each time they stopped by to see her. When Sister AJ told Grace she thought this was "an ill advised practice," she responded, "But, of course, I know I have to buy them!"[11]

Sister AJ not only relished these cherished memories of Grace's humor and her impact on St. Mary's, but she also recalled her friend's life of serious commitment to social justice that went beyond her work on campus. "She wasn't just entertaining," Sister AJ said of Grace. "She was a good, strong, bright woman of principle and morality and spirituality." Those principles included Grace's early refusal to inform for the FBI and her many years of challenging her friends, like Father Emeric and Dr. Breitenbucher, to understand her approach to social change. Sister AJ appreciated that approach: "Her aphorisms and expression of obligations and guiding principles for one who commits to a cause bigger than oneself were pithy and powerful and useful well beyond the Socialist Workers party. Many of the self-centered practices of the rebels of the 60's annoyed and distressed her, precisely because they seemed to be self-centered." Sister AJ acknowledged that "Grace was not so great a supporter of the 'do-good-to-the-individual victim' as she was deeply committed to change the system, economic and political." In her daily work that translated into educating future generations of women for professional careers and for lives as informed and engaged citizens who tackled the pressing issues of the day by challenging the sources of economic and political power.[12]

Yet for all of Grace's seriousness when it came to political matters, she was also deeply committed to her friends and family. Her "faithfulness and devotion to all her friends, and especially to Gilbert in his illnesses and incapacities before he died were truly inspiring and beautiful." And although Sister AJ did not articulate it in these exact words, Grace was also faithful to all parts of her identity—her Catholic activism, her brand of feminism, and her Marxist understanding of political and economic power and change—"at the core and to the end."[13]

ACKNOWLEDGMENTS

I am grateful to the many people who helped make this book happen. For helping me locate important archival records, I want to thank the reference librarians and staff at the Minnesota Historical Society Library, the St. Catherine University Archives and Special Collections, the Archdiocese of St. Paul, and the interlibrary loan teams at the Wisconsin Historical Society and Hunter College. At the Archives of Congregation of the Sisters of St. Joseph of Carondelet (CSJ) in St. Paul I want especially to thank Sister Mary Kraft, CSJ, and Michelle Hueg, who went above and beyond the call to track down leads for me. I also appreciate the research assistance of David Attali and Loris Sofia Gregory. And thank you to Ruth Brombach, Alumnae Liaison at St. Catherine University, for helping me connect with Grace's former students. Raymond Schultz, Peter D'Heilly, Bill Morgan, Patrick Quinn, and Laure Campbell kindly shared their memories of Grace and her family with me, for which I am very grateful. I also want to express special appreciation to David Sundeen, Linda Leighton, and Mary and Jim Dunne for opening their home and hearts to me and sharing stories and photos of their grandparents, Vincent Raymond Dunne and Jennie Dunne.

For supporting this project from the beginning by giving me a forum to discuss my early findings, I need to thank Peter Rachleff of the East Side Freedom Library in St. Paul and David Riehle. Special thanks, too, to Mary Wingerd, Tom Beer, and Tom O'Connell, who came to my talk and provided helpful leads and encouragement. Elizabeth Raasch-Gilman not only has been an enthusiastic supporter since day one but also generously gave me all her notes and her interview material from her work on the Holmes sisters. Thanks, too, to Michael Koncewicz for inviting me to present portions of this work at New York University's Cold War Seminar and to Alice Kessler-Harris for her insightful comment at that meeting. Thank you to Leon Fink and Eric Arnesen for hosting me at the DC Area Labor and Working-Class History Seminar, to Sue Levine and

Robyn Muncy for their probing critiques, and to all the seminar participants, especially Jay Driskell, for their feedback. I would like to single out Robyn, who kindly also read an additional chapter and shared her very helpful insights with me. The final work is a much better product as a result. The same holds true for the comments I received from my new colleagues at the CUNY Graduate Center after presenting my work there. Special thanks to Joel Allen and the Department of History Membership Committee for the invitation. And I must thank Matthew Pehl, Leslie Woodcock Tentler, Alan Wald, and Steve Rosswurm, who generously took time out of their busy schedules to read portions of the manuscript and send me their thoughts. Steve also read the manuscript in its entirety as a referee for NYU Press, and I am deeply grateful to him, and to Eileen Boris, who did the same. My work has benefited from the insights of all of these good colleagues. And special thanks to Clara Platter and Veronica Knutson at NYU Press for supporting me through the publication process and to Jim O'Brien for preparing the index.

Although it has been many decades since I walked the halls of St. Patrick School in Smithtown, New York, and of the Academy of St. Joseph in Brentwood, New York, the lessons I learned from the Sisters of St. Joseph at both institutions about the value of hard work and the importance of serving others have certainly remained with me and, no doubt, informed my understanding of Grace's life. More recently, it is the moral support I have received from my colleagues at Hunter for which I am also deeply appreciative. In the course of my work on this book, my father, Mario Truglio, passed away after an all-too-short battle with stage-four cancer. I am saddened that he will not get to read my version of Grace's story, but perhaps she is regaling him with her take as they dwell among the communion of saints. I am also very grateful for the love and support I have received during these trying times from my siblings, Maria Truglio and Joseph Truglio, from my cousins, Mary Bennis and Marianne LaCroce, and from my dear friends, Andrew Horgan and Alex Choong. Maria, my fellow academic, also provided helpful feedback on portions of the manuscript. I thank my mother, Rose Truglio, for being, as one dear friend noted, "stronger than she looks," and for providing a constant source of love and support for all of us. And, as always, gratitude to Dylan and Josie for putting up with "the Grace book" for so long and for being my home and my heart.

ABBREVIATIONS

AFC, NYU Avery Fisher Center, New York University Library, New York University, New York, NY

CCSS, TAMIMENT Collection of Communist and Socialist Serials, Tamiment Library and Robert F. Wagner Labor Archives, Elmer Holmes Bobst Library, New York University, New York, NY

CP, MHS Grace Holmes Carlson Papers, Minnesota Historical Society, St. Paul, MN

CSJ ARCHIVES Sisters of St. Joseph of Carondelet & Consociates, St. Paul Province Archives, St. Paul, MN

IBT, WHS International Brotherhood of Teamsters Records, Wisconsin Historical Society, Madison, WI

MHS Minnesota Historical Society, St. Paul, MN

RG 21, KC Records of the District Courts of the United States, RG 21, National Archives at Kansas City, Kansas City, MO

RG29 Records of the Bureau of the Census, RG29, National Archives, Washington, DC, reprinted by Ancestry.com

RHR, MHS Rockwell and Carstater Hearing Files, Commissioner's Office, Education Department, Minnesota Historical Society, St. Paul, MN

SCUA-SC St. Catherine University Archives and Special Collections, St. Paul, MN

SWP 146-1-10 Socialist Workers Declassified Papers 146-1-10, General Records of the Department of Justice, RG 60, National Archives at College Park, MD

WHS Wisconsin Historical Society, Madison, WI

NOTES

INTRODUCTION

1. Anne Joachim Moore, "Remembering Grace Holmes Carlson," November 25, 1992, p. 5, f. SMJC Faculty, Grace Carlson, box 4, SMJC Collection, Sisters of Saint Joseph of Carondelet & Consociates, St. Paul Province Archives, St. Paul, Minnesota (hereafter cited as CSJ Archive).
2. Through my use of this interpretive framework, informed by wider use of archival sources, I make arguments and draw conclusions in my biography of Carlson that differ from those of Traci Swenson's unpublished work, even though we address some of the same formative episodes in Carlson's life. See Traci D. Swenson, "Grace Carlson: A Life of Rebellion," MFA in Liberal Studies, Hamline University, St. Paul, Minnesota, May 2004.
3. Elizabeth Faue, "Re-Imagining Labor: Gender and New Directions in Labor and Working-Class History," in *Rethinking U.S. Labor History: Essays on the Working-Class Experience, 1756–2009*, ed. Donna T. Haverty-Stacke and Daniel J. Walkowitz (New York: Continuum, 2010), 278.
4. See, for example, Elizabeth Fones-Wolf and Ken Fones-Wolf, *Struggle for the Soul of the Postwar South: White Evangelical Protestants and Operation Dixie* (Urbana: University of Illinois Press, 2015), and Matthew Pehl, *The Making of Working-Class Religion* (Urbana: University of Illinois Press, 2016).
5. On the call to examine such histories, see Linda Kerber, "'I Was Appalled': The Invisible Antecedents of Second-Wave Feminism," *Journal of Women's History* 14:2 (Summer 2002): 93–94. On such history see, for example, Dorothy Sue Cobble, *The Other Women's Movement: Workplace Justice and Social Rights in Modern America* (Princeton, NJ: Princeton University Press, 2004).
6. Susan Ware, "Writing Women's Lives: One Historian's Perspective," *Journal of Interdisciplinary History* 40:3 (Winter 2010): 413–14.
7. James R. Barrett, "*Was* the Personal Political? Reading the Autobiography of American Communism," *IRSH* 53 (2008): 396, 418–23.
8. Nick Salvatore, "Biography and Social History: An Intimate Relationship," *Labour History* 87 (November 2004): 190.
9. Ross had served on the National Committee of the Communist Party USA during the 1940s. He conducted a series of interviews with former Socialists and Communists during the 1980s (including with Carlson) for the Twentieth-Century Radicalism in Minnesota Oral History Project housed at the Minnesota Historical Society (hereafter MHS). See http://collections.mnhs.org (accessed July 12, 2019).

10 On these histories see, for example, Kate Weigand, *Red Feminism: American Communism and the Making of Women's Liberation* (Baltimore, MD: Johns Hopkins University Press, 2001), and Daniel Horowitz, *Betty Friedan and the Making of the Feminine Mystique: The American Left, the Cold War, and Modern Feminism* (Amherst: University of Massachusetts Press, 1998).

11 On the importance of private relationships to the political Left more broadly between 1919 and 1950, see Kathleen A. Brown and Elizabeth Faue, "Social Bonds, Sexual Politics, and Political Community on the U.S. Left, 1920s–1940s," *Left History* 7:1 (Spring 2000): 9–45.

12 One exception is Alice Kessler-Harris's biography of Lillian Hellman, *A Difficult Woman: The Challenging Life and Times of Lillian Hellman* (New York: Bloomsbury, 2012).

CHAPTER 1. BEGINNINGS

1 Interview with Grace Holmes Carlson, by Carl Ross, July 9, 1987, transcript pages 1 and 2, Twentieth-Century Century Radicalism in Minnesota Project, MHS.

2 On historical subjects grappling with public and private forces, see Salvatore, "Biography and Social History," 190. On working-class subjects defining themselves in the past, see Faue, "Re-Imagining Labor," 278.

3 Mary Lethert Wingerd, *Claiming the City: Politics, Faith, and the Power of Place in St. Paul* (Ithaca, NY: Cornell University Press, 2001), 72.

4 See, for example, Grace Carlson to James Cannon, December 1, 1940, f. 1, box 1, Grace Holmes Carlson Papers, Minnesota Historical Society (hereafter cited as CP, MHS); Bea Janosco to Grace Carlson, January 21, 1945, f. 11, box 1, CP, MHS.

5 Samuel Holmes, 1850, Lebanon, Dodge, Wisconsin, *Seventh Census of the United States, 1850*, National Archives Microfilm Publication M432, roll M432_996, page 147A, image 291, Records of the Bureau of the Census, RG29, National Archives, Washington, DC, reprinted by Ancestry.com (hereafter RG29).

6 Jay P. Dolan, *The Irish in America: A History* (New York: Bloomsbury, 2008), 85.

7 Minnesota Department of Health, Division of Vital Statistics, *Certificate of Death: James A. Holmes*, September 3, 1951, registered no. 26926.

8 S. J. Holmes, *Hollands' Fond Du Lac City Directory for 1872–1873*, Ancestry.com. S. J. Holmes, *Centennial Directory of Fond Du Lac, Wisconsin, 1876*, Ancestry.com. Samuel J. Holmes, 1880, Fond Du Lac, Fond Du Lac, Wisconsin, *Tenth Census of the United States, 1880*, National Archives Microfilm Publication T9, roll 1426, page 234B, enumeration district 042, RG29.

9 Samuel J. Holmes, 1880, Fond Du Lac, Fond Du Lac, Wisconsin, *Tenth Census of the United States, 1880*, National Archives Microfilm Publication T9, roll 1426, page 234B, enumeration district 042, RG29.

10 Script by Paul Nelson, edited by Tony Andrea. Video by East End Productions, "Rice Street: An Introduction," *Saint Paul Historical*, http://saintpaulhistorical.com (accessed September 21, 2018).

11 Wingerd, *Claiming the City*, 41.

12 Forty-three percent of Irish residents in St. Paul were unskilled in 1900. See Wingerd, *Claiming the City*, 40.
13 Samuel Holmes, 1895, St. Paul Ward 9, Ramsey, Minnesota, *Minnesota, Territorial and State Censuses*, microfilm edition reel V290_90, MHS.
14 James A. Holmes, *St. Paul, Minnesota, City Directory, 1895* (helper/driver for U.S. Express Co.), *St. Paul, Minnesota, City Directory, 1901* (packer for A. Booth and Co.), *St. Paul, Minnesota, City Directory, 1908* (laborer), Ancestry.com. James A. Holmes, 1900, St. Paul Ward 9, Ramsey, Minnesota, *Twelfth Census of the United States*, National Archives Microfilm Publication T623, roll 786, page 10A, enumeration district 0145, RG29. James A. Holmes, 1910, St. Paul, Ward 8, Ramsey, Minnesota, *Thirteenth Census of the United States*, National Archives Microfilm Publication T264, roll T624_719, page 9A, enumeration district 0115, RG29.
15 James A. Holmes, *St. Paul Minnesota, City Directory, 1919*, Ancestry.com; James Holmes, 1920, St. Paul Ward 8, Ramsey, Minnesota, *Fourteenth Census of the United States*, National Archives Microfilm Publication T625, roll T625_855, enumeration district 98, RG29. James Holmes, 1930, St. Paul, Ramsey, Minnesota, *Fifteenth Census of the United States*, National Archives Microfilm Publication T626, roll 1119, page 21A, enumeration district 0109, RG29.
16 On the craft of boilermaking, see Colin J. Davis, *Power at Odds: The 1922 National Railroad Shopmen's Strike* (Urbana: University of Illinois Press, 1997), 17, 18.
17 Mary Nuebel, 1900, St. Paul Ward 8, Ramsey, Minnesota, *Twelfth Census of the United States*, National Archives Microfilm Publication T623, roll 785, page 14B, enumeration district 0128, RG29.
18 Frank Nuebel, 1885, Redwing, Minnesota, *Minnesota, Territorial and State Censuses*, microfilm edition reel MNSC_26, MHS. Frank P. Nuebel, December 14, 1891, *U.S. Find a Grave Index, 1600s–Current*, Ancestry.com. Mary Nuebel, 1900, St. Paul Ward 8, Ramsey, Minnesota, *Twelfth Census of the United States*, National Archives Microfilm Publication T623, roll 785, page 14B, enumeration district 0128, RG29.
19 Mary Nuebel, 1895, St. Paul Ward 8, Ramsey, Minnesota, *Minnesota, Territorial and State Censuses*, microfilm edition reel V290_89, MHS. Frank Nuebel, *St. Paul, Minnesota, City Directory*, 1895, Ancestry.com.
20 Frank Nuebel, *St. Paul, Minnesota, City Directory*, 1895, *St. Paul, Minnesota, City Directory*, 1897, *St. Paul, Minnesota, City Directory*, 1900, Ancestry.com.
21 Casper, Frank, Henry, Joseph, and Mary Nuebel, *St. Paul, Minnesota, City Directory*, 1901, Ancestry.com. Debra Graden, comp., "Joseph F. Nuebel, U.S. Army, Fourth Cavalry," *Minnesota Volunteers in the Spanish American War and the Philippine Insurrection*, p. 499, Ancestry.com. Joseph F. Nuebel, *U.S. Army, Register of Enlistments 1901*, National Archives Microfilm Publication M233, Records of the Adjutant General's Office 1780s–1917, RG 94, National Archives, Washington, DC, Ancestry.com.
22 Wingerd, *Claiming the City*, 36.
23 Carlson interview with Ross, July 9, 1987, 5.

24 James Holmes and Mary Neibel [sic], St. Paul, Ramsey, Minnesota, July 20, 1904, *Minnesota, Marriages Index*, FHL film number 1313337, Ancestry.com.
25 James A. Holmes, *St. Paul, Minnesota, City Directory, 1908*, Ancestry.com. James Holmes, 1910, St. Paul Ward 8, Ramsey, Minnesota, *Thirteenth Census of the United States*, National Archives Microfilm Publication T624, roll T624_719, page 9A, enumeration district 0115, RG29.
26 Henry J. Nuebel, *St. Paul, Minnesota, City Directory, 1902*, Ancestry.com. Frank Nuebel, *St. Paul, Minnesota, City Directory*, 1903, Ancestry.com. Frank Nuebel, 1910, St. Paul Ward 8, Ramsey, Minnesota, *Thirteenth Census of the United States*, National Archives Microfilm Publication T624, roll T624_719, page 11B, enumeration district 0111, RG29. Frank Nuebel, 1920, St. Paul Ward 8, Ramsey, Minnesota, *Fourteenth Census of the United States*, National Archives Microfilm Publication T625, roll T625_855, page 12A, enumeration district 93, RG29.
27 Baptismal certificate for Grace Mary Holmes, December 9, 1906, St. Peter Claver, St. Paul, Minnesota, Archives of the Archdiocese of Saint Paul and Minneapolis. Baptismal certificate for Helen Dorsey Holmes, January 2, 1906, St. Peter Claver, Saint Paul, Minnesota, Archives of the Archdiocese of Saint Paul and Minneapolis. *Historical Souvenir: St. Peter Claver's Church St. Paul, Minnesota Golden Jubilee, October 18*, 1942, 18.
28 *Historical Souvenir*, 15.
29 Wingerd, *Claiming the City*, 77.
30 *Historical Souvenir*, 15, 18.
31 By 1930 no more than 48 percent of St. Peter's parish was black. See Wingerd, *Claiming the City*, 79.
32 Archbishop John Ireland also grew up in a racially mixed community in St. Paul and was considered "ahead of his time" when it came to civil rights: *History of St. Peter Claver Church, Saint Paul, Minnesota* (1992), 52; Wingerd, *Claiming the City*, 78; and, Marvin R. O'Connell, *John Ireland and the American Catholic Church* (St. Paul: Minnesota Historical Society Press, 1988), 268–69.
33 Wingerd, *Claiming the City*, fn. 25, p. 288. There were "350 colored and white members" when Rev. Printon took over in 1897, see *Historical Souvenir*, 18.
34 "History and Architecture—Church of St. Agnes," http://churchofsaintagnes.org (accessed September 12, 2018).
35 Henry J. Nueble [sic], *St. Paul, Minnesota, City Directory*, 1914, Ancestry.com. James A. Holmes, *St. Paul, Minnesota, City Directory*, 1916, Ancestry.com.
36 James Holmes, 1920, St. Paul Ward 8, Ramsey, Minnesota, *Fourteenth Census of the United States*, National Archives Microfilm Publication T625, roll T625_855, enumeration district 98, RG29.
37 James Holmes, 1920, St. Paul Ward 8, Ramsey, Minnesota, *Fourteenth Census of the United States*, National Archives Microfilm Publication T625, roll T625_855, enumeration district 98, RG29. In 1920, James would have been earning seventy-two cents per hour as a shopman. See Davis, *Power at Odds*, 46.
38 Carlson interview with Ross, July 9, 1987, 3.

39 Carlson interview with Ross, July 9, 1987, 3.
40 Carlson interview with Ross, July 9, 1987, 3–4.
41 Carlson interview with Ross, July 9, 1987, 5.
42 Carlson interview with Ross, July 9, 1987, 1.
43 "Carlson Reports on Success in Rochester during Her Tour," unidentified newspaper clipping, f. SWP, Women in Prison Speech, box 1, CP, MHS.
44 Baptismal certificate for Grace Mary Holmes, December 9, 1906.
45 Casper J. Nuebel, 1940, St. Paul, Ramsey, Minnesota, *Sixteenth Census of the United States*, National Archives Microfilm Publication T627, roll m-t0627, page 13A, enumeration district 90–178, RG29. Grace said the newspaper in question was the *Daily Worker*, but given the years in question, it was most likely the *Socialist Appeal*.
46 Carlson interview with Ross, July 9, 1987, 2, 3.
47 Carlson interview with Ross, July 9, 1897, 2, 3.
48 *Eightieth Anniversary Homecoming: Church of St. Vincent de Paul, St, Paul Minnesota, September 15, 1968* (St. Paul, MN: The Church, 1968), 12, 13.
49 Wingerd, *Claiming the City*, 133. On the impact of Irish republican politics on first- and second-generation Irish immigrants, see Laura Murphy, "'An Indestructible Right': John Ryan and the Catholic Origins of the U.S. Living Wage Movement, 1906–1938," *LABOR: Studies in Working-Class History of the Americas* 6:1 (Spring 2009): 66.
50 Wingerd, *Claiming the City*, 130–32. O'Connell, *John Ireland*, 517.
51 Carol K. Coburn and Martha Smith, *Spirited Lives: How Nuns Shaped Catholic Culture and American Life, 1836–1920* (Chapel Hill: University of North Carolina Press, 1999), 20–24.
52 Directives quoted in Coburn and Smith, *Spirited Lives*, 23.
53 Margaret McGuinness, *Called to Serve: A History of Nuns in America* (New York: NYU Press, 2013), 45. See also Sister Helen Angela Hurley, *On Good Ground: The Story of the Sisters of St. Joseph in St. Paul* (Minneapolis: University of Minnesota Press, 1951), 44.
54 Coburn and Smith, *Spirited Lives*, 53. In the 1850s, 104 women from the United States joined the congregation: see McGuiness, *Called to Serve*, 46.
55 Hurley, *On Good Ground*, 9. Coburn and Smith, *Spirited Lives*, 100. Hurley notes, "By the turn of the [twentieth] century there were 428 sisters in the province [of St. Paul] to staff the twenty-five institutions then under the charge of the Sisters of St. Joseph." See Hurley, *On Good Ground*, 173.
56 Coburn and Smith, *Spirited Lives*, 101.
57 As McGuinness argues, "With the exception of celebrating Mass or administering the sacraments, sisters were more actively involved in the everyday lives of Catholics than priests." See McGuinness, *Called to Serve*, 8.
58 Coburn and Smith, *Spirited Lives*, 130–31.
59 Rev. Laurence Cosgrove, *A Popular History of St. Vincent's Parish: For Eighteen Years from 1889 to 1907* (n.p.), 42. *Eightieth Anniversary Homecoming*, 18.

60 Cosgrove, *A Popular History*, 4, 12–13. *Golden Jubilee: The Church of St. Vincent, 1888–1938* (St. Paul, MN: n.p., 1938), 17, 22.
61 Cosgrove, *A Popular History*, 17.
62 Cosgrove, *A Popular History*, 11.
63 Cosgrove, *A Popular History*, 12, 13.
64 Evelyn Savidge Sterne, *Ballots and Bibles: Ethnic Politics and the Catholic Church in Providence* (Ithaca, NY: Cornell University Press, 2004), 3–5. On women's participation in St. Vincent's parish, see *Golden Jubilee*, 22, 27–28.
65 *Eightieth Anniversary Homecoming*, 3.
66 *Golden Jubilee*, 19, 37.
67 Quotation from the Prayer to St. Vincent: see "Appendix" in Cosgrove, *A Popular History*, 29.
68 Shared celebrations remained important as the immigrant Church in America matured after 1900, but private devotions became more popular too, as did more frequent mass attendance. See James P. McCartin, *Prayers of the Faithful: The Shifting Spiritual Life of American Catholics* (Cambridge, MA: Harvard University Press, 2010), 23–33, 43–61.
69 Rev. Patrick F. O'Brien quoted in Cosgrove, *A Popular History*, 19. On Cosgrove's missionary work, see Cosgrove, *A Popular History*, 18.
70 Cosgrove, *A Popular History*, 36.
71 Iris Chang, *The Chinese in America: A Narrative History* (New York: Penguin, 2003), 141. On the nativist hostility that fueled the passage of these laws, see Chang, *The Chinese in America*, 130–56.
72 Cosgrove, *A Popular History*, 36–38.
73 Wingerd, *Claiming the City*, 57–62. O'Connell, *John Ireland*, 5–60, 136, 378–80, 411–12.
74 Murphy, "'An Indestructible Right,'" 69. See also O'Connell, *John Ireland*, 229–39, 247–248, 394; and, Francis L. Broderick, *Right Reverend New Dealer: John A. Ryan* (New York: Macmillan, 1963), 19–20.
75 Murphy, "'An Indestructible Right,'" 68.
76 Murphy, "'An Indestructible Right,'" 66–68. Broderick, *Right Reverend New Dealer*, 1–50.
77 Murphy, "'An Indestructible Right,'" 71, 72.
78 Murphy, "'An Indestructible Right,'" 71.
79 Ryan became one of the most well-known proponents of the living wage on the national stage through his work on the National Catholic Welfare Conference and during the New Deal. See Murphy, "'An Indestructible Right,'" 80–86.
80 According to Francis Broderick, "During the thirteen years, 1902–1915, that the young theologian spent on the faculty, the student body passed two hundred." See Broderick, *Right Reverend New Dealer*, 36.
81 Wingerd, *Claiming the City*, 105.
82 *Golden Jubilee*, 15.

83 Wingerd, *Claiming the City*, 215, 105. On Ryan's influence once he was at Catholic University, see also Tom Beer and Tom O'Connell, "Father Francis Gilligan and the Struggle for Civil Rights," *Minnesota History* (Summer 2011): 206.
84 Wingerd, *Claiming the City*, 105.
85 Wingerd, *Claiming the City*, 145.
86 Wingerd, *Claiming the City*, 4.
87 Wingerd, *Claiming the City*, 70, 72, 85–91.
88 Wingerd, *Claiming the City*, 41, 125–26.
89 Wingerd, *Claiming the City*, 127–28.
90 Wingerd, *Claiming the City*, 130. O'Connell, *John Ireland*, 517.
91 Ireland coined this slogan. See Kathleen Sprows Cummings, *New Women of the Old Faith: Gender and American Catholicism in the Progressive Era* (Chapel Hill: University of North Carolina Press, 2009), 72.
92 Hurley, *On Good Ground*, 202–20. O'Connell, *John Ireland*, 105–14, 249–51, 386.
93 Timothy Walch, *Parish School: American Catholic Parochial Education from Colonial Times to the Present* (New York: Crossroad, 1996), 81, 84–99. O'Connell, *John Ireland*, 290–316.
94 Hurley, *On Good Ground*, 202.
95 Such displays of patriotism were common in parish schools at the turn of the twentieth century. See Walch, *Parish School*, 72–73.
96 Cosgrove, *A Popular History*, 6–10.
97 *Pioneer Press* quoted in Cosgrove, *A Popular History*, 16–17.
98 Wingerd notes that Ireland "joined the Patriotic League, as did all his subordinates in the chancery." See Wingerd, *Claiming the City*, 130–32. The same may not have been true for all the priests at the parish level and was most certainly not true for the women religious who taught Grace. On the need to appreciate the heterogeneity of priests and their politics, see Leslie Woodcock Tentler, "On the Margins: The State of American Catholic History," *American Quarterly* 45:1 (March 1993): 121.
99 Carlson interview with Ross, July 9, 1987, 4. On the Patriotic League see Wingerd, *Claiming the City*, 127–28.
100 Wingerd, 159–64. David M. Kennedy, *Over Here: The First World War and American Society* (New York: Oxford University Press, 2004), 24, 67–68.
101 Carlson interview with Ross, July 9, 1987, 4.
102 Wingerd, *Claiming the City*, 136, 160–63.
103 Wingerd, *Claiming the City*, 161–63.
104 Carlson interview with Ross, July 9, 1987, 4, 5.
105 Carlson interview with Ross, July 9, 1987, 5.
106 Carlson interview with Ross, July 9, 1987, 2.
107 Carlson interview with Ross, July 9, 1987, 5.
108 *Golden Jubilee*, 24.
109 Carlson interview with Ross, July 9, 1987, 5.

110 Class tensions erupted in St. Paul during the 1917 streetcar strike, too, but Grace does not comment on that event as having affected her or her family. On the 1917 streetcar strike, see Wingerd, *Claiming the City*, 179–205.
111 Davis, *Power at Odds*, 11.
112 Davis, *Power at Odds*, 21.
113 Davis, *Power at Odds*, 26–27.
114 Davis, *Power at Odds*, 34–47.
115 Davis, *Power at Odds*, 48–53.
116 Davis, *Power at Odds*, 58–63. Quotation from page 63.
117 Davis, *Power at Odds*, 67, 77–78.
118 *Tribune* quoted in Davis, *Power at Odds*, 102.
119 Davis, *Power at Odds*, 71–76, 83–86, 89–96, 27–28.
120 Davis, *Power at Odds*, 130–35.
121 Davis, *Power at Odds*, 139.
122 Davis, *Power at Odds*, 141.
123 Grace Carlson, "Value Based Schools," 10/8/81, handwritten notes, f. SMJC, Speech and Lecture Notes, box 1, CP, MHS.
124 Grace Carlson to Sister Ann Thomasine, May 11, 1983, f. Correspondence and Memoirs, box 2, CP, MHS.
125 Mary Jo Richardson, "School to Remember. St. Joseph's Academy: The Legacy Lives On," *Ramsey County History* (2012): 21, 23. Sister Mary Lucida Savage, *The Century's Harvest: Gathered by the Sisters of St. Joseph of Carondelet in the United States* (1936), 103–5. Sister Elizabeth Marie, CSJ, *Academy for a Century: A History of Saint Joseph's Academy Located in St. Paul, Minnesota* (St. Paul, MN: North Central Publishing, 1951), 8–16.
126 Marie, *Academy for a Century*, 15, 20. Savage, *Century's Harvest*, 106.
127 Richardson, "School to Remember," 23. Marie, *Academy for a Century*, 19–20.
128 On Sr. Seraphine, see Hurley, *On Good Ground*, 216–17, and Cummings, *New Women of the Old Faith*, 72–74. On SJA's curriculum, see Savage, *Century's Harvest*, 106; *St. Joseph's Academy Handbook* (1933), 8; and *The Sixty-Ninth Annual Catalogue: St. Joseph's Academy: A Day School for Girls Conducted by the Sisters of St. Joseph* (1921), 10–11. On the accreditation see *St. Joseph's Academy Handbook* (1933), 8–9; Marie, *Academy for a Century*, 22–23; and, Savage, *Century's Harvest*, 106.
129 *The Sixty-Ninth Annual Catalogue*, 6.
130 *The Sixty-Ninth Annual Catalog*, 6.
131 Marie, *Academy for a Century*, 23.
132 *St. Joseph's Academy Handbook* (1933), 17. *School of Happy Memories: A Pictorial History, 1851–1971* (St. Paul: Minnesota Historical Society, 1971), 24, 25. *The Seventy-Second Annual Catalogue: St. Joseph's Academy: A Day School for Girls Conducted by the Sisters of St. Joseph* (1924), 7.
133 Katharine E. Harmon, "The Liturgical Movement and Catholic Action: Women Living the Liturgical Life in the Lay Apostolate," in *Empowering the People of God:*

Catholic Action before and after Vatican II, ed. Jeremy Bonner, Christopher D. Denny, and Mary Beth Fraser Connolly (New York: Fordham University Press, 2014), 50–52. McCartin, *Prayers of the Faithful*, 59–61.
134 Grace Carlson, "Value Based Schools," 10/8/81, handwritten notes, f. SMJC: Speech and Lecture Notes 4, box 1, CP, MHS.
135 Harmon, "Liturgical Movement," 52.
136 *The Sixty-Ninth Annual Catalogue*, 10–11. *St. Joseph's Academy Handbook* (1933), 26, 18–19.
137 Richardson, "School to Remember," 27.
138 Marie, *Academy for a Century*, 46.
139 *St. Joseph's Academy Handbook* (1933), 12.
140 *St. Joseph's Academy Handbook* (1933), 18. Marie, *Academy for a Century*, 38–39. *The Academy* (June 1924): 29.
141 Richardson, "School to Remember," 27.
142 Marie, *Academy for a Century*, 34. *St. Joseph's Academy Handbook* (1933), 27. *School of Happy Memories*, 28.
143 Grace Holmes, transcript, St. Joseph's Academy, box 4, Early Student Records Not Microfilmed, 1923–1926, #901–1275, St. Catherine University Archives and Special Collections, St. Paul, Minnesota (hereafter cited, SCUA-SC). *The Sixty-Ninth Annual Catalog*, 7, and *The Seventy-Second Annual Catalogue*, 8.
144 On shopmen's pay in 1920 and 1922 see Davis, *Power at Odds*, 46, 60.
145 *Academy* (June 1923): 27. *Academy* (April 1924): 36.
146 *Academy* (November 1923): 9–11.
147 *Academy* (April 1924): 10–12.
148 *Academy* (April 1924): 25–27.
149 *Academy* (June 1924): 7–10.
150 *Academy* (June 1924): 38–39.
151 *Academy* (June 1924): 44.
152 *Academy* (June 1924): 29.
153 Carlson interview with Ross, July 9, 1987, 5.
154 See Coburn and Smith, *Spirited Lives*, 147, 165.

CHAPTER 2. CONVERSION

1 I thank Steve Rosswurm for suggesting Max Weber's concept of elective affinity here. In elective affinity, "The contents of one system of meaning engender a tendency for adherents to build and pursue the other system of meaning." "Elective affinity," *Oxford Reference*, www.oxfordreference.com (accessed November 1, 2019).
2 Jane Lamm Carroll, Joanne Cavallaro, and Sharon Doherty, "Introduction: Taking Catholic Women Seriously," in *Liberating Sanctuary: 100 Years of Women's Education at the College of St. Catherine*, ed. Jane Lamm Carroll, Joanne Cavallaro, and Sharon Doherty (New York: Lexington Books, 2012), 1.
3 Carroll, Cavallaro, and Doherty, "Introduction," 3.

4 Hurley, *On Good Ground*, 229, 234. Jane Lamm Carroll, "Extravagantly Visionary Leadership: The Irelands and Sister Antonia McHugh," in *Liberating Sanctuary*, 23–31.
5 Coburn and Smith, *Spirited Lives*, 184. Hurley, *On Good Ground*, 244–51. Carroll, "Extravagantly Visionary Leadership," 33–35.
6 On the "Ideology of Catholic Womanhood," see Paula M. Kane, *Separatism and Subculture: Boston Catholicism, 1900–1920* (Chapel Hill: University of North Carolina Press, 1994), 145–99. For examples of the contemporary articulation of this ideology, see George Deshon, "Advice for Catholic Young Women," Rev. F. X. Lasance, "Rest Content with the Position God Has Ordained," and Archbishop William O'Connell, "On the Meaning of Mary," in *Gender Identities in American Catholicism*, ed. Paula M. Kane, James J. Kenneally, and Karen Kennelly, CSJ (New York: Orbis Books, 2001), 47–55, 57–59, 83–84.
7 Carroll, "Extravagantly Visionary Leadership," 19.
8 Carroll, "Extravagantly Visionary Leadership," 18–19.
9 On Josephites' earning doctorates, see Carroll, "Extravagantly Visionary Leadership," 25, 30.
10 Joanne Cavallaro, Jane Lamm Carroll, and Lynne Gildensoph, "What a Woman Should Know, What a Woman Can Be: Curriculum as Prism," in *Liberating Sanctuary*, 97.
11 *La Concha: The College of St. Catherine Yearbook* (1926): 124, SCUA-SC.
12 *La Concha* (1927): 124, SCUA-SC.
13 See, for example, *La Concha* (1926): 114, and *La Concha* (1929): 184, SCUA-SC.
14 *La Concha* (1929): 67, SCUA-SC.
15 Paula Fass, *The Damned and the Beautiful: American Youth in the 1920s* (New York: Oxford University Press, 1977), 23, 73–78.
16 On the ways in which working-class women were more than mere "bystanders" to the construction of gender, see Kathy Peiss, *Cheap Amusements: Working Women and Leisure in Turn-of-the-Century New York* (Philadelphia: Temple University Press, 1986), 6–8.
17 Fass, *The Damned and the Beautiful*, 76–77.
18 Leslie Woodcock Tentler, *Catholics and Contraception: An American History* (Ithaca, NY: Cornell University Press, 2009), 57–72.
19 Tentler, *Catholics and Contraception*, 50–51, 101–9.
20 Barrett, "*Was* the Personal Political?" 395–407.
21 See, for example, Grace's marriage noted in *Ariston* 28:4 (1934): 45 and others in *Ariston* 24:9 (1929): 49–50 and 24:2 (1930): 42, 46, 60, SCUA-SC.
22 See for example, *Ariston* 24:1 (1929): 6; *Ariston* 25:2 (1931): 45–48; *Ariston* 27:1 (1932): 43–44; *Ariston* 25:3 (1931): 43–44; *Ariston* 26:2 (1932): 49, 56; and *Ariston* 25:4 (1932): 32, SCUA-SC.
23 Cavallaro, Carroll, and Gildensoph, "What a Woman Should Know," 101.
24 Julie Balamut and Virginia Steinhagen "Learning and Earning: The Work-Study Experience," in *Liberating Sanctuary*, 161–63.

25 Cavallaro, Carroll, and Gildensoph, "What a Woman Should Know," 95–119. John Fleming, "Portrait of a Daughter of St. Joseph, Sister Jeanne Marie Bonnett," in *Liberating Sanctuary*, 46.
26 Cavallaro, Carroll, and Gildensoph, "What a Woman Should Know," 98.
27 Cavallaro, Carroll, and Gildensoph, "What a Woman Should Know," 95–103.
28 The College of St. Catherine, College Record of Carlson (Grace Holmes), College Records, box 4: Early Student Records Not Microfilmed, 1923–1926, #901–1275, SCUA-SC.
29 College of St. Catherine, College Record of Carlson.
30 Raymond Schultz, e-mail to author, October 3, 2016.
31 State of Minnesota, Department of Vital Statistics, *Certificate of Death: Mary J. Holmes*, May 1, 1926, registered no. 02411.
32 "Grace Carlson: Forever an Activist," *Good News* 8:2 (Winter 1988): 5.
33 See, for example, *Ariston* 22:2 (Winter 1928): 2 and *Ariston* 23:3 (April 1929): 25, SCUA-SC.
34 *La Concha* (1929): 112, SCUA-SC.
35 *Ariston* 23:2 (February 1929): 52 and *La Concha* (1929): 154–55, SCUA-SC.
36 *La Concha* (1929): 116; *Ariston* 25:4 (June 1931): 53; *Ariston* 25:3 (1931): 43, SCUA-SC.
37 *Ariston* 25:3 (1931): 44, SCUA-SC.
38 *Ariston* 26:4 (Summer 1932): 32, SCUA-SC.
39 *La Concha* (1929): n.p., SCUA-SC.
40 For references to these events, see, for example, *La Concha* (1926): 11; *La Concha* (1927): 102; *La Concha* (1928): 62, 161, 162; *La Concha* (1929): 150, 164, 169, SCUA-SC.
41 Russell Conners, Joyce K. Dahlberg, Catherine Litecky, CSJ, Mary Lou Logsdon, and Thomas West, "Theology Fit for Women: Religious Wisdom, St. Catherine's Style," in *Liberating Sanctuary*, 125.
42 *Ariston*, 26:3 (Spring 1932): 44, SCUA-SC.
43 "Grace Holmes Carlson," *SCAN* (Spring 1986): 12. Moore, "Remembering Grace Holmes Carlson," f. SMJC Faculty, Grace Carlson, box 4, SMJC Collection, CSJ Archive. There is no record in the CSJ Archive that Grace ever entered the convent: see Michelle Hueg, e-mail to author, April 1 and 12, 2019.
44 See, for example, the directory page that lists Grace and Dorothy in 1929: *La Concha* (1929): 136.
45 Carlson interview with Ross, July 9, 1987, 5.
46 "Grace Holmes Carlson," *SCAN* (Spring 1986): 12.
47 Carlson, interview with Ross, July 9, 1987, 2.
48 University of Minnesota, Office of the Registrar, Transcript Record for Grace Marie Holmes. See also "Biographical Sketch: Grace Carlson," f. biographical information, box 1 CP, MHS.
49 Grace Holmes, "A Statistical Study of a New Type of Objective Examination Question" (MA thesis, University of Minnesota, July 1930). Quotation from p. 13.

50 Grace Marie Holmes, "A Study on Work Decrement" (PhD diss., University of Minnesota, June 1933). Quotation from p. 124.
51 Holmes, "A Study on Work Decrement," "Acknowledgements" page (unnumbered), and pp. 35, 39, 45, 52, 55, 58, 67, 75, 82, 103.
52 "The Biennial Report of the President of the University of Minnesota to the Board of Regents, 1934–1936," 107, 110, https://conservancy.umn.edu (accessed October 18, 2018).
53 On the early years of the Depression and the first hundred days, see David M. Kennedy, *Freedom from Fear: The American People in Depression and War, 1929–1945* (New York: Oxford University Press, 2005), 70–189.
54 Carlson interview with Ross, July 9, 1987, 6.
55 Carlson interview with Ross, July 9, 1987, 25.
56 W. Philips Shively, "In Memoriam: Benjamin Evans Lippincott," *PS: Political Sciences & Politics* (March 1989): 99–100. William C. Smith, review of *On the Economic Theory of Socialism* by Oskar Lange, Fred M. Taylor, and Benjamin E. Lippincott, *Social Science* 16:4 (October 1941): 399.
57 Grace Carlson to Bill Morgan, 1973, f. Misc. info. on SWP, box 1, CP, MHS.
58 Charles Rumford Walker, *American City: A Rank and File History of Minneapolis* (Minneapolis: University of Minnesota Press, 2005), 84–85.
59 Carlson interview with Ross, July 9, 1987, 25.
60 Iric Nathanson, "Olson, Floyd B. (1891–1936)," MNopedia, Minnesota Historical Society, http://www.mnopedia.org (accessed October 19, 2018).
61 Tom O'Connell, "Minnesota Farmer-Labor Party, 1924–1944," MNopedia, Minnesota Historical Society, http://www.mnopedia.org (accessed October 19, 2018). On the origins of the Farmer-Labor movement, see also Wingerd, *Claiming the City*, 209–10, 218, 220–21, 232, 240–42.
62 Interview with Grace Holmes Carlson, by Carl Ross, July 14, 1987, transcript page 30, Twentieth-Century Radicalism in Minnesota Project, MHS. "Grace Carlson, New York" (New York: Paris/Ram Productions, 1987), Avery Fisher Center, New York University Library, New York University, New York, NY (hereafter, AFC, NYU).
63 Robert Cohen, *When the Old Left Was Young: Student Radicals and America's First Mass Student Movement, 1929–1941* (New York: Oxford University Press, 1993). Ralph S. Brax, *The First Student Movement: Student Activism in the United States during the 1930s* (Port Washington, NY: Kennikat Press, 1981), 28–61. George W. Garlid, "The Antiwar Dilemma of the Farmer-Labor Party," *Minnesota History* 40:8 (Winter 1967): 365–69.
64 Cohen, *When the Old Left Was Young*, 22, 31–38, 94–95.
65 Carlson interview with Ross, July 9, 1987, 25.
66 Paul LeBlanc, "Trotskyism in the United States: The First Fifty Years," in *Trotskyism in the United States: Historical Essays and Reconsiderations*, ed. George Breitman, Paul LeBlanc, and Alan Wald (Chicago: Haymarket Books, 2016), 12–16. Fraser M. Ottanelli, *The Communist Party of the United States: From Depression to

World War II (New Brunswick, NJ: Rutgers University Press, 1991), 9–48. Bryan D. Palmer, *James P. Cannon and the Origins of the American Revolutionary Left, 1890-1928* (Urbana: University of Illinois Press, 2007). James A. Barrett, *William Z. Foster and the Tragedy of American Radicalism* (Urbana: University of Illinois Press, 1999).

67 Palmer, *James P. Cannon*, 334–49. Constance Ashton Myers, *The Prophet's Army: Trotskyists in America, 1928-1941* (Westport, CT: Greenwood, 1977), 32–41. Philip A. Korth, *The Minneapolis Teamsters Strike of 1934* (East Lansing: Michigan State University Press, 1995), 8.

68 Carlson interview with Ross, July 14, 1987, 41.

69 On the third period, see Ottanelli, *The Communist Party of the United States*, 18–48, and Bryan D. Palmer, *Revolutionary Teamsters: The Minneapolis Truckers' Strikes of 1934* (Chicago: Haymarket Books, 2013), 275–76. On physical fights see, for example, the discussion of the Madison Square Garden riot in 1934 in Ottanelli, *The Communist Party of the United States*, 56–57, and of the Communist attack on various CLA members in Minneapolis in 1929 in Palmer, *Revolutionary Teamsters*, 277–78.

70 Carlson interview with Ross, July 14, 1987, 30.

71 On creation of the Workers Party through the merging of the Communist Left Opposition and the American Workers Party in late 1934, see LeBlanc, "Trotskyism in the United States," 27. Quotation from Carlson interview with Ross, July 9, 1987, 6.

72 A garage at 1900 Chicago Avenue served as strike headquarters during the May strike. Headquarters for the July strike were at 215 South Eighth Street. See Palmer, *Revolutionary Teamsters*, 83–86, 154.

73 "Grace Carlson, New York," AFC, NYU. "Grace Holmes Carlson," *SCAN* (Spring 1986): 12. Carlson interview with Ross, July 9, 1987, 6.

74 Grace Carlson to Bill Morgan, 1973, f. Misc. info on SWP, box 1, CP, MHS.

75 Grace Carlson to Bill Morgan, 1973.

76 Henry Schultz, 1910, Minneapolis Ward 9, Hennepin, Minnesota, *Thirteenth Census of the United States, 1910*, NARA Microfilm Publication T624, roll T624_704, page 2B, RG29. FBI file on Henry Schultz, 100–1078, St. Paul, 11/6/44, p. 1, FOIA, in author's possession.

77 On the meeting, see "Grace Carlson, New York," AFC, NYU. On Schultz's role in the strike, see Farrell Dobbs, *Teamsters Rebellion* (New York: Pathfinder, 2004), 164.

78 Carlson to Morgan, 1973, f. Misc. info on SWP, box 1, CP, MHS.

79 On the CA, see Philip A. Korth, *The Minneapolis Teamster Strike of 1934* (East Lansing: Michigan State University Press, 1995), 13–22; William Millikan, *Union against Unions: The Minneapolis Citizens Alliance and Its Fight against Organized Labor, 1903-1947* (St. Paul: Minnesota Historical Society Press, 2003); and George Dimitri Tselos, "The Minneapolis Labor Movement in the 1930s" (PhD diss., University of Minnesota, 1970), 12–25.

80 On Dunne's background, see interview with Vincent Raymond Dunne by Lila Johnson Goff, April 27, 1969, MHS. Farrell Dobbs, *Teamster Rebellion* (New York: Pathfinder, 1972; repr. 2004), 38. On Skoglund see interview with Carl Skoglund, Twentieth-Century Radicalism in Minnesota Oral History Project, interviewer unidentified, n.d., MHS. *Who Are the 18 Prisoners in the Minneapolis Labor Case?* (New York: Civil Rights Defense Committee, 1944), 27.

81 Palmer, *Revolutionary Teamsters*, 3–9.

82 *Who Are the 18?* 15–17.

83 On DeBoer see Palmer, *Revolutionary Teamsters*, 165–66. On Dobbs, see his "Notes on 'Funeral Address—for Grant John Dunne' October 7, 1941," Minneapolis, Minn., f. 3, 1941, box 8 Speeches and Writings, Farrell Dobbs Papers, 1928–1983, Wisconsin Historical Society Library (hereafter cited as WHS).

84 James Green, *The World of the Worker: Labor in Twentieth-Century America* (Urbana: University of Illinois Press, 1998), 140–48.

85 Korth, *Minneapolis Teamsters Strike*, 58–64. Interview with V. Dunne by Goff, April 27, 1969. Dobbs, *Teamster Rebellion*, 58–70.

86 Dobbs, *Teamster Rebellion*, 70–86. Korth, *Minneapolis Teamsters Strike*, 80–81.

87 Dobbs, *Teamster Rebellion*, 94–126. Korth, *Minneapolis Teamsters Strike*, xii, 92–105. Palmer, *Revolutionary Teamsters*, 87–125. Green, *World of the Worker*, 143–46.

88 Dobbs, *Teamster Rebellion*, 127–45. Palmer, *Revolutionary Teamsters*, 137–57.

89 "Grace Carlson, New York," AFC, NYU.

90 Le Sueur quoted in Palmer, *Revolutionary Teamsters*, 163. Palmer, *Revolutionary Teamsters*, 159–65.

91 Palmer, *Revolutionary Teamsters*, 164.

92 "Grace Carlson, New York," AFC, NYU.

93 Korth, *Minneapolis Teamsters Strike*, 162–63. Palmer, *Revolutionary Teamsters*, 219–22. Thaddeus Russell, *Out of the Jungle: Jimmy Hoffa and the Remaking of the American Working Class* (Philadelphia: Temple University Press, 2001), 36–37.

94 University of Minnesota, "Commencement Convocation Winter Quarter 1933," 26, https://conservancy.umn.edu (accessed June 25, 2018).

95 Carlson interview with Ross, July 14, 1987, 30.

96 "Grace Carlson, New York," AFC, NYU.

97 "Gilbert Edward Carlson, Birth Record," certificate number 1909-36261, April 6, 1909, Minnesota, Birth Index, 1900–1934, MHS. Gilbert Carlson, 1910, St. Paul Ward 6, Ramsey, Minnesota, *Thirteenth Census of the United States, 1910*, NARA Microfilm Publication T624, roll T624_719, page 3B, RG29. For location of West St. Paul in this era, see map in Wingerd, *Claiming the City*, 74–75.

98 Gilbert Carlson, 1920, St. Paul Ward 6, Ramsey, Minnesota, *Fourteenth Census of the United States, 1920*, NARA Microfilm Publication T625, roll T625_853, page 6B, RG29.

99 "Minneapolis, Minnesota, City Directory, 1921," entry for Gilbert E. Carlson, Ancestry.com.

100 Gilbert Carlson, 1930, St. Paul, Ramsey, Minnesota, *Fifteenth Census of the United States, 1930*, NARA Microfilm Publication T626, roll T626, page 19A, RG29. "St. Paul, Minnesota, City Directory, 1931," entry for Gilbert E. Carlson, Ancestry.com.
101 Dorothy Holmes Schultz, interview with Elizabeth Raasch-Gilman, December 29, 1994, in author's possession.
102 Carlson interview with Ross, July 9, 1987, 29–30, 6. *Program and Constitution of the Non-Partisan Labor Defense*, Non-Partisan Labor Defense, 1934–1935, SWP Records, micro 2050 reel 48, SWP Records, WHS.
103 Carlson interview with Ross, July 9, 1987, 29–30, 6.
104 Charles Walker to Herbert Solow, May 28, 1936, f. Walker, Charles, Correspondence, Charles Walker Papers, MHS.
105 Robert Schrank, *Wasn't That a Time? Growing Up Radical and Red in America* (Cambridge, MA: MIT Press, 1998), 126.
106 Certificate of Marriage, Gilbert E. Carlson to Grace M. Holmes, 28 July 1934, Ramsey County, Minnesota, Book 177, page 469, microfilm reel 49, MHS.
107 *Minneapolis Star*, July 29, 1934, 7, section 15.
108 Elizabeth Faue, *Writing the Wrongs: Eva Valesh and the Rise of Labor Journalism* (Ithaca, NY: Cornell University Press, 2002), 5.
109 Marriage notation (February 18, 1937) on Baptismal Certificate for Helen Dorsey Holmes, January 2, 1906, St. Peter Claver, Saint Paul, Minnesota, Archives of the Archdiocese of Saint Paul and Minneapolis.
110 Mary Lethert Wingerd, interview with Dorothy Holmes, August 31, 1995, summarized in Wingerd, *Claiming the City*, fn.7, pp. 314–15.
111 The reconstitution was connected to the Trotskyists' entry into the Socialist Party in 1936. See Alan M. Wald, *The New York Intellectuals: The Rise and Decline of the Anti-Stalinist Left from the 1930s to the 1980s* (Chapel Hill: University of North Carolina Press, 2017), 110.
112 Carlson interview with Ross, July 9, 1987, 6. Walker, *American City*, 64.
113 Grace Carlson to Sarah Colvin, September 29, 1939, f. Pre-SWP Correspondence, box 1, CP, MHS. On Colvin, see Sarah Tarleton Colvin, *A Rebel in Thought* (New York: Island Press, 1944).
114 "Grace Holmes Carlson," *SCAN* (Spring 1986): 12.
115 "Named to Direct Rehabilitation Work," *Journal*, November 11, 1935, n.p. Clipping in f. Pre-SWP Correspondence, box 1, CP, MHS.
116 Grace H. Carlson and Donald H. Dabelstein, "The Vocational Rehabilitation of the Tuberculous: A Preliminary Report," *American Review of Tuberculosis* 42:5 (November 1940): 674–81.
117 "Unemployment Conference Was Huge Success," *Advocate*, March 1, 1940, and "Unemployment Called Government Problem," *St. Paul Pioneer Press*, March 1, 1940, clippings in f. Pre-SWP Correspondence, box 1, CP, MHS.
118 Mrs. Grace Carlson, "What the St. Paul Labor Movement Is Doing in Workers' Education," in "Report of Saint Paul Fifth Annual Workers' Education Conference Held February 10, 1940—Saint Francis Hotel," page 5, f. Pre-SWP Correspon-

dence, box 1, CP, MHS. "More Than 150 Delegates Attend Fifth Annual Workers' Education Conference: New Plans Approved," *Minnesota Union Advocate*, February 15, 1940, and "Benefits of Labor Education Cited," *St. Paul Pioneer Press*, February 11, 1940, f. Pre-SWP Correspondence, box 1, CP, MHS.

119 Tom Beer and Tom O'Connell, "Father Francis Gilligan and the Struggle for Civil Rights," *Minnesota History* (Summer 2011): 205–10.

120 "Report of Saint Paul Fifth Annual Workers' Education Conference," page 1, and "More Than 150 Delegates Attend."

121 On the "range of perceptions and commitments" that make up a revolutionary Marxist viewpoint, see Paul LeBlanc, "Leninism in the United States and the Decline of American Trotskyism," in *Trotskyism in the United States: Historical Essays and Reconsiderations*, ed. George Breitman, Paul LeBlanc, and Alan Wald (Chicago: Haymarket Books, 2016), 218.

122 George Breitman, "The Liberating Influence of the Transitional Program: Three Talks," in *Trotskyism in the United States*, 133–34. James Cannon, *History of American Trotskyism, 1928–1938: Report of a Participant* (New York: Pathfinder, 1944), 287.

123 Breitman, "The Liberating Influence," 134. Cannon, *History of American Trotskyism*, 287–306.

124 LeBlanc, "Trotskyism in the United States," 32.

125 Carlson interview with Ross, July 9, 1987, 6.

126 "Declaration of Principles and Constitution of the Socialist Workers Party," pp. 3–10, f. 41, box 169, Collection of Communist and Socialist Serials, Tamiment Library and Robert F. Wagner Labor Archives, Elmer Holmes Bobst Library, New York, NY (hereafter, CCSS, Tamiment).

127 "Declaration of Principles," 10–11, 19, f. 41, box 169, CCSS, Tamiment.

128 Breitman, "The Liberating Influence," 134.

129 Wald, *The New York Intellectuals*, 168–71.

130 Wald, *The New York Intellectuals*, 170.

131 Palmer, *James P. Cannon*, 195–98.

132 "Grace Carlson, New York," AFC, NYU.

133 On the fears of Nazi subversion see Francis MacDonnell, *Insidious Foes: The Axis Fifth Column and the American Home Front* (New York: Oxford University Press, 1995). On the little red scare's origins, see Donna T. Haverty-Stacke, *Trotskyists on Trial: Free Speech and Political Persecution since the Age of FDR* (New York: NYU Press, 2015), 27–30. On FDR's orders to the FBI, see Douglas M. Charles, *J. Edgar Hoover and the Anti-Interventionists: FBI Political Surveillance and the Rise of the Domestic Security State, 1939–1945* (Columbus: Ohio State University, 2007), 31, 33–34, and Frank J. Donner, *The Age of Surveillance: The Aims and Methods of America's Political Intelligence System* (New York: Vintage, 1980), 53. On support for federal restrictions on alleged security threats, see Richard W. Steele, "Fear of the Mob and Faith in Government in Free Speech Discourse, 1919–1941," *American Journal of Legal History* 38:1 (January 1994): 55–83. On Dies, see Richard

Gid Powers, *Not without Honor: The History of American Anticommunism* (New Haven, CT: Yale University Press, 1995), 124–25, and Michal R. Belknap, *Cold War Political Justice: The Smith Act, the Communist Party, and American Civil Liberties* (Westport, CT: Greenwood, 1977), 21. On the way the little red scare functioned in the public and private sector, see Robert Justin Goldstein ed., *Little "Red Scares": Anti-Communism and Political Repression in the United States, 1921–1946* (Surrey, UK: Ashgate, 2014).

134 Carlson interview with Ross, July 9, 1987, 24.
135 John G. Rockwell to Grace Carlson, April 1, 1940, f. Pre-SWP Correspondence, box 1, CP, MHS.
136 On Rockwell keeping aloof, see Colvin, *A Rebel in Thought*, 205. On Rockwell's later explanation, see *St. Paul Pioneer Press*, August 3, 1940, clipping in f. Rockwell Case—Supreme Court file #33143, Plaintiff's Exhibits 1941, box 2, Rockwell and Carstater Hearing Files, Commissioner's Office, Education Department, MHS (hereafter RHR, MHS).
137 Grace Carlson to John G. Rockwell, April 1, 1940, f. Pre-SWP Correspondence, box 1, CP, MHS.
138 Grace Carlson to D. H. Dabelstein, August 21, 1940, f. Pre-SWP Correspondence, box 1, CP, MHS.
139 State of Minnesota, Civil Service Department, "Report of Separation" for Grace H. Carlson, signed August 25, 1940, f. Pre-SWP Correspondence, box 1, CP, MHS.
140 Grace Carlson to Dr. E. S. Mariette, August 27, 1940, f. Pre-SWP Correspondence, box 1, CP, MHS.
141 John G. Rockwell to Grace Carlson, August 28, 1940, f. Pre-SWP Correspondence, box 1, CP, MHS.
142 Grace Carlson to John G. Rockwell, August 29, 1940, f. Pre-SWP Correspondence, box 1, CP, MHS.
143 "Grace Carlson Is Full-Time Party Worker Now," *Militant*, September 7, 1940, 4. Program from the Leon Trotsky Memorial Meeting, August 29, 1940, f. SWP, Minneapolis, Minn. Papers, Campaign Literature and Printed Materials, 1939–48, box 1, SWP Minnesota Section Records, MHS.
144 "In the Matter of the Removal of John G. Rockwell—Defendant—as Commissioner of Education, by the Board of Education, State of Minnesota—Plaintiff," transcript of hearings December 26 and 27, 1940, pages 3 and 4, box 1, RHR, MHS. *State ex. Rel. Rockwell v. State Board of Education*, 6N.W. 2d 251 (Minn. 1942).
145 "In the Matter of the Removal of John G. Rockwell," transcript of hearings March 5, 1941, pp. 3076–3184, and December 26, 1940, p. 29, box 1, RHR, MHS.
146 *Zumbrota News*, September 6, 1940, n.p., reproduced in f. Clippings, 1938–1941, box 2, RHR, MHS.
147 For supportive press coverage, see, for example, Mary Herrick, "Dr. Rockwell vs. Minnesota Spoils," *American Teacher*, 10–12, f. Clippings, 1938–1941, box 2, RHR, MHS. On the state supreme court's final decision, see *State ex. Rel. Rockwell v. State Board of Education*, 6N.W. 2d 251 (Minn. 1942).

148 On the state aid and teachers' certification controversies, see *State ex. Rel. Rockwell v. State Board of Education*, 6N.W. 2d 251 (Minn. 1942).
149 Carlson interview with Ross, July 9, 1987, 24.
150 Carlson interview with Ross, July 9, 1987, 7.
151 Carlson interview with Ross, July 9, 1987, 7, and July 14, 1987, 28. "Grace Carlson, New York," AFC, NYU. On Gilbert's continued work as an attorney for the Trotskyist-led Teamsters, see *Minneapolis Star*, March 11, 1938, 1; *Minneapolis Star Journal*, June 17, 1941, 1; *Minneapolis Star*, September 19, 1941, 1; and, *Minneapolis Star Journal*, February 11, 1942, 17.

CHAPTER 3. SISTERHOODS

1 Brown and Faue, "Social Bonds, Sexual Politics," 11, 14.
2 Dorothy Schultz to Grace Carlson, January 23, 1944, f. 3, box 1, CP, MHS.
3 On the variants of feminisms during the 1940s and 1950s, see Joanne Meyerowitz ed., *Not June Cleaver: Women and Gender in Postwar America* (Philadelphia: Temple University Press, 1994); Leila J. Rupp and Verta Taylor, *Survival in the Doldrums: The American Women's Rights Movement, 1945–1960* (New York: Oxford University Press, 1987); and, Cobble, *The Other Women's Movement*.
4 Carlson interview with Ross, July 14, 1987, 38, and July 9, 1987, 12.
5 Carlson interview with Ross, July 14, 1987, 32, and July 9, 1987, 14.
6 George Novack quoted in LeBlanc, "Trotskyism in the United States," 34.
7 LeBlanc, "Trotskyism in the United States," 34.
8 Grace Carlson, V. R. Dunne, and Carlos Hudson, "Minnesota Answers the Minority," Minutes—Political Committee/National Committee/National Conventions, micro 596 reel 1, SWP Records, WHS.
9 Le Blanc, "Trotskyism in the United States," 34. James P. Cannon, "The Convention of the Socialist Workers Party, April 1940," in *James P. Cannon: Writings and Speeches; The Socialist Workers Party in World War II* (New York: Pathfinder Press, 2002), 31–37.
10 "Grace Carlson, New York," AFC, NYU.
11 Elizabeth Faue, *Community of Suffering and Struggle: Women, Men, and the Labor Movement in Minneapolis, 1915–1945* (Chapel Hill: University of North Carolina Press, 1991), 19, 120–21, 122–24, 142. Marjorie Penn Lasky, "'Where I Was a Person': The Ladies' Auxiliary in the 1934 Minneapolis Teamsters' Strikes," in *Women, Work, and Protest: A Century of Women's Labor History*, ed. Ruth Milkman (New York: Routledge, 1985), 181–205.
12 Grace Carlson, "Biographical Sketch," f. Pre-SWP Correspondence, box 1, CP, MHS.
13 The party touted Grace's working-class and trade union background. See "Meet the SWP Candidate," *Militant*, August 24, 1946, n.p., Scrapbook Vol. 6: SWP 1946 Election Campaign, SWP Minnesota Section Records, 1914–1980, MHS.
14 "Grace Holmes Carlson," *SCAN* (Spring 1986): 12.
15 Linda K. Kerber, "Separate Spheres, Female Worlds, Woman's Place: The Rhetoric of Women's History," *Journal of American History* 75:1 (June 1988): 9–39. Barbara

Welter, "The Cult of True Womanhood: 1820–1860," *American Quarterly* 18:2, part 1 (Summer 1966): 151–74. Linda Kerber, "The Republican Mother: Women and the Enlightenment—An American Perspective," *American Quarterly* 28:2 (Summer 1976): 187–205.

16 Eleanor Flexner and Ellen Fitzpatrick, *A Century of Struggle: The Woman's Rights Movement in the United States*, enlarged edition (Cambridge, MA: Belknap, 1996). Louise A. Tilly and Patricia Gurin, "Introduction: Women, Politics, and Change," in *Women, Politics, and Change*, ed. Louise A. Tilly and Patricia Gurin (New York: Russell Sage Foundation, 1990), 3–32.

17 See, for example, Nancy A. Hewitt, *Women's Activism and Social Change: Rochester, New York, 1822–1872* (Ithaca, NY: Cornell University Press, 1984); Mari Jo Buhle, *Women and American Socialism, 1870–1920* (Chicago: University of Illinois Press, 1981); Annelise Orleck, *Common Sense and a Little Fire: Women and Working-Class Politics in the United States, 1900–1965* (Chapel Hill: University of North Carolina Press, 1995).

18 Susan Ware, *Holding Their Own: American Women in the 1930s* (Boston: Twayne, 1982), 95–96.

19 Susan M. Hartmann, *The Home Front and Beyond: American Women in the 1940s* (Boston: Twayne, 1982), 149–50.

20 Hartmann, *The Home Front and Beyond*, 152–53.

21 *Socialist Appeal*, September 21, 1940, 1; October 12, 1940, 3; and, October 26, 1940, 2.

22 *Socialist Appeal*, November 9, 1940, 1.

23 *Socialist Appeal*, November 2, 1940, 2.

24 *Socialist Appeal*, October 12, 1940, 3.

25 James P. Cannon, *Socialism on Trial: The Official Court Record of James P. Cannon's Testimony in the Famous Minneapolis Sedition Trial*, 2nd edition (New York: Pioneer Press, 1944), 44.

26 David M. Kennedy, *Freedom from Fear: The American People in Depression and War, 1929–1945* (New York: Oxford University Press, 2005), 426–64.

27 Kennedy, *Freedom from Fear*, 459.

28 *Socialist Appeal*, September 21, 1940, 1.

29 On the 1940 platform, see *Socialist Appeal*, September 21, 1940, 1. On the Trotskyists' position on civil rights, see "Negroes and Other Oppressed Groups" in "Declaration of Principles and Constitution of the Socialist Workers Party," p. 22, f. 41, box 169, CCSS, Tamiment. On Grace's membership in the NAACP, see Ledger Book, Volume 1, page 134, and Volume 2, page 34, Saint Paul Branch of the NAACP Records, MHS. On Grace's appeal to women, see *Socialist Appeal*, December 14, 1940, 1.

30 "General Election Returns for Minnesota, Tuesday, November Fifth 1940," http://www.leg.state.mn.us (accessed November 28, 2018).

31 *Socialist Appeal*, November 30, 1940, 1.

32 Grace Carlson to Rose Karsner, November 13, 1940, f. 1, box 1, CP, MHS.

33 *Militant*, February 8, 1941, 4.
34 Grace Carlson to Natalia Sedova, November 13, 1940, f. 1, box 1, CP, MHS.
35 Grace Carlson to Farrell Dobbs, November 13, 1940, and Grace Carlson to James Cannon, December 1, 1940, f. 1, box 1, CP, MHS.
36 On "woman leader," see postscript added to letter from Carlson to Sedova, November 26, 1940, f. 1, box 1, CP, MHS. On "place for you," see Farrell Dobbs to Grace Carlson, September 17, 1940, f. 1, box 1, CP, MHS.
37 Dobbs to Carlson, November 13, 1940, and November 28, 1940, f. 1, box 1, CP, MHS.
38 James Cannon to All Locals and Branches, December 3, 1940, f. 1, box 1, CP, MHS.
39 Dobbs to Carlson, April 15, 1941, f. 1, box 1, CP, MHS.
40 *Militant*, February 8, 1941, 2.
41 "Declaration of Principles and Constitution of the Socialist Workers Party," p. 29, f. 41, box 169, CCSS, Tamiment. On Grace's election as an alternate, see the handwritten list of National Committee members, October 1941, f. 15 National Committee, Oct. 10–12, 1941, box 14, George Breitman Papers, Tamiment Library and Robert F. Wagner Labor Archives, Elmer Holmes Bobst Library, New York, NY (hereafter, Breitman Papers, Tamiment).
42 National Committee Minutes (October 2–4, 1942), f. 19, box 14, Breitman Papers, Tamiment.
43 U.S. Congress, Senate, Subcommittee of the Committee on the Judiciary, Hearing on H.R. 5138, *Crime to Promote the Overthrow of Government*, 76th Cong., 3rd sess., May 17, 1940, 1–5.
44 *St. Paul Dispatch*, June 28, 1941, 1, 3.
45 *Star Journal Tribune*, June 29, 1941, 2.
46 *Minneapolis Star Journal*, July 11, 1941, n.p., f. SWP, 1941 Sedition Trial Newspaper Clippings, box 1, CP, MHS.
47 On the FBI's infiltration see, for example, Robert Hawn to Daniel J. Tobin, April 17, 1941, f. Local 544, Minneapolis 1939–1941, box 44, series II, International Brotherhood of Teamsters Records, WHS (hereafter, IBT WHS).
48 FBI 100–1022, St. Paul, 4/5/41, Perrin, f. 1, box 108, Socialist Workers Declassified Papers 146-1-10, General Records of the Department of Justice, RG 60, National Archives at College Park, Maryland (hereafter, SWP 146-1-10). FBI 100–1246, St. Paul, 7/26/41 by R. T. Noonan, f. 3, box 108, SWP 146-1-10. *Minneapolis Star Journal*, June 28, 1941, 1, 8.
49 *U.S. v. Dunne et al.* (8th Cir. 1941) Abstract of the Record (microfilm: 1 reel) 5–12, Tamiment Library and Robert F. Wagner Labor Archives, Elmer Holmes Bobst Library, New York, NY (hereafter *U.S. v. Dunne et al.*).
50 "The FBI-Gestapo Attack on the Socialist Workers Party," *Fourth International* 2:6 (1941): 163–66. *Minneapolis Morning Tribune*, July 25, 1941, 20. *Minneapolis Star Journal*, July 17, 1941, 15. "Civil Liberties in Minneapolis," *New Republic*, July 28, 1941, 103–4. I. F. Stone, "The G-String Conspiracy," *Nation*, July 26, 1941, 66–67.

51 *Militant*, October 11, 1941, 1, 4. Carlson to Sedova, October 20, 1941, f. 1, box 1, CP, MHS.
52 Farrell Dobbs, notes on "Funeral Address—for Grant John Dunne," October 7, 1941, f. 3, 1941, box 8, Speeches and Writings, Dobbs Papers, WHS.
53 Haverty-Stacke, *Trotskyists on Trial*, 93–104.
54 *U.S. vs. Dunne et al.*, 854–57.
55 Haverty-Stacke, *Trotskyists on Trial*, 109–22.
56 *Minneapolis Times*, November 25, 1941, 1.
57 *U.S. vs. Dunne et al.*, 488–89, 522–24, 588–90, 618, 792–96, 822–23, 1093–95.
58 *U.S. vs. Dunne et al.*, 1112–15.
59 *U.S. vs. Dunne et al.*, 1114.
60 Haverty-Stacke, *Trotskyists on Trial*, 104–5, 109. Richard Polenberg, *Fighting Faiths: The Abrams Case, the Supreme Court, and Free Speech* (Ithaca, NY: Cornell University Press, 1987) and Geoffrey R. Stone, *Perilous Times: Free Speech in Wartime from the Sedition Act of 1798 to the War on Terrorism* (New York: Norton, 2004), 192–212.
61 Schweinhaut's closing argument, p. 19, f. 2 #7256 US v. Dunne, box 194, Records of the District Courts of the United States, RG 21, National Archives at Kansas City, Kansas City, MO (hereafter cited as RG 21, KC).
62 Schweinhaut's closing argument, p. 19, f. 2 #7256 US v. Dunne, box 194, RG 21, KC, 23.
63 Haverty-Stacke, *Trotskyists on Trial*, 134–37.
64 C. Charles, telegram December 8, 1941, micro 596 reel 27, SWP Records, WHS.
65 Haverty-Stacke, *Trotskyists on Trial*, 139–41.
66 Carlson to Sedova, February 17, 1942, and February 21, 1942, f. 1, box 1, CP, MHS.
67 *Militant*, February 21, 1942, 1.
68 United States Circuit Court of Appeals, Eighth Circuit, Opinion, No. 12,195, *Vincent Raymond Dunne et al. vs. United States of America*, 1317–21, in Albert Goldman Papers (microfilm edition: reel 1), WHS.
69 *United States Law Week*, vol. 12, sec. 3 (November 23, 1943): 3149, n.p., 3187.
70 "Rehearing Denied," *United States Law Week*, vol. 12, sec. 3 (November 23, 1943): 3187. Eric A. Posner and Adrian Vermeule, *Terror in the Balance: Security, Liberty, and the Courts* (New York: Oxford University Press, 2007), 16.
71 *Militant*, January 1, 1944, 1, 5.
72 Carlson to Sedova, December 16 and 30, 1943, f. 2, box 1, CP, MHS.
73 "Carter" does not come up on the list of party pseudonyms kept by George Breitman, most likely because Braverman did not publish under that name. Several factors, including the timing of her activities in New York and references to her husband, Harry, identify Carter as Braverman nonetheless. Use of such "mailing names" to protect one's identity from the state was not uncommon among members of the SWP. See "List of Pseudonyms," f. 14, box 62, Breitman Papers, Tamiment.

74   Telegram from New York Local SWP to Grace Carlson, December 28, 1943, and Carlson to Sedova, December 30, 1943, f. 2, box 1, CP, MHS.
75   *Militant*, January 8, 1944, 1, 5.
76   *Militant*, January 8, 1944, 1, 5.
77   *Militant*, January 8, 1944, 5.
78   *Militant*, January 8, 1944, 1.
79   Grace Carlson to Evelyn Anderson, January 7, 1944, f. 3, box 1, CP, MHS. Carlson interview with Ross, July 9, 1987, 7.
80   Grace Carlson to Dorothy and Henry Schultz, December 11, 1943, f. 2, box 1, CP, MHS.
81   Carlson to Anderson, January 7, 1944, f. 3, box 1, CP, MHS.
82   Carlson to Schultz, January 16, 1944, f. 3, box 1, CP, MHS.
83   Carlson to Schultz, January 16, 1944, f. 3, box 1, CP, MHS.
84   Mary B. Harris, *I Knew Them in Prison* (New York: Viking, 1936), 285. See also Rose Giallombardo, *Society of Women: A Study of a Women's Prison* (New York: Wiley, 1966), 21–28.
85   Harris, *I Knew Them*, 372–73. On work assignments and classes at the time Grace was incarcerated, see her copy of "Greetings to a Newcomer: Alderson West Virginia," pp. 4 and 5, f. 3, box 1, CP, MHS.
86   L. Mara Dodge, "Discipline, Resistance, and Social Control at the Illinois Reformatory for Women, 1930–1962," *Incarcerated Women: A History of Struggles, Oppression, and Resistance in American Prisons*, ed. Erica Rhodes Hayden and Theresa R. Jach (New York: Lexington Books, 2017), 101–2.
87   Harris, *I Knew Them*, 296–97.
88   Carlson to Schultz, January 16, 1944, f. 3, box 1, CP, MHS. Requests to the Bureau of Prisons for Grace's inmate file from Alderson prison have gone unanswered.
89   Department of Justice, Penal and Correctional Institutions, "Sentence Notice to Inmate," to Grace Carlson, no. 6512-W, f. 3, box 1, CP, MHS.
90   Helen Bryan, *Inside* (Boston: Houghton Mifflin, 1953), 8–12.
91   Carlson to Schultz, January 16, 1944, f. 3, box 1, CP, MHS.
92   Carlson to Schultz, January 30, 1944, f. 3, box 1, CP, MHS.
93   Brown and Faue, "Social Bonds, Sexual Politics," 22.
94   Giallombardo, *Society of Women*, 94.
95   Carlson to Schultz, January 23, 1944, f. 3, box 1, CP, MHS.
96   United States Penal and Correctional Institutions, Alderson, "List of Authorized Correspondents," Grace Carlson, #6512, f. 3, box 1, CP, MHS.
97   Carlson to Schultz, February 27, 1944, f. 3, box 1, CP, MHS.
98   Carlson to Evelyn Anderson, January 30, 1944; Carlson to Bea Janosco, February 20, 1944; Carlson to Carter, February 27, 1944, f. 3, box 1, CP, MHS. Carlson to Elaine Roseland, March 5, 1944, f. 4, box 1, CP, MHS. Anderson to Carlson, May 5, 1944, f. 6, box 1, CP, MHS. Roseland to Carlson, November 10, 1944, f. 10, box 1, CP, MHS.

99   Giallombardo, *Society of Women*, 96.
100 Carlson to Schultz, February 13, 1944, f. 3, box 1, CP, MHS.
101 Carlson to Schultz, June 4, 1944, f. 7, box 1, CP, MHS. Carlson to Schultz, July 23, 1944, f. 8, box 1, CP, MHS.
102 Carlson to Carter, February 6, 1944, f. 3, box 1, CP, MHS.
103 Carlson to Schultz, January 30, 1944, f. 3, box 1, CP, MHS. Carlson to Anderson, March 12, 1944, f. 4, box 1, CP, MHS.
104 Carlson to Janosco, February 20, 1944, f. 3, box 1, CP, MHS. Carlson to McCallum (Roseland), March 5, 1944, f. 4, box 1, CP, MHS. Henrietta Geller to Schultz, June 29, 1944, f. 7, box 1, CP, MHS. Carter to Carlson, July 22, 1944, and Carlson to Carter, August 27, 1944, f. 8, box 1, CP, MHS.
105 Carter to Carlson, March 26, 1944, f. 4, box 1, CP, MHS. Carlson to Schultz, April 2, 1944, f. 5, box 1, CP, MHS.
106 Carter to Carlson, March 11, 1944, f. 4, box 1, CP, MHS.
107 Carter to Carlson, April 8, 1944, f. 5, box 1, CP, MHS. Carter to Carlson, May 4, 1944, f. 6, box 1, CP, MHS. Carter to Carlson, June 15, 1944, f. 7, box 1, CP, MHS. Carter to Carlson, July 28, 1944, f. 8, box 1, CP, MHS.
108 Anderson to Carlson, March 6, 1944, f. 4, box 1, CP, MHS. Anderson to Carlson, June 1, 1944, f. 7, box 1, CP, MHS.
109 This was true for other branches around the country too. LeBlanc, "Trotskyism in the United States," 37.
110 Janosco to Carlson, November 29, 1943, Schultz to Carlson, December 1, 1943, Carlson to Janosco, December 1, 1943, and Carlson to Winnie Nelson, December 3, 1943, f. 2, box 1, CP, MHS.
111 Janosco to Carlson, March 17, 1944, and Carlson to Janosco, March 25, 1944, f. 4, box 1, CP, MHS.
112 Roseland to Carlson, May 5, 1944, Janosco to Carlson, May 12, 1944, Janosco to Carlson, May 22, 1944, f. 6, box 1, CP, MHS. Janosco to Carlson, June 7, 1944, f. 7, box 1, CP, MHS.
113 Janosco to Carlson, November 10, 1944, f. 10, box 1, CP, MHS.
114 Janosco to Carlson, November 24, 1944, f. 10, box 1, CP, MHS.
115 On Dorothy's speaking at forums and the May Day meeting, see Schultz to Carlson, March 6, 1944, f. 4, box 1, CP, MHS. Schultz to Carlson, May 1, 1944, f. 6, box 1, CP, MHS. Janosco to Carlson, December 5, 1944, f. 10, box 1, CP, MHS. On her encouraging Roseland, see Schultz to Carlson, December 6, 1943, f. 2, box 1, CP, MHS. On Dorothy's work as an organizer, see Schultz to Carlson, March 19, 1944, f. 4, box 1, CP, MHS, and Schultz to Carlson, October 10, 1944, f. 9, box 1, CP, MHS. On her work on the WDL and NAACP, see Schultz to Carlson, May 8, 1944, f. 6, box 1, CP, MHS; Roseland to Carlson, September 28, 1944, f. 9, box 1, CP, MHS; Schultz to Carlson, May 18, 1944, f. 6, box 1, CP, MHS. On Carlson's pushing Schultz, see Carlson to Schultz, February 13, 1944, f. 3, box 1, CP, MHS, and November 5, 1944, f. 10, box 1, CP, MHS.
116 Carlson to Schultz, July 30, 1944, f. 8, box 1, CP, MHS.

117 Carlson to Carter, April 2, 1944, f. 5, box 1, CP, MHS.
118 Schultz to Carlson, January 30, 1944, f. 3, box 1, CP, MHS. Schultz to Carlson, March 19, 1944, f. 4, box 1, CP, MHS. Roseland to Carlson, April 17, 1944, f. 5, box 1, CP, MHS. Schultz to Carlson, October 10, 1944, f. 9, box 1, CP, MHS.
119 Janosco to Carlson, July 30, 1944, and Carlson to Janosco, July 30, 1944, f. 8, box 1, CP, MHS.
120 Carlson to Anderson, November 5, 1944, f. 10, box 1, CP, MHS.
121 Schultz to Carlson, June 15, 1944, f. 7, box 1, CP, MHS.
122 Carlson to Schultz, June 17, 1944, f. 7, box 1, CP, MHS.
123 Schultz to Carlson, June 18 and June 23, 1944, f. 7, box 1, CP, MHS.
124 Carlson to Schultz, June 25, 1944, f. 7, box 1, CP, MHS.
125 Carlson to Schultz, July 2, 1944, f. 8, box 1, CP, MHS.
126 Schultz to Carlson, July 3, 1944, f. 8, box 1, CP, MHS.
127 Karsner to Carlson, July 3, 1944, f. 8, box 1, CP, MHS.
128 Karsner to Carlson, April 18, 1944, f. 5, box 1, CP, MHS. Karsner to Carlson, May 5, 1944, f. 6, box 1, CP, MHS. Karsner to Carlson, July 18, 1944, Carlson to Anderson, July 24, 1944, Anderson to Carlson, July 27, 1944, and Karsner to Carlson, August 3 and 20, 1944, f. 8, box 1, CP, MHS.
129 Evelyn Anderson, "My Visit to Grace Carlson," April 26, 1944, f. 5, box 1, CP, MHS.
130 Carlson to Anderson, June 18, 1944, f. 7, box 1, CP, MHS.
131 Henrietta Geller to Grace Carlson, June 29, 1944, f. 7, box 1, CP, MHS.
132 George Novack to Dorothy Schultz, July 15, 1944, and Schultz to Carlson, August 20, 1944, f. 8, box 1, CP, MHS. Carter to Carlson, September 29, 1944, f. 9, box 1, CP, MHS. Schultz to Carlson, November 24, 1944, f. 10, box 1, CP, MHS.
133 Giallombardo, *Society of Women*, 100.
134 Carlson to Schultz, February 27, 1944, f. 3, box 1, CP, MHS.
135 Hironimus succeeded Harris in 1941. On the May Act, see Elizabeth Raasch-Gilman, "Sisterhood in the Revolution: The Holmes Sisters and the Socialist Workers Party," *Minnesota History* (Fall 1999): 367. Prior to this law, most inmates at Alderson were imprisoned for narcotics violations, followed by counterfeiting and forgery (statistics for 1935). See Harris, *I Knew Them*, 260.
136 Carlson to Anderson, January 30, 1944, f. 3, box 1, CP, MHS.
137 Carlson to Anderson, March 12, 1944, f. 4, box 1, CP, MHS.
138 Carlson to Anderson April 16, 1944, f. 5, box 1, CP, MHS.
139 Carlson to Carter, May 7, 1944, f. 6, box 1, CP, MHS.
140 Carlson to Schultz, August 6, 1944, quoted in Raasch-Gilman, "Sisterhood in the Revolution," 368.
141 On social roles in Alderson, including homosexual relationships, see Giallombardo, *Society of Women*, 105–89.
142 Henrietta Geller, "Report on Visit to Grace Carlson, June 28, 1944," f. 7, box 1, CP, MHS.
143 Carlson to Anderson, July 2, 1944, f. 8, box 1, CP, MHS.

144 Carlson to Schultz, May 4, 1944, f. 6, box 1, and Carlson to Schultz, August 19, 1944, f. 8, box 1, CP, MHS.
145 Carlson to Schultz, January 23, 1944, f. 3, box 1, CP, MHS.
146 Carlson to Carter, June 25, 1944, f. 7, box 1, CP, MHS.
147 On "inmate cops" see Giallombardo, *Society of Women*, 112–15.
148 See, for example, Dorothy Sproul to Grace Carlson, January 24, 1945, January 28, 1945, February 2 and 4, 1945, February 7, 1945, and Carlson to Sproul, January 30, 1945, f. 11, box 1, CP, MHS.
149 Carlson to Schultz, July 23, 1944, f. 8, box 1, CP, MHS.
150 Carlson to Sedova, December 31, 1944, quoted in Raasch-Gilman, "Sisterhood in the Revolution," 371.
151 Lara Vapneck, *Elizabeth Gurley Flynn: Modern American Revolutionary* (Boulder, CO: Westview), 159–62.
152 Elizabeth Gurley Flynn, *The Alderson Story: My Life as a Political Prisoner* (New York: International Publishers, 1963), 44–56, 77, 106–23, 164–65.
153 Schultz to Carlson, December 22, 1944, f. 10, box 1, CP, MHS.
154 Carter to Carlson, January 11, 1945, f. 11, box 1, CP, MHS.
155 Carlson to Schultz, January 14, 1945, f. 11, box 1, CP, MHS.
156 Program for "Homecoming Banquet," January 28, 1945, and "8 Ex-Prisoners Get $150 Gifts," unidentified newspaper clipping, f. 11, box 1, CP, MHS.
157 Carlson interview with Ross, July 9, 1987, 9. "Ms. Carlson Speaks on Women in Prison," *Minneapolis Times*, September 10, 1945, n.p., and Carlson's notes for her "Women in Prison" speech, f. SWP, "Women in Prison" Speech Tour, June–September 1945, box 1, CP, MHS.
158 *Militant*, June 9, 1945, 1, 7; June 16, 1945, 1, 3; June 23, 1945, 4; July 7, 1945, 6; July 14, 1945, 4; July 21, 1945, 6; July 28, 1945, 6; August 11, 1945, 6; August 25, 1945, 7; September 8, 1945, 6; September 22, 1945, 6.
159 *Militant*, June 30, 1945, 1; July 7, 1945, 6; September 22, 1945, 6.
160 Grace Carlson, handwritten notes, "Constitution Day—Camphor Church, 9-16-45," f. SWP, "Women in Prison" Speech Tour, June–September 1945, box 1, CP, MHS.
161 *Militant*, June 9, 1945, 1, and June 16, 1945, 1.
162 *Militant*, July 14, 1945, 4, and July 21, 1945, 6. Up until her tour, the party had not engaged with the specific issue of women prisoners: see Diane Feeley, Annotated Bibliography of articles from the *Militant* and *Socialist Appeal* on or by women from 1928 to 1968, f. 6, box 63, Breitman Papers, Tamiment.
163 *Socialist Appeal*, September 21, 1940, 1.
164 Carlson to Sedova, January 7, 1942, f. 1, box 1, CP, MHS. Janosco to Carlson, August 14, 1944, f. 8, box 1, CP, MHS.
165 Carlson to Sedova, October 20, 1942, f. Pre-SWP Correspondence, box 1 CP, MHS.
166 Schultz to Carlson, December 13, 1943, and January 23, 1944, f. 2 and January–February 1944, box 1, CP, MHS. See also Schultz to Carlson, January 28, 1944,

Schultz to Carlson, February 3, 1944, Schultz to Carlson, February 13, 1944, f. 3, box 1, CP, MHS. Schultz to Carlson, March 17, 1944, f. 4, box 1, CP, MHS.

167 Schultz to Carlson, February 23, 1944, February 29, 1944, f. 3, box 1, CP, MHS. Schultz to Carlson, March 4, 1944, f. 4, box 1, CP, MHS. Schultz to Carlson, May 9, 1944, f. 6, box 1, CP, MHS.

168 Schultz to Carlson, September 13, 1944, f. 9, box 1, CP, MHS. According to Raymond Schultz, Jim did not agree with their mother's version of events. See Raymond Schultz, e-mail to author, October 3, 2016, and June 1, 2017.

169 Brown and Faue, "Social Bonds, Sexual Politics," 10–17.

170 Janosco to Carlson, August 18, 1943, f. 8, box 1, CP, MHS.

171 Janosco to Carlson, November 29, 1943, f. 10, box 1, CP, MHS.

172 Schultz to Carlson, January 21, 1944, and January 30, 1944, f. 3, box 1, CP, MHS.

173 Schultz to Carlson, January 30, 1944, f. 3, box 1, CP, MHS. Janosco to Carlson, March 22, 1944, f. 4, box 1, CP, MHS.

174 Janosco to Carlson, January 21, 1945, f. 11, box 1, CP, MHS.

175 Grace Carlson, "'Learn to Relax by Cultivating Hobby' Is Radio Advice to Overworked Mothers," *Militant*, March 17, 1945, 4.

176 Carlson, "Poor Mothers Advised to Patch, Darn, and Sew," *Militant*, May 12, 1945, 3; Carlson, "When Housewives Dream," *Militant*, February 8, 1947, 6.

177 Carlson, "Poorly-Housed Workers Long for 'Dream Home,'" *Militant*, March 31, 1945, 4.

178 Carlson, "Why Millions of Women Workers Don't Have That American Look," *Militant*, June 9, 1945, 4. On Konikow, see LeBlanc, "Trotskyism in the United States," 16, 52.

179 Carlson, "Poverty Robs Many Women of Right to Health and Beauty," *Militant*, April 21, 1945, 4.

180 On the variants of feminisms during the 1940s and 1950s, see Meyerowitz, ed., *Not June Cleaver*; Rupp and Taylor, *Survival in the Doldrums*; and Cobble, *The Other Women's Movement*.

181 Feeley, Annotated Bibliography, f. 6, box 63, Breitman Papers, Tamiment.

182 Antoinette Konikow, "Birth Control Is No Panacea," *Militant*, February 1, 1941, 5.

183 Larissa Reed, "Equal Rights Bill," *Militant*, January 23, 1943, 1.

184 Konikow, "Women Workers Suffer Double Exploitation," *Militant*, June 2, 1945, 6; Marie Taylor, "Women in Industry," *Militant*, January 2, 1943, 2; Ruth Johnson, "Problems of Women Workers in War Industry," *Militant*, March 11, 1944, 2; Mary Kane, "Nursery Closures Hit Minneapolis Mothers," *Militant*, September 22, 1945, 8; "Why Some Mothers Can't Stay Home to Take Care of Children," *Militant*, September 1, 1947, 5. On the socialist vision of communal facilities, see Alice Patton, "The Slavery of a Housewife," *Militant*, September 28, 1946, 6.

185 Mille Fredreci, "My Day—Experiences of a Working Mother," *Militant*, August 17, 1945, 5; Fredreci, "A Working Mother Gets a Politician's Letter," *Militant*, August 24, 1945, 5; Fredreci, "Working Mother Writes of Day in N.Y. Court," *Militant*, September 7, 1945, 5.

186 Quotation from "War Intensifies Women's Role," *Militant*, April 25, 1942, 3. See also Lydia Beidel, "'Woman's Place'—It's in the Factories Now," *Militant*, April 18, 1942, 3; Marie Taylor, "Women in Industry," *Militant*, November 28, 1942, 3; Marie Taylor, "Women in Industry," *Militant*, February 6, 1943, 2; Antoinette Konikow, "Employment of Women in Industry and What It Means for the Working Class," *Militant*, July 29, 1944, 4; Ruth Johnson, "Problems of Women Workers in War Industry," *Militant*, March 11, 1944, 2; E. Landi (letter to the editor), "Women Appreciate SWP Program," *Militant*, October 5, 1945, 5.

187 On Inman, see Kate Weigand, *Red Feminism: American Communism and the Making of Women's Liberation* (Baltimore, MD: Johns Hopkins University Press, 2001), 28–45.

188 Weigand, *Red Feminism*, 68–89.

189 Hawes laid out this vision in her 1943 book, *Why Women Cry; or, Wenches with Wrenches*. See the discussion of Hawes in Michael Denning, *The Cultural Front: The Laboring of American Culture in the Twentieth Century* (New York: Verso, 2000), 146–50.

190 Clara Fraser, *Which Road towards Women's Liberation? A Radical Vanguard of a Single-Issue Coalition?* 2nd edition (Seattle, WA: Radical Women Publications, 2003). Myra Tanner Weiss, *The Bustelo Incident: Marxism and Feminism* (New York: Onward Press, 1987). Myra Tanner Weiss, Oral History, April 29, 1983, OH 002, Tamiment Library and Robert F. Wagner Labor Archives, Elmer Holmes Bobst Library, New York, NY.

191 Jack Bustelo, "Sagging Cosmetic Lines Try a Face Life," in *Cosmetics, Fashions, and the Exploitation of Women*, ed. Joseph Hansen, Evelyn Reed, and Mary-Alice Waters (New York: Pathfinder, 1986), 43–46.

192 Louise Manning, "Cosmetics and the Women," in *Cosmetics, Fashions, and the Exploitation of Women*, 47–48.

193 F.J., "Lives in World as It Is Today," in *Cosmetics, Fashions, and the Exploitation of Women*, 53. Sam Stern, "We Have to Know What Women Want," in *Cosmetics, Fashions, and the Exploitation of Women*, 60. Helen Baker, "Cosmetics and Economic Pressure," in *Cosmetics, Fashions, and the Exploitation of Women*, 54.

194 Marjorie McGowan, "Letter on Bustelo Article," in *Cosmetics, Fashions, and the Exploitation of Women*, 69.

195 Evelyn Reed, "The Woman Question and the Marxist Method," in *Cosmetics, Fashions, and the Exploitation of Women*, 79–80. On Reed's "traditionalist approach" to feminist issues, see Gilbert Abcarian, "On the Political Theories of Radical and Socialist Feminism on the U.S.A," *Il Politico* 47:2 (1982): 419–20.

196 Reed, "The Woman Question," 90–91.

CHAPTER 4. POLITICS AND LOVE ON THE LEFT

1 On the variety of sexual nonconformity among Trotskyists in the postwar period, and the Cold War pressures that contributed to its being forgotten, see Alan

Wald, "Bohemian Bolsheviks after World War II: A Minority within a Minority," *Labour/Le Travail* 70 (Fall 2012): 159–86. Quotation from p. 168.
2. Brown and Faue, "Social Bonds, Sexual Politics," 9–45.
3. FBI Report 100-1334, Detroit, 9/27/46, f. 21, box 110, SWP 146-1-10. "Fraction" is the term the SWP used to refer to its groups within labor unions.
4. Le Blanc, "Trotskyism in the United States," 39.
5. Green, *World of the Worker*, 193–94.
6. Grace Carlson, "A GM Striker's Story," *Militant*, n.d., n.p., f. SWP, Grace Carlson articles on health, box 1, CP, MHS.
7. Grace Carlson, "A GM Striker's Story," *Militant*, n.d., n.p., f. SWP, Grace Carlson articles on health, box 1, CP, MHS.
8. Carlton Jackson, *Child of the Sit-Downs: The Revolutionary Life of Genora Dollinger* (Kent, OH: Kent State University Press, 2008), 67–70.
9. Dorothy Schultz to Morris Stein, January 22, 1946, and Morris Stein to Henry Schultz, February 8, 1946, micro 2050 reel 15, SWP Records, WHS.
10. L. Lynn to Farrell Dobbs, June 15, 1946, and M. Stein to L. Lynn, June 28, 1946, micro 2050 reel 15, SWP Records, WHS. *St. Paul Pioneer Press*, July 1, 1946, n.p., scrapbook vol. 6, SWP Minnesota Section Records, MHS.
11. C. K. Johnson, press release, July 31, 1946, and "The Socialist Workers Party in Minn. Election," *Wilmar Daily Tribune*, July 31, 1946, n.p., scrapbook vol. 6, box 7, SWP Minnesota Section Records, MHS.
12. *St. Paul Pioneer Press*, August 1, 1946, n.p., and *Militant*, August 24, 1946, n.p., scrapbook vol. 6, SWP Minnesota Section Records, MHS.
13. *Twin City Observer*, September 20, 1946, *St. Paul Pioneer Press*, September 21, 1946, and September 28, 1946, *Minneapolis Morning Tribune*, September 28, 1946, *St. Paul Recorder*, October 11, 1946, *Twin City Observer*, October 18, 1946, *St. Paul Recorder*, November 1, 1946, *Militant*, October 3, 1946, and November 2, 1946, n.p., scrapbook vol. 6, SWP Minnesota Section Records, MHS.
14. C. K. Johnson, press release, July 31, 1946, clipping, scrapbook vol. 6, SWP Minnesota Section Records, MHS. *Belle Plaine Herald*, August 8, 1946, *Virginia Range Facts*, October 10, 1946, n.p., scrapbook vol. 6, SWP Minnesota Section Records, MHS.
15. *Militant*, November 30, 1946, 1. "Our Party Vote" state map, scrapbook vol. 6, SWP Minnesota Section Records, MHS.
16. Ellen Schrecker, *Many Are the Crimes: McCarthyism in America* (Princeton, NJ: Princeton University Press, 1998), 154–59.
17. Stone, *Perilous Times*, 343–44.
18. Ellen Schrecker, "Labor and the Cold War: The Legacy of McCarthyism," in *American Labor and the Cold War: Grassroots Politics and Postwar Political Culture*, ed. Robert W. Cherny, William Issel, and Kieran Walsh Taylor (New Brunswick, NJ: Rutgers University Press, 2004), 7–24. Richard Gid Powers, *Not without Honor: The History of American Anticommunism* (New Haven, CT: Yale University Press, 1995), 201.

19 Goldman and Cannon quoted in Paul LeBlanc, "Leninism in the United States and the Decline of American Trotskyism," in *Trotskyism in the United States: Historical Essays and Reconsiderations*, ed. George Breitman, Paul LeBlanc, and Alan Wald (Chicago: Haymarket Books, 2016), 215–17.
20 LeBlanc, "Trotskyism in the United States," 38–40. James P. Cannon, *The Coming American Revolution* (New York: Pioneer Publishers, 1947), 31.
21 Farrell Dobbs to Vincent Dunne, May 19, 1947, and Farrell Dobbs to Joe Olman, June 4, 1947, micro 2050 reel 15, SWP Records, WHS.
22 *Militant*, March 1, 1948, n.p., scrapbook vol. 7, box 7, SWP Minnesota Section Records, MHS.
23 Carlson diary-activity book, entries for June 23–July 1, 1948, f. Meeting flyers and related papers, box 1, CP, MHS.
24 *Minneapolis Star*, July 3, 1948, n.p., scrapbook vol. 7, box 7, SWP Minnesota Section Records, MHS.
25 "Acceptance Speech of Grace Carlson," July 3, 2:30–3:30 p.m., f. 1948 Pres. Campaign, Carlson's Speeches, box 1, CP, MHS.
26 Andrew E. Busch, *Truman's Triumphs: The 1948 Election and the Making of Postwar America* (Lawrence: University Press of Kansas, 2012), 71–73, 112–18.
27 "Acceptance Speech of Grace Carlson," July 3, 2:30–3:30 p.m., f. 1948 Pres. Campaign, Carlson's Speeches, box 1, CP, MHS.
28 "Acceptance Speech of Grace Carlson," July 3, 2:30–3:30 p.m., f. 1948 Pres. Campaign, Carlson's Speeches, box 1, CP, MHS.
29 Carlson diary-activity book, entries for July 4–12, 1948, f. Meeting flyers and related papers, box 1, CP, MHS.
30 Carlson diary-activity book, entries for July 13–18, 1948, f. Meeting flyers and related papers, box 1, CP, MHS. *St. Paul Dispatch*, July 15, 1948, 1, and *Minneapolis Morning Tribune*, July 19, 1948, n.p., scrapbook vol. 7, box 7, SWP Minnesota Section Records, MHS.
31 *Minneapolis Star*, July 39, 1948, n.p., scrapbook vol. 7, box 7, SWP Minnesota Section Records, MHS.
32 On her 1948 campaign tour, see newspaper clippings in f. 1948 Pres. Campaign, Newspaper clippings & Magazine articles, March–November, box 1, CP, MHS.
33 Carlson, "SWP Election Tour: Seattle and Milwaukee," *Militant*, n.d., n.p., clipping, f. 1948 Pres. Campaign, Newspaper clippings, box 1, CP, MHS.
34 *Buffalo Courier Express*, September 16, 1948, n.p., f. Newspaper clippings, 1944–54, box 3, SWP Minnesota Section Records, MHS.
35 Thomas W. Devine, *Henry Wallace's 1948 Presidential Campaign and the Future of Postwar Liberalism* (Chapel Hill: University of North Carolina Press, 2013), 242–46.
36 Carlson, "SWP Election Tour: Barnstorming in Buffalo," *Militant*, n.d., n.p., f. 1948 Pres. Campaign, Newspaper clippings, box 1, CP, MHS.
37 Carlson, "SWP Election Tour: Seattle and Milwaukee," "SWP Election Tour: From the Arrowhead Country," "SWP Election Tour: Crowded Days," "SWP Election

Tour: A Week in Ohio," *Militant*, n.d., n.p., f. 1948 Pres. Campaign, Newspaper clippings, box 1, CP, MHS.
38 *Detroit Times*, October 12, 1948, n.p., f. Newspaper clippings, box 3, SWP Minnesota Section Records, MHS.
39 The party also identified her with "the fight for women's rights in America." See *Militant*, September 6, 1948, 2.
40 "Friends of the Radio Audience," n.d., f. 1948 Pres. Campaign, Carlson Speeches, box 1, CP, MHS.
41 On the Berlin crisis and the war scare, see Busch, *Truman's Triumphs*, 69–71.
42 "The Only Road to Peace," August 13, 1948, f. 1948 Pres. Campaign, Carlson's Speeches, box 1, CP, MHS.
43 On the CPUSA and Hiss cases, see Powers, *Not without Honor*, 221–27. On Kutcher, see Robert Justin Goldstein, *Discrediting the Red Scare: The Cold War Trials of James Kutcher, "The Legless Veteran"* (Lawrence: University of Kansas Press, 2016), 18–25.
44 Grace Carlson to President Harry Truman, August 26, 1948, f. Meeting flyers and related papers, box 1, CP, MHS.
45 On the failed letters, see Haverty-Stacke, *Trotskyists on Trial*, 194–95.
46 "Friends of the Radio Audience," September 8, 1948, and September 10, 1948, f. 1948 Pres. Campaign, Carlson's Speeches, box 1, CP, MHS.
47 Powers, *Not without Honor*, 214–21, 229–33. Ellen Schrecker, *The Age of McCarthyism: A Brief History with Documents*, 2nd edition (New York: Bedford, 2002), 80–85.
48 *St. Cloud Sentinel*, March 20, 1948, *Le Sueur News-Herald*, March 24, 1948, *Good Thunder Herald*, March 25, 1948, n.p., scrapbook vol. 7, box 7, SWP Minnesota Section Records, MHS.
49 Erika Falk, *Women for President: Media Bias in Nine Campaigns* (Urbana: University of Illinois Press, 2010).
50 "Woman Is Candidate for Vice President," *Detroit Times*, October 12, 1948, n.p., and "Socialist Workers' Candidate to Talk," *Cleveland Plain Dealer*, August 24, 1948, n.p., f. 1948 Pres. Campaign, Newspaper clippings, box 1, CP, MHS. "See Slavery Aim in Marshall Plan," *Milwaukee Journal*, October 8, 1948, n.p.; "She'll Answer Wallace," *Buffalo Evening News*, September 15, 1948, n.p., f. Newspaper clippings, box 3, SWP Minnesota Section Records, MHS.
51 Falk, *Women for President*, 60, 62.
52 Falk, *Women for President*, 88.
53 *Minneapolis Morning Tribune*, July 21, 1948, n.p.; *Cleveland News*, August 24, 1948, n.p.; *Cleveland Press*, August 24, 1948, n.p.; *Cleveland Plain Dealer*, July 11, 1948, n.p.; *Pittsburgh Press*, September 10, 1948, n.p.; *Detroit Times*, October 12, 1948, n.p., f. 1948 Pres. Campaign, Newspaper clippings, box 1, CP, MHS. *Evening Telegram*, September 28, 1948, n.p., f. Newspaper clippings, box 3, SWP Minnesota Section Records, MHS.
54 *Picture News*, October 21, 1948, n.p., f. Newspaper clippings, box 3, SWP Minnesota Section Records, MHS.

55 "Pretty Woman," *Milwaukee Deutsche Zeitung*, October 12, 1948 (translation), n.p., f. Newspaper clippings, box 3, SWP Minnesota Section Records, MHS.
56 On framing and status conferral see Falk, *Women for President*, 16–29.
57 Carlson, "A Week in Ohio," *Militant*, n.p., n.d., f. 1948 Pres. Campaign, Newspaper clippings, box 1, CP, MHS.
58 On Brehm, see J. David Gillespie, *Challengers to Duopoly: Why Third Parties Matter in American Two-Party Politics* (Columbia: University of South Carolina Press, 2012), 156.
59 Falk, *Women for President*, 37.
60 On references to "woman candidate," "first woman," or "only woman," see, for example, *Seattle Post Intelligence*, October 6, 1948, n.p.; *Stillwater Daily Gazette*, October 4, 1948, n.p.; *New York Post*, October 27, 1948, n.p.; *Wilmer Daily Tribune*, September 16, 1948, n.p.; *Pittsburgh Press*, September 9, 1948, n.p.; *Buffalo Evening News*, September 15, 1948, n.p., f. Newspaper Clippings: Political Campaign, box 3, SWP MN Section Records, MHS. See also, clippings from f. 1948 Pres. Campaign, Newspaper clippings, box 1, CP, MHS.
61 On references to the "only woman" in SWP publicity, see, for example, flyers advertising her campaign events from the Cleveland, Chicago, Youngstown, and St. Paul branches, f. SWP, Minneapolis, MN, Campaign Literature and Printed Materials, 1939–48, box 1, SWP MN Section Records, MHS.
62 *Minneapolis Morning Tribune*, July 21, 1948, n.p., and *Milwaukee Sentinel*, October 9, 1948, n.p., f. 1948 Pres. Campaign, Newspaper clippings, box 1, CP, MHS.
63 *Pontiac Daily Times*, August 9, 1948, n.p., f. 1948 Pres. Campaign, Newspaper clippings, box 1, CP, MHS.
64 *Minneapolis Morning Tribune*, July 21, 1948, n.p., f. 1948 Pres. Campaign, Newspaper clippings, box 1, CP, MHS.
65 Haverty-Stacke, *Trotskyists on Trial*, 179–86.
66 Grace Carlson to Farrell Dobbs, June 15, 1948, and Morris Stein to Grace Carlson, June 19, 1948, SWP Records, micro 2050 reel 15, WHS.
67 "National Campaigner for Dobbs and Carlson," August 23, 1948, f. Meeting flyers and related papers, box 1, CP, MHS.
68 Busch, *Truman's Triumphs*, 155.
69 Ibid., ix.
70 Grace Carlson, "Friends of the Radio Audience" and "A Socialist America: The Only Road to Peace," f. 1948 Pres. Campaign, box 1, CP, MHS.
71 Michael Levy, "United States Presidential Election of 1948," https://www.britannica.com (accessed January 29, 2019).
72 Carlson interview with Ross, July 14, 1987, 38.
73 Schrecker, *Many Are the Crimes*, 158–59, 240–65.
74 Hoover to Assistant Attorney General T. L. Caudle, August 4, 1945, Hoover to Attorney General, September 14, 1945, f. 17, box 109, SWP 146-1-10. Hoover to Caudle, November 20, 1945, Hoover to Caudle, November 28, 1945, f. 18, box 109, SWP 146-1-10. Hoover to Attorney General, March 26, 1945, f. 20, box 110, SWP

146-1-10. Hoover to Attorney General, August 6, 1946, and September 24, 1946, f. 21, box 110, SWP 146-1-10. Hoover to Attorney General, October 29, 1946, and November 7, 1946, f. 22, box 110, SWP 146-1-10. Hoover to Caudle, February 17, 1947, and February 20, 1947, and Hoover to Attorney General, March 13, 1947, f. 23, box 110, SWP 146-1-10. Hoover to Attorney General, November 15, 1947, and Hoover to Assistant Attorney General, December 20, 1947, and January 14, 1948, f. 25, box 110, SWP 146-1-10. Hoover to Attorney General, June 13, 1948, and July 7, 1948, f. 27, box 110, SWP 146-1-10.

75 Schrecker, *Many Are the Crimes*, 208.
76 Stone, *Perilous Times*, 335.
77 Schrecker, *Many Are the Crimes*, 208. SAC Minneapolis to Director, June 10, 1955, tabbing Dunne as DETCOM in his SI file, Dunne's FBI file, 100–18341, FOIA request, in author's possession. SAC New York to Director, January 30, 1950, and SAC Chicago to Director, January 30, 1953, tabbing Dobbs as DETCOM in his SI file, and SAC Chicago to Director, May 14, 1951, tabbing Dobbs as COMSAB (a designation that is then removed in June), Dobbs's FBI file 100–21226, FOIA request, in author's possession.
78 On Palmquist, see Edward Palmquist's FBI file 146-7-1214, report for 1/22/46, FOIA request, in author's possession; Ed Palmquist's FBI file, AN 74–10, Anchorage, 11/7/47, FOIA, in author's possession; Ed Palmquist's FBI file, AN 100–1381, Anchorage, 2/7/48, 5/7/48, 4/2/48, 12/4/48, and 8/22/50, 11/5/54, p.1, FOIA, in author's possession; Ed Palmquist, FBI file, SU 100–9142, Salt Lake City, 5/6/57, pp. 1, 6–8, FOIA, in author's possession. On Skoglund, see interview with Carl Skoglund, Twentieth-Century Radicalism in Minnesota Oral History Project, OF30.64, interviewer unidentified, n.d. MHS; George Novack to All National Committee Members, April 30, 1949, f. Skoglund, 1943–51, box 2, CRDC Records, WHS; *Militant*, August 22, 1949, 3, and September 12, 1949, 1; George Novack to Grace and Vincent, September 6, 1949; Vincent Dunne to George Novack, September 26, 1949, October 10, 1949, and October 15, 1949, f. Skoglund—Correspondence, 1943–1951, box 2, CRDC Records, WHS; CRDC press release, December 15, f. Skoglund—Correspondence, 1943–1951, box 2, CRDC Records, WHS; George Novack to Friend (CRDC Members), July 15, 1954, and November 22, 1954, f. Skoglund Correspondence, 1952–1957, box 2, CRDC Records.
79 J. A. A. Burnquist, Minnesota Attorney General, to Hon. Mike Holm, July 17, 1944, and Grace Carlson to William Warde, June 21, 1950, micro 2050 reel 15, SWP Records, WHS.
80 *Minneapolis Tribune*, September 30, 1950, n.p., f. SWP, Minneapolis, Minn. Papers, Campaign Literature, 1949–64, box 1, SWP Minnesota Section Records, MHS. Grace Carlson to Comrade, October 1, 1950, SWP Records, micro 2050 reel 15, WHS.
81 *Minneapolis Star*, October 7, October 21, and October 23, 1950, n.p., and "Support the Fight for Civil Rights: Vote for Grace Carlson," f. SWP, Minneapolis, Minn. Papers, Campaign Literature, 1949–64, box 1, SWP Minnesota Section Records, MHS.

82 Grace Carlson to William Warde, October 27, 1950, SWP Records, micro 2050 reel 15, WHS. *Minneapolis Star*, October 31 and November 1, 1950, n.p., f. SWP, Minneapolis, Minn. Papers, Campaign Literature, 1949–64, box 1, SWP Minnesota Section Records, MHS.
83 Grace Carlson to M. J. Myer, November 9, 1950, micro 2050 reel 15, SWP Records, WHS.
84 Brown and Faue, "Social Bonds, Sexual Politics," 10–11, 14–16. Carlson interview with Ross, July 9, 1987, 13.
85 Carlson interview with Ross, July 9, 1987, 7, and July 14, 1987, 28.
86 Gilbert Carlson to Grace Carlson, December 6, 1943, f. 2, box 1, CP, MHS.
87 Gilbert Carlson to Grace Carlson, December 6, 1943, f. 2, box 1, CP, MHS.
88 "Letters from Gilbert," notebook entry, f. SWP, Carlson's Notebook, Prison, 1943–1944, box 1, CP, MHS.
89 See her reference to this letter in Grace Carlson to Dorothy Schultz, June 25, 1944, f. 7, box 1, CP, MHS.
90 Schultz to Carlson, March 4, 1944, March 14, 1944, and March 20, 1944, f. 4, box 1, CP, MHS; Schultz to Carlson, April 9, 1944, and April 20, 1944, f. 5 box 1, CP, MHS; and Carlson to Schultz, August 25, 1944, f. 8, box 1, CP, MHS.
91 Gilbert Carlson to Grace Carlson, January 3, 1945, f. 11, box 1, CP, MHS.
92 Carlson to Schultz, March 5, 1944, f. 4, box 1, CP, MHS.
93 Carlson to Schultz, May 28, 1944, f. 6, box 1, CP, MHS.
94 Linda Leighton, Memories of Jennie Octavia Holm, e-mail to author June 6, 2018, July 10, 2018, and January 29, 2019. "Jennie Dunne at 74, Dies in Minneapolis," *Militant*, January 18, 1960, 4. State of Minnesota, County of Hennepin, "Marriage Certificate of Vincent R. Dunne and Jennie of Holmes [sic]," May 29, 1914, David Sundeen and Linda Leighton private collection, copy in author's possession. Minnesota Birth Index, "Vincent Raymond Dunne," June 9, 1918, certificate number 1918–44837. Vincent Raymond Dunne, 1930, Minneapolis, Hennepin, Minnesota, *Fifteenth Census of the United States, 1930*, National Archives Microfilm Publication, page 18A, RG29.
95 Linda Leighton, Memories of Jennie Octavia Holm, e-mail to author, July 10, 2018. "Vincent R. Dunne," *Minneapolis, Minnesota, City Directory, 1941*, Ancestry.com.
96 Carlson interview with Ross, July 9, 1987, 7, and July 14, 1987, 28. "Grace Carlson, New York," AFC, NYU.
97 Tentler, *Catholics and Contraception*, 43–129.
98 St. Paul Archbishop John Gregory Murray's order that all Catholics in the archdiocese had to "withdraw membership from any birth-control or sterilization organization or face excommunication" was read from all pulpits on August 18, 1935: see Mary Losure, "'Motherhood Protection' and the Minnesota Birth Control League," *Minnesota History* (Winter 1995): 365–66.
99 Antoinette Konikow, *Voluntary Motherhood: A Study of the Physiology and Hygiene of Prevention of Conception* (Boston: Buchholz Publishing, 1923).
100 Losure, "'Motherhood Protection,'" 359–70.

101 FBI file for Dorothy Schultz, 100-1894 St. Paul, 9/28/44, p. 3, in HQ-100-159217, FOIA, in author's possession.
102 Grace Carlson to Natalia Sedova, October 20, 1942, f. 1, box 1, CP, MHS.
103 Carlson to Sedova, June 19, 1943; envelope from Mexico with Grace's New York City address; and Bea Janosco to Grace Carlson, August 18, 1943, f. 2, box 1, CP, MHS. FBI file for Vincent Raymond Dunne, 100-18341, p. 204, FOIA, in author's possession.
104 Schultz to Carlson, January 31, 1944, f. 3, box 1, CP, MHS.
105 Carlson to Schultz, February 6, 1944, f. 3, box 1, CP, MHS.
106 Schultz to Carlson, March 19, 1944, f. 4, box 1, CP, MHS.
107 Schultz to Carlson, March 19, 1944, f. 4, box 1, CP, MHS. The poem is about a sixteen-year-old girl and her older male lover and may have resonated with Grace and Ray because of their age difference: he was seventeen years her senior.
108 Carlson to Schultz, March 26, 1944, f. 4, box 1, CP, MHS.
109 Carlson to Schultz, February 6, 1944, February 20, 1944, and March 5, 1944, f. 3 and f. 4, box 1, CP, MHS.
110 Schultz to Carlson, April 23, 1944, f. 5, box 1, and November 9, 1944, f. 10, box 1, CP, MHS. Elaine Roseland to Grace Carlson, July 5, 1944, f. 8, box 1, CP, MHS.
111 Leighton, e-mail to author, July 10, 2018. Schultz to Carlson, January 28, 1944, f. 3, box 1, CP, MHS.
112 Schultz to Carlson, May 15, 1944, f. 6, box 1, CP, MHS.
113 Bea Janosco to Grace Carlson, December 17, 1944, f. 10, box 1, CP, MHS.
114 Schultz to Carlson, December 28, 1944, f. 10, box 1, CP, MHS.
115 Brown and Faue, "Social Bonds, Sexual Politics," 9–45. Fraser M. Ottanelli, *The Communist Party of the United States: From Depression to World War II* (New Brunswick, NJ: Rutgers University Press, 1991), 44–46.
116 Carlson to Schultz, March 5, 1944, f. 4, box 1, CP, MHS.
117 Schultz to Carlson, March 19, 1944, f. 4, box 1, CP, MHS.
118 Carlson to Schultz, March 26, 1944, f. 4, box 1, CP, MHS.
119 Carlson to Schultz, April 29, 1944, f. 5, box 1, CP, MHS.
120 Carlson to Schultz, February 13, 1944, f. 3, box 1, CP, MHS.
121 Schultz to Carlson, December 29, 1944, f. 10, box 1, and Janosco to Carlson, January 3, 1945, f. 11, box 1, CP, MHS.
122 FBI file for Vincent Raymond Dunne, St. Paul-100-932, 5/21/45, pp. 3–4, FOIA, in author's possession. The informant may have been a postal worker: the FBI most likely had a mail cover on Dunne. On mail covers see Frank J. Donner, *The Age of Surveillance: The Aims and Methods of America's Political Intelligence System* (New York: Vintage, 1981), 129–30.
123 FBI file for Vincent Raymond Dunne, 100-18341, p. 293, FOIA. in author's possession.
124 FBI file for Vincent Raymond Dunne, St. Paul-100-932, 10/30/45, p. 1, FOIA, in author's possession.
125 FBI file for Vincent Raymond Dunne, 100-18341, pp. 300, 309, 317–18, 320, 324, 332, FOIA, in author's possession.

126 FBI file for Vincent Raymond Dunne, NY-100–59477, 7/25/46, p. 2, FOIA, in author's possession. George [Novack] to Myra Tanner Weiss, June 9, 1946, f. 1, box 2, Weiss Papers, Tamiment Library, New York University, New York, NY.
127 Carlson to Sedova, March 9, 1943, and Dr. Wittich to Grace Carlson, September 9, 1943, f. 1, box 1, CP, MHS. Wittich to Evelyn Anderson (with enclosed medical report from December 28, 1943), June 23, 1944, f. 7, box 1, CP, MHS.
128 Farrell Dobbs to James Cannon, June 13, 1946, micro 2033 reel 7, James P. Cannon Papers, WHS.
129 Vincent Dunne to James Cannon, July 23, 1946, micro 2033 reel 7, Cannon Papers, WHS.
130 See, for example, *Minneapolis Daily Times*, September 19, 1946, n.p.; *Twin City Observer*, September 20, 1946, n.p.; *St. Paul Pioneer Press*, September 21, 1946, n.p., scrapbook vol. 6, SWP Minnesota Section Records, MHS.
131 FBI file for Vincent Raymond Dunne, 100–18341, pp. 5, 348, 349, 357, 363, 368, 371, FOIA, in author's possession.
132 FBI files for Vincent Raymond Dunne, 100–18341, p. 393; St. Paul-100–932, 6/12/47, p. 3; St. Louis-100–7629, 7/23/47, p. 1; and St. Paul-100–932, 11/8/47, pp. 1–3, FOIA, in author's possession.
133 Grace Carlson, diary-activity book, January 1–November 1, 1948, f. Meeting flyers and related papers, box 1, CP, MHS.
134 FBI file on Dr. Grace Carlson, St. Paul-100–166, 9/20/46, pp. 2–3, SWP 146-1-10. On the use of "Temporary symbols" for informants, see FBI file on Dunne, 100–59477, New York 12/20/45, p. 5, FOIA, in author's possession. On the electronic surveillance of the Schultz home, see memos requesting continuation of technical surveillance in 1946 and 1947 in FBI file on Dorothy Schultz, 100–159217, Correlation Summary, April 11, 1955, pp. 21 and 28A, FOIA, in author's possession. On Grace's residing with Dorothy, see FBI file on Dorothy Schultz, 100–159217, Correlation Summary, April 11, 1955, p. 19, FOIA, in author's possession.
135 FBI file for Vincent Raymond Dunne, 100–18341, p. 399, FOIA, in author's possession.
136 FBI file for Vincent Raymond Dunne, St. Paul 100–932, 3/19/48, p. 2, FOIA, in author's possession.
137 Brown and Faue, "Social Bonds, Sexual Politics," 15.
138 FBI file for Vincent Raymond Dunne, St. Paul-100–932, 3/1/49, p. 2, FOIA, in author's possession.
139 FBI file for Vincent Raymond Dunne, 100–18341, p. 467, FOIA, in author's possession.
140 FBI file for Vincent Raymond Dunne, 100–18341, p. 482, FOIA, in author's possession.
141 FBI file for Vincent Raymond Dunne, Minneapolis-100–932, 11/16/49, p. 1, FOIA, in author's possession.
142 On Dunne's tour, see SAC Minneapolis to Director, December 3, 1949, subject Vincent Raymond Dunne, in FBI file on Vincent Raymond Dunne, 100-18341-55,

FOIA, in author's possession. On being at the headquarters almost daily, see FBI file on Vincent Raymond Dunne, Minneapolis-110–932, 5/16/50 and 10/23/50, FOIA, in author's possession. On dominating the local, see FBI file on Vincent Raymond Dunne, Minneapolis-110–932, 1/15/51, p. 11, and 4/9/51, p. 2. On the other events see, for example, FBI file on Vincent Raymond Dunne, Minneapolis-110–932, 1/15/51, p. 2, and 1/23/51, pp. 2–4.

143 See, for example, Schultz to Carlson, February 28, 1944, and February 29, 1944, f. 3, box 1; Elaine Roseland to Grace Carlson, April 17, 1944, Schultz to Carlson, April 23, 1944, Janosco to Carlson, April 24, 1944, Schultz to Carlson, April 25, 1944, f. 5, box 1; Roseland to Carlson, May 5, 1944, Schultz to Carlson, May 8, 1944, Schultz to Carlson, May 15, 1944, May 18, 1944, May 22, 1944, f. 6, box 1; Schultz to Carlson, June 7, 1944, f. 7, box 1; Schultz to Carlson, July 25, 1944, July 28, 1944, August 7, 1944, August 22, 1944, f. 8, box 1; Schultz to Carlson, September 3, 1944, September 12, 1944, September 13, 1944, September 17, 1944, September 27, 1944, September 28, 1944, and Roseland to Carlson, September 28, 1944, f. 9, box 1; Schultz to Carlson, December 14, 1944, December 28, 1944, and Janosco to Carlson, December 26, 1944, f. 10, box 1, CP, MHS.

144 Raymond Schultz, e-mail to author, October 3, 2016, and June 1, 2016. On the various meetings, parties, and Marxist study groups held by SWP members in the Schultz home, see, for example, FBI file for Dorothy Schultz, 100–1894 Minneapolis, 8/15/52 pp. 9–10.

145 James R. Barrett argues that children's experiences in the party varied by family and time period but could be quite pressured. See Barrett, "Was the Personal Political?" 416–18.

146 Palmer, *James P. Cannon*, 196.

147 James P. Cannon, *Letters from Prison* (New York: Merit, 1968).

148 Jessie Lloyd O'Connor, *Harvey and Jessie: A Couple of Radicals* (Philadelphia: Temple University Press, 1988), 188, 220.

149 Palmer, *James P. Cannon*, 313–15.

150 Jackson, *Child of the Sit-Downs*, 71–73.

151 Myra Tanner Weiss to Murry Weiss, June 18, 1953, f. Correspondence—Murry Weiss–Myra Tanner Weiss, 1948–1958, box 1, Myra Tanner Weiss Papers, Tamiment Library, New York University, New York, NY.

152 Wald, "Bohemian Bolsheviks," 168–69.

153 Janosco to Carlson, July 23, 1944, and Roseland to Carlson, July 28, 1944, f. 8, box 1, CP, MHS.

154 Norman Nelson later informed for the FBI. See INS, Report of Investigation, St. Paul, Minn., 4/13/54, f. Misc. info on SWP, box 1, CP, MHS.

155 FBI files for Ed Palmquist, AN 74-10, Anchorage, 11/7/47; AN 100–1381, Anchorage, 11/30/56, pp. 1–2; and, SU 100–9142, Salt Lake City, 5/6/57, pp. 1, 6–8, FOIA, in author's possession.

156 Fragment of letter from Grace Carlson to unidentified subject, 1947, micro 2050 reel 15, SWP Records, WHS.

157 Constance Webb, *Not without Love: Memoirs* (Hanover, NH: University Press of New England, 2003), 33.
158 Webb, *Not without Love*, 246–47, 253. On C. L. R. James and the Johnson-Forest tendency see LeBlanc, "Trotskyism in the United States," 32, 42. According to LeBlanc, "The Johnson-Forest tendency, led by C. L. R. James and Raya Dunayevskaya (whose party names were J. R. Johnson and F. Forest), left [the SWP] in 1951, in part due to differences on how to analyze the USSR, China and other such countries (which the Johnson-Forest tendency viewed as 'state capitalist'), but perhaps even more out of a frustrated sense that life in the SWP was preventing them from reaching out to masses of working people who would, they believed, respond more readily to the insights being developed" by those in the tendency.
159 Webb, *Not without Love*, 253.
160 Webb, *Not without Love*, 169, 180–81, 195–97, 261.
161 Raasch-Gilman, "Sisterhood in the Revolution," 370. Janosco to Carlson, September 17, 1944, f. 9, box 1; Roseland to Carlson, September 26, 1944, f. 9, box 1; Janosco to Carlson, October 15, 1944, and October 23, 1944, October 30, 1944, f. 9, box 1; Roseland to Carlson, October 27, 1944, f. 9, box 1; Schultz to Carlson, November 1, 1944, f. 10, box 1; Janosco to Carlson, November 10, 1944, and November 24, 1944, f. 10, box 1; Schultz to Carlson, November 24, 1944, f. 10, box 1; Roseland to Carlson, December 1, 1944, f. 10, box 1, CP, MHS.

CHAPTER 5. THE BREAK

1 Carlson interview with Ross, July 14, 1987, 37.
2 On the "bombshell" effect, see Raasch-Gilman, "Sisterhood in the Revolution," 373.
3 *Minneapolis Morning Tribune*, July 1, 1952, 8. Carlson interview with Ross, July 14, 1987, 38. She does not mention her father's death in her official resignation letter sent to Cannon on June 18: Grace Carlson to James P. Cannon, June 18, 1952, micro 2050 reel 15, SWP Records, WHS.
4 "Holmes, Jas. A.," *St. Paul Minnesota, City Directory*, 1944, and "Holmes, Jas. A.," *St. Paul Minnesota, City Directory*, 1950, Ancestry.com.
5 Raymond Schultz, e-mail to author, October 3, 2016.
6 Dorothy Schultz to Grace Carlson, n.d., f. 1, box 1, and January 5, 1945, f. 11, box 1, CP, MHS.
7 Minnesota Department of Health, Division of Vital Statistics, *Certificate of Death: James A. Holmes*, September 3, 1951, registered no. 26926.
8 *Minneapolis Morning Tribune*, July 1, 1952, 8.
9 Carlson interview with Ross, July 14, 1987, 38. "Grace Holmes Carlson," *SCAN* (Spring 1986): 14.
10 James Holmes was in good standing with the Church when he died and was buried in Calvary Cemetery in St. Paul on September 6, 1951. Linda K. Radtke, Calvary and St. Mary's Cemeteries, e-mail to author, May 8, 2019.
11 *Minneapolis Morning Tribune*, July 1, 1952, 1, 8.

12 *Minneapolis Morning Tribune*, July 1, 1952, 8. "Carlson," *SCAN* (Winter 1986): 25.
13 Pauline Lambert, *In the Heart of the City: The Story of Saint Olaf Catholic Church, Minneapolis, Minnesota, 1941–2001* (Minneapolis: Japs-Olson, 2001), 5–6, 8–14.
14 See, for example, Grace Carlson to James P. Cannon, March 18, 1952, and Morris Stein to Grace Carlson and Vincent Dunne, March 24, 1952, micro 2050 reel 15, SWP Records, WHS.
15 *Militant*, September 10, 1951, 1, 3; February 11, 1952, 1, 2; February 18, 1952, 1.
16 Carlson to Cannon, June 18, 1952, micro 2050 reel 15, SWP Records, WHS.
17 *Minneapolis Star*, June 30, 1952, 1, 10.
18 *Minneapolis Star*, June 30, 1952, 1, 10. Notes from telephone call from Cannon in Minneapolis, June 20, 1952, micro 2050 reel 15, SWP Records, WHS.
19 *Minneapolis Star*, June 30, 1952, 1, 10. Letter to all locals and branches, re. Resignation of Grace Carlson, from James P. Cannon, July 1, 1952, micro 2050 reel 15, SWP Records, WHS.
20 "How We Won Grace Carlson and How We Lost Her," *Militant*, July 7, 1952, 1. Notes from telephone call from Cannon in Minneapolis, June 20, 1952, micro 2050 reel 15, SWP Records, WHS.
21 *Minneapolis Star*, June 30, 1952, 1. "How We Won," 1.
22 "Priest, Party Clash on Mrs. Carlson," *Minneapolis Morning Tribune*, July 1, 1952, 8.
23 Carlson to Schultz, June 25, 1944, f. 7, box 1, CP, MHS.
24 Carlson to Schultz, April 9, 1944, f. 5, box 1, CP, MHS.
25 Thomistic theology was revived in Catholic academia in the 1880s and peaked (including at CSC) during the 1930s and 1940s. As one student observed, it taught that "reason worked with faith, not against it." See Russell Conners, Joyce K. Dahlberg, Catherine Litecky, CSJ, Mary Lou Logsdon, and Thomas West, "Theology Fit for Women: Religious Wisdom, St. Catherine's Style," in *Liberating Sanctuary: 100 Years of Women's Education at the College of St. Catherine*, ed. Jane Lamm Carroll, Joanne Cavallaro, and Sharon Doherty (New York: Lexington Books, 2012), 128–30.
26 "Carlson," *SCAN* (Winter 1986): 25. The article does not comment on whether Grace went to confession before receiving communion. The "automatic" excommunication of Trotskyists mentioned in this article refers to the "Decree against Communism" that the Supreme Sacred Congregation of the Holy Office issued on July 1, 1949, which, as Peter C. Kent explains, indicated that "members or supporters of the Communist party, or those who publish, read, write or disseminate printed materials in support of communist doctrine and practice, would be excommunicated." See Peter C. Kent, *The Lonely Cold War of Pope Pius XII: The Roman Catholic Church and the Division of Europe, 1943–1950* (Montreal: McGill-Queen's University Press, 2002), 242.
27 "Carlson," *SCAN* (Winter 1986): 25.
28 *Minneapolis Morning Tribune*, July 1, 1952, 8.
29 Carlson interview with Ross, July 14, 1987, 39.

30 *Minneapolis Star*, June 30, 1952, 1. Carlson interview with Ross, July 14, 1987, 38.
31 "Carlson," *SCAN* (Winter 1986): 25.
32 Steve Rosswurm, *The FBI and the Catholic Church, 1935–1962* (Boston: University of Massachusetts Press, 2009), 83–86. Schrecker, *Many Are the Crimes*, 74, 192–97, 248.
33 Kathryn S. Olmsted, *Red Spy Queen: A Biography of Elizabeth Bentley* (Chapel Hill: University of North Carolina Press, 2002). Schrecker, *Many Are the Crimes*, 172. Schrecker, *The Age of McCarthyism*, 33. Rosswurm, *The FBI and the Catholic Church*, 83.
34 Olmsted, *Red Spy Queen*, 114–71.
35 On Sheen's communications with the FBI, see Rosswurm, *The FBI and the Catholic Church*, 83–86.
36 FBI file on Grace Carlson, 73-HQ-14643, November 15, 1963, SA William P. Effertz, 13, FOIA, in author's possession. "Carlson," *SCAN* (Winter 1986): 25.
37 "Report of Investigation, INS," St. Paul, Minn., 4-13-54 and Redacted heading, St. Paul, Minn., 4-13-54, f. Misc. info. on SWP and FBI reports, box 1, CP, MHS.
38 Carlson interview with Ross, July 14, 1987, 38.
39 *Good News* 8:2 (Winter 1988): 4.
40 Carlson quoted in "Carlson," *SCAN* (Winter 1986): 25.
41 FBI 73-HQ-14643, 16–18, FOIA, in author's possession.
42 *Minneapolis Morning Tribune*, July 1, 1952, 8.
43 Carlson interview with Ross, July 14, 1987, 14.
44 FBI 73-HQ-14643, 4 and 17, FOIA, in author's possession.
45 FBI 73-HQ-14643, 17, FOIA, in author's possession.
46 FBI file for Vincent Raymond Dunne, Minneapolis 100-932, February 24, 1961, 40–41, FOIA, in author's possession.
47 FBI 100-932, December 24, 1952, 5, FOIA, in author's possession.
48 Patrick M. Quinn, e-mail to author, March 7 and 8, 2019. The Trotskyists in question were Harry DeBoer and Jake Cooper.
49 Grace Carlson to Father Timothy McCarthy, November 2, 1968, f. General Correspondence and Misc., box 2, CP, MHS.
50 *Minneapolis Morning Tribune*, July 1, 1952, 8.
51 Carlson interview with Ross, July 14, 1987, 39.
52 Father McDonough to Grace Carlson, March 24, 1959; McDonough to Grace, n.d. (Christmas note in which he pokes fun at "conservatives in Washington and Rome"); McDonough to Grace, June 16, 1969; McDonough to Grace, n.d. (re. shared progressive interests), f. General Correspondence and Misc., box 2, CP, MHS.
53 Carlson interview with Ross, July 14, 1987, 39.
54 On Newman, see https://www.britannica.com (accessed March 21, 2019). On the centers, see https://www.uscatholic.org (accessed March 21, 2019).
55 *Minneapolis Star*, June 30, 1952, 1. FBI 73-HQ-14643, 3, 7, FOIA, in author's possession.

56 Schrecker, *Many Are the Crimes*, 74. Olmsted, *Red Spy Queen*, 153–54, 185. Rosswurm, *The FBI and the Catholic Church*, 83–86.
57 Carlson interview with Ross, July 9, 1987, 11.
58 "Carlson," *SCAN* (Winter 1986): 25.
59 It is now the site of the University of Minnesota Medical Center, West Bank Campus. On the hospital's ties to the Josephites, see Carroll, "Extravagantly Visionary Leadership," 18.
60 FBI 73-HQ-14643, 7–8, FOIA, in author's possession. *Catherine Wheel*, September 28, 1955, 3.
61 *Catherine Wheel*, December 15, 1955, 5; December 6, 1956, 3; and April 11, 1957, 4.
62 *Catherine Wheel*, April 12, 1956, 3. Grace H. Carlson, "Monthly Report for Staff Card," f. S9A Alumnae Awards, Carlson, Grace, box 93, Alumnae Awards, SCUA-SC.
63 B. W. Lohmar to Grace Carlson, September 17, 1953, Ulric Scott to Grace Carlson, October 2, 1953, and Carlton R. Cronin to Grace Carlson, August 11, 1953, f. General Correspondence and Misc., box 2, CP, MHS. Grace H. Carlson, "Monthly Report for Staff Card" and "Community Service, Conventions, Committee Meetings Attended," f. S9A Alumnae Awards, Carlson, Grace, box 93, Alumnae Awards, SCUA-SC. On the Serra Clubs, see https://serraus.org (accessed March 21, 2019).
64 Grace H. Carlson, "Monthly Report for Staff Card" and "Community Service, Conventions, Committee Meetings Attended," f. S9A Alumnae Awards, Carlson, Grace, box 93, Alumnae Awards, SCUA-SC.
65 Carlson, "The Paradox of Communism," March 20, 1957, and June 23, 1957, f. SMJC Speech and Lecture Notes, box 1, CP, MHS.
66 FBI 73-HQ-14643, 7–8, FOIA, in author's possession.
67 St. Mary's provided the clinical training for nurses after CSC took over the degree in the 1940s until the two institutions split again in 1958. See Carroll, "Extravagantly Visionary Leadership," 18. "The College of St. Catherine, Department of Nursing Instructor's Contract, Grace Carlson," April 20, 1957, f. S9A Alumnae Awards, Carlson, Grace, box 93, Alumnae Awards, SCUA-SC.
68 "Sister Mary Jane, re. Mrs. Grace Carlson," February 7, 1958, f. S9A Alumnae Awards, Carlson, Grace, box 93, Alumnae Awards, SCUA-SC.
69 Grace Carlson, "Marks of an Educated Woman," March 23, 1956, notes, f. SMJC, Speech and Lecture Notes, box 1, CP, MHS.
70 Grace Carlson, "The School as Learning Community," December 1, 1956, notes, f. SMJC, Speech and Lecture Notes, box 1, CP, MHS.
71 Deborah Churchill and Thelma Obah, "Opening Doors: Sister AJ and the Minneapolis Campus," in *Liberating Sanctuary: 100 Years of Women's Education at the College of St. Catherine*, ed. Jane Lamm Carroll, Joanne Cavallaro, and Sharon Doherty (New York: Lexington Books, 2012), 57–59.
72 Churchill and Obah, "Opening Doors," 59–61.
73 Sister A J Moore, "A Bit of Background Chronology re. the Minneapolis Campus," f. SMJC, Faculty, Grace Carlson, box 4, SMJC Collection, CSJ Archive.

74 "The St. Mary's Plan," f. St. Mary's School of Nursing, box 3, St. Mary's School of Nursing Materials, SCUA-SC.
75 "The St. Mary's Plan," f. St. Mary's School of Nursing, box 3, St. Mary's School of Nursing Materials, SCUA-SC.
76 On Grace's perspective at SMJC, see Churchill and Obah, "Opening Doors," 62–63.
77 Peter D'Heilly, e-mail to author, October 4, 2018.
78 Bill Morgan, e-mail to author, February 21, 2019.
79 Bill Morgan, e-mail to author, February 21, 2019.
80 Sister Fides to Grace Carlson, n.d.; Grace Carlson to Arleen, April 6, 1959; Sister M. Germaine to Grace Carlson, n.d., and August 10, 1958; Sister Margaret Clare to Grace Carlson, n.d.; Sister Aimee to Grace Carlson, n.d.; Sister Agnes Leon to Grace Carlson, n.d.; Sister Richard to Grace, January 4, 1959; Sister Marguerite to Grace Carlson, n.d., f. General Correspondence and Misc., box 2, CP, MHS.
81 FBI 73-HQ-14643, 9, FOIA, in author's possession. Peter D'Heilly, e-mail to author, October 4, 2018. George Garrelts to Grace Carlson, August 31, 1951, October 14, 1958, November 3 and April 28 (no years), f. General Correspondence and Misc., box 2, CP, MHS. George Garrelts to Grace Carlson, February 24, 1961, f. Correspondence and Memoirs, 1961–1984, box 2, CP, MHS.
82 George Garrelts to Grace Carlson, October 14, 1958, f. General Correspondence and Misc., box 2, CP, MHS.
83 Grace H. Carlson, "Monthly Report for Staff Card," f. S9A Alumnae Awards, Carlson, Grace, box 93, Alumnae Awards, SCUA-SC. Father McDonough to Grace Carlson, n.d., f. General Correspondence and Misc., box 2, CP, MHS.
84 Peter D'Heilly, e-mail to author, October 4, 2018. "SMJC Catalog, 1975–1977," p. 90, f. St. Mary's School of Nursing, box 3, St. Mary's Administration, SCUA-SC.
85 Father McDonough to Grace Carlson, n.d. ("campfire singing friend in the Sacristy") and McDonough to Carlson, n.d. (Christmas card), f. General Correspondence and Misc., box 2, CP, MHS.
86 "ACC Rally, February 22nd–23, 1958, Tentative Program Outline," and Rev. Raymond Lucker to Grace Carlson, January 27, 1958, f. General Correspondence and Misc., box 2, CP, MHS.
87 Grace Carlson, "The Layman and the Crisis of the Modern World," February 22, 1958, notes, f. SMJC Speech and Lecture Notes, box 1, CP, MHS.
88 Rev. Raymond Lucker to Grace Carlson, March 11, 1958, f. General Correspondence and Misc., box 2, CP, MHS.
89 Peter M. Butler and H. Warren Bahr to Grace Carlson, December 10, 1958; Sister Loyola to Grace Carlson, October 9, 1958; and Virgil Welna to Grace Carlson, November 10, 1958, f. General Correspondence and Misc., box 2, CP, MHS.
90 Peter D'Heilly, e-mail to author, October 4, 2018. Father George Garrelts to Grace Carlson, November 3 (no year), f. General Correspondence and Misc., box 2, CP, MHS.

91 Peter D'Heilly, e-mail to author, October 4, 2018.
92 *Minneapolis Morning Tribune*, July 1, 1952, 8.
93 "Carlson, Gilbert," *St. Paul, Minnesota, City Directory, 1950*, and Gilbert Carlson, 1940, St. Paul, Minnesota, roll m-t0627-02003, page 9B, *Sixteenth Census of the United States, 1940*, RG29.
94 "Grace Carlson, New York" (New York: Paris/Ram Productions, 1987), AFC, NYU. Carlson interview with Ross, July 9, 1987, 11.
95 *Good News* 5:4 (Summer 1985): 11. *Good News* 5:4 (Summer 1979): 1.
96 "Carlson," *SCAN* (Winter 1986): 25. Bill Morgan, e-mail to author, February 21, 2019.
97 Raymond Schultz, e-mail to author, October 3, 2016.
98 Carlson quoted in *Minneapolis Tribune*, July 1, 1952, 1.

CHAPTER 6. "CARLSON'S CONTINUING COMMENTARY"

1 Grace Carlson, "Our Share in the Building," 1981, f. SMJC Programs 3, 1980–84, box 2, CP, MHS.
2 Carlson, "Nurse and the Parish," 1957, f. SMJC Speech and Lecture Notes 1, box 1, CP, MHS.
3 Carlson, "The Lay Apostle," 1958, f. SMJC Speech and Lecture Notes 2, box 1, CP, MHS.
4 Carlson, "Christianity and Communism in the World Today," 1958/1959/1960, f. SMJC Speech and Lecture Notes 2, box 1, CP, MHS.
5 Carlson, "Christianity and Communism in the World Today," 1960 and 1963, f. SMJC Speech and Lecture Notes 3, box 1, CP, MHS. Carlson, "Confrontation between Communism and Christianity," 1965, f. SMJC Speech and Lecture Notes 3, box 1, CP, MHS. Riga was a professor of theology at St. John Vianney Seminary in East Aurora, New York. See "Priest Criticizes Catholics' Indifference to Social Ills," *Advocate*, April 11, 1963, 5.
6 Jeremy Bonner, Christopher D. Denny, and Mary Beth Fraser Connolly, eds., "Introduction," in *Empowering the People of God: Catholic Action before and after Vatican II* (New York: Fordham University Press, 2014), 1–2. Christopher D. Denny, "From Participation to Community: John Courtney Murray's American Justification for Catholic Action," in *Empowering the People of God*, 112–13.
7 Bonner et al., "Introduction," 3.
8 James P. McCartin, *Prayers of the Faithful: The Shifting Spiritual Life of American Catholics* (Cambridge, MA: Harvard University Press, 2010), 61–62.
9 On Catholic Action and the liturgical movement, see Bonner et al., "Introduction," 8, and Katherine E. Harmon, "The Liturgical Movement and Catholic Action: Women Living the Liturgical Life in the Lay Apostolate," in *Empowering the People of God: Catholic Action before and after Vatican II* (New York: Fordham University Press, 2014), 48–52. On the Catholic Worker movement, see Mel Piehl, *Breaking Bread: The Catholic Workers and the Origin of Catholic Radicalism in America* (Philadelphia: Temple University Press, 1982), 95–143.
10 McCartin, *Prayers*, 97.

11 McCartin, *Prayers*, 96–97. Carlson, "Confrontation between Communism and Christianity," 1965, f. SMJC Speech and Lecture Notes 3, box 1, CP, MHS. Peter D'Heilly, e-mail to author, May 18, 2019.
12 Lambert, *In the Heart of the City*, 42. On correspondence with Diekmann and Lawrence, see, for example, Carlson to Lawrence, Feast of St. Teresa 1968, and Diekmann to Carlson, April 6, 1959, f. Gen. Correspondence and Misc., box 2, CP, MHS.
13 Bonner et al., "Introduction," 17.
14 Chester Gillis, *Roman Catholicism in America* (New York: Columbia University Press, 1999), 86–90.
15 McCartin, *Prayers*, 114.
16 Tom Beer and Tom O'Connell, "Father Francis Gilligan and the Struggle for Civil Rights," *Minnesota History* (Summer 2011): 205–15. McGuinness, *Called to Serve*, 162–66.
17 *Good News* 5:4 (Summer 1979): 1.
18 Carlson to Father David, February 23, 1969, f. Gen. Correspondence and Misc., box 2, CP, MHS.
19 George C. Herring, *America's Longest War: The United States and Vietnam, 1950–1975*, 2nd edition (New York: Knopf, 1986). William H. Chafe, *The Unfinished Journey: America since World War II*, 3rd edition (New York: Oxford, 1995), 256–301.
20 Simon Hall, *Rethinking the American Anti-War Movement* (New York: Routledge, 2012), 4–11, 12–28.
21 Carlson, "Commencement Address," n.d., Nursing School, 8/1/65, f. SMJC Speech and Lecture Notes 3, box 1, CP, MHS.
22 Charles Meconis, *With Clumsy Grace: The American Catholic Left, 1961–1975* (New York: Seabury Press, 1979), 2–15.
23 Meconis, *With Clumsy Grace*, 15–60. On the criticisms of the Catholic Left, see pp. 36–38.
24 Carlson to Emeric Lawrence, August 31, 1970, f. Gen. Correspondence and Misc., box 2, CP, MHS.
25 Carlson to Emeric Lawrence, August 31, 1970, f. Gen. Correspondence and Misc., box 2, CP, MHS.
26 Emeric Lawrence to Grace and Gilbert Carlson, September 21, 1970, f. Gen. Correspondence and Misc., box 2, CP, MHS.
27 Carlson to Emeric Lawrence, October 12, 1970, f. Gen. Correspondence and Misc., box 2, CP, MHS.
28 Carlson, "Review of Catholics and the Left," 11/13/68, f. SMJC Speech and Lecture Notes 3, box 1, CP, MHS.
29 Peter D'Heilly, e-mail to author, October 4, 2018.
30 Andrew Hunt, "How New Was the New Left?" in *The New Left Revisited*, ed. John McMillian and Paul Buhle (Philadelphia: Temple University Press, 2003), 142–46.

31 Carlson to Breitenbucher, May 29, 1968, f. Gen. Correspondence and Misc., box 2, CP, MHS.
32 Jeremy Bonner, "Who Will Guard the Guardians: Church Government and the People of God, 1965–1969," in *Empowering the People of God: Catholic Action before and after Vatican II*, ed. Jeremy Bonner, Christopher D. Denny, and Mary Beth Fraser Connolly (New York: Fordham University Press, 2014), 238–39.
33 Carlson to Breitenbucher, May 29, 1968, f. Gen. Correspondence and Misc., box 2, CP, MHS.
34 Carlson to Lawrence, (n.d.) 1968, f. Gen. Correspondence and Misc., box 2, CP, MHS.
35 Carlson to Mary Berres, n.d., f. Gen. Correspondence and Misc., box 2, CP, MHS. James Patrick Shannon was an auxiliary bishop of St. Paul and Minneapolis who spoke out against the war in Vietnam and in support of civil rights. In 1968 he resigned as bishop because of his opposition to *Humane Vitae*. See https://www.latimes.com (accessed November 23, 2019).
36 Carlson, "Review of Catholics and the Left," 11/13/68, and "Contemporary Atheism," 4/14/67, f. SMJC Speech and Lecture Notes 3, box 1, CP, MHS.
37 Jay P. Corrin, *Catholic Progressives in England after Vatican II* (Notre Dame, IN: University of Notre Dame Press, 2013), 216–17, 228.
38 On her criticism of Day, see Carlson interview with Ross, July 14, 1987, 39. On *Slant* at SMJC, see *Good News* 5:4 (Summer 1979): 1, and Peter D'Heilly, e-mail to author, May 18, 2019.
39 Carlson to Lawrence, August 31, 1970, f. Gen. Correspondence and Misc., box 2, CP, MHS.
40 Memo from SAC, Minneapolis (73–330) to Director, FBI, 10/16/63, p. 2, in FBI 73-IIQ-14643, FOIA, in author's possession. On voter registration drives, see Sister A J Moore, "Remembering Grace Holmes Carlson," November 25, 1992, p. 3, f. SMJC Faculty. Grace Carlson, box 4, SMJC Collection, CSJ Archives.
41 FBI 73–14643, Minneapolis, 11/15/63, William P. Effertz, p. 1, in FBI 73-HQ-14643, FOIA, in author's possession.
42 Reed Cozart, Pardon Attorney, to J. Edgar Hoover, October 20, 1965, in FBI 73-HQ-14643, FOIA, in author's possession.
43 Peter D'Heilly, e-mail to author, October 4, 2018.
44 On recruiting difficulties, see "Farrell Dobbs's Testimony," in *FBI on Trial: The Victory in the Socialist Workers Party Suit against Government Spying*, ed. Margaret Jayko (New York: Pathfinder, 1988), 286. On the fear of legal reprisals, see Vincent Dunne to Harry Press, May 19, 1950, micro 2050 reel 15, SWP Records, WHS. On financial constraints, see Vincent Dunne to James Cannon, December 1, 1948; Grace Carlson to Morris Stein, March 29, 1949; Morris Stein to Grace Carlson, November 21, 1951, micro 2050 reel 15, SWP Records, WHS. On the "dog days," see Vincent Dunne to Farrell Dobbs, May 5, 1955, micro 2050 reel 15, SWP Records, WHS.

45 On "spats," see Henry Schultz to Farrell Dobbs, June 17, 1956, and on "fratricidal," see Tom Kerry to Charles Sheer, April 30, 1958, micro 2050 reel 15, SWP Records, WHS.
46 Dorothy Schultz interview with Elizabeth Raasch-Gilman, December 29, 1994, in author's possession.
47 Carl Feingold to Farrell Dobbs, January 30, 1959, February 8, 1959, February 15, 1959, February 17, 1959, February 23, 1959, March 19, 1959, March 22, 1959, May 7, 1959, and Carl Feingold to James Cannon, March 4, 1959, micro 2050 reel 16, SWP Records, WHS. On Cochran faction, see Le Blanc, "Trotskyism in the United States," 43.
48 Le Blanc, "Trotskyism in the United States," 42–44.
49 Schultz interview with Raasch-Gilman, December 29, 1994.
50 FBI file for Henry Schultz, 100–1078 Minneapolis, 6/17/60, pp. 3–4 in 100-HQ-21325, FOIA, in author's possession.
51 FBI file for Henry Schultz, 100–1078 Minneapolis, 12/20/60, p. 2, in 100-HQ-21325, FOIA, in author's possession.
52 Raymond Schultz, e-mail to author, October 3, 2016.
53 FBI file on Dorothy Schultz, 100–1894 Minneapolis, 9/30/61, p. 2, in 100-HQ-159217, FOIA, in author's possession.
54 Raymond Schultz, e-mail to author, June 1, 2017. "U.W. News" 3/2/66, http://digital.library.wisc (accessed June 3, 2019). FBI 73–14643, Milwaukee, 11/15/63, Baier, pp. 1 and 2, and FBI 73–14643, Minneapolis, 11/15/63, Effertz, p. 4, in FBI 73-HQ-14643, FOIA, in author's possession. FBI file on Henry Schultz, 100–13832 Milwaukee, 11/29/63, cover page c, in 100-HQ-21325, FOIA, in author's possession. Memo from SAC Milwaukee to Director, 12/27/65 re. Dorothy Mary Schultz, in 100-HQ-159217, FOIA, in author's possession.
55 FBI 73–14643, Milwaukee, 11/15/63, Baier, pp. 1–6, in FBI 73-HQ-14643, FOIA, in author's possession. Schultz, e-mail to author, June 1, 2017.
56 FBI 73–14643, Minneapolis, 11/15/63, Effertz, p. 4, in FBI 73-HQ-14643, FOIA, in author's possession. FBI 100-HQ-422072 v. 1, pp. 3–191, FOIA, in author's possession.
57 Raymond Schultz, e-mail to author, October 3, 2016, and June 1, 2017. On Henry's unemployment during the late 1950s, see FBI 100-HQ-21325 v. 2, pp. 59–82, FOIA, in author's possession.
58 Carlson interview with Ross, July 14, 1987, 41–42.
59 On her antiwar involvement, see Raymond Schultz, e-mail to author, June 1, 2018. On her political campaign work, see Patrick Quinn, e-mail to author, March 7, 2017 (she financially supports local SWP candidates and strikes) and Schultz to Carlson, March 8 (n.d.), f. Gen. Correspondence and Misc., box 2, CP, MHS (she did house-to-house work for Eugene McCarthy).
60 Raymond Schultz, e-mail to author, June 1, 2017. Memo from SAC Milwaukee to FBI Director, 7/29/68, in 100-HQ-21325, FOIA, in author's possession.

61 Dorothy Schultz to Grace Carlson, Friday (no year); Schultz to Carlson, March 8 (1968?); and Schultz to Carlson, Friday (no year), f. Gen. Correspondence and Misc., box 2, CP, MHS.
62 Schultz to Carlson, Sunday morning (n.d.), f. Gen. Correspondence and Misc., box 2, CP, MHS.
63 Raymond Schultz, e-mail to author, June 1, 2017.
64 Schultz to Carlson, Wednesday (n.d.); Schultz to Carlson, Friday, March 8 (1968?), f. Gen. Correspondence and Misc., box 2, CP, MHS. Raymond Schultz, e-mail to author, June 1, 2017.
65 FBI 100-HQ-422072 v. 1, pp. 212–52 and v. 3 pp. 2–20, FOIA, in author's possession. Schultz to Carlson, Tuesday (n.d.), f. Gen. Correspondence and Misc., box 2, CP, MHS.
66 Schultz to Carlson, Friday, March 1 (1969?), f. Gen. Correspondence and Misc., box 2, CP, MHS.
67 Hillel Aron, "The Story of This Drug Rehab-Turned-Violent Cult Is *Wild, Wild Country*–Caliber Bizarre," *Los Angeles Magazine*, April 23, 2018, https://www.lamag.com (accessed May 23, 2019). On the original positive press, see, for example, "A Tunnel Back into the Human Race," *Life*, March 9, 1962, 52–66, and "Letters to the Editors," *Life*, March 30, 1962, 19.
68 Schultz to Carlson, Sunday morning (1969?), f. Gen. Correspondence and Misc., box 2, CP, MHS.
69 Aron, "The Story of This Drug Rehab." "Life at Synanon Is Swinging," *Time*, December 26, 1977, 20.
70 Susan Rimby Leighow, "An 'Obligation to Participate': Married Nurses' Labor Force Participation in the 1950s," in *Not June Cleaver: Women and Gender in Postwar America, 1945–1960*, ed. Joanne Meyerowitz (Philadelphia: Temple University Press, 1994), 38–41.
71 Carlson, "The Professional Woman Today," 1/15/60, f. SMJC Speech and Lecture Notes 2, box 1, CP, MHS.
72 Mary J. Henold, *Catholic and Feminist: The Surprising History of the American Catholic Feminist Movement* (Chapel Hill: University of North Carolina Press, 2008), 6.
73 Carlson, "The Catholic Woman's Apostolate," 1/28/59, f. SMJC Speech and Lecture Notes 2, box 1, CP, MHS.
74 Carlson, "The Professional Woman Today," 1/15/60, and "The Need for Commitment," 9/16/59, f. SMJC Speech and Lecture Notes 2, box 1, CP, MHS.
75 Fraser, *Which Road towards Women's Liberation?* Weiss, *The Bustelo Incident*. Weiss, Oral History, April 29, 1983, OH 002, Tamiment Library, New York University, New York, NY.
76 On Grace's affiliation with women's groups, see *Good News* 5:4 (Summer 1979): 1 On the links between the Old Left and second wave feminism, see Horowitz, *Betty Friedan and the Making of the Feminine Mystique*, and Weigand, *Red Feminism*.
77 Cobble, *The Other Women's Movement*, 121–44.

78 Leighow, "An 'Obligation to Participate,'" 46–51.
79 Carlson, "Women's Role," 1/27/72, f. SMJC Speech and Lecture Notes 2, box 1, CP, MHS.
80 Julie Ann Bloemnedaal to Grace Carlson, Easter (n.d.); Joanie Machart to Grace Carlson, n.d. (1959); Nina Leewright to Grace Carlson, July 1, 1970, f. Gen. Correspondence and Misc., box 2, CP, MHS. Laure Campbell, e-mail to author, October 5, 2018.
81 "Grace Carlson: Forever an Activist," *Good News* 8:2 (Winter 1988): 5. Peter D'Heilly, e-mail to author, October 4, 2018.
82 Grace Carlson, "Carlson's Continuing Commentary," *Good News* 6:1 (Fall 1979): 2; Carlson, "Commentary," *Good News* 6:3 (Spring 1980): 3; Carlson, "Commentary," *Good News* 1:1 (Fall 1980): 3–4.
83 See, for example, Staff meeting minutes, November 7, 1980, October 24, 1980, October 10, 1980, f. SMJC, Programs 3, 1980–1984, box 2, and lists and planning sheets for 1981 alumni day, f. Alumnae Relations 3: 1981–1984, box 2, CP, MHS.
84 Carlson to Dr. Hedrick, January 27, 1984, and February 17, 1984; Dr. Hedrick to Carlson, February 3, 1984, and February 24, 1984, f. Alumnae Relations 3: 1981–1984, box 2, CP, MHS.
85 Carlson, "Continuing Commentary," *Good News* 2:2 (Winter 1981): 11–12. On PSR, see https://www.psr.org (accessed May 31, 2019).
86 Lawrence S. Wittner, *Confronting the Bomb: A Short History of the World Nuclear Disarmament Movement* (Stanford, CA: Stanford University Press, 2009), 122, 132–33, 138–39. Helen Broinowski Caldicott, *A Desperate Passion: An Autobiography* (New York: Norton, 1996), 133–78, 198–214, 253. When Caldicott demanded a nuclear freeze and the abolition of weapons, others in PSR disagreed. She was pressured into resigning from her role as president of PSR in 1983, and the history of the organization was rewritten to exclude her. See Caldicott, *A Desperate Passion*, 270–91. See also the history of PSR on its website: https://www.psr.org (accessed May 31, 2019).
87 Carlson, "Continuing Commentary," *Good News* 2:2 (Winter 1981): 11–12. On the PSR, see letter from John Mahan Jr., MD, to "prospective member," n.d., f. Gen. Correspondence and Misc., box 2, CP, MHS, and https://www.psr.org (accessed May 31, 2019).
88 Carlson, "Our Share in the Building," May 1981, f. SMJC Programs 3, 1980–1984, box 2, CP, MHS. Sisters Angelica Schreiber and Mary Heinen to Mrs. Carlson, March 27, 1981, and Sisters Angelica Schreiber and Mary Heinen to Mrs. Carlson, May 12, 1981, f. Gen. Correspondence and Misc., box 2, CP, MHS.
89 *Annotated by Carlson Cookbook* (SMJC, 1970) and *Carlson's Curry Cookbook* (SMJC, 1984). Frances Sontag, "St. Catherine Alumna Award: Grace Holmes Carlson," *SCAN* (Winter 1986): 25.
90 Peter D'Heilly, e-mail to author, October 4, 2018.
91 Peter D'Heilly, e-mail to author, October 4, 2018.
92 *Good News* 5:4 (Summer 1979): 1.

93 *Good News* 5:4 (Summer 1979): 1.
94 Joanie Machart to Mr. and Mrs. Carlson, n.d., f. Gen. Correspondence and Misc., box 2, CP, MHS.
95 On Grace's health, see Peter D'Heilly, e-mail to author, October 4, 2018. On Gilbert, see Gerald Mullin to Grace Carlson, September 11, 1973, and October 4, 1973, f. Gen. Correspondence and Misc., box 2, CP, MHS.
96 "Home Health Care," *Bells*, August–September 1978, 1, 4–5.
97 On chain smoking, see Peter D'Heilly, e-mail to author, October 4, 2018. On Gilbert's wishes, see Moore, "Remembering Grace Holmes Carlson," November 25, 1992, pp. 5–6, f. SMJC Faculty. Grace Carlson, box 4, SMJC Collection, CSJ Archives. Minnesota State Department of Health, *Certificate of Death for Gilbert E. Carlson*, May 13, 1985, no. 2285012490.
98 Grace Carlson to Miriam Braverman, August 26, 1970, and Grace Carlson to Jean and Bill Brust, November 6, 1970, f. Gen. Correspondence and Misc., box 2, CP, MHS. On Miriam's background, see http://www.mjfreedman.org (accessed December 18, 2018) and LeBlanc, "Trotskyism in the United States," 42–43. On the Brusts, see biographical note for the Bill Brust Papers, MHS, http://www2.mnhs.org (accessed May 29, 2019).
99 Bea Janosco to Grace Carlson, October 20, 1981, f. Gen. Correspondence and Misc., box 2, CP, MHS.
100 George Breitman to Grace Carlson, March 5, 1981, f. Misc. info. on SWP, box 1, CP, MHS.
101 Leonard B. Boudin, "Forward," in *FBI on Trial: The Victory in the Socialist Workers Party Suit against Government Spying*, ed. Margaret Jayko (New York: Pathfinder, 1988), 10.
102 On COINTELPRO's goals, see Athan Theoharis, *Spying on Americans: Political Surveillance from Hoover to the Huston Plan* (Philadelphia: Temple University Press, 1978), 136. On the measures needed to release the files, see Boudin, "Forward," 10.
103 Margaret Jayko, "Introduction," in *FBI on Trial*, 13–14.
104 David Cole and James X. Dempsey, *Terrorism and the Constitution: Sacrificing Civil Liberties in the Name of National Security*, 3rd ed. (New York: New Press, 2006), ibook edition, chap. 7, p. 124 of 342.
105 Alan Wald to Grace Carlson, September 20, 1983, October 4, 1983, and October 20, 1983; Grace Carlson to Alan Wald, September 28, 1983, and October 12, 1983, f. Misc. info. on SWP, box 1, CP, MHS. Richard Valelly to Grace Carlson, September 20 (no year), f. Misc. info. on SWP, box 1, CP, MHS.
106 Carlson interview with Ross, July 14, 1987, 42–43.
107 "Grace Carlson, New York" (New York: Paris/Ram Productions, 1987), AFC, NYU.
108 "Grace Carlson: Forever an Activist," *Good News* 8:2 (Winter 1988): 5.
109 Raymond Schultz, e-mail to author, June 1, 2017. On the campus protests, see "A Turning Point: Six Stories from the Dow Chemical Protests," https://1967.wisc.edu

(accessed May 28, 2019) and Teryl Franklin, "From the Archives: University of Wisconsin Students Protest the Vietnam War," *Wisconsin State Journal*, September 25, 2017, https://madison.com (accessed May 28, 2019).

110 Ruth Bleier, "History of the Association of Faculty Women—Madison: A Participant's View," in *Women Emerge in the Seventies*, ed. Marian J. Swoboda and Audrey J. Roberts (Madison, WI: U.W. System, Office of Women, 1980), 14. Sue Searing, "Women's Studies Librarian," in *Women on Campus in the Eighties: Old Struggles, New Victories*, ed. Marian J. Swoboda, Audrey J. Roberts, and Jennifer Hirsch (Madison, WI: Office of Equal Opportunity Programs and Policy Studies, 1993), 41 fn. 2.

111 Raymond Schultz, e-mail to author, October 3, 2016, and June 1, 2017. Dorothy Schultz to Carlson, March 8 (1968?), f. Gen. Correspondence and Misc. box 2, CP, MHS. Ann's daughter, Laura, graduated medical school and began a practice elsewhere.

112 Peter D'Heilly, e-mail to author, October 4, 2018. "Carlson, Dr. Grace H," Obituary, *Star Tribune*, July 9, 1992, and *St. Paul Pioneer Press*, July 9, 1992, clippings, f. Biographical info., box 1, CP, MHS. Moore, "Remembering Grace Holmes Carlson," 6.

CONCLUSION

1 "Carlson, Dr. Grace H," Obituary, *Star Tribune*, July 9, 1992, and *St. Paul Pioneer Press*, July 9, 1992, clippings, f. Biographical info., box 1, CP, MHS.

2 "Dedication and Spirit Endears Staff and Students to Carlson," *Good News* (Fall 1992): 6.

3 On the ways labor and working-class historians have tended to overlook the role of faith in their subjects' lives, see Joseph A. McCartin, "The Force of Faith: An Introduction to the Labor and Religion Special Issue," *Labor: Studies in Working-Class History of the Americas* 6:1 (Spring 2009): 1–4. On the ways in which labor historians and scholars of US Catholic history have tended to work in isolation from each other, see James P. McCartin and Joseph A. McCartin, "Working-Class Catholicism: A Call for New Investigations, Dialogue, and Reappraisal," *Labor: Studies in Working-Class History of the Americas* 4:1 (Spring 2007): 99–110. Some works that address the role of faith in workers' lives include Sterne, *Ballots and Bibles*, Wingerd, *Claiming the City*, and Pehl, *The Making of Working-Class Religion*.

4 Carlson to Breitenbucher, May 29, 1968, f. Gen. Correspondence and Misc., box 2, CP, MHS.

5 Carlson to Breitenbucher, May 29, 1968, f. Gen. Correspondence and Misc., box 2, CP, MHS. Carlson to Lawrence, August 31, 1970, f. Gen. Correspondence and Misc., box 2, CP, MHS.

6 "Grace Carlson: Forever an Activist," *Good News* 8:2 (Winter 1988): 5.

7 Friedrich Engels, *The Origins of the Family, Private Property, and the State* (1884; New York: Penguin Books, 2010; reprint, Lawrence & Wishart, 1972). Evelyn

Reed, *Problems of Women's Liberation: A Marxist Approach*, 5th edition (New York: Pathfinder Press, 1971).
8 Schultz to Carlson, January 23, 1944, f. 3, box 1, CP, MHS.
9 "Thanksgiving Remembrances" program, November 25, 1992, f. SMJC Faculty, Grace Carlson, box 4, SMJC Collection, CSJ Archives, St. Paul, Minnesota.
10 Moore, "Remembering Grace Holmes Carlson," 1–3.
11 Moore, "Remembering Grace Holmes Carlson," 2–4.
12 Moore, "Remembering Grace Holmes Carlson," 4–5.
13 Moore, "Remembering Grace Holmes Carlson," 5–6.

INDEX

Italic references to figures indicate photographs between pages 118–19.

African Americans, 188; in St. Paul, 13–14, 21–22; SWP and, 84, 85–86, 126–27. *See also* NAACP
Alderson federal prison, 93, 94–96, 107, *Fig. 7* —Grace in, 94–107, 144; correspondence during, 5, 80, 97–103, 138, 141–43, 153; and fellow prisoners, 5, 102, 103–9, 116. *See also* "Women in Prison" speaking tour
American Civil Liberties Union (ACLU), 91, 108, 163
American Federation of Labor (AFL), 25, 30, 57, 69
American Workers Party (AWP), 70
Americanization, 26
Anderson, Evelyn, 92, 97, 102–3, 108, 124, 125, 143; Grace's correspondence with, 93–94, 97, 98, 99, 101, 103, 104, 145
Anderson, Victor, 88
antinuclear movement, 7, 211–12, 213
antiwar movement: in 1930s, 56, 85, 90; against Vietnam War, 189–92, 201, 203, 218
Aquinas, St. Thomas, 158, 162
Association of Catholic Trade Unionists (ACTU), 185
Association of Christians for Church Renewal (ACCR), 193–94

Barrett, James, 3
Beidel, Lydia, 113, 116
Benson, Elmer, 86

Bentley, Elizabeth, 163, 164–65, 170
Berres, Mary, 194
Berrigan, Father Daniel, 191, 192, 223
Berrigan, Father Philip, 191, 192, 223
birth control, 45, 113–14, 140–41, 263n98
blacklisting, 122, 135, 153; of Grace, 6, 156, 166, 170
Bloemendaal, Julie Ann, 209
Braden, Mark, 155
Brandeis, Louis, 90
Braverman, Harry, 198
Braverman, Miriam, 92, 98, 205; as friend of Grace, 92, 97, 98–99, 103, 104, 107, 108, 215; pseudonym "Carter" used by, 251n73
Brehm, Marie C., 132
Breitenbucher, Robert, 193–94, 226
Breitman, George, 71, 216
Brennan, Sister Rita Clare, 170, 182, *Fig. 11*
Broderick, Mary, 225
Browder, Earl, 86
Brown, Kathleen A., 80, 110, 136, 137, 149, 150
Brown, William, 62
Brust, Bill, 151, 197–98, 215
Brust, Jeanne, 151, 197–98, 215
Budenz, Louis, 163–65, 170
Burnham, James, 81–82
Busch, Andrew E., 133
Bustelo incident, 117–18, 208
Byran, Helen, 96

Caldicott, Helen, 212
Campbell, Laure, 209

Cannon, James P., 72–73, 81–82, 85, 141, 154; in early years of Trotskyist movement, 57, 73; marriage of, 150, 151–52; as friend of Grace, 5, 6, 72, 86–87, 92, 119, 125, 136, 146, 152, 159–61; in Smith Act trial, 89, 91; in SWP factional conflicts, 81–82, 123, 198

Carlson, Edward (Gilbert's father), 64, 181

Carlson, Gilbert, 59, 180, *Fig. 12*; family background of, 64–65; as a lawyer, 59, 64, 65, 78, 181; and Catholicism, 66, 78, 89, 137; service of, in World War II, 137, 138; and St. Mary's Junior College, 181–82, 214; illness and death of, 184, 214–15, 217, 219, 226

—marriage of, to Grace, 41, 46, 51, 67; romance leading to, 64, 65–66; long separation in, 6, 41, 78–79, 136–37, 139–41; during Grace's prison term, 97, 137, 138, 162; restoration of, 7, 156, 180–82, 222; after reconciliation, 180–82, 188, 200, 213–14, 215

Carlson, Grace Holmes: family background of, 9–17; working-class consciousness of, 32, 39, 40, 70, 78; and sister Dorothy, *see under* Schultz, Dorothy Holmes; Catholic education of, *see under* Sisters of St. Joseph; and university, *see under* University of Minnesota; marriage of, *see under* Carlson, Gilbert; in Minnesota Department of Education, 4–5, 67–69, 73–78, 166, 222; in SWP, *see under* Socialist Workers Party; romance of, with Ray Dunne, *see under* Dunne, Vincent Raymond; feminism of, 5–6, 80–81, 113, 116, 118, 182, 207–8, 224; in 1941 Smith Act trial, 1, 5, 80, 87–88, 89, 92, 139, 192, *Fig. 6*; in prison, *see under* Alderson federal prison; and FBI, *see under* Federal Bureau of Investigation; return of, to Catholic Church, 1, 2, 6–7, 156–63, 168–72,

224; and St. Mary's Junior College, *see under* St. Mary's Junior College; post-1952 speeches and lectures by, 171–72, 173, 179, 185, 191–93, 195, 207; criticisms by, of New Left, 7, 192–95, 223; last years of, 214–19; eulogy for, 1, 225–26

Carlson, Ida Tessier (Gilbert's mother), 64, 181

Carroll, Jane Lamm, 43–44

Carter, Jimmy, 212

Catholic Action movement, 35, 185–86, 190; influence of, on Grace, 7, 183, 206, 222

Catholic Interracial Council (CIC), 194

Catholic Left, 190–96

Catholic Marxism, 7, 193, 194–95, 196, 223. See also *Slant* movement

Catholic Worker movement, 172, 186, 187

Chambers, Whittaker, 128

China, 134

Chinese immigrants, 21

Citizens Alliance (CA), 25, 60

Civil Rights Defense Committee (CRDC), 91, 92, 97, 99, 102, 108, 143

Clarke, George, 125, 149

Cobble, Dorothy Sue, 208

Coburn, Carol K., 19, 39

Cochran, Bert, 103

Cohen, Robert, 56

COINTELPRO, 216

Coleman, Father James, 158

College of St. Catherine (CSJ), 34, 41, 42–53; Grace as student in, 4, 15, 42–53, 170, *Fig. 3*; Grace teaching in, 172–73, 174

Colvin, Sarah Tarleton, 67–68, 77

Communist International (Comintern), 58, 70, 73

Communist Left Opposition, 56, 57, 61, 70, 73, 112

Communist Party (CPUSA), 72, 115–16, 119, 136, 143; founding of, 57, 73;

expulsion of Trotskyists from, 56, 57, 70, 73, 152; in the Depression, 57–58; and Second Red Scare, 128, 129, 134, 163–64
Corrin, Jay P., 195
Cosgrove, Father Laurence, 21, 22, 23, 27, *Fig. 1*
Cowley, Father Leonard, 158; and Grace's return to Catholic Church, 158, 159, 161–62, 168, 169
Creel, Marie, 153–54
Creel, Warren, 121, 154
Cretin, Bishop Joseph, 19, 22
Crowley, Father Timothy, 23

Dabelstein, D. H., 67, 68, 75
Dante, Mary, 113, 116
Davis, Colin J., 30, 31, 32
Day, Dorothy, 186, 187, 195
DeBoer, Harry, 6, 61, 83, 92, 101
Dennis, Peggy, 116
Dewey, Thomas E., 131, 133
D'Heilly, Peter, 176, 196, 219, 221; on Grace's role at St. Mary's Junior College, 176, 178, 180, 193, 210
Diekman, Father Godfrey, 187
Dies, Martin, 74
Dobbs, Farrell, 61, 123–24, 134, 197; in 1934 Teamsters strikes, 61, 62; as friend of Grace, 5, 6, 119, 136, 146; in Smith Act trial, 89, 90–91; as SWP presidential candidate, 119, 124, 125, 128, 129, 133, 159
Dobbs, Marvel, 125
Dodge, L. Mara, 95
Dolan, Jay P., 11
Dollinger, Genora, 120–21, 150, 152, 153
Dollinger, Sol, 120, 150, 152, 153
Dunne, Bill, 201
Dunne, Grant, 61, 88
Dunne, Jeannette, 139, 143
Dunne, Jennie Holm, 6, 138–39, 142–43
Dunne, Miles, 61, 82, 108

Dunne, Vincent Raymond, 71, 73, 138–39, 154, 155, 167–68, 201; background of, 60–61; as a leader in 1934 Teamster strikes, 61, 62; in SWP, 61, 73, 135, 197, *Fig. 9*; FBI reports on, 141, 145, 146, 149, 167
—romance of, with Grace, 6, 120, 138, 139–40, 141–50, 155; secrecy of, 6, 120, 139; and shared political work, 120, 137, 144–45, 150, 155; conflicts in, 147–50; ending of, 167–68

Eagleton, Terry, 195
Effertz, William P., 165, 196
Elizabeth Marie, Sister, 33, 53
Engels, Friedrich, 59, 113, 115, 224

Falk, Erika, 130, 132
Farmer-Labor Party, 42, 55, 57, 59, 86, 121
Fass, Paula, 45
Faue, Elizabeth, 66, 80, 110–11, 136, 137, 149, 150
Federal Bureau of Investigation (FBI), 74, 134–35, 164–65, 191, 203; SWP as a target of, 87, 88, 89, 134, 153, 197, 199, 216
—and Grace, 127, 134, 140–41, 145, 146, 147–50; after break from SWP, 6, 156, 165–68, 170–71, 172, 196, 215–16, 226
Federal Employee Loyalty Program, 122, 128
Feingold, Carl, 197–98
feminism, 3, 6, 8; Grace's, 5–6, 80–81, 113, 116, 118, 182, 207–8, 224; second wave, 116, 208, 224. *See also* Marxist feminism
Finch, Dr. Frank, 67
Flaherty, Jewell, 82
Flynn, Elizabeth Gurley, 106–7
Foreign Agents Registration Act (1938), 134

Fourth International, 72, 82, 123, 134
Fraser, Clara, 117, 208
Fredreci, Mille, 113
Frosig, George, 62

Galazan, Gene, 202–3
Garrelts, Father George, 178, 180
Gaudium et Spes decree (1965), 187–88
Geller, Henrietta, 103, 105
German Americans, 11, 14, 131; and Grace's heritage, 2, 4, 10, 12–13, 28, 32; and World War I, 25, 28, 32
Giallombardo, Rose, 97
Gibbons, James Cardinal, 26
Gilligan, Father Francis J., 69, 188
Goldman, Albert, 89–90, 91, 123, 145
Golos, Jacob, 164
Good Thunder Herald, 129
Great Depression, 41, 53, 54, 55, 67, 68, 139
Great Northern Railway, 25; as Grace's father's employer, 2, 9, 14, 30, 32; and 1922 shopmen's strike, 9, 30, 31–32
Great Society, 174
Green, William, 69
Griesa, Thomas, 216
Griffin, Father Martin, 23, 66

Hansen, Joseph, 117, 118, 208. *See also* Bustelo incident
Hardy, Samuel, 14
Harmon, Katherine E., 186
Harris, Mary, 95, 107
Hartmann, Susan M., 83–84
Hawes, Elizabeth, 116
Hebl, Father John, 221
Hedrick, Dr. William, 211
Hironimus, Helen, 104
Hiss, Alger, 128, 164
Holmes, James A. (Grace's father), 11–14, 15–16, 36, 107; death of, 6, 156, 157–58 —as railroad worker, 2, 12, 16, 30, 37; and 1922 shopmen's strike, 4, 9, 30, 32, 37, 63
Holmes, Mary Neuber (Grace's mother), 9, 12–13, 14, 15, 48–49; influence of, on Grace, 15, 33, 36, 49, 223–24
Holmes, Oliver Wendell, 90
Home of the Good Shepherd, 177; Grace and, 177, 178, 180, 182, 188, 201, 223
Hoover, J. Edgar, 134
House Un-American Activities Committee (HUAC), 122, 127; formally House Committee to Investigate Un-American Activities, 74

Immigration and Naturalization Service (INS), 135, 165, 166
Industrial Workers of the World (IWW), 57, 61, 72
Inman, Mary, 115, 116
International Labor Defense, 73
Ireland, Archbishop John, 10, 18, 22–24, 26, 27–28, 222, 234n32; and Catholic education, 34, 36, 37, 42
Ireland, Ellen, 34
Irish Americans, 25, 28, 32; and Grace's heritage, 4, 10, 11–12, 29, 32

Jackson, Carlton, 152
James, C. L. R., 154
Janosco, Bea, 99, 141, 143, 145, 153, 207; in friendship network within SWP, 80, 100–101, 103, 109, 111, 126, 151, 155, 205; correspondence of, with Grace, 97, 99–100, 103, 143, 215; work of, in SWP, 99–100, 109, 111
Janosco, John, 151, 165
Jeanne Marie, Sister, 53
John XXIII, Pope, 187, 190
Johnson, Chester K., 84, 121
Johnson, Lyndon B., 174, 189, 196
Jones, Claudia, 107, 116
Josephites. *See* Sisters of St. Joseph
Joyce, Matthew, 89
Judd, Walter, 135–36

Karsner, David, 73
Karsner, Rose, 57, 72, 102, 141; and James Cannon, 73, 150, 151–52, 153; and Grace, 72, 80, 86, 92, 93, 97, 102; writings by, on women's issues, 113, 116
Killen, Marcella, 136
Konikow, Antoinette, 57, 112, 113–14, 116, 140
Korean War, 163, 166
Kutcher, James, 128

Laski, Harold, 54
Lawrence, Father Emeric, 187, 190, 191–92, 194, 196, 223, 226
League of Women Voters, 49–50
Leewright, Nina, 209
Lenin, Vladimir, 57, 59, 72, 87, 115, 192
Leo XIII, Pope, 22
Leonard, Tom, 199–200, 202
Le Sueur, Meridel, 63
Le Sueur News-Herald, 129
Liber, Mary, 170, 171
Lippincott, Benjamin, 54, 58
"little red scare," 73–75, 76, 77, 129–30
liturgical movement, 7, 183, 185–86, 187, 190, 222
Lloyd, Jessie, 152
Lucker, Rev. Raymond, 179
Lumen Gentium decree (1964), 187–88

Machart, Joanie, 209
Makimson, Lista, 72, 73
Manning, Louise, 117
Mariette, Dr. E. S., 75
Marxist feminism, 113–18, 205, 208, 224; Grace's, 5–6, 81, 113, 116, 118, 182, 207, 224
McCarran Act (1950), 134
McDonough, Father Michael, 169, 177, 178–79
McGee, Sister Alberta, 29
McGowan, Marjorie, 117
McHugh, Sister Antonia, 42–43, 44, 48, 49, 50

Merton, Thomas, 190, 191
Michel, Father Virgil, 185–86
Militant, the, 92, 93, 98, 108–9, 117–18, 151, 152; Grace's writing in, 5, 81, 111–15, 116, 131–32; Dorothy and, 99, 100; explanation for Grace's break from SWP, 160–61
Millard, Betty, 115–16
Milwaukee Deutsche Zeitung, 131
Milwaukee Sentinel, 132
Minneapolis Morning Tribune, 132, 157–58, 161, 163, 167, 180
Minneapolis Star, 159, 160, 163, 167
Minnesota Commission for Public Safety, 28
Minnesota Department of Education (DoE), 42, 67–69, 76–78; Grace's employment by (1935–1940), 4–5, 67–69, 73–78, 166, 222
Moore, Sister Anne Joachim ("Sister AJ"), 173–75, 177, 188, 219, *Fig. 13*; eulogy for Grace by, 1, 225–26
Morgan, Bill, 176, 181
Morrow, Felix, 91, 123, 145, 217
Mundelein, Bishop George, 26
Murray, Archbishop John, 50
Muste, A. J., 193
Myer, Mike, 136
"Mystical Body of Christ" concept, 7, 184–87

NAACP, 99; Dorothy in, 100, 103; Grace in, 14, 85, 103, 104, 121, 124, 127, 188
Nash, Helen, 28
National Catholic Welfare Conference (NCWC), 185
National Industrial Recovery Act (NIRA), 61
Nelson, Norman, 153
Nelson, Winnie, 99, 108, 151, 153
Neubel, Casper (Grace's uncle and godfather), 12, 13, 14, 16–17, 22, 52
New Deal, 53, 61

New Left, 6, 7, 189–90, 192–93, 223
Newman Center (at University of Minnesota), 169–70; Grace and, 169–70, 177, 178, 180, 201
Newman, John Henry, 169
Non-Partisan Labor Defense (NPLD), 65, 66, 67, 137. *See also* Workers Defense League
Novack, George, 92, 93, 125, 153, 217

O'Connell, Tom, 55
O'Connor, Harvey, 152
Olmsted, Kathryn S., 164
Olson, Floyd, 55, 64, 67–68, 73, 74

Pacem in Terris encyclical (1963), 190
Paine, Thomas, 128
Palmer, Bryan, 63, 151, 152
Palmquist, Ed, 82, 135, 153
Patriotic League of St. Paul, 26, 28
Physicians for Social Responsibility (PSR), 211–12, 221
Pius X, Pope, 34, 186
Pius XI, Pope, 186
Pius XII, Pope, 179
Postal, Kelly, 111
presidential pardon, 98, 99, 133; granted to Grace (1965), 196
Printon, Father Thomas, 13
Progressive Party, 126, 136, 198
Prohibition Party, 132, 133

Reagan, Ronald, 212
red scares. *See* "little red scare"; Second Red Scare
Reed, Evelyn, 118, 153, 208
Reed, Larissa, 113, 114, 116
Regan, John, 86
Rerum Novarum encyclical, 22, 23–24, 36, 55
Riga, Father Peter, 185, 272n5
Rockwell, Dr. John G., 53, 67, 74–78, 166
Roosevelt, Eleanor, 114

Roosevelt, Franklin D., 53, 74, 85, 88
Roseland, Elaine, 80, 93, 101, 109, 151, 207; as friend of Grace, 80, 93, 97, 99, 100, 103, 109, 124, 141, 155, 207
Ross, Carl, 4, 46, 140, 163, 217, 231n9
Royayne, Rita, 211
Ryan, Father John, 22–24, 55, 69, 222, 236n79

Saari, Joan K., 211
St. Cloud Sentinel, 129
St. John's Abbey, 186, 187
St. John's University, 171, 173, 187
St. Joseph's Academy high school, 33–39, *Fig. 2*; Grace in, 10, 15, 18, 33, 36–39, 221
St. Leo's parish (St. Paul), 188–89, 213, 221, 223
St. Mary's Hospital, 7, 170, 172, 214, 215; nursing school of, 170–71, 173–75. *See also* St. Mary's Junior College
St. Mary's Junior College (SMJC), 173–77; Gilbert and, 181–82, 214
—Grace and, 2, 173–77, 182, 193, 201, 208–14, 217, 221, *Fig. 13*, *Fig. 14*; in founding of, 173–76, 188; influence of, on students, 7–8, 195–96, 205–7, 208–10, 224, 225; and alumnae, 7, 183, 210–11; memorial service for, 1, 225–26
St. Mary's Plan, 174–75, 176, 177, 188, 225
St. Olaf Catholic Church, 158, 165, 169; Grace and, 158, 159, 177, 178, 180, 182, 187
St. Paul Dispatch, 87–88
St. Paul Labor College, 69
St. Paul Seminary, 22–23, 69
St. Paul Trades and Labor Assembly (TLA), 25, 68–69, 73, 82, 176
St. Peter Claver's parish, 13–14, 21
St. Vincent's parish, 19–22, 23, 26–27, 66, 221, *Fig. 1*. *See also* St. Vincent's school
St. Vincent's school, 17–18, 39; Grace in, 10, 14, 17–18, 32, 33, 36, 221–22; Sisters of St. Joseph and, 17–18, 29

Salvatore, Nick, 3
Schrecker, Ellen, 170
Schultz, Ann, 92, 97, 110, 143, 151, 157, 199; as an adult, 199–200, 202–5, 218
Schultz, Dorothy Holmes, 5, 65, 157, 199, 217; childhood and education of, 13, 14, 16, 36, 47, 49–51, 53–56, 58; and Catholic Church, 13, 50, 66; and 1934 Teamster strikes, 59–60, 62–63, 64; in Madison, Wisconsin, in later years, 184, 196, 199–205, 218–19
—closeness of, with sister Grace, 92, 96, 107, 143, 156; during Grace's imprisonment, 93, 97–105, 138, 139, 141–42, 143–44; interruption of, 156, 160, 166, 167, 169, 182, 200; resumption of, 183–84, 196–97, 201–5, 218–19
—and Henry Schultz, 6, 59–60, 62–63, 101, 107, 110, 139; wedding of, 66; children with, 92, 110. *See also* Schultz, Ann; Schultz, James; Schultz, Raymond; Schultz, Vincent
—in SWP, 81–82, 91, 99, 100–102, 121–22, *Fig. 5*, *Fig 6*; as part of friendship network including Grace, 6, 80, 99, 100–102, 109–11, 150–51, 155; and Smith Act trial, 87, 88, 89, 91, *Fig. 6*; after Grace's break from party, 160, 166, 167, 169, 182, 196–99, 200
Schultz, Henry, 6, 59–60, 62–63, 72, 92, 103, 107, 139, 141–43, 157; as electrician, 59–60, 199, 201; and Dorothy Schultz (*see under* Schultz, Dorothy Holmes); and SWP, 6, 81–82, 110–11, 150–51, 154, 159, 167, 196, 197–99, 200, *Fig. 9*; illnesses and death of, 101–2, 105, 151, 162, 201–2, 203, 205
Schultz, James, 110, 151, 157, 199, 204, 218
Schultz, Raymond, 110, 121, 199, 200; family memories shared by, 151, 157, 182, 200, 201, 202, 217, 218

Schultz, Vincent, 110, 121, 151, 157, 199, 200, 204, 218
Schweinhaut, Henry, 90
Second Red Scare, 122, 128–30, 134, 164–66; and Grace, 156, 160, 164–65, 170–71; impact of, on SWP, 119, 128, 134, 150, 156, 197
Second Vatican Council (1962–1965), 7, 187–88, 190; liberalizing currents in Catholic Church prior to, 4, 183, 185, 186, 187, 222
Sedova, Natalia, 86, 106
Seiler, Rose, 82, 153, *Fig. 6*
separate spheres, ideology of, 43
Shachtman, Max, 81–82, 123
Sheen, Monsignor Fulton, 163–64
Shipstead, Henrik, 86
shopmen's strike of 1922, 9, 30–32; Grace's father and, 4, 9, 30, 32, 37, 63; influence of, on Grace, 9, 24, 30, 32, 63, 222
Silvermaster, Nathan, 164
Sisters of St. Joseph, 18–19, 50, 170, 174–75, 235n55; Grace and, after her return to Catholic Church, 1, 2, 170–71, 174–75, 177, 213; schools run by, *see* College of St. Catherine; St. Joseph's Academy; St. Mary's Junior College; St. Vincent's school
—and Grace's education, 2, 10, 19, 33–39, 174, 186, *Fig. 1*; as role models for Grace, 10, 42; and challenge to gender norms, 42, 43–44, 47–48, 66, 224, *Fig. 3*; and commitment to social justice, 10, 18, 33, 36, 221–22
Skoglund, Carl, 61–62, 91, 108, 135, 216
Slant movement, 7, 194–96, 201, 223
Smith, Martha, 19, 39
Smith Act (1940), 106, 128–29, 164. *See also* Smith Act trial of 1941
Smith Act trial of 1941, 87–91, 92, 139, 192, *Fig. 6*; Grace in, 1, 5, 80, 87–88, 89, 92, 139, 192, *Fig. 6*
Socialist Labor Party, 56, 133, 136

Socialist Party of America (SP), 56–57, 73, 86, 133; Trotskyists in, 42, 70–71

Socialist Workers Party (SWP), 5, 199–200, 202–3; background of, 71–72, 81–82 (*see also* Communist Left Opposition); founding convention of, 5, 71–72, 73; friendship networks in, 5–6, 80–81, 92–94, 97–103, 107, 110–11, 125, 136, 143, 156, 166; gender dynamics in, 2–3, 8, 80–87, 99–100, 111–15, 116–18, *Fig. 8*; Marxist feminism in, 5–6, 80–81, 113, 114–15, 116–18, 205; government actions against, 87, 88, 89, 134–35, 149–50, 153, 197, 199, 216. *See also* Smith Act trial of 1941

—Grace in, 1, 73, 74–77, 81, *Fig. 5*, *Fig. 6*; attraction to, 41–42, 58–59, 64, 68–70; ; as delegate to founding convention, 5, 71, 73; as electoral candidate, 84–86, 91, 121–23, 124–33, 135–36, 155, *Fig. 5*, *Fig. 10*; and friendship network within, 5–6, 80–81, 92–94, 97–103, 107, 110–11, 125, 136, 143, 156, 166; and her marriage, 78–79; and the *Militant*, writings for, 5, 81, 111–13, 116, 120, 126, 131–32; in prison (*see under* Alderson federal prison); romance of, with Ray Dunne (*see under* Dunne, Vincent Raymond); speaking tours by, 87; withdrawal from party (1952), 1, 2, 6, 118, 156–63, 164–69, 172, 182. *See also* "Women in Prison" speaking tour

Soviet Union, 122, 134, 164–66, 212; Trotskyists' views on, 81–82, 127; and World War II, 74, 81

Sproul, Dorothy, 106

Stalin, Josef, 57, 70, 72, 76, 123, 127

Stassen, Harold, 73

Sterne, Evelyn Savidge, 20

Stone, I. F., 193

strike wave of 1945–1946, 120–21

Studer, Father Jim, 212

Sullivan, Father John, 23

Synanon, 204, 205

Taft-Hartley Act, 122, 125, 127

Taylor, Marie, 113, 114, 116

Teamster strikes of 1934 (Minneapolis), 59–64, 82, 139, *Fig. 4*; Grace and, 41–42, 51, 59, 60, 62–63, 64; Trotskyist leadership of, 57, 59, 60–64

Teilhard de Chardin, Pierre, 187

Tentler, Leslie Woodcock, 45

Thomas, Norman, 86

Thurmond, Strom, 124, 133

Tobin, Daniel J., 88, 217

true womanhood, ideology of, 43–44

Truman, Harry S., 122, 124, 128; and Cold War, 122, 127; in 1948 election, 131, 133

United Auto Workers (UAW), 120–21

University of Minnesota ("the U"), 65, 134, 199

—Grace at: as graduate student, 2, 4, 41, 51–56, 64; as lecturer, 53, 56, 64; and the Newman Center, 169–70, 177, 178, 180, 201; Social Problems Club at, 54–55, 56, 58, 59, 64, 65

Valelly, Richard, 216

Vatican II. *See* Second Vatican Council

Vietnam War, 189; movement in protest of, 189–92, 201, 203, 218

Vincent de Paul, Saint, 20

Wald, Alan, 153, 216

Walker, Adelaide, 65

Walker, Charles, 54, 65

Wallace, Henry, 126, 123, 198

War on Poverty, 174

Ware, Susan, 3, 83

Warren, Earl, 131

Webb, Constance, 154
Weigand, Kate, 115
Weiss, Murry, 150, 152, 153
Weiss, Myra Tanner, 117, 150, 152, 153, 208
White, Harry Dexter, 164
Wingerd, Mary Lethert, 24, 25
Wittich, Dr. Fred, 146
"woman question," 5–6, 109, 113–18, 224. *See also* Marxist feminism
"Women in Prison" speaking tour (1945), 108–9, 120, 145; and working-class Marxist feminism, 5–6, 81, 108–9, 116

Workers Defense League (WDL), 67, 99, 100, 108, 121, 137, 153–54. *See also* Non-Partisan Labor Defense
Workers Party (WP), of Shachtman, 82, 123
Workers Party of the United States (WPUS), 70
Works Progress Administration (WPA), 69
World War I, 24–26, 27–31, 56, 88; and Grace's evolving political views, 4, 10, 17–18, 24, 29, 32, 222
World War II, 1, 74, 81, 84–85, 113–14; Gilbert in, 137, 138

ABOUT THE AUTHOR

Donna T. Haverty-Stacke is Professor of History at Hunter College and the Graduate Center, CUNY, where she teaches courses in US cultural, urban, labor, and legal history. Haverty-Stacke is the author of *America's Forgotten Holiday: May Day and Nationalism, 1867–1960* and *Trotskyists on Trial: Free Speech and Political Persecution since the Age of FDR*. She is coeditor with Daniel J. Walkowitz of *Rethinking U.S. Labor History: Essays on the Working-Class Experience, 1756–2009*.

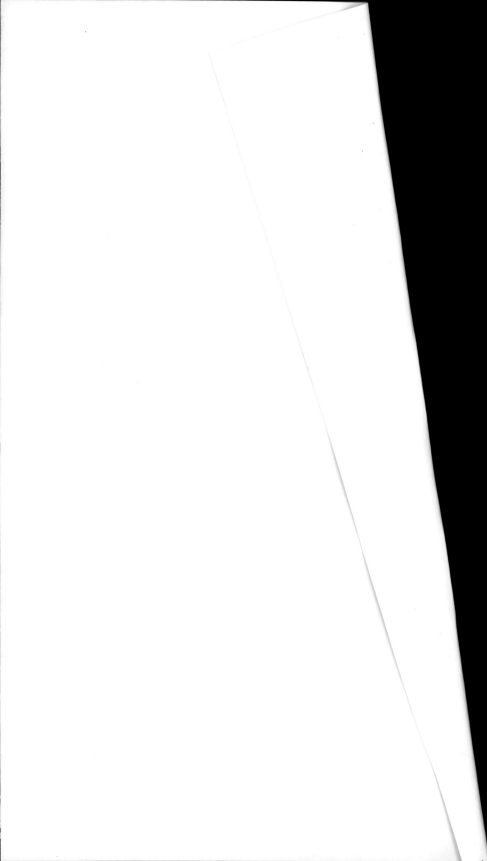